# Latin America

## The Peoples and Their History

### SECOND EDITION

**WILLIAM H. BEEZLEY**
University of Arizona

**COLIN M. MACLACHLAN**
Tulane University

THOMSON
™
WADSWORTH

Australia • Brazil • Canada • Mexico • Singapore
Spain • United Kingdom • United States

## THOMSON
™
## WADSWORTH

*Latin America: The Peoples and Their History,* **Second Edition**
*William H. Beezley and Colin M. MacLachlan*

Publisher: Clark Baxter
Senior Acquisitions Editor: Ashley Dodge
Assistant Editor: Paul Massicotte
Editorial Assistant: Kristen Jusy
Technology Project Manager: David Lionetti
Marketing Manager: Lori Grebe Cook
Marketing Assistant: Teresa Jessen
Marketing Communications Manager: Tami Strang
Project Manager, Editorial Production:
   Katy German
Creative Director: Rob Hugel
Art Director: Maria Epes

Print Buyer: Rebecca Cross
Permissions Editor: Roberta Broyer
Production Service: International Typesetting
   and Composition
Photo Researcher: Terri Wright
Copy Editor: Chris Thillen
Cover Designer: Bartay
Cover Image: Courtesy of the Latin America
   Library at Tulane University
Compositor: International Typesetting
   and Composition
Printer: Courier-Stoughton

Printed in the United States of America
1 2 3 4 5 6 7 09 08 07 06

Library of Congress Control Number: 2006900661

ISBN 0-495-05016-4

**Thomson Higher Education**
**10 Davis Drive**
**Belmont, CA 94002-3098**
**USA**

For more information about our products, contact us at:
**Thomson Learning Academic Resource Center**
**1-800-423-0563**
For permission to use material from this text or product, submit a request online at
**http://www.thomsonrights.com**
Any additional questions about permissions can be submittted by e-mail to
**thomsonrights@thomson.com**

*To Blue*

# Contents

# Preface

For many years, Frank Tannenbaum's *Ten Keys to Latin America* (1962) offered a provocative introduction to the history and culture of the region. Tannenbaum selected ten topics, which he thought offered a general, yet systematic orientation. Our familiarity with that book and its value for introductory students, travelers, and general readers persuaded us that the time had come for a new, similar volume.

In the first edition of *Latin America: The Peoples and Their History* (1999), we organized the book around five themes: peoples, places, economies, politics, and cultures (religious and popular). We learned from that edition that most readers prefer a chronological ordering, even within a topical organization; so, for this second edition, we have modified the sequence of topics and chapters.

Doing this new edition allowed us to rethink not just the order of chapters, but the general themes we have included. We have revised the text to follow our unstated goal of integrating newly developed historical themes into the general narrative. In our initial effort, we wanted to move both women's and gender history out of the compensatory category by using them to enrich and revise the general history of the region, so we included them along with our discussion of ethnicity and class in the two chapters on peoples. In this new edition, we have also continued this approach by dropping the compensatory separation of popular religions and popular cultures in separate chapters. We replaced the two original chapters on these topics with new ones on religions and cultures. This allows us to talk about the more significant and interesting topics of the interplay between the formal, organized religions with popular practices, and of the constant cross-fertilization of high and popular cultures in Latin America.

We look forward to the reaction of our colleagues to the new organization and chapter topics. Just as we profited from the beneficial criticism of the first edition by Mark Wassermann and other anonymous reviewers, we welcome comments on this second edition. We use this book to teach introductory surveys to Latin America, and we want to learn about the experiences that others have with it.

We acknowledge the helpful assistance we have received from our students at the University of Arizona and Tulane University. Both graduate and undergraduate students have provided intelligent and insightful criticism of the book. Emily Wakild, in particular, made helpful comments on the environmental chapter. We also benefited from the professional advice of the publisher—especially the history editor for Latin America, Ashley Dodge, and her assistants. Ashley gave us editorial recommendations in the midst of fashion suggestions. We heeded the former and neglected the latter. The production process went smoothly, and for that we thank the Project Manger, Sam RC at International Typesetting and Composition.

Over the years, our ideas and interpretations of Latin America and its peoples have been shaped through conversations with friends at professional meetings, both in the United States and Latin America, and with colleagues in our university departments. Although the footnotes identify some of these influences, we want to recognize several individuals who must share responsibility for the contents of this book. These persons are members of our cohort—John Hart, Jaime Rodríguez, and Chris Archer—as well as others from a younger cohort, participants in the Oaxaca Summer Institute, and our colleagues Bill French, Linda Curcio-Nagy, and Susan Deeds.

# Introduction

U nderstanding Latin America today requires knowing who the Latin Americans are and how they evolved. It demands an understanding of their expectations and aspirations. Although the future cannot be predicted, we are able to suggest the possibilities. An historical trajectory points to the future with general reliability, although the details may be surprising. The journey into the past inevitably offers an enriched understanding of the present.

Indigenous cultures achieved variety, elegance, commercial and political sophistication, and, in some cases, grand architecture. These cultures partially survived the European conquest, enduring through the peoples and their daily practices of family life, preparation of ordinary foods, and common knowledge of agriculture. The Iberian conquerors imposed their crusading religion, vernacular languages, and social—including gender—patterns in the creation of a hybrid society that existed for three centuries. The intermingling of peoples and cultures from the Americas, Europe, Africa, and Asia created a rich and complex society. As individuals Latin Americans found an identity within tribal, national, ethnic, or racial groups and the extended family. The 300-year colonial period witnessed the formation of social and political habits that would endure after independence, remnants of which can be recognized today in the form of the indigenous and colonial heritage.

After independence (collectively about 1824), new national leaders attempted to create regimes with stable politics, economies based on exploitation of natural resources, and populations with a greater European character. They directed a drive to attract supposedly superior immigrants with the skills to help create modern economies and to change the ethnic character of the populations. About 1870, many changed the way they saw themselves and their societies. The social and economic elites and the urban middle sectors struggled to define their social position by adopting cosmopolitan European practices. They contrasted themselves sharply with the lower orders of Indians, blacks, peasants, and the poor, whose behavior they considered inappropriate. Argentine and Mexican leaders, among others, launched campaigns to reform these people into model citizens as defined by national elites.

Latin Americans have always considered themselves city people who constructed urban centers, creating a distinctive built environment. Pre-Columbian, Iberian, and colonial traditions of urban living can be found in every urban concentration in the Americas, although new urban traditions also are evident. After independence in Latin America, urban life acquired enhanced meaning as national capitals and secondary centers acted as magnets for those seeking opportunities of all sorts. The growth of modern cities created mounting pressure to provide opportunities and services to meet basic needs. This has become a staggering task today.

The physical and natural setting for Latin America's history has undergone constant transformation caused by both natural and human actions. Consequently, how Latin Americans viewed their surroundings also repeatedly changed. At various times, people have viewed their environment as a threatening, dangerous place; at other times, they have seen it as a storehouse of natural wealth in minerals and plant or animal life. The rain forest, for example, has been viewed as home, as an obstacle to progress, as an economic opportunity, and increasingly as an environmental asset. Many political and economic controversies have origins in different interpretations of the environment.

Latin American economies from the pre-Columbian era until the world depression of 1929–1930 revolved around three interlocking themes: growing economic specialization; control of labor and property; and the nineteenth-century rise of an economy based on exporting raw materials (minerals, coffee, bananas, and sugar) and importing commodities and capital goods (luxury items like fashions, pianos, champagne, and machinery, including tools). "Boom" economies, with such products as rubber in Brazil and Bolivia, guano in Peru, nitrates and copper in Chile, and petroleum in Venezuela and Ecuador, occurred throughout the hemisphere. World War I delivered a body blow to the export-import economy, and the world depression of 1929–1930 delivered a knockout punch. Nevertheless, struggling free of a commodity-based economy and moving toward a diversified economic model has not been easy.

After 1930, as it became evident that traditional liberal economic solutions (balanced budgets and reduced expenses) had failed to revive their economies, Latin American national governments intervened directly in the economy. Only then did recovery begin. The Keynesian revolution (a program of government investment and deficit spending based on the economic principles of John Maynard Keynes) brought Latin American central governments into direct economic contact with the people. National governments sought to direct investment; select exports and imports; calibrate wages, prices, and profits; and regulate management and marketing. National governments bypassed state and local administrations and interacted with people at the grassroots level. This economic system continued into the 1980s, when overwhelming international debts crushed confidence in it. Latin American governments moved not only toward privatization (returning the economy to private hands) of state-owned enterprises, national corporations, and investment agencies but also toward decentralization of social services, in a pattern called Neoliberalism. Traditional politics, entrenched bureaucracies, and ingrained state paternalism resulted in violence and widespread protests to privatization. Populism returned to suggest that a paternalistic state based on a government-controlled economy could address the problems of poverty, public health, and inadequate living standards.

Leaders throughout Latin America's history have defined their societies, by developing plans either to incorporate or to ignore various peoples. In pre-Columbian societies, the Aztecs sought only economic integration of conquered peoples through tribute payments. The Incas pursued unification of subject peoples under their control by demanding linguistic, religious, and economic incorporation and holding hostages as guarantees. The Iberians went about the incorporation of individuals by converting them to Roman Catholicism and placing them within a social hierarchy. After independence patriotic leaders imagined new national identities and initiated campaigns to integrate or exclude people as citizens. They identified worthy members of their nation, excluding many indigenous peoples as "barbarians," and promoted European immigration, attempting to reduce the Afro- and Indo-American character of the population. Beginning about 1880, new forces began to shape Latin American politics. National leaders aggressively sought to introduce new facets of western European culture. Then, beginning in the 1920s, populist leaders decided to incorporate all their people into the nation, to some extent merely by appropriating their everyday behavior as a national activity. Three overlapping stages became evident: First, the eruption of popular groups into national politics such as the Mexican Revolution of 1910. Second, the rise of populist movements composed of the disenfranchised people, recent immigrants from abroad and villagers flooding into the cities, and the rural poor in the countryside. Third, reaction against foreign economic demands personalized by the existence of enclaves from oil camps, mining towns, and posh city neighborhoods for foreigners. The Latin American countries all have experienced mass political movements, popular-based revolutionary campaigns, militarism, and mass political parties. For Latin American governments, the essential political question remains that of determining how to integrate their people into national life and raise the standard of living.

Religious culture serves as the organizing framework of daily life, shaping social, political, economic, and family activities throughout Latin America. Since the sixteenth century, Latin America has been regarded as a Roman Catholic region, but this is correct only as an overarching generalization. Latin American Catholicism has a unique community character resulting from modifications that incorporated pre-Columbian and African practices. Local faiths have combined community practices with Roman Catholic narratives to explain life and death, and to obtain divine help with sickness, romance, and other puzzles of everyday life. Today millions profess nonorthodox beliefs and African-based religions, and 4 out of 10 Latin Americans belong to evangelical groups. Nevertheless, the entire population functions within a loose *mestizo* Catholic framework put in place in the colonial period. The distinctive character of local beliefs emerged from the mixtures of attitudes, assumptions, and taken-for-granted convictions. Local miracles, parish holy men and women, and community tales of divine intervention and retribution have combined in unique expressions of religion.

The essayist Carlos Monsaváis spoke for all Latin Americans when he wrote that Mexicans have the ability "to assimilate, without being assimilated," when they encounter useful or interesting foreign practices. This trait expresses Latin

America's characteristic experience of constant merging cultures from pre-Columbian times to the present. Indigenous groups absorbed each other's cultures to build impressive civilizations in South and North America. When the Europeans arrived, cultural interaction continued, creating mixed or mestizo cultures that fused indigenous, western European, African, and Asian cultures. In more recent times, the cultural marketplace offers a wide range of influences, many of them transnational in origin, including movie fashions, television programs, musical performances, and comic book stories. What people emulate cannot be forced on them by government officials or social betters. The constant evolution of culture always includes the preservation of what individuals regard as essential practices. The reincorporation of surviving indigenous and African customs and the revival of native languages that function within the nation is an example of the ongoing modification that creates the rich cultures of the region.

Since the arrival of the first migrating peoples from Asia cross the land bridge to the Americas, Latin Americans have been mobile societies, constantly interacting with other communities and societies. This interaction developed a global character with the arrival of Europeans, who were followed by Africans and Asians. The increasing transnational character of Latin American societies has been a major theme since the independence era. The new nations experienced diplomatic, commercial, cultural, and military interaction with other nations, especially the United States. The inescapable theme that runs through relations between Latin America and the United States is captured in the lament, "Poor Mexico. So far from God, so near the United States." Since independence, the U.S. government has attempted to exercise its influence throughout the Americas. Policy decisions and formal treaties displayed both self-righteous self-interest, for example, the Monroe Doctrine and Caribbean debt collection and well-meaning assistance (aid to Benito Juárez to confront foreign invaders and the Peace Corps program). Diplomacy notwithstanding, commercial, cultural, and tourist relationships have provided more widespread interaction between the United States and Latin America. Trade has received the greater attention of these unofficial interactions, especially in an attempt to explain the region's national problems through a theory of economic dependency on the United States (and to a lesser degree Western Europe). Less well known, but equally significant, are forms of cultural relationships between the United States and Latin America. These relationships have countless expressions, ranging from U.S. scientific, artistic, and botanic expeditions (the latter, for example, organized to gather potentially valuable plants) to Latin Americans resident in the United States as students and as refugees fleeing both revolutionary and reactionary political regimes and long-standing economic disadvantages. Those who returned home took with them their experiences in the United States; those who stayed became increasingly prominent in U.S. politics and culture. Tourists have become an important factor since World War II. The nature of United States–Latin American relations has shown persistent themes since the era of independence in the hemisphere, but modern communications and transportation have made them more visible and pressing.

The key for understanding this composite of such a diverse, complex, and captivating past remains the community, just as it was during the eras of indigenous, colonial, nineteenth, and twentieth-century life.

# 1

# The Indigenous
# and Colonial Legacies

Latin Americans today, in 21 separate nations, have developed national identities that incorporate both local indigenous and colonial legacies. These traditions constitute community expressions of the nation's history and have deep roots in the geography of each nation. Location provides an essential key to understanding the historical evolution of Latin America's nations and peoples.

## LATIN AMERICA'S GEOGRAPHIC SETTING

Latin America's physical setting frames the central drama of the region's cultural, political, and social life. Geological and geographical factors influence culture, but do not determine it. These features, even geology, can never be static. Changes, as imperceptible as plate tectonics or as apparent as changes in the tropical rain forest, occur continually. The nature of the land and the diversity of the environment are easy enough to overlook when we focus on historical patterns, but they should not be forgotten.

The traveler, moving from north to south, passes through all possible climatic and physical zones. Northern Mexico forms part of a vast, wind-eroded, arid, high tableland crisscrossed by deep canyons that make passage difficult and access to water a daily challenge. The plateau extends from an altitude of 4,000 to 8,000 feet in the south, before dropping to an insignificant 600 feet, about sea level, in the Isthmus of Tehuantepec. Rainfall, when it comes, arrives inland, driven by strong storms across the tableland's mountain barriers. Moisture-starved plants dot a barren landscape. Baja California constantly struggles to obtain adequate water, whereas to the east the Sonoran Desert, caught between mountain ranges, exists almost without it. When storms penetrate into the interior, rain comes in torrents, drenching the parched land without being absorbed. The coastal strips of the Gulf of Mexico and the Pacific Ocean receive rain in ever-increasing amounts as one moves south along the coast. In general, Mesoamerica (the region of Mexico and Central America) has water only in extremes, either not enough or too much. Few districts have conditions close to optimal for agriculture. Only an estimated 13 percent of Mexico has sufficient rain on a year-round basis, and only approximately 10–15 percent of the land surface (about the area of the U.S. state of Kansas) is ideally usable for agricultural purposes. Expensive dams, irrigation systems, and technology must be utilized to bring more land under cultivation.

Snow-covered peaks ring Mexico's central valleys. Orizaba, Ixtaccihuatl, Popocatepetl, and other impressive volcanoes add beauty to the countryside, complicate transportation, and occasionally threaten villages. The region's geological formation continues. Paricutín, a new volcano, dramatically made this point in 1943, when it burst from a cornfield 150 miles west of Mexico City. It eventually rose to 8,248 feet. Popocatepetl, affectionately referred to as Popo, began smoking in the early 1990s and now threatens to erupt with uncertain consequences for life in the central valley. Earthquakes periodically rumble through the land. A major quake in 1985 leveled large blocks of Mexico City. The central government's weak response to the needs of victims inspired spontaneously organized community groups to dig people out of the rubble and establish temporary shelters. The "sons of the shaking earth," to use anthropologist Eric Wolf's evocative term for the people of the region, constantly confront nature and frequently lose.

Central America, from Mexico to Panama, means mountain ranges. Guatemala's Tajumulco rises some 14,000 feet. Of this country's 33 volcanoes, 4 remain active, especially Pacaya, which has erupted continually since 1960. Costa Rica has several volcanic peaks that reach above 12,000 feet; the other republics have impressive sierras over 7,000 feet in altitude. Mountains run down Central America, forming a geological spine that separates the land into strips along both coasts. Central America has few navigable rivers or good natural harbors on either coast because of these ranges. Movement into and out of the interior requires major effort and modern engineering. Most of the population lives at an elevation between 3,000 and 8,000 feet to take advantage of the more temperate climate, with the exception of Panama. San José, Costa Rica, is typical at some 4,000 feet, and even San Salvador, El Salvador, near the coast, stands at 2,238 feet.

Natural threats to the people run the gamut from torrential rains to mudslides, drought, lava flows, hurricanes, and earthquakes. Although roads, crops, dwellings, and human beings are often swept away, nature supplies physical features of magical beauty as compensation. Lovely volcanic lakes such as Guatemala's Atitlán, Huehuetenango, and Amatitlán are some of nature's jewels. Lowland lakes with their lush shorelines suggest a tropical Garden of Eden, whereas other lakes, such as Nicaragua and Managua, are almost inland seas. Volcanic soils are rich and productive. As a consequence, Central American coffee and other crops require minimal soil improvement. All in all, nature has the upper hand, giving and taking away in unpredictable sequence.

## Major Landforms

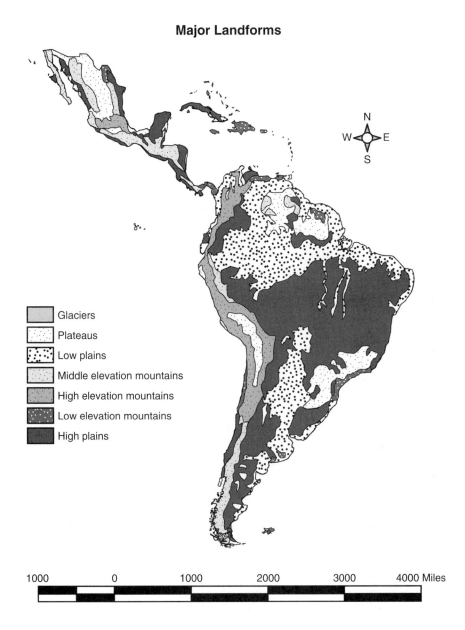

Glaciers

Plateaus

Low plains

Middle elevation mountains

High elevation mountains

Low elevation mountains

High plains

1000        0        1000        2000        3000        4000 Miles

South America has stunning geology and geography. Again, mountains, the Andes, define the region, extending down the western coast from Colombia to the Straits of Magellan. Major spurs cut Colombia into three distinct segments, eventually becoming two ranges as one moves southward. The Andes vary in width from 120 miles in Ecuador to 500 in Bolivia. Aconcagua in Chile is the highest peak at some 23,000 feet, with many others rising to 16,000 and most reaching 14,000 feet. Major Andean cities are located at 6,000- to 14,000-foot elevations, with snowcapped mountains as a backdrop. A high tableland (the *Altiplano*) beginning slightly north of Lake Titicaca runs southward some 500 miles. Lake Titicaca, atop this plateau, helps moderate the Altiplano's otherwise bitter cold. Titicaca and Lake Poopó, farther south, provide relatively favorable agricultural conditions to a series of plains stretching from their shorelines. Farther east, steep river valleys, the *yungas*—descending from 8,200 to 3,200 feet—feel the impact of Amazonian winds, making them suitable for temperate and semitropical agriculture.

The mountain barrier determines regional rainfall by blocking clouds from the east. Only the northern region of the west coast receives sufficient moisture. As one travels down the coast south of the equator, rainfall becomes sparse, then nonexistent, turning the land into a parched coastal desert. A few rivers channel rain and melting snows to the Pacific. The valleys of these rivers make human habitation possible. Lima, Peru's capital, sprawls across one such valley. A mantle of cool mist (*La Garúa*) cloaks the capital from April through December. Chile appears to slither down the coastal plain bordered by the forbidding Andes to the east and the much less daunting southern Pacific. Chile's geological isolation points it toward Oceania and Australia, rather than to its immediate neighbors, making the country a decidedly Pacific Rim nation both in a physical and a psychological sense. The hemisphere's western coast from Tierra del Fuego at the Straits of Magellan to Alaska in the extreme north is geologically active, subject to almost undetected but constant tremors, severe earthquakes, and volcanic activity.

Rainfall increases dramatically on the eastern slope of the northern Andes. Perpetual rain characterizes the *montaña* region that drops steeply into the Amazon basin. Here life becomes almost unbearable until one reaches the drier lower elevations. South America's Amazon basin appears to stretch into infinity over some 2,000,000 square miles of land only slightly above sea level. Indeed, the river drops a mere one-eighth of an inch per mile in its last 500 miles to the sea.

The east coast of South America is less intimidating than the Pacific side. Nevertheless, it presents a number of challenges to would-be inhabitants. In the north, the Guiana highlands provide a thin strip of coastal land, whereas south of the Amazon region the Brazilian highlands begin. From Salvador da Bahia to the southernmost state of Rio Grande do Sul, the escarpment averages 2,600 feet with areas where the mountains rise from 7,000 to an extreme of 9,000 feet. The entire coastal plain receives plentiful rain, in certain regions enough to create rain forests. Inland from the coast the northern area becomes arid, a place of scrub vegetation and dry grasslands often made worse by severe droughts occurring on a more or less 12-year cycle. Inland south-central Brazil's hilly terrain is a favored coffee region with a temperate climate, although it is occasionally cold enough for a hard frost. Extreme southern Brazil is part of the fertile *pampa* running through Uruguay into Argentina. Here the rains decrease as they move inland making irrigation increasingly necessary.

Massive river systems drain the South American continent, creating a watery maze, which comes close to being interconnected. Over the years, innumerable proposals to connect the rivers with a series of canals have been put forward. The main Amazonian system, composed of the Amazon and Solimões-Ucayali rivers, extends slightly longer than the Nile system. Approximately 1,000 tributaries feed the main river, creating a combined flow discharging an estimated 200,000 cubic meters of water per second into the South Atlantic. This amount represents some 15.5 percent of the world's freshwater flowing into the oceans. In comparison, the Mississippi discharges only 1.5 percent into the Gulf of Mexico. One of the Amazon's major tributaries, the Marmoré-Madeira, is 3,000 miles long. Oceangoing vessels can navigate over 40,000 miles, penetrating as far as Iquitos, Peru.

Three other impressive river systems, each unique, drain the continent in addition to providing access to the interior. The Río de la Plata, with Buenos Aires at its mouth, constitutes a back door for the Andean nations of Peru and Bolivia and links Paraguay with the sea. Venezuela's Orinoco and Colombia's Magdalena complete the continent's major rivers. South America's rivers and mountain chains form the armatures for the ecosystems of South American civilization.

Submerged mountains extend into the Caribbean Sea, occasionally breaking through the surface to create the Antilles. The largest islands, Cuba, Hispaniola (today the nations of Haiti and the Dominican Republic), and Puerto Rico, exemplify patterns of high, dominant mountains, rivers that allow little navigation, and rich soils. The mountains contained minerals that attracted Spaniards and others. Initially, those who followed Columbus joined gold rushes in both Cuba and Hispaniola. Mining remains an important Caribbean enterprise from diverse metals in Cuba to chromium in Jamaica. Trinidad and Tobago's oil industry developed after World War II. The fertile soils created a sugar boom in the sixteenth century of worldwide consequence. Europeans introduced sugarcane, initiated the slave trade that ripped Africans from their homelands, and furnished sugar, fiery rum, and coffee to consumers across Europe. Eventually, New World profits drove Europeans into dazzling colonial projects across Asia. The shipments of sugar, silver, and other valuables soon provoked the worldwide practice of piracy, especially in the Caribbean. Coffee and other products followed in boom cycles. The economic patterns of the region were established by the end of the colonial period, dependent on the physical geography. The major change in the region has been the twentieth-century development of tourism. Tourists are drawn to the Caribbean by the beauty of the mountains, rivers, and especially the beaches.

Of all the human modifications to the natural environment, the city may be the most important. Some large cities, especially capitals, appear to have absorbed the nation itself by drawing talent, money, and resources from throughout the country. Latin Americans have always been city people. Their urban experience reflects pre-Columbian, Iberian, and colonial patterns of living. Although they shared urban traditions, each community also had its own unique social, economic, political, spatial pattern, and building style. After independence in Latin America, about 1824, national capitals became magnets for those seeking opportunities of all sorts. The growth of cities pressured governments to create opportunities and provide services to meet basic needs. This has become a staggering challenge today.

Cities, from their origins, have served as focal points of Latin American history and culture. Today, political, financial, demographic, and cultural resources are concentrated in megacities, such as Mexico City and São Paulo (Brazil), and other large capital cities, such as Montevideo (Uruguay) and Bogotá (Colombia). These urban centers generate tremendous opportunities and present overwhelming problems, including human congestion, air pollution, and environmental degradation. Moreover, the cities exemplify the severe socioeconomic distortions evident throughout Latin America: the very rich and the very poor, the educated and the illiterate, those with high-tech skills and those without—living side by side.

## THE INDIGENOUS LEGACIES

Latin American history and culture reflect the region's people and the social organizations that have roots extending to their pre-Columbian past. These indigenous peoples defined themselves, lived as families, formed communities, and built cities. From the arrival of the first prehistoric men and women from Asia in the Americas, the intermingling of peoples has provided the overriding theme of social interaction beyond the family. Individuals shaped their identities and sought opportunities within tribal, ethnic, or racial groups, and within the extended family.

The first prehistoric men and women came to the Americas from Asia. Their constant intermingling provided the overriding theme of social interaction during this era. Distinct indigenous cultures flourished before the Europeans arrived in the Western Hemisphere in 1492. From north to south, the societies included the Aztecs in central Mexico; the Mayas in a band across Yucatán, southern Mexico, and northern Central America; the Incas in Andean and coastal South America; and the Tupí-Guaraní in the lowlands of Brazil, Argentina, Paraguay, and Uruguay. In these cultures, each dramatically different in social complexity, population size, and economic specialization, the basic unit was the family.

Unlike nomadic hunting and gathering groups in which all members engaged in communal practices, sedentary societies developed specialized activities. Those at the top of the social hierarchy, the political and religious elites, dominated those at the lower levels. They did not expect or permit broad participation in governing society. Nevertheless, the entire community shared certain basic values and cultural practices, typically those involving language and religion. Family values and familial relationships remained paramount, even as fabulous empires rose in the high Andes (the Incas), the Yucatán (the Mayas), and central Mexico (the Aztecs).

### Pre-Columbian Families

Creating a family made a person, man or woman, an adult and a full-fledged member of society. The man in his late teens or early twenties married a suitable woman in her midteens after their families negotiated the appropriate match. The social responsibility of this new family translated into support for kinship groups and, through them, for the political and religious leaders who governed society. The family in the Aztec and Mayan cultures existed as a patriarchy. The ideal wife worshiped the gods, served her husband, raised her children, and acted in a chaste and modest fashion. The ideal husband was responsible for the material well-being of the family. In theory, he dominated the family, and his wife and children acceded to his wishes. As head of the household, he received from the community the right to work a plot of land to provide for his family. Nevertheless, all family members worked the fields. Children rounded out the family. They learned respect for their parents, elders, and gods. Parents taught their children family values that included obedience to authority, respect for established leaders, and acceptance of adversity. An orderly, productive, and obedient society exhibited behaviors learned as children in the family.

Among the Incas, a term referring to several Andean groups, the family performed the same basic role as in Mexico. As a married person, the man gained access to communal land for cultivation. The Inca family formed the base of a rigid social hierarchy and heredity continued to determine the individual's lifetime place within this stratified society. Kinship contributed to Inca imperial politics. The leaders demanded that newly conquered peoples send hostages to the Inca capital of Cuzco. This system fused kinship and politics.

## Pre-Columbian Cities

The first great leap toward civilization, many experts believe, came when people in the Americas and elsewhere, nearly simultaneously, domesticated crops and settled in permanent locations. Well before the arrival of Europeans in the hemisphere, cities and crops were the basis for the formation of important religious, political, and economic centers. Mayan cities, such as Chichén Itzá and Palenque, achieved political and religious splendor based on a productive economy and regional trade that reached from Oaxaca to the Pacific coast of present-day Nicaragua and into what is now Panama.

The great Aztec capital city Tenochtitlán, founded in 1325 and now the site of Mexico City, soon dominated other cities across central Mexico, including Texcoco and Azcapotzalco. Tenochtitlán, described as a splendid city by the first Europeans to enter it, had an elaborate water supply system, large sprawling markets, and causeways that linked the island city with the lakeshore. Tribute and trade stimulated the growth of a complex economic system, with some manufacturing and processing activities. Consumers within the city and throughout Mesoamerica provided a market for embroidered fabrics, fine jewelry, feather work, cotton cloth, copper goods, and other finished products. Aztec military conquest made it possible to draw resources from great distances, making Tenochtitlán partially independent of the surrounding rural areas. Nevertheless, the need for basic commodities, including foodstuffs, tied the city to the countryside. The city served as the economic and political center of a distinct region. Thus, European conquerors rebuilt on the ruins of the Aztec urban center of Tenochtitlán in order to control the valley of Mexico.

In South America, the Inca Empire stretched inland from what is today the southern region of Colombia to the fringe of the Amazon basin, down along the coast of the Pacific, to Chile. A series of roads connected the capital city, Cuzco, with the towns of Tambomachay, Pisac Calca, and Ollantaytambo, each with its own subordinate road systems and settlements. In effect, two strings of urban centers, stretching along the coast and down the Andes, provided the political and administrative spine of the Inca Empire. Inca population centers and the surrounding rural territory developed a closer relationship than the towns in Mesoamerica because of the physical obstacles that made trade and commerce difficult. Mountainous terrain made trade too costly except for luxury goods or exotic novelties. Consequently, Inca settlements relied on regional resources and did not engage in significant trade with other areas. *Cuzco* (meaning "navel" in the Inca language) may have been the empire's political center, but in economic terms it functioned only as one of many separate regional economies. Conflict, rebellion, and civil war, constant occurrences in the Inca Empire, were an outcome of competition among regional economic centers. Geography joined with the limitations of the barter system to create a fragmented imperial economy.

## Indigenous Economies

Indigenous economic development reached complex specialization in several places; in other regions it remained at rudimentary levels. At one extreme, hunter-gatherers of the Amazon basin exchanged polished stone cheek and lip plugs, whereas the specialized production and elaborate commerce of the Aztec, Mayan, Mixtec, and Zapotec peoples represented the other. Variations in economic diversity and productive sophistication stretched along the spectrum between the extremes.

The Aztec empire, based on tribute payments from subject towns and peoples, established a widespread commercial network rooted in trade fairs that were larger and more sophisticated than those in Spain. The peoples of central Mexico, although reliant on *maize,* beans, and squash agriculture, had developed specialized production. They reworked raw materials obtained from a variety of places to produce cotton cloth, leather goods, copper items, semiprecious and precious jewelry, and exquisitely designed feather cloaks and ornamentation. These manufactured items provided value-added consumer goods.

The Aztecs traded products throughout Mesoamerica. Tenochtitlán, their political and economic capital, relied on a complex market system that served 60,000–80,000 consumers daily. Incredulous Spaniards later compared the city's sprawling Tlatelolco market to Castile's international commercial hub at Medina del Campo. Smaller neighborhood markets rotated on set days throughout Tenochtitlán as they still do in Mexico City. *Tiangis,* the Nahuatl term for these traveling markets, remains in use today.

The multiplicity of goods produced to meet consumer demand in the fifteenth century had pushed the barter system to the point of collapse. Although many large wholesale transactions effectively employed barter, secondary distribution needed a more flexible exchange system. As a consequence, to facilitate retail exchange, the Aztecs developed a uniform system to set values and prices. They created a rudimentary form of money, using small copper items, gold dust packaged in turkey quills, cacao beans, and cotton cloth. The Aztecs hovered on the verge of replacing barter with a monetary system based on market value.

Aztec merchants emerged as a class promoting the expanding economic activities. They sought the means for greater economic flexibility, wealth creation, and commodity specialization. Trade with distant regions based on caravans of porters functioned as a monopoly of the hereditary caste of merchants, the Pochteca. They provided luxuries and exotic goods for Tenochtitlán and distributed reworked products throughout Mexico and Central America. The Pochteca acquired considerable wealth, but Aztec society made it difficult for them to enjoy or even display their possessions. How one dressed and lived depended on group status, not the individual's wealth. Only nobles could wear sumptuous clothes and precious jewels. Restricted in dress and housing, the Pochteca occupied an increasingly ambivalent social position that did not correspond to their wealth. An outlet for earned and accumulated wealth could not be long delayed.

The concept of private property existed in nascent form. Nobles depended on a constantly growing number of suitable positions for sons and grandsons, but the empire, no longer expanding, could not offer sufficient places. In somewhat the same fashion as the Pochteca, the Aztec nobility had reached a critical point. In response to pressures from members of this privileged group, a type of private landholding with putative title vested in an individual rather than a social position had developed. A serf class (*mayeques*) attached to these emerging private estates added productive value. This represented a step toward transforming land into a transferable commodity and endowing individuals with independent wealth they could use at their personal discretion.

The Maya shared many economic characteristics with the Aztecs and in a similar fashion responded to the opportunities that commerce offered. Mayan activity centered on market cities in Yucatán. From these towns, trade routes extended westward into central and southern Mexico and southward through Central America. Once Mayan traders reached modern Panama, they probably met Inca coastal traders. In addition to the proto-money they used in the central valley of Mexico, the Maya also used Pacific coast oyster shells from coastal Nicaragua. Both Mayan and Aztec officials struggled with counterfeiters, who hollowed out cacao beans, refilled them with dirt, and circulated them among the unwary. Reflecting its damage to commerce, the crime carried the death penalty.

In Inca Peru, geography determined the nature of production and geologic obstacles the extent of trade. Rugged mountain terrain and deep valleys limited long-distance trade to the exchange of exotic goods. Agricultural production reflected elevation, called by geographers the cold (*tierra fría*), temperate (*tierra templada*), and tropical (*tierra caliente*) zones. Some trade developed between elevation regions. Tierra fría or high-elevation peoples cultivated root crops, including an amazing array of potatoes, and raised herds of *llama, alpaca,* and *vicuña.* They exchanged meat, wool, and tubers for fish, corn, fruit, beans, and coca leaves from temperate and tropical coastal areas. This trade between climatic zones should not be confused with the far-flung commerce possible in other parts of the hemisphere such as Mesoamerica.

The exception to the limited trade in the Andes came when Inca tax collectors used *corvée* laborers to haul large shipments of foodstuffs or low-value fabricated items from one region to another. Only imperial taxation and unpaid porters made this possible. Rows of storehouses (*qollqa*), well-ventilated one-room structures, marked the hillsides; archaeologists have identified more than 10,000 storehouses across the expanse of the Inca Empire. Taxes provided the resources needed for irrigation canals, hillside terracing, roads, and fortifications. At Ollantaytambo, 70 kilometers from Cuzco, taxes paid for a rural retreat for the Inca elite. This opulent estate covered some 10 square kilometers and has been compared to Versailles, the seventeenth-century palace built by Louis XIV. The Inca elite lived on the tax revenues derived from the production of different agricultural zones, which functioned largely independently of each other. In this fragmented, state-directed economy, the need for a monetary system was not as pressing as in Mesoamerica.

In what is now Brazil, the pre-Columbian economy operated at a more rudimentary level. The first exchange between the Indians and the Portuguese indicated the region's economic limits. Approaching the shore, the Portuguese landing party dared not pass through the rough surf, so they threw their hats, beads, and other trinkets to the Indians they saw on the beach. In return, the Portuguese received polished stones, feathers, and stone-tipped weapons. The Europeans, excited by this exotic encounter, at first ignored the economic disparity between themselves and their accidental trading partners.

Brazil's hunting and gathering economy did not produce a large enough surplus to encourage significant trade. Brazilians extracted food, medicines, and hunting poisons from the forest. Their productivity matched their needs, skills, technology, and understanding of nature. The small population and its low reproductive rate, controlled by limited food resources and continuous warfare, exerted little pressure to develop a more complex system of production or develop regional networks of supply and consumption.

Indigenous peoples in the region today recognized as Latin America developed complex interactions with the environment well before the age of global maritime exploration in the fifteenth century. In what would become the two poles of Spain's empire, Peru and Mexico, indigenous peoples achieved a remarkable level of social organization based on intensive agriculture. Effective crop cultivation, beginning sometime around 1500 B.C., supported complex nonagricultural activities. Occupational differentiation, development of a religious base, and the need for a political structure led to the creation of a managerial class. Formation of territorial units or provinces subject to an imperial entity demanded impressive organizational skills. Inhabitants of what are now the modern nations of Mexico, Guatemala, most of El Salvador, Honduras, Nicaragua, Ecuador, Peru, and Bolivia created societies based on surplus agricultural production, all of which depended on control of natural resources.

Intensive agricultural practices produced surpluses of corn, beans, squash, chilies, potatoes (in Andean South America), and some specialty plants, such as avocados (in Mexico) and cacao for chocolate. Large harvests of these crops in many cases required sophisticated techniques to modify the land through terracing, irrigation, and natural fertilization. Native peoples, especially the Aztecs and Incas, made a lasting impact on the environment by attempting to control and remake it. The Aztec capital, Tenochtitlán, built on an island and reclaimed land from Lake Texcoco, offered testimony to their ability and willingness to engineer the physical circumstances.

Less complex Indian societies existed on the distant fringes of these empires. Many depended on hunting and gathering, which required only a limited political system and only minor occupational differentiation and a corresponding lesser need to modify nature. These peoples moved across a wide area in search of food, leaving only their footsteps behind. Many nomadic groups, particularly in what is today Brazil, functioned at a proto-tribal level. In some areas, natural food resources supported only small extended family groups. Other Indians, such as the Araucanians in Chile, functioned within a fully elaborated tribal system, effectively controlled a defined expanse of territory, and, subsequently, had a greater impact on the natural setting. Tribal and proto-tribal groups possessed complex beliefs and some remarkable technology, which indicated their place within the ring of human civilization. Nevertheless, their physical impact was limited mainly because they did not extensively alter their environment to support a large population or create cities.

The indigenous patterns of family, commerce, and agriculture, and the language used to describe these practices continued into the colonial era, and, in some instances, have survived to the present day.

## THE EUROPEAN ERA, 1492–1703

Christopher Columbus, intrepid sailor, poor mathematician, and horrible geographer, had studied maps of the earth, calculated distances across the open sea to Asia, and persuaded the Spanish monarchs, especially Isabella, to invest in his commercial voyage. His landfall in the Western Hemisphere in October 1492 opened the era of European conquest in the Americas and European imperialism throughout Asia and Africa. Following Columbus, Hernán Cortés and Francisco Pizarro conquered the Aztecs (1519–1521) and the Incas (1535–1550) respectively. The few Spanish conquerors succeeded by using swords, guns, and horses against the massive numbers of indigenous peoples who lacked all three. Smallpox and measles epidemics, as the invisible allies of the Spaniards, ravaged American peoples. Although the Spaniards had little resistance to these diseases, indigenous peoples had no immunity at all. Portuguese explorers, no less rapacious, met less resistance from the Tupí-Guaraní, and quickly founded trading posts in what today is Brazil. Within 60 years of Columbus's first voyage, Europeans had established the broad outlines of their colonies in the Americas.

Europeans, during the colonial era, came in surprisingly small numbers to the Western Hemisphere. Nevertheless, because perhaps as many as 7 out of 10 were males and they occupied important political, military, and economic positions, they introduced an era of tremendous ethnic and cultural intermingling. Once Europeans arrived, they forced Africans to come as slaves and later provided the means for a smaller migration from Asia. All these groups joined the American human hodgepodge. The encounter of European, African, and indigenous peoples prompted both Spain and Portugal to impose political and economic institutions and acculturate them.

Spaniards, just as they had in the Iberian lands reconquered from the Moors, especially Granada, evangelized the Indians and Africans. Forced conversion to Catholicism resulted in rudimentary devotion by African and indigenous peoples. More often, it yielded only a surface Catholicism. If scratched, it revealed a number of other religious beliefs and vestiges of religious practices that when combined with Catholicism resulted in the local community faith. For example, as Hernán Cortés carried out his conquest of the central part of Mexico, he destroyed idols and replaced them with Catholic altars and crucifixes. When he and his troops departed, they left local indigenous leaders in charge of the new shrines. From that time forward, these local leaders interpreted religion in the absence of missionaries or priests.

A handful of missionaries attempted to evangelize indigenous populations and convert African slaves. Techniques that used locally recognized sacred practices to explain Catholic practices made the process relatively effective, but subject to spiritual confusion. Music, especially drumming and dancing, ritual dramas, and even puppet shows were part of the campaign by missionaries to convert non-Christian peoples. Equivalents drawn between women goddesses and apparitions of the Virgin Mary, use of indigenous religious terms to define Catholic saints, rituals, and practices, combined with a limited number of priests in rural areas, created a variety of Catholic beliefs and practices. The small number of missionaries foreshadowed the chronic shortage of priests in modern times. The scarcity of priests left many parishioners, often barely knowledgeable about the faith, without much guidance beyond a once-a-year confession, communion, and mass. These variants received validity from local leaders who interpreted religious practices.

The Church, well aware of the reality, exempted Indians from the Inquisition normally in charge of assuring orthodoxy, placing them under the jurisdiction of bishops. Unique local modifications are best observed today in local village festivals. Church music incorporated European, Native American, and African influences. Gaspar Fernández, music director and organist at the Puebla, Mexico, cathedral (1606–1620), composed works of which 568 pages remain extant. His compositions are especially rich in *Guineos* (a reference to individuals from Guinea) and works in Indian forms. His music included songs with lyrics reflecting both Guinea and Indian dialects. A similar form of sacred music, with lyrics referring to Guinea peoples, Roman Catholicism, and festivals, was composed in Brazil in 1647. An example of Indian influence is Manuel Blasco's *Versos con duo para chirimías* (a *chirimía* is an Andean wind instrument), written in 1684 in Quito. The eminent composer Gutiérrez Fernández Hidalgo spent his career in the Andean towns of Bogotá, Quito, Cuzco, and Sucre. The five volumes of his compositions, one devoted entirely to Holy Week, reveal Spanish, Andean, and African influences.[1]

The evangelical campaign faced a challenge in the eighteenth century with the spread of Enlightenment ideas. The latter promoted the cult of reason, which in practical terms meant the spread of useful knowledge to replace the spiritual explanations of everyday life. The adoption of useful information split the Church from the state, but in more spectacular ways it divided churchmen and pitted Enlightened officials against bureaucrats. More important, believers could not be easily convinced to relinquish local beliefs and adopt the practical programs of Enlightened philosophers. In a critical development, Enlightenment officials supported individual piety. In a reflection of the Protestant movement, individualism undercut the society of castes and orders and moved from external religious display to internal personal spirituality. This process in Latin America made an appeal to intellectualism as a reform of what was described as female emotions that demanded spectacle and public performance of religion. Adding the dimension of gender to reforms in part created the foundation for the nineteenth-century Liberal definition of citizenship as a male prerogative.

Religion remained strong in the eighteenth century, even as Enlightened reformers pressed for new religious expressions. The rise of medical doctors as a part of the Enlightenment did not eliminate the need for popular healers and midwives, both usually women; the former in fact often resorted to *santiguadra,* the treatment of illness by making the sign of the cross. If the healer proved unsuccessful or too slow, patients often reported the practitioner to the Inquisition, making this religious court serve as a malpractice review board.[2]

Popular religion also created the context for significant political events. The clarion call of Mexican independence by Father Miguel Hidalgo came in the town of Dolores (known today as Dolores Hidalgo) during the predawn hours of September 16, 1810. Hidalgo organized the rebellion the night of the feast of the town's patron saint, the Virgin of Dolores, when villagers had spent the evening celebrating after breaking the fast and attending mass. A group of celebrants, tired and drunk, heard their parish priest incite them to rebellion, and they immediately marched off, seized a banner of the Virgin in her avocation as Guadalupe, and started the Mexican revolution that culminated in independence from Spain.

## Colonial Peoples

Once Europeans arrived in the Western Hemisphere, they replaced ethnicity with race as the means to differentiate groups. Europeans, long familiar with other races as a result of Mongol and Moslem invasions, explorations along the African coast, and spice trade with the Levant, identified the New World's native

---

[1] See liner notes, *Festival of Early Latrine American Music.* Roger Wagner Chorale and the Sinfornia Chamber Orchestra (El Dorado/UCLA Latin American Center), USR 7746.

[2] See Pamela Voekel, "Sensibility and Piety in the Making of the Veracruz Gente Sensata, 1780–1810," in William H. Beezley and Linda Curcio-Nagy, eds., *Latin American Popular Culture: An Introduction* (Wilmington, DE: SR Books, 2000), p. 23.

population as a different racial group. Putting aside Columbus's insistence that he had reached India, leading to the inaccurate designation of *Indians,* Europeans still recognized indigenous peoples as a distinct group.

Iberian attitudes toward race and miscegenation, from 1492 to 1800, are difficult to understand in present-day terms. The legal designation of purity of blood (*limpieza de sangre*), shared by both the Spanish and Portuguese, rested on the conviction that racial purity established a superior individual, whereas racial mixture combined the least desirable traits of both parents. As a complement to this attitude, Spaniards promoted the superiority of Christians and the inferiority of non-Christians.

Nevertheless, Spain and Portugal, their claims notwithstanding, lacked racial purity. Cultural and biological mixture, beyond anyone's ability to unravel it, long characterized the Iberian Peninsula. Visigoths, Romans, Vikings, Jews, Moors, and Iberians all contributed to this mélange, making the religious claim critically important. Race alone did not convey advantage. Superiority could not be asserted without Christianity. This fragile syllogism became the rationalization to overturn Indian empires and build a new society.

Despite theoretical notions about racial purity, a *mestizo,* or biologically mixed, society emerged in Latin America. The early Spanish and Portuguese explorers were almost exclusively men, who took advantage of the initial absence of European women and the temporary collapse of sexual mores to cohabit with Indian and African women. Widespread intermixing and illegitimacy accompanied the violence and confusion of armed conquest and early settlement. By the time European gender ratios came closely into balance, many who claimed European heritage were in fact mestizos.

Many mestizos took part in the final stages of the Spanish conquest, particularly in South America. Both Francisco Pizarro and Diego Almagro, the conquerors of Peru, had mestizo sons who inherited their fathers' prestige and their violent temperaments. The Spaniards accorded high status to intermarriage with the Indian nobility. The mestizo offspring of the *conquistadores* enjoyed a position that made their mixed parentage immaterial. In Paraguay, some 600 European settlers intermarried so completely that by 1600 almost the entire non-Indian population were mestizos. Their pragmatic mix resulted from illegitimacy and polygamy despite church efforts to force the conquistadores to establish monogamous families.

In colonial society, illegitimacy and miscegenation mattered little at the lower social levels. In society's higher registers, the payment of a fee could erase either impediment. An individual could purchase a royal decree, called a *cédula de gracias al sacar,* to alter biological and legal categories. This compromise provided the social flexibility often needed in a mestizo community. The Spanish introduced large numbers of African slaves on their islands in the Caribbean and on the coast of what is now Mexico, Venezuela, and Colombia. Publicly the Spaniards tried to avoid contact with blacks, but in private they established numerous relationships. Miscegenation quickly became a common practice.

Portuguese-American society differed from that of Spanish Americans because no great indigenous civilizations existed in Brazil. The Portuguese encountered

## The Atlantic Slave Trade 1451–1871

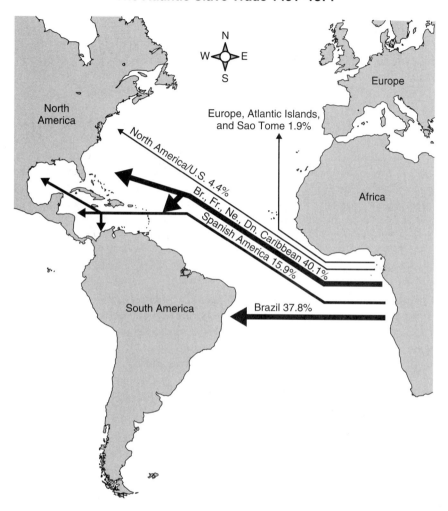

tribal Indians, mainly engaged in hunting and gathering. The sparse population numbered no more than a million scattered across the wide expanse of Brazil, and the societies lacked the social and economic complexity of the Aztecs, Incas, and other groups encountered by the Spaniards. Portuguese miscegenation with Indian peoples occurred, but not on the scale it did in Spanish America, nor did it result in a mestizo society. In the absence of a large indigenous population, the Portuguese turned to African slavery as a source of labor. This decision totally changed the demographic composition of Brazil. European and African peoples provided the major racial and cultural components that intermixed in the emerging Luso-Brazilian society.

Racial preference emerged in a two-tier system as a result of African slavery in Brazil. Portuguese law did not link slavery to race, but Brazil's complete reliance on African slavery for labor inevitably did so. Miscegenation had both a public and a private face. Luso-Brazilian men mingled with black and mulatto women in private, but in public they avoided too close an identification with Afro-Brazilians.

## Colonial Environments

The Spanish and the Portuguese, once they arrived in the Western Hemisphere, accelerated the human impact on the environment that had begun in major ways with the domestication of crops. Over the next 300 years, Europeans and their successors used their crops and animals to effect ecological imperialism, creating "neo-Europes" in the temperate regions of the Americas. European plants (wheat especially) and a variety of animals (including cattle, hogs, and chickens) had an indelible impact in the hemisphere.[3] Immigrants brought fewer changes to the American tropics and alpine zones, where both indigenous products and peoples remained in the majority. The European arrivals, nevertheless, brought about a radical transformation of the ecological systems of the temperate regions of the Americas.

Massive migration from Europe and Africa to the Americas brought about great ecological change in the hemisphere. Spaniards and Portuguese came in search of adventure, riches, and the chance to serve their church. They attempted to build an improved version of their homelands, not just a replica. In the process of incorporating the Africans they brought as slaves and the indigenous peoples, along with and their living and material cultures, the Spaniards and Portuguese created new mestizo or parallactic environments.[4] During the colonial years, this mestizo environment meant different things to different peoples. The one-time corn patch converted to sugarcane represented agricultural progress to Spaniards, environmental ruination to Indians, and the horrors of enslavement to Africans. Even in these Europeanized fields, elements of African and indigenous origin, even if unrecognized, shaped this mestizo environment.

Although changes in the environment resulted from activities of indigenous cultures, the Europeans and Africans brought different changes, which made dramatic alterations as a result of the new plant and animal life they introduced. They made some efforts to preserve the environment. For example, in 1775, the Spanish colonial governor of Costa Rica, don Juan Fernández de Bobadilla, issued

---

[3] Alfred W. Crosby, *Ecological Imperialism: The Biological Expansion of Europe, 900–1900* (New York: Cambridge University Press, 1986), pp. 2–7; Elinor G. K. Melville, *An Environmental History of Latin America* (Albuquerque: University of New Mexico Press, forthcoming) and *A Plague of Sheep: Environmental Consequences of the Conquest of Mexico* (New York: Cambridge University Press, 1994).

[4] Elinor Melville, a leading thinker on topics of landscapes, environments, and ecological history of Latin America, recently developed the thesis that the arrival of Europeans and Africans in the Western Hemisphere resulted in the creation of a series of environments in the same space. She calls these overlapping landscapes "hybrid environments," which were understood and appreciated differently depending on one's location in the space. Thus, this concept might be termed parallactic environmentalism.

a proclamation against burning fields and forests, "since the practice is followed by sterility of the soil." The decree, like many others, remained unenforced.[5]

## European Economic Modifications

The existing economic situation in the Americas to a large extent determined the nature of European innovations. The changes introduced by the newcomers varied from one region to another. Both the Spanish and the Portuguese had market demands and consumer tastes that they grafted onto the Indian economy. In particular, the Europeans made immediate demands for land and labor.

When Columbus arrived in the Western Hemisphere, land and labor were not separate commodities as they were in Europe. Indians in general perceived real property and labor as inseparable. The Iberians saw them as distinct commodities. In Europe, land constituted the basic capital unit upon which all else rested. It produced wealth for its individual owner, could be mortgaged, sold to raise capital to purchase other land, or switched to another economic activity. For the Spaniards the absence of private property made the creation of individual wealth impossible. To have value in their terms, land required individual ownership. The Indian system—communal work on commonly held village lands—created static wealth, not the individual profits that propelled the European economy.

Dissolving the communal ties between land and labor constituted the first and most difficult change attempted in the Americas. Modification required implementing concepts of personal property and individual work for wages. To do this, Spaniards fell back on the *encomienda,* an institutional device developed during the Christian reconquest of Moorish Spain (711–1492) to incorporate Moslems as peasants into the Spanish political and economic order. The Spanish-American encomienda created mutual obligations between Spanish trustees and Indian wards. It assigned Indian male heads of household, who paid tribute (tax) to a Spanish *encomendero,* who assumed responsibility, in theory, for their well-being and loyal conduct. The Crown required the Indians to pay tribute in both goods and labor. The encomienda proved useful in getting Indians accustomed to land detached from their lands. The cultural disruption caused by the arrival of the Europeans and the use of the encomienda gradually created a pool of workers available for wage hire. Where they could, Indians persisted in traditional labor practices. For example, they preferred to work in groups directed by an Indian foreman. As early as the 1540s, Indians in Guatemala worked under notarized contracts that specified their foremen, labor conditions, and payment. Once mining became widespread, it relied on large numbers of both free and tribute workers.

For largely political reasons, the Crown essentially abolished use of the encomienda as a labor system in 1549 and replaced it with the *repartimiento.* This system required villages to send a percentage of their adult male workers

---

[5]David Rains Wallace, *The Quetzal and the Macau: Costa Rica's National Parks* (San Francisco: Sierra Club, 1996), p. 8.

each week to work on what the Spaniards considered projects for the common good, for the most part defined as work on wheat farms, in silver mines, and, in Mexico City, on drainage projects. The workers received minimal weekly wages that more or less matched the new head taxes assessed by the Crown as tribute. The repartimiento accustomed workers to wage labor, but by the 1630s, because of village depopulation, this system began to fail. Workers increasingly fled with their families to work on Spanish-owned estates or in the mines. They received contracts from Spanish owners that specified wages and offered benefits such as minimal housing and credit to desperate families. This latter system, called *gañan* or contract labor, continued for the rest of the colonial era.

Plantation agriculture boomed in the tropical zones (the *tierra caliente*), especially with the introduction of sugarcane. The sugar industry resulted in such onerous labor demands that only slavery could provide sufficient workers. Indian slaves quickly died due to the harsh working conditions, compounded by European diseases. The Spaniards and the Portuguese then turned to African slaves. By the mid-sixteenth century, African slaves made up the majority of the population throughout the tropical zones and became an important population component of domestic labor in the cities of the temperate region for the rest of the colonial period.

Land constituted the other half of the European economic equation. Roman tradition and Spanish law recognized the Crown as the ultimate owner of all lands in the kingdoms. This provided the necessary authority to the monarch to issue legal titles. The Crown recognized the legal existence of Indian communal property, thereby preventing its simple seizure. The king also disposed of abandoned property (*tierras baldías*) and made grants of unoccupied territory. Fraud, theft, and intimidation of residents all played a part in the transfer of ownership. Surveying and granting land titles often concealed tremendous skullduggery. Indigenous population decline under the impact of epidemic disease and cultural trauma opened up significant amounts of land that, ignoring communal ownership, could be classified as abandoned. The Indians quickly grasped the concept of land ownership. As land transferred in all directions, individual Indians sought titles from the Crown, and Indian groups defended their property in royal courts. When necessary, they hired legal assistance and manipulated the concept of private property to their own advantage.

Colonial landholdings varied greatly in size and productivity. Variables such as fertility, water, and distance from markets determined land values and the type and extent of production. The *hacienda,* an overused label for a great estate, functioned as a mixed enterprise of crops and cattle. Its size ranged from a few hundred hectares in fertile, well-watered locations to vast sprawling spreads in arid regions that supported only one animal per hectare (2.4 acres). Some haciendas produced handsome profits, but all required considerable attention, market knowledge, and of course a little luck. Proximity to large towns or roads reaching the mines provided the best guarantee of success. Smaller units, with a variety of names such as *ranchos, labores,* and *chacras,* were usually intensively farmed and supplied fruits, vegetables, and cereals for subsistence.

## Colonial Economy

Although new perceptions of land and labor had the greatest economic impact in the Americas, the economy of the Spanish colonies depended on precious metals to sustain both the internal and export sectors and to meet the fiscal demands of the empire. The mining industry created an extensive market for food, animals, clothing, hides, and transportation. This demand drove the internal colonial economy. Silver and other precious metals enjoyed high demand in Europe and had enough value to support the cost of mining and transportation. Agricultural products, in contrast, did not have an immediate export market in Europe or elsewhere. Rather than shipping produce to Europe, Spaniards introduced American crops such as maize and potatoes to their homeland. Exotic products, for example, cacao to make chocolate and tobacco to sniff or smoke, required decades to attract consumers. Initially only a limited number of American commodities went to Europe, but eventually demand grew for products such as cacao, tobacco, cotton, indigo, and later sugar. Silver and cochineal (for scarlet dye) remained the major exports.

Europeans introduced wheat, barley, oats, cattle, sheep, goats, and commercial sugarcane to the Americas. Heavy draft animals, absent before the arrival of the Spaniards, along with deep furrow plows made for a significant increase in agricultural productivity. Horses and mules revolutionized the transport of goods. Although human porters, carrying heavy loads while navigating steep and narrow trails, continued to be used along with *llamas* in the Andes, Spanish transport expanded the carrying trade. Coastal shipping in large sailing vessels replaced pre-Columbian rafts. Not long after the Spaniards arrived, enterprising Indian traders sailed aboard Spanish ships loaded with indigenous goods.

The growing demand for food, clothing, mules, horses, and hides in the mining regions created prosperity in distant regions that produced these goods. The mining zones drew resources from virtually every part of Spain's empire, including Chinese silk and other luxuries channeled through the Spanish Philippines. Central Mexico—Puebla, Atlixco, and the San Pablo region—specialized in European agricultural production. A century after Cortés arrived, Indian workers on Spanish haciendas each year produced 375,000 bushels of wheat in the central valley for Mexico City as well as some 60,000 bushels exported to Cuba. Livestock multiplied at a fantastic rate, providing hides and cheap meat. In the process, the sheep and cows caused tremendous environmental changes by destroying native grasses, which prompted soil erosion and forest reduction.

In South America, the mines were located in the high Andes. Provisioning centers to support them quickly developed in what are now Argentina's interior provinces. Agricultural entrepreneurs raised food, grapes, horses, mules, and oxen, and prepared hides that supplied the miners of what is now modern-day Peru and Bolivia. In a similar fashion, Spaniards in Chile produced wheat for the Peruvian market.

Quito, Ecuador, and its surrounding valley contained 150,000 sheep and goats, 30,000 cattle, 12,000 hogs, and 2,000 mules and horses. Quito also drew wool from the adjacent valleys of Latacunga and Riobamba, which supported another 600,000 sheep. Regional wool and cotton supplies provided the basis for a thriving textile industry. Quito's merchants shipped textiles to Andean regions, Panama, and Cartagena, and Chileans in turn obtained these fabrics and transported them to western Argentina. Labor-intensive factories, called *obrajes,* employed some 30,000 workers in Quito. Mineral wealth effectively capitalized industry, trade, and commerce across the hemisphere.

Manufacturing constituted an important segment of the colonial economy. By the last decades of the sixteenth century, Spain's colonists produced almost all their everyday needs, such as furniture, leather goods, glass, and textiles (mainly woolen work clothing and some cotton products). As a result, they achieved a certain degree of independence from Spain. Most of the American production depended on small workshops employing one or two individuals. Textile operations tended to be larger. Obrajes that produced fine as well as common-quality cloth employed 100–200 workers. Small operations with one or two looms, called *trapiches,* catered to specialty demands or limited local markets.

## Imperial Trade

Trade between Spain and the Americas depended on shipping, organized in a convoy system. Individual vessels occasionally received permission to sail on their own schedule. Pirates, who first appeared off the coast of North Africa, later around the Azores, and subsequently in the Caribbean, created the need for convoys of merchant ships escorted by naval vessels. Well-armed men-of-war defended convoys carrying tools, finished goods, and European luxuries to the Americas and silver on the return trip. In the early days, ships carried immigrants and tools, agricultural implements, seeds, domesticated animals, and casks of wine, olive oil, and flour—all the items needed to establish a European lifestyle. By the middle of the sixteenth century, cargos shifted from basic supplies to manufactured goods. Spanish merchants eventually faced competition from domestic goods produced in ever greater quantities.

Spain sent two fleets, the *flota* and the *galeones,* to the Americas. The galeones sailed in May, destined for Mexico and Central America. When the fleet entered the Caribbean, ships bound for Honduras and the islands of the Greater Antilles split off, and the remaining vessels continued to Veracruz. The flota, or South American fleet, sailed in August for Panama. Once loaded with silver, this fleet sought refuge in the safe and fortified port of Cartagena. Both fleets gathered in Havana for the return voyage to Spain the following summer, hoping to avoid the hurricane season. The system had obvious drawbacks. Wholesalers in the Americas, receiving vast quantities of goods all at one time, could bargain for lower prices, then store the merchandise in warehouses and sell it as prices rose between convoys. When shipping remained idle for an extended period, during European wars, for example, the expense of refitting warships and merchant vessels required burdensome taxes. During the first two centuries, security concerns made the convoy system necessary, but it lingered after it had outlived its usefulness. Finally, the Crown ended the convoys in the latter half of the eighteenth century.

Latin America's integration into the broader world economy began in a gradual fashion and gained momentum by the eighteenth century. Smuggling, encouraged by the amount of silver available, pulled Spanish America into the world economy beyond Spain's economic control. Imperial reforms between 1765 and 1800 acted to increase trade in the empire, but Spain could not supply its American colonies with all the consumer goods they wanted, nor absorb their raw materials.

## Creation of the Luso-Brazilian Economy

The Portuguese settled a land of unknown prospects, peopled by inhabitants who had little need for trade and commerce. Early sharp-eyed Portuguese prospectors identified dyewood trees, similar to those imported at great cost from the Far East. Wood samples sent back to Portugal confirmed its value as a textile dye. As the first viable export, Brazilwood also supplied the name for the vast new land.

The Portuguese needed workers to sustain the steady production required to support the European market for dyewood. The enterprise required heavy work, cutting the dense dyewood, trimming logs, moving them to the beach, and loading them aboard ships. Brazilian hunter-gatherers made reluctant workers with little interest in European-style labor. The Portuguese bartered for trade goods, metal axes, shirts, hats, even firearms, but this worked only for a short time. The Tupí-Guaraní, well adapted to their environment, had little desire for surplus goods or wages offered by Portuguese traders. The Portuguese soon changed the early ad hoc labor system from barter to slavery.

Rapid establishment of a colonial economy required government involvement, planning, and encouragement. The Portuguese monarch employed the captaincy system to entice developers to invest in the creation of colonies. The Crown, for its part, granted them huge tracts of land, sufficient authority to enforce order, and the right to certain monopolies, and urged them to get on with the task. As one of these developers carped, the king granted them land by the league and they had to conquer it by inches. Only two of the captaincies succeeded. Of the others, many never moved beyond the talking stage and several existed in name only.

In 1549, the Crown established a colonial capital in Bahia, took control of the undeveloped captaincies, dispatched troops and immigrants, and pushed Brazil to a new economic stage, the sugar era. The Portuguese had gained experience with this crop in southern Portugal and on the island of Madeira. An expanding European market that promised high profits motivated them to try sugar cultivation in Brazil. Once again, the Portuguese sought workers to do the hard, continuous work required in cutting trees, clearing land, planting, harvesting, and preliminary processing. The Portuguese demand quickly exceeded available workers from the small Amerindian population, whether enslaved or not. The planters promptly turned to African slavery. Sugar and slaves created the Portuguese plantation economy. Dutch ships carried most of the sugar to Europe and provided much of the marketing expertise. Plantation sugar became a wildly profitable export. Such success led the Crown to oppose crop diversification. Nevertheless, tobacco, rice, cotton, indigo, and *aguardiente* (cane spirits) entered the trade. Cane alcohol became a commercial item within Brazil and in the African trade.

Sugar remained dominant until the 1680s when competing production in the English, French, and Dutch Caribbean undercut prices and drastically reduced demand. Sugar's collapse in Brazil plunged much of the coastal region into economic depression. The last decade of the seventeenth century demonstrated the dangers inherent in relying on one export product and excessive dependence on overseas markets (called monoculture). This lesson was easy to comprehend, but painfully difficult to do much about. Sugar experienced a moderate recovery in the eighteenth century, but declined once again in the early decades of the next century.

Luso-Brazilians developed a cattle industry exclusively for the internal market. Livestock met the demand for dried meat to feed slave workers, oxen and mules to supply motive power, and hides used for packaging. The Portuguese Crown, anxious to maximize profits during the sugar boom, prohibited stock raising on the coast to preserve land for cane production. Brazil's backlands appeared well suited for cattle, oxen, horses, and mules. Herds driven in all directions established a series of trails that crisscrossed the interior from north to south. The cattle industry, through its well-established herding network, acted to tie Brazil together. Cattle ranches spanned vast territories, especially in arid regions. Burning trees to create pastureland occurred in areas where rainfall could support a permanent grass cover. This pastoral endeavor produced roving herdsmen, who later took on folkloric stature roughly equal to U.S. cowboys and Argentine *gauchos.*

The discovery of gold and diamonds in the last decade of the seventeenth century created a new boom cycle in Brazil. The rush to mining zones shifted the economic center away from the sugar coast to the south-central region where it remains today. Gold flowed to Portugal, lingered briefly, and then went to London. Portugal, and through it Brazil, had been pulled into the English trading system. The Methuen Treaty of 1703 capped the process of economic dependency on Great Britain. The treaty opened Portugal to British manufactured goods in return for establishing a market for Portuguese wines and agricultural products. As a consequence, Brazil's wealth helped fuel the Industrial Revolution in England and made London the financial capital of the world. The amount of gold extracted from Brazil equaled the amount mined in the entire hemisphere from 1492 to the California gold rush of 1849. Although gold rescued the grim economic situation, it drastically unbalanced trade between Portugal and its American colony. Portugal ran a trade surplus with Great Britain, thanks to gold transshipments, but a large and growing deficit developed with Brazil. The distortion caused by the gold trade completely undercut Portugal's role as middleman and created a parasitic connection. Gold production tapered off around 1760, but the damage to the Portuguese economy could not be reversed. Brazil's move into the international system under British tutelage made political independence probable.

## Colonial Cities

The approach Spain and Portugal took to urbanization differed little from that of pre-Columbian empires. The Iberian tradition, derived from Roman practice, required that those who worked the land reside in villages and not live scattered across the landscape in dispersed family holdings. No matter how humble, population centers functioned as the core of an agricultural district, providing the initial collection point for labor and produce. Larger settlements became regional marketing centers. Each Iberian town and its surrounding area constituted a single economic, political, and psychological unit. The Iberians brought this urban blueprint with them to the Western Hemisphere, where the pattern of urban-based development closely linked to the surrounding hinterland meshed with similar pre-Columbian practices.

Early European settlements in the New World served as outposts, either for penetration of the interior, as in Portuguese America (Brazil), or for political control of Indian societies, as in the Spanish regions. Conquistadores moved swiftly to take control of Indian centers such as Cuzco and Tenochtitlán. When necessary, they founded new settlements in strategic locations such as Lima. This urban strategy enabled them to control the populated and productive parts of the New World.

Spanish-American cities, complete with royal charters, sprang up with stunning rapidity. Initial settlements in the Antilles, beginning with Santo Domingo (1496), served to consolidate the European presence and provided a springboard for the wave of conquest that swept the mainland. The municipality of Veracruz, established on the Mexican coast (1519), became the first of many mainland coastal settlements. Trujillo, Honduras (1525), Santa Marta (1529), Maracaibo (1529), Cartagena (1533), Guayaquil (1535), Callao (1537), Valparaíso (1544), and other port settlements provided the all-important maritime link with the European world. Yet, although the port cities were important from a logistical standpoint, the inland centers had more political importance for the Spaniards. Mexico City (1521), Cochabamba (1536), Asunción (1537), Bogotá (1538), Guadalajara (1541), Santiago (1541), La Paz (1548), Córdoba (1573), and Spanish Cuzco, established on the massive stone foundation of the former Inca capital, represented the inland jewels of the emerging empire. Indeed, all major Spanish-American cities, with the exception of Montevideo, Medellín, and the modern shadow cities created by displaced urban poor, have sixteenth-century roots.

Not all settlements remained in the same location. Havana, for example, relocated from Cuba's southern coast to its present site in 1591. Relocations resulted from discoveries of more suitable environments (protected from storms, for example), concern for security, changing conditions such as demographic decline or increase, or economic developments. Functional needs determined the site as well as its permanence, and when functions changed so did location. The status and importance of settlements also shifted over time. For example, Frontera de Cáceres, founded in the interior of Honduras in order to establish a European presence in the demographic center of the Olancho valley near the Indian towns of Telica Chiquita and Escamilpa Chiquita, subsequently lost out to San Jorge de

Olancho on the other side of the Patuca River. Then, with the irresistible attraction of silver in the 1580s, Tegucigalpa became the economic and political center of Honduras.

Urban planning responded to political and economic realities in a pragmatic fashion. Colonial cities, whether built from scratch, such as Lima (1535) and Puebla (1531), or superimposed on existing Indian cities, such as Mexico City, were also meant to demonstrate European permanence and strength. Although not physically walled in, they did serve as unmistakable bastions of European power.

King Felipe II codified the establishment of settlements in his "Ordinances Concerning New Discoveries and Settlements," issued in 1573. His decrees prudently noted that settlements should have easy access to both land and sea routes to facilitate trade and enable settlers to govern and defend themselves. The ordinances ordered the settlers to lay out the towns on a grid pattern, incorporating a central plaza with regularly spaced blocks extending outward from the four sides of the plaza. The corners of the grid were oriented to the four cardinal points; this way, every street had sunlight and heat at some time during the day and some shade during most of the summer months. This orientation also prevented the streets, often lined with two-story houses, from becoming wind tunnels during storms. The main plaza (*plaza mayor* or *plaza de armas*) housed the state authority. The municipal building (*palacio municipal*), a church (or cathedral if a bishop resided there), the governor's palace (in a viceregal capital, the viceroy's palace), and the high court (*audiencia*) were located around the main plaza. Although geography might require some modifications, all cities followed the general grid pattern.

Inevitably, best-laid plans failed to anticipate the future. As Bernabé Cobos, who described the city of Lima in 1629, observed, the urban expanse had greatly exceeded the area so carefully allotted by the original designers. In that year, Lima had 4,000 houses sheltering some 5,000–6,000 Spanish inhabitants with a fluctuating Indian population adding as many as 25,000 more residents. Lima's growth amazed Cobos and he saw no end in sight. He proved prophetic.

A hierarchy of urban centers existed. A municipality's political jurisdiction extended far beyond its urban core to the boundary of another municipality or to a point where political jurisdiction appeared unnecessary. Only the principal cities had a municipal council (*cabildo* or *ayuntamiento*). At the end of the eighteenth century, for example, New Spain (Mexico) had fewer than 20 such town councils. Councillors, along with nobles and churchmen, constituted the traditional three estates of feudal Europe and were entitled to meet as a parliament (called a *Cortes* in Spain), when convened by the monarch.

In the New World, the councillors of Lima, Mexico City, and other political centers understood that they occupied an important place within the political structure. Wealthy citizens (*vecinos*) dominated the municipality, and among them a few families usually served as members of the municipal council. Their wealth and social prestige made them an urban-based elite. Ownership of property in the city and in surrounding rural areas supported their claims to political and social authority. Mexico City leaders, less than a decade after the destruction of Tenochtitlán, pressed

Carlos V to extend to New World municipalities the right to convene as a Cortes in the same manner as in Spain. The major American cities jealously guarded their rights and maintained lobbyists in Madrid to protect and further their interests. When Lima's representatives arrived to see the king in 1692, they entered the royal chambers after ceremoniously being urged, "Enter city of Lima, His Majesty awaits you."

Cities at the top of the political structure had authority over surrounding towns (*villas*), which in turn had their own dependent villages (*pueblos*) that controlled tiny outlying settlements called simply places (*lugares*). A regional or district capital served as administrative center (*cabecera*) for a network of towns with smaller populations and their rural areas. Over time an urban center's status might change. Havana, established as a villa, became a city in 1592. The primacy of major cities over lesser centers reinforced their dominant economic and political importance.

One function of early Spanish-American cities was to control the Indians and incorporate them into the new imperial structure. Others soon emerged. Many small villages were created when missionary friars settled several Indian groups in one place to facilitate religious indoctrination and social control. Such artificial settlements, often an assembly of many different Indian groups, contributed to the weakening of Indian cultural bonds. Some inhabitants fled, but, unable to return to their old villages, they drifted away to the cities. The growth of the Indian barrios of Mexico City and Lima reflected this pattern despite the efforts of colonial authorities to discourage such migration.

City formation also followed economic impulses. In Mexico, silver strikes drew people northward, creating frontier mining camps that soon developed into cities, such as Zacatecas, Guanajuato, San Luis Potosí, Real de Monte, and Pachuca, among others. Towns established along the routes between silver settlements and New Spain's political and agricultural center offered protection against nomadic northern Indian raiders and served as supply centers. Silver mining created demand and supplied wealth to establish the urban network.

In Upper Peru (now Bolivia) Europeans began to work Potosí's mountain of silver ore in 1545. Silver wealth spawned a fantastic city. The silver mountain that created Potosí rose some 16,000 feet above sea level, an altitude that proved difficult for human settlement. Nevertheless, staggering mineral wealth overcame terrain and elevation to create the largest city in South America, with approximately 120,000 inhabitants by 1650. Potosí's fame spread throughout the world. Antonio de León Pinelo, Spain's royal cosmographer and chronicler, in the early seventeenth century described Potosí as a paradise containing sufficient silver to construct a bridge from Potosí across the Atlantic Ocean to Madrid. Stunned by the wealth and grandeur of the New World, he asserted that the Amazon, Magdalena, Orinoco, and, appropriately, the *Río de la Plata* (Silver River) were in fact the four rivers of the Bible. León Pinelo claimed that Noah's ark had been constructed near Lima in the Andes. Obviously silver not only dazzled the eye but also swept away scholarly prudence. Half a world away, Chinese cartographers drawing an imperial world map accurately located Potosí. The Spanish king, Carlos V, who was also Holy Roman Emperor, responded to both the glamorous aspect of the mountain of silver and its economic contribution to his kingdom, when he designated Potosí as an Imperial City. Lavish excesses characterized life in the world's greatest mining town. In 1556, the city celebrated King Felipe II's coronation with a civic extravaganza that lasted 24 days and cost 8 million pesos. A more practical expenditure of 3 million pesos for a water system indicated that frivolous excess could be balanced by more useful endeavors.

Potosí epitomized the New World's promise of social and economic opportunity. A flood of eager immigrants, anxious for quick wealth, turned a rough mining camp into a city. More refined ways of making a living soon changed Potosí into a complex urban center, home to merchants, artisans, and others not directly involved in mining. By the early seventeenth century hundreds of professional gamblers did their best to share the wealth of carefree miners. At least 120 courtesans offered the pleasure of their company to residents of the city. Doña Clara, a woman of great beauty and intelligence, created an elegant salon furnished with Oriental and European luxuries. Potosí's richest miners literally showered her with silver as they ardently competed for her favors. Unfortunately, silver declined and with it the city. By the early nineteenth century, only the mystique of Potosí remained. In 1825, Simón Bolívar, along with General José Antonio Sucre and their entourage, climbed to the summit to proclaim victory for the independence movement in South America at the site of "Spain's treasury for three hundred years."[6]

Potosí was the most extravagant mining center, but there were other mining towns. Silver strikes across Peru created mining camps where miners extracted over 400 million pesos of silver between 1533 and 1635. These mining activities supported an extensive network of secondary supply and market cities.

Colonial cities engaged in nonagricultural activities such as mining had a direct link to raw materials and food resources from surrounding agricultural areas. Of course, they also relied on trade, including overseas products. Mining settlements produced little except ore, thus providing strong markets for virtually everything. Silver mining in Peru, Mexico, and elsewhere constituted the economic engine of the Spanish-American empire. Supplemental trade with distant settlements tied cities and regions together, which stimulated a sense of belonging to the larger Spanish kingdom.

**City Living**    Life in the city ranged from the grand and ostentatious style of the elites, to the well-off respectability of the artisans and petty merchants, to the daily struggle for survival of the lower-class workers, transients, and recent, especially Indian, arrivals. Destruction of pre-Columbian agricultural production, detachment from ethnic communities, and the association of the city with the notion of Spanish progress pushed and pulled individuals and their families into colonial cities. The reception of poor newcomers—Indians, Africans, mulattoes, and mestizos at the bottom of society—passed from tolerance to indifference,

---

[6]Lewis Hanke, *The Imperial City of Potosí: An Unwritten Chapter in the History of Spanish America* (The Hague: Martinus Nijhoff, 1996), pp. 1–42.

disapproval, and hostility. Eventually, municipal authorities expressed alarm at the growing mixed population.

Cities consisted of distinct social layers. Residential zones ringed the main plaza and reflected the social hierarchy. The first ring, in close proximity to the physical seat of power, contained the mansions of the wealthy and high officials. Capital city streets in this area were paved and lighted after dark. The most prestigious convents could also be found in this district. The second ring contained the stores and houses of petty merchants, artisans, and government clerks. These residents generally lived above or behind businesses. Beyond this ring lived the poorest residents, a mixture of ethnic groups and penniless newcomers hoping to survive in the city.

The residential layout did not stop the constant interaction among classes. Water carriers, porters, servants, peddlers, beggars, and pickpockets plied their trades in all neighborhoods. The desperate poor often built lean-tos and shacks against church or convent walls, hoping the proximity to religion would make their eviction less likely. An underclass made up of the underemployed, jobless, and hopeless roamed throughout the city, enduring periodic scrapes with the law or within the sudden reach of military impressment gangs. Malnutrition, alcoholism, and endemic disease, particularly respiratory ailments and skin afflictions, served as emblems of this large and visible group.

In Portuguese America, the establishment of cities followed a pattern different from that in Spanish America. The need to replace Indian political control of pre-Columbian cities did not exist. Brazil's indigenous population had not developed large settlements or extensive political organizations. Brazil in 1500 presented a densely forested coastline with a population of warlike hunters and gatherers who depended on root crops and the natural bounty of the land. Early Portuguese settlements huddled insecurely on this coast, their inhabitants barely able to penetrate inland. In many respects, Brazilian colonists followed a pattern similar to that of British North Americans; both made many failed attempts before a permanent colony could be secured.

The first Portuguese settlements struggled to develop an economic base. These tenuous outposts could not rely on the chronically impoverished Portuguese monarchy for assistance. Nor did the Indians of Brazil possess great treasures, resources, or agriculture, as did the Incas and Aztecs. Dyewood, also called brazilwood, found a market in Europe that created small lumber-cutting settlements, but these lasted only as long as the supply of dyewood trees. Excessive demands on the limited number of Indians as workers and on available food resources soon brought the new arrivals into violent conflict with the local population, making it even more difficult to establish permanent settlements. Moreover, brazilwood soon attracted the French to the South Atlantic, who threatened Portugal's tenuous grip on Brazil.

The Portuguese Crown had to find a way to lure colonists or lose control over Brazil. São Vicente (1532), near present-day Santos, along with a tiny settlement that became modern São Paulo, were the first permanent outposts of Portuguese America. To stimulate other settlements, the Crown divided Brazil into 15 captaincies, conveyed as quasi-private holdings to 12 individuals (*donatarios*). In theory, the donatarios would use their own resources to establish colonies. Only two of these captaincies succeeded—Pernambuco, around the population core of Olinda-Recife, and São Vicente. Settlements, strung up and down the coast like a strand of pearls, eventually provided the beachheads for movement into the backlands. Salvador da Bahia, eventually the largest city in the Luso-Brazilian world after Lisbon, developed because of direct Crown investments, despite the captaincy program. Bahia became the colonial capital in 1549 and remained so until 1763 when economic factors led to the transfer of the capital to Rio de Janeiro in the south. Portuguese-American cities served mainly as ports to funnel plantation agriculture and raw materials to the European market.

Bahia, on the *Baía de Todos os Santos* (Bay of All Saints), one of the world's best anchorages, depended directly on the surrounding agricultural area for its prosperity. The initial site of the city, deemed too exposed, was abandoned in favor of an area atop a cliff. A defensive wall completed in 1551 protected the new settlement. The city developed two distinct parts—the lower harbor district, which was soon filled with warehouses and merchant offices; and the upper city, the site of official buildings and residences of the inhabitants. Four steep paths ascended the cliff and a windlass raised or lowered cargo. Bahia expanded, its growth restricted only by natural obstacles. Portuguese officials did not follow the rigid grid layout with the zeal of Spanish planners. Without a large and complex Indian population to govern, city officials lacked the status and civic legitimacy enjoyed by Spanish-American councilmen.

Colonists leaped into Brazil's interior with the discovery of gold in 1695 and the subsequent diamond strike. Wild fantasies of wealth lured speculators, miners, adventurers, and merchants into the backlands to create rough mining camps. Most of these boomtowns disappeared with the exhaustion of the ore, but a few remained as towns and cities. In the sixteenth century, only 4 cities and 37 towns existed; the gold rush stimulated the establishment of 3 cities and 118 towns. *Villa Rica de Ouro Prêto* (the Rich Town of Black Gold), established by Antonio de Albuquerque in 1711, represented the prototypical mining settlement. Founded as a gold camp—a crude collection of huts filled with recent arrivals from Portugal, Luso-Brazilians from the coast, Indians, various population mixtures, and African slaves—Ouro Prêto evolved into a stable settlement over the next few decades. Royal officials intent on squeezing taxes from the residents, price-gouging merchants anxious to accommodate spendthrift miners, entertainers, and prostitutes all eventually provided a civic base. Ouro Prêto had a population of approximately 100,000 by 1750.

Luso-Brazilian cities, more interesting than grand, provided prosperity for the fortunate and hope of survival for the less so. Vagrants and beggars afflicted towns. They made passage through the streets unpleasant during the day and perilous after dark.

Beyond human dangers, Brazil harbored an amazing array of diseases. The existence of an ill-treated slave population with poor nutrition and unhealthy living conditions provided the human fodder for epidemic disease. Yellow fever, malaria, smallpox, and cholera could suddenly sweep through the population whether rich, poor, free, or slave. Even under day-to-day circumstances, public health conditions verged on the disastrous. *Mal do bicho* (getting the bug), acute dysentery that caused ulceration of the intestines and rectal gangrene became a common scourge throughout Portuguese America. Preventive medicine for dysentery consisted of a shot of *cachaça* (crude cane brandy) upon rising in the morning—the so-called *mata-bicho* (bug killer), a name and practice still remembered in modern-day Brazil and Angola.

Public hygiene, or rather the lack of it, threatened community health. Public squares often served as convenient places to abandon garbage and refuse of all types. At night slaves, known as *tigres,* carried baskets of human excrement on their heads to dump into the ocean or rivers, polluting stretches of the beaches or riverbanks. Tidal swamps and rivers acted as breeding grounds for diseases that assaulted the public's health. The wind carried both awful smells and dried fecal matter back into the cities to attack the senses, clog the lungs, and spread disease.

Burial practices contributed to the general unsanitary conditions. The rich and powerful were entombed within the Church until the late eighteenth century when the practice came under attack as dangerous to the health of the living. Faithful middle-class individuals could count on a private burial in hallowed ground, but the lower classes and slaves often suffered the indignity of mass burial. Trenches remained open until filled with cadavers, guaranteeing the spread of pestilence. Tropical and subtropical climates provided ideal breeding conditions for both epidemic and endemic diseases.

The Spaniards avoided some of the health problems found in Portuguese America by locating many of their cities at higher altitudes. Nevertheless, coastal cities such as Panamá, Cartagena, Veracruz, and Havana experienced the ravages of disease compounded by poor public health practices. Occasionally firing cannons in the belief that the sulfuric fumes would purify the air did little but startle the inhabitants. The Enlightenment, with its emphasis on scientific experimentation and observation, led to a better understanding of disease and its causes. By the end of the eighteenth century a smallpox vaccination had been developed and Spanish officials had introduced its use in the American empire. The cause of mosquito-borne diseases, such as yellow fever and malaria, remained a mystery until the end of the nineteenth century.

For all their problems and dangers, colonial cities attracted foreign and rural migrants willing to take their chances. Illiteracy and limited skills, perhaps a fatal combination in modern times, could be overcome in a society where basic skills could be acquired rapidly. One might begin selling a few items displayed on a blanket in the street, then turn to activity as an itinerant peddler, then rent a market space or even a stall, and perhaps eventually become a small shop owner.

Cities offered opportunities for individuals to advance socially and economically. Daring and ambitious individuals took on new ethnic identities and higher social status. Indians changed clothes, abandoning their distinctive regional dress for European fashions, and, in doing so, became cultural mestizos. Indian languages gave way to the city's *lingua franca* of Spanish. European immigrants to the New World, who came primarily from humble beginnings, preferred the city for similar reasons. The escape from the hereditary rigidity of the Old World, along with the psychological sense of a new beginning, made many things seem possible. In these circumstances, Europeans of modest attainments could insist on being addressed as *don,* in Spain a courtesy reserved for those of noble status. The city naturally promoted intermarriage and miscegenation and promised a chance for social and economic advancement.

The same process occurred in Portuguese America, although the vast number of African slaves restricted both the promise and the reality of social and economic mobility. Yet, some free Afro-Brazilians became small shop owners. Often women who began life as slaves turned their personal understanding of slave culture into profitable businesses, extending tiny bits of credit and buying smuggled gold and diamonds. Through their enterprise, they raised themselves socially and helped modify the economic and social structure of colonial Brazil. Race mixture, although it occurred frequently in Brazil, did not readily provide for mobility because of the inevitable restrictions of a society and economy based on slavery. Nevertheless, terms such as *branco de Bahia* (Bahian white) indicate a level of social mobility based on miscegenation.

The vitality and impressive population growth of colonial cities reflected the fact that the conquest of space in the New World began with urban settlements. Towns and cities became central to New World development and the major element in the symbiotic relationship between the productive countryside and its market.

## Colonial Families

European colonial families desired a secure position for themselves, their children, and ultimately their extended family. They sought to create a social, gender, and economic structure that not only mirrored the familiar European model but also went beyond it with respect to status, patriarchy, and wealth. They found a powerful appeal in the Old World notions of primogeniture, nobility, and entailed estates, even if they could not fully attain them. Attenuated grants of encomienda and titles of nobility experienced renewed vitality in the Americas. The enco-mienda had been employed during the reconquest of Spain from the Moors, but had lost its purpose. In the New World, during the conquest it offered a method of rewarding the conquistadores, elevating family status, and providing an economic foundation for the colonies. The encomienda placed the Indian within a system of mutual obligation: the Indian paid tribute to the patron, who, in theory, afforded protection and conversion to Christianity to the Indian dependents. Imperial celebrities, such as Hernán Cortés, received in encomienda (that is, in trust) thousands of tribute-paying heads of household. Lesser conquistadores averaged approximately 2,000 tribute-paying individuals, although on rare occasions a few Spaniards received as few as half a dozen Indians in trust. The Crown viewed the encomienda as a type of pension given for the lifetime of the original grantee. Encomienda holders often succeeded in petitioning the monarch to extend the grant for several generations. Eventually, by 1549, owing to staggering population decline as a result of European diseases and increasing labor demands because of plantation agriculture and silver mining, the Crown largely eliminated the institution. Still, the encomienda represented an early attempt by colonial elites to secure permanent economic and social advantage for themselves and their families based on subjugation of Indian peoples.

The colonial family functioned as a protective socioeconomic association encompassing the nuclear unit, relatives, and dependents. This extended family might well comprise several subordinate families and distant relatives connected through marriage or consanguinity. The family provided social and economic security. Elite families revolved around the male head of household, the patriarch who held authority within the family. The patriarch not only supported immediate relatives but also provided jobs, financial support, and modest dowries for distant and poorer relatives. Occasionally, a powerful widow directed the allocation of resources, planning and executing family strategies including marriages. Poorer relations, anxious to please, served as managers or trusted agents in family enterprises. Women helped in the household, or in schooling the children, and provided companionship. Of course, orphans were cared for as needed.

Servants also relied on the family patriarch. Both men and women found permanent or temporary employment in domestic service. For many, a position as a servant constituted a useful apprenticeship. Domestics, beyond cleaning house and waiting tables, learned to make items for household use that in modern times would be purchased. This way, the job provided training that could be useful elsewhere, perhaps even to enable the servant to become an independent artisan. Wages, although low, included room and board. In the sixteenth century, a household included from 1 to 40 servants. Long-term servants evolved into loyal retainers, adding to the strength and effectiveness of the family unit. Paternalistic ties of mutual obligation and formal affection gave many servants a sense of belonging to a respected social entity.

Actual household size varied greatly in the number of individuals living under the same roof. The family and its retainers constituted the important element, not the physical site occupied by its members. Economic success for the family might be capped by the purchase of a title of nobility and establishment of an entailed estate. Families without such dramatic wealth could use less grandiose techniques to preserve resources and create opportunities to improve their economic and social position. Astute as well as ambitious patriarchs formed alliances with powerful individuals through god-parentage (*compadrazgo*). Rich and poor alike sought out suitable individuals to become their children's godparents at baptism. Godparents also had a role at marriages and burials. The practice of selecting godparents for such occasions established networks of obligation between families linked in symbolic consanguinity. Any achievement, even if indirectly attained, translated into civic influence, social privilege, and material advantage. Honor constituted a tangible asset not to be jeopardized cavalierly or carelessly bestowed, and always to be closely guarded.

**Marriage**  Unmarried daughters and sons represented major family assets. These single family members served as pawns to be moved across the social chessboard for the family's collective advantage. Suitable marriages strengthened the family and provided social mobility. The dowry served several purposes. It acted as an economic restraint on the temptation to overreach social categories, but, above all, it provided economic security for the bride and established, at least in terms of wealth, equality between the two matrimonial partners and their families. Although the groom could invest the dowry, it remained the bride's property. Nevertheless, the dowry represented a transfer of property the impact of which had to be calculated closely.

Individuals such as Antonio López de Quiroga, a silver grandee of seventeenth-century Potosí, could afford to indulge the whims of their families and lavish wealth upon them. Don Antonio endowed his daughter with 20 sacks of silver coins and 1.5 tons of silver bars valued at some 100,000 pesos. Of course, few individuals could afford such ostentatious gestures. Often the groom had to resort to a lawsuit to collect the dowry, and on occasion the amount fell short of the terms of the marriage agreement. Tadeo Díez de Medina, who became one of the richest men in eighteenth-century La Paz, received only 2,250 pesos of the agreed 10,721 pesos. Dowries at the lower end of the social scale could be quite modest: a few chairs, some cooking utensils, or perhaps several farm animals. Lower-class marriages or consensual unions might carry only symbolic dowries.

Families developed various devices to counter the potential loss of resources. Endogamy, a fairly common practice, involved such arrangements as an uncle marrying a niece or a brother marrying a deceased brother's widow. Spaniards who became well-to-do merchants in Mexico or Peru often sent home to Spain for poor but able nephews to help in the business. If all went well they married them to their daughters, thereby maximizing both managerial and financial resources. Today such marriage strategies appear to overemphasize economics, but colonial families had few other mechanisms at their disposal by which they could advance socially or protect themselves in case of some economic disaster.

Romantic love existed despite the best-laid family plans, close parental supervision, and constant warnings about the consequences of an unsuitable alliance. Elopement and abduction (also called bride rape) could change family calculations. Smitten or ambitious suitors manipulated the importance of honor to gain admittance to the family by abducting an unmarried daughter. The family's honor, especially related to that of the daughter, was socially compromised by elopement, whether or not she had been sexually assaulted. A quickly performed marriage brought the abductor into the family. Elopement or abduction, both highly calculated acts, succeeded only when the pretender to family membership accurately assessed the situation. A totally unacceptable predator could expect little except punishment—including death at the hands of male family members.

Married women surrendered most of their day-to-day rights to their husbands. A woman's legal position varied according to social status and class. Prenuptial agreements allowed for many exceptions and variations. Personality and unique talents obviously came into play and influenced important family activities regardless of legal technicalities. Most women married between the ages of 14 and 18, although girls of 12 or even younger could be married if their fathers deemed it advantageous. Early marriage agreements allowed the

Individuals who engaged in bride abduction or rape, a danger for any young heiress and her family, manipulated the highly important concept of family honor to force their way into a socially and economically privileged family. Perhaps this colonial Ecuadorian chair back served as a reminder of the danger.

family almost total control of biological and financial resources, minimizing the possibility of elopement or bride rape, and determined the terms of the pre-nuptial agreement. Delivery of a very young bride, the actual ceremony, and consummation of the union could be delayed until a reasonable future date, at which time the dowry became due. Such agreements offered advantages at no immediate cost.

**Convents**   For some women, retreat into a convent, along with its implied divine protection as a bride of Christ, offered an attractive escape. Fear of an unwanted marriage, or of age disparities in an arranged union, acted as a moti-vator in many instances. In addition, the well-understood risks of repeated childbirth provided another incentive to avoid marriage. High infant mortality and childbirth complications made motherhood a risky gamble. A novice had a wide selection of convents to choose from, from those with minimal demands to those with rigorous requirements. Some nuns ran schools for young girls (the *Escuela de Amigas*) and engaged in other pious or charitable activities. Sor Juana Inés de la Cruz, the most famous Spanish colonial nun, often evoked today as a feminist symbol, spent much of her time writing poetry and discussing intellectual topics with the archbishop and other learned friends. In her last years, she gave in to pressure to behave more saintly and adopted a harsh regimen of self-denial. Her poetry, complex and poignant, remains a treasured intellectual legacy.

   Life in a convent might be forced on a woman as part of her family's eco-nomic strategy. Although the family had to allot a dowry to the convent, the amount often was considerably less than that required in a marriage. A family with several daughters could choose to concentrate resources on one and dispatch the others to a convent. The social as well as the religious importance of convents made them favored recipients of bequests. Colonial Brazilians constantly pressured the Crown to permit the establishment of additional convents as demand for openings exceeded the supply. In Spanish America the number of convents appears to have been sufficient.

**Black and Indian Families**   For the black and Indian populations, family patterns, including marriage customs and child rearing, depended to some extent on location. The Spanish and Portuguese crowns and the Catholic Church recognized the sanctity of slave families, but enslaved workers on sugar plantations in the Caribbean and in the Brazilian tropics could not count on this recognition. Indian women working as domestics might be forced into concubinage relationships, without regard to their marital status and with no intention of ever regularizing the relationship. Both the Spanish Crown and the Church during the colonial years attempted to force Spaniards to marry or give up their companions, but in practice illicit unions continued and illegitimacy grew apace among the mixed population.

Freed slaves and runaways resorted to remembered or invented African patterns of marriage in the communities they established beyond the reach of colonial authorities. Those Indians who managed to elude Spanish bureaucrats and missionaries, in Peru's remote Andes and Mexico's Lacandon forests, for example, successfully continued pre-Columbian cultural patterns, including family practices, for years. Royal officials considered these communities rogue settlements that threatened the rest of colonial society.

**Gender and Honor**   Gender-based behavioral restrictions varied across colonial society. Those who constituted the *gente decente* (respectable people), or perceived themselves as such, tended to have a rigid set of standards. As a group they struggled to preserve appearances, clinging to traditional religious and social values. They viewed violations of acceptable behavior as damaging to their carefully constructed social status. Their ruthless reaction to perceived transgressions reflected their slippery grip on the social ladder (see the Profile, "A Hapless Bigamist," page 39). How they expected to be regarded, and how they viewed others, depended on outward appearances rather than actual circumstances. In a society in which downward mobility appeared a constant threat, respectability and honor provided an important psychological barrier against a decline in social standing.

Society recognized different standards of conduct for men and women based on cultural perceptions, myths, biological differences, social status, age, civil conditions, and economic factors. Differences in expected behavior did not necessarily lead to tensions within the family, but the rigidity of the behavioral code made women transgressors exceedingly vulnerable. Society divided women into two categories, "decent" and "indecent." These served as both moral and social distinctions. At the lower end of the social scale the negative assumptions made lower-class women more vulnerable than others.

## PROFILE    A Hapless Bigamist

The experience of the hapless Francisco del Valle, entrapped by his own passion, demonstrates the importance of marriage and honor in colonial Latin America. A Spaniard, whose family lived in Mexico City and had long-held Crown appointments, Francisco had served as a district governor, judge, and militia officer.

His ordeal began pleasantly enough with the seduction of Clara Ochoa, of a well-to-do family from near Puebla. Francisco, on his way back to the capital where his invalid wife resided, secured lodging in doña Clara's house. It is not clear whether he used the ploy of a promise of marriage or some other means to accomplish his conquest, but his success soon became evident as he settled comfortably and openly in Clara's home. After several months the woman's family decided that the liaison jeopardized its honor and only marriage could erase the blot. The fact that Francisco already had a wife would not be allowed to stand in the way of rescuing family honor.

To set the stage, the family circulated rumors that Francisco's wife had died. A messenger arrived to inform Francisco of the unfortunate, if timely, death. Local officials rushed to offer condolences. The wily Francisco countered with a request for verification of the death and the publication of the wedding banns in Mexico City, where he felt sure someone would object and rescue him. Local clerical authorities denied his request. Adding pressure, the determined relatives demanded that Francisco marry Clara, or repay a debt of 2,300 pesos immediately, or be imprisoned and have his property seized. Now a prisoner of love, the desperate Francisco attempted to secure a horse in order to escape under cover of darkness. The plan was uncovered and thwarted. The episode ended with Clara's brother holding the reluctant groom at dagger point as he married Clara and restored the family's honor. Immediately after the wedding, Francisco fled to Mexico City. Now a bigamist, in 1656, he had difficulty explaining what had happened to officials of the Inquisition—the church court that investigated breaches of religious orthodoxy.

SOURCE: Richard Boyer, *Lives of the Bigamists: Marriage, Family and Community in Colonial Mexico* (Albuquerque: University of New Mexico Press, 1995).

Only women from wealthy families could flout many, but not all, social conventions without harming the family's social standing. Those with everything to lose clung to behavioral rigidity. Sexual misconduct by women constituted the most feared attack on family status, one perceived to require swift and harsh measures in order to salvage as much honor as possible. In contrast, the assumed absence of honor among the lower classes gave them freedom from social convention, but also suggested that because they had nothing to lose they could be abused, denied respect, or exploited sexually.

Individually, women did not possess honor in a positive sense, but they could dishonor their families by their conduct. Adultery or other forms of sexual misconduct could be avenged by violence, even murder, with little fear of judicial punishment. Expulsion from the protective family net constituted a harsh response. Any woman cut off from her family lost all social standing and was considered little better than a prostitute. Men, on the other hand, enjoyed the luxury of being both saints and sinners. The male incorporated and, in theory, balanced the extremes of good and evil within himself. But as an imperfect human being, at any given time, the man might succumb to temptation. Although women might be subjected to similar temptation, in them weakness could not be tolerated. As the moral and biological anchor of the family, the woman was subject to a restrictive social code, one closely connected with her socioeconomic standing.

Chastity in the New World became even more highly prized than in Europe because of miscegenation. Families could tolerate no doubts concerning the paternity of children for fear of the loss of status. Because differences in complexion and physical features were common in most families, legitimacy of birth mattered. This exaggerated concern for legal and racial purity provided the dramatic tension and humorous confusion in novels about the society. The Brazilian mulatto Machado de Assis captured the melodrama of uncertain paternity in his early nineteenth-century novel *Helena*. The beautiful and talented Helena met a tragic end, which proved suitable, at least, for the anxieties and pretensions of a society organized by racial categories.

In retrospect, the forging of a mestizo culture seems quite extraordinary. The diverse peoples formed the region's richest resource, and Latin America had much to be proud of on the eve of independence. Baron Alexander Von Humboldt, the astute Prussian observer who traveled extensively throughout early nineteenth-century America, expressed admiration and confidence that a brilliant future lay ahead for Spanish America. He saw a self-sustaining society and economy, composed of an educated, skilled people.

The New World and its population appeared to be the most dynamic and promising component of the Spanish system. Few, perhaps no one, could have predicted that the people of this region would have to endure a destructive civil war to gain independence, and a painful restructuring of the economy and society to survive. Brazilians avoided such a struggle because of the transfer of the Portuguese monarchy to Rio de Janeiro in 1808, which effectively established Brazil as the capital of the Portuguese world. Independence came in 1822 with little violence. Although fortunate politically, from a social standpoint Brazil desperately needed change. Slavery, though understood to be an unjust and archaic institution, persisted virtually undisturbed into the nineteenth century and remained the shame of Brazil until 1888.

## Town Councils and Kingdoms, the Colonial Heritage

The municipal council, called the *ayuntamiento* or *cabildo* in Spanish America and the *senado da câmara* in Brazil, constituted the fundamental political institution. Municipal officers exercised executive, legislative, and judicial authority. More people came into contact with these officials on a daily basis than with any other authority, including the Church. The council regulated many aspects of daily life: it assured an adequate food supply (meat, corn, and beans), potable water, public sanitation, and street maintenance; controlled markets, such as honest weights and measures; licensed taverns; and dealt with street crime. The council also collected taxes, organized militias, and directed a host of other activities that touched individuals daily.

Both the Portuguese and Spanish crowns depended on municipal councils but disliked their tendency for independent action. Consequently, in Spanish

America, Crown magistrates, called *alcaldes mayores,* were appointed to serve as presidents of the councils. Many New World cities at first resisted this royal official, but only Lima succeeded in remaining largely independent of direct royal control throughout the colonial period. The Crown also tried naming permanent councilmen, but this decision failed to alter the political culture of municipalities. When the nearly insolvent King Felipe II sold municipal posts, he converted them into private assets, inadvertently strengthening the council's independence, and allowing American-born individuals to dominate the councils throughout the colonies.

Spanish-American councilmen jumped to defend local interests. Early disputes with colonial administrators revolved primarily around the issue of Indian labor but soon broadened to include taxes. Because the council had to review revenue measures, inevitable haggling developed between royal officials and councilmen. Spain's extension of the sales tax (*alcabala*), which started in Mexico in 1571, caused major municipal protest, especially in South America. In Quito, Ecuador, the municipal council rallied public opposition. Riots swept the Andean region, leading some bolder protestors to suggest breaking with Spain and forming some form of protective relationship with England. In the end, the Crown used force to quell the so-called Revolution of the Alcabala and introduced a 2 percent sales tax. Eventually the tax crept up to 8 percent.

In Portuguese America, the absence of a large Indian population and the slow trickle of Europeans delayed the appearance of councils. São Vicente established the first *senado da câmara* in 1532, three decades after the Portuguese arrived. The second, in Bahia, established 17 years later, became the most powerful council because the city served as the capital of colonial Brazil. Other municipal bodies formed slowly but, as in Spanish America, they dominated daily life.

Identifying individuals to serve as councilmen involved an elaborate selection procedure culminated by placing a series of wax balls representing nominees in separate pockets for each office. On New Year's Day, a young boy was called in from the street to pluck one ball from each pocket. The individuals thus selected had to serve. Crown officials claimed that because of this system, Bahia's first council included exiles sent to Brazil for having committed crimes, some whose ears had been clipped as punishment. Eventually, more respectable sugar planters dominated the council.

Just as Spain imposed royal agents, hoping to bring ayuntamientos under control, Portuguese officials in 1696 replaced municipal judges with a *juiz de fora* (crown district magistrate), who served as the council's president. Nevertheless, Crown penury undercut royal control. Municipal councils often assumed duties that technically belonged to the Crown. Bahia's senado da câmara, for example, shouldered the responsibility for almost 70 years of paying, provisioning, and clothing the local garrison.

Municipal councils constantly complained about high customs duties, Portuguese monopolies, and Crown activities they believed to be injurious. Any practice deemed to discriminate against Brazilian-born individuals provoked loud protests, and municipal councils carried their complaints all the way to the king. Such complaints, carefully crafted as petitions for relief, led one exasperated

Lisbon official to complain in 1678 that councilmen in Bahia acted as if they shared the governance of the empire equally with the Crown.

## Spanish-American Imperial Structure

Above the municipal councils, the imperial system incorporated the colonial population in general. Newcomers—Europeans, including those born in the Americas (*criollos*), mestizos, Africans, and mulattoes—had shallow roots in the hemisphere. As the spawn of empire, they functioned within an oceanic imperial system that linked Europe, Asia, Africa, and America. Native Americans, in sharp contrast, functioned within a crumbling universe. Survival for Indians under siege depended on merging their culture—language, religion, and laws—with that of the newcomers. The Spanish Crown accepted responsibility for the well-being of its Indian subjects, but only within a European context. Indians quickly learned to defend their interests and manipulate the new system. They hired lawyers, petitioned the Crown, registered land titles, and in many other ways engaged colonial society on its own terms. In the process, the Indians became cultural mestizos unavoidably linked to the empire. The Europeanized political culture of Spanish America functioned as an all-embracing hybrid.

A viceroyalty served as an umbrella territorial unit that covered a vast area with several kingdoms, each with its own captain–general functioning with little direct contact with the viceroy. Poor communications created a patchwork of Crown institutions over which a thin veneer of viceregal authority rested. Only in the core kingdom of a viceroyalty did the viceroy have direct governing functions. There he balanced imperial political interests with those of society.

The high court or *audiencia* at the next level down functioned as a civil and criminal court as well as a political arena for the colonial elite to influence imperial policy. The court's political functions, in addition to its judicial authority, gave it a wide reach. Judges mediated disputes between merchants, made tours of inspection, and monitored aspects of the district's economic, social, and political life along the lines of inspector generals. Crown regulations designed to insulate judges from local elites proved ineffectual. For example, although forbidden to marry within their jurisdiction, they often did. After the Crown began to sell audiencia seats in 1687, American-born judges dominated the courts. When independence came, although the courts failed to survive, Spanish America often fragmented into new nations along the jurisdictional lines of the audiencias and the cities in which they functioned.

Lower-ranking officials served nominally under the orders of their superiors. Nevertheless, as Crown agents they communicated directly with Spain, making it difficult to control them. The Hapsburgs provided a flexible, adaptable political system with a variety of ways to influence officials in the New World and Crown policy as it was formulated in Madrid.

In the eighteenth century, the new Bourbon dynasty viewed politics as nonproductive and as a hindrance to economic development and tax collection. The Bourbons hoped to replace viceroys with more efficient administrators. Even labels changed to emphasize that Spain now saw the New World as a colony, not as a series of kingdoms. The monarch's traditional title "King of the Spains (acknowledging the several kingdoms in the peninsula) and the Indies" changed to "King of Spain (unified and singular) and Emperor of America (dominant and fused into one)." Reforms, particularly under Carlos III (1759–1788), encountered widespread opposition. In the end, enlightened reformers damaged the political system, especially the prestige of Crown officials, in the disruptive efforts to impose a new bureaucracy.

## Political Structure of Portuguese America

Imperial institutions functioned weakly in Portuguese America because of financial limitations. Whereas Spain drew upon a productive Indian peasantry for labor and taxes, the Portuguese encountered a seminomadic population with limited resources. As a result, revenues barely supported a royal presence in Brazil. No other European empire functioned with so few personnel for so long. Consequently, governing responsibilities fell to those who assumed power. Cattle barons in the backlands imposed their will, establishing a self-interested stability by force. The Crown proffered them royal commissions, creating the illusion of control. These so-called *mestres de campo* favored their order over abstract justice.

After Bahia became the capital of Portuguese America in 1549, independent authority gradually gave way to Crown agents. A hierarchy of authority slowly and haltingly put down roots. The high court, *relação,* was permanently established in 1652. It remained the most important court until the colonial capital moved to Rio de Janeiro in 1763. In the absence of strong authority, politics fell to the lower levels in Brazil or rested with distant authorities in Portugal.

Other institutions assumed political functions. Religious lay brotherhoods attracted a large number of adherents. These brotherhoods formed a sociopolitical network only nominally linked to the Church as they set standards of conduct and responsibility for society. The Third Order of St. Francis and the Carmelites enjoyed high status, but other brotherhoods enrolled the lower classes, including slaves. The most notable brotherhood, Our Lady, Mother of God, Virgin Mary of Mercy, founded in Lisbon in 1498, was commonly called the *Misericordia*. It soon had a presence in virtually every settlement in the overseas empire. This brotherhood provided charity, arranged burials, cared for orphans, and occasionally supplied dowries to encourage family formation. Even with royal patronage, it relied upon monies from donations and wills for operating expenses. Bahia's Misericordia received generous support from sugar planters until the late seventeenth century, when merchants assumed responsibility for its financial well-being.

The manner in which Spanish and Portuguese America achieved independence had a direct impact on the nineteenth century's political process. For both empires the crucial moment came when Napoleon's armies invaded the Iberian Peninsula. The French arrested the monarch and occupied much of Spain. The Portuguese royal family and government, however, escaped to Brazil and transformed Rio de Janeiro into the capital of the Portuguese world. The subsequent return of the Portuguese king in 1821 resulted in Crown Prince Pedro's guiding Brazil through an almost bloodless transition to independence in 1822. Consequently, the old political system remained virtually intact as Brazil had a constitutional monarch until the creation of the republic in 1889. Significantly, Emperor Pedro sent Brazil's first constitution, the Constitution of 1824, to all the major municipalities for approval.

The Spanish Crown, in contrast, entered the nineteenth century as a Napoleonic toy. Emperor Napoleon bestowed the crown of Spain on his brother Joseph. With the loss of a legitimate king, Spaniards formed committees, or *juntas,* to resist the French occupation. In the New World, municipal councils declared they were holding government in trust for the imprisoned Fernando VII. They did not immediately move toward radical change.

In Spain, a central resistance committee called for the empire to select and dispatch delegates to a general assembly. The American provinces elected delegates to a Spanish parliament (called the *Cortes*), which met in 1810. American and Spanish deputies wrote the Constitution of 1812, creating a unified state governed by a legislative body under laws applicable across the entire Spanish world. The constitution gave the American provinces a large measure of home rule. It expanded the number of recognized municipal councils, providing wider local representation.

The restoration of King Fernando and his old regime destroyed this system in the making. The monarch understood that pressing the colonies back into an imperial structure could be accomplished only by force, but he miscalculated how many troops and the level of resources required. Eventually, reacting against the American campaign, Spanish army officers in 1820 revolted and forced a restoration of the constitution. This action allowed revolutionaries in the Americas to move toward independence.

The events following the Napoleonic invasion of the peninsula created two political traditions in America—one based on force directed by a dominant individual and the other a civic tradition of legislated legitimacy. Northern South Americans, liberated by self-appointed generals, most notably Simón Bolívar, found it difficult to extricate themselves from the tradition of force. Bolívar personified the strong hand of imposed authority. In Chile and Argentina, only lightly touched by revolutionary armies, civilians soon established legislative oligarchies. Mexicans, deeply influenced by the Constitution of 1812, created a hybrid political system, one tilted in favor of legislative bodies and a federal republic.

A complex legacy of indigenous and colonial patterns passed into the nineteenth century, particularly at the community and family levels. Many of these practices survived the struggle for independence and some remain recognizable at the beginning of the twenty-first century.

# 2

# Politics

Politics express the configuration of power and the exercise of authority; the nature of politics shapes the interactions of Latin American peoples. The programs leaders use in an attempt to control, include, and exclude people cast silhouettes that reveal the images of politics. Leaders throughout Latin America's history have defined their societies and developed plans to either incorporate or ignore peoples. In the newly independent societies, the leaders, knowingly or unknowingly, drew on indigenous and colonial legacies as they attempted to create new nations and new nationalities. In nearly every case, the politicians had to grapple with the roles of the Roman Catholic Church and the military as institutions in the nation. Moreover, politicians pursued three major campaigns with respect to the general population. First, patriotic leaders imagined new national identities and initiated campaigns to integrate and exclude people as citizens. Second, they identified those they deemed civilized members of their nations and excluded others, especially many indigenous peoples, as "barbarians." Third, they promoted European immigration in an attempt to reduce the Afro- and Indo-American character of the population.

Beginning about 1880, new forces began to shape Latin American politics. In particular, national leaders addressed the issue of integration by planning campaigns that would introduce civilization to all the nation's peoples. Civilization was defined in many ways, of course, but primarily as a variant of Western European culture. Then, beginning in the 1920s, new government leaders determined to nationalize all their people, to some extent by taking popular, everyday behavior and declaring it the expression of the nation. Four overlapping influences became evident: (1) the eruption of popular groups into national politics, such as the Mexican Revolution of 1910, rather than more local sporadic and isolated uprisings, such as the Canudos Rebellion in Brazil; (2) the rise of populist political movements composed of disenfranchised peoples, immigrants from abroad, and rural migrants new to burgeoning cities; (3) rising expectations and resentments created by better education, the sensational mass media, and growing foreign economic enclaves such as oil camps, mining towns, and posh city neighborhoods; and (4) the increasing incorporation of Latin America into the North Atlantic and the global political and economic marketplace. Of course, these factors affected Latin American countries differently and at different times, but all the nations experienced to some extent mass political movements, popular revolutionary campaigns, militarism, and mass political parties. Some countries have experienced all these political movements, often inspired by charismatic leaders. For Latin American governments, how to integrate the people into national life without revolutionary violence or undue dependency on foreign powers remains the essential political dilemma.

Finding the answer has been difficult because the masses are divided by location (rural, urban, and capital city), ethnicity (indigenous, African, European, and mixed cultures), and mobility (nomadic working families, urban migrants, mobile young men, and the sedentary elderly). One solution, although risky, was to ignore the masses. Another option was to somehow incorporate them into the political structure, but this, of course, raised the difficult issue of how and to what extent to make them a part of the system. The latter approach led to policies of public education, land reform, local sovereignty, regional clientelism, and patriarchal politics. Popular mobilization, at times mere indoctrination and at times mere affirmation, may result in effective political participation.

From the top-down perspective of central political authority, politics in independent Latin American nations have passed through four broad periods: (1) Enlightened and independent states, to ca. 1850; (2) liberal regimes and revolutionary eras, ca. 1850–1929; (3) heyday of the nation-state, 1930 to the 1980s; and (4) democratization and local regimes, 1980 to the present. These periods offer a convenient structure to examine how different regimes grappled with the issue of which people formed part of the political system.

## ENLIGHTENED AND INDEPENDENT STATES, TO CA. 1850

Bourbon Spanish administrators (1753–1820) and later nationalist independence leaders (1808–1850) participated in the drive toward an Enlightened society. These groups included both Church and civic officials who shared a concern about the threat represented by the lower classes, especially the indigenous peoples and blacks. Creole fear of what they regarded as the bottom rungs of the social ladder, slaves and nomadic Indian groups, *mestizos,* and blacks, appeared confirmed by two violent outbreaks, the Tupac Amaru rebellion in Andean South America (1780–1783) and the independence insurrection in Haiti (1790–1804). Although the Andean rebellion included Europeans and individuals from all classes, in the popular perception it represented a revolt from below. Both outbreaks appeared to demonstrate the danger of suppressed peoples who expressed their identity through their race or ethnicity. Rumors of caste or race war sent shivers down the spines of colonial officials and early national politicians. Preemptive efforts to overcome racial or ethnic identity markers resulted in campaigns to organize society through patriarchal networks and patriotic mobilization. These concerns explained elite opposition to the early phases of the independence movement (1810–1815), which many interpreted as an uprising of lower classes. This was especially the case in Mexico, where Padre Miguel Hidalgo rallied a horde of Indian and mestizo followers (1810–1811), who were soon defeated.

As the struggle for independence continued, hard-pressed leaders, especially José de San Martín in South America, began recruiting both black and indigenous troops with the promise of an end to head taxes and slavery. Even in Mexico, where more conservative elements dominated the struggle, Emperor Agustín Iturbide (1821–1822) removed racial and ethnic labels from all public records. After independence, new leaders had to work out the meaning of citizenship, the definition of political rights, and application of the law.[1] Simón Bolívar's aristocratic suspicion of the masses prompted him to plan some reward for the enlisted men in his armies. In many places the people expected to have an opportunity to participate in the politics of the new nations, but for the most part, the new national leaders ignored popular expectations.

An exceptional case occurred in Peru. After independence (1824), leaders moved decisively to restrain the pretensions of the masses. The majority of the country's Indian and mestizo peoples and the substantial black population in Lima and along the coast threatened the political and social claims of elites. The new leaders reacted to these threats by reinstating the head tax on Indian peoples and reinstituting slavery of Afro-Peruvians throughout the nation.

A more general response in the new Spanish American nations to restrict the mass mobilization associated with popular sovereignty came through the legal system. Vagrancy laws resulted from the desire of elites to reinstate public order following the wars of independence. In Mexico, for example, the national congress in 1828 established a special court solely to prosecute vagrants, who personified disorder to elites.

New national leaders placed renewed emphasis on the colonial pattern of client–patron systems and found ways to allow popular groups to participate in politics without actually offering them influence. One technique was to promote festivals as celebrations of national identity. The Brazilian emperor instituted an

---

[1]See, for one example, Sarah C. Chambers, "Crime and Citizenship: Judicial Practice in Arequipa, Peru, during the Transition from Colony to Republic," in Carlos Aguirre and Robert Buffington, eds., *Reconstructing Criminality in Latin America* (Wilmington, DE: SR Books, forthcoming).

imperial celebration of the new nation that permitted participation without influence. To commemorate the first anniversary of independence on December 1, 1823, dom Pedro I founded the "Society of the Knights of Fun." He ordered a grand parade consisting of royal carriages, allegorical floats, and costumed characters representing important figures in Brazilian history. As the spectacular parade passed his reviewing stand, the ecstatic emperor himself indulged in the frivolity by throwing lemon-sized wax balls containing perfumed ether at the young, lovely, costumed ladies riding on the floats. The evening festivities for the Brazilian court included eating, drinking, and dancing to the latest waltzes and polkas, whereas ordinary Brazilians turned to the disorderly and unruly behavior associated with the *entrudo* (a celebration involving practical jokes, mischief, and throwing buckets of water, sewage, paint, flour, cheap perfume, liquor, and vinegar). This way, Brazilians affirmed their support for the political system.[2] Conservatives in Brazil and throughout Spanish America feared that even these ritual celebrations might result in riots, with the masses turning to disorder. This concern caused the police in Rio de Janeiro to focus their attention on victimless public order offenses.[3]

In Spanish America, new leaders found ways to organize political allegiance without allowing much political participation. This discussion explains the process of governing and shows how the unique political leader of this era, the *caudillo,* became so popular. Independence resulted at first in a period of confused and disjointed political campaigns. Ambitious and idealistic politicians sought authority and legitimacy from corporate bodies and followers from popular groups. The great caudillos built alliances with popular groups, either Indian, black, mestizo, or a combination of these populations, depending on the nation. They often mobilized followers by supporting municipal autonomy, recognizing land titles, or, above all, offering relief to the most common grievance of the era—taxes, charged in money, goods, or labor. Caudillos who challenged the governments mobilized campesinos or urban mobs with promises of reform, restoration, or relief from government demands, especially taxes and national military service.[4]

No leader better exemplifies the nature of political leadership during the first half century after independence than Juan Manuel Rosas of Argentina. Rosas, who ruled from 1829 to 1852 (except for the interval, 1832–1835), epitomizes the caudillo. He built a political machine using the people on the lower rungs of the social ladder. In Buenos Aires, these were the mestizos and blacks; in rural areas, the *gauchos,* a group that included many mestizos, Afro-Argentines, and acculturated indigenous peoples. His techniques for mobilizing widespread support included the use of patriotic celebrations, called *fiestas federales,* which served as a pedagogy of politics. This instruction drew on traditional forms of expression that combined popular religion and patriotic republicanism to foster support for

---

[2]Alexander Orloff, *Carnival, Myth and Cult* (Worgl, Austria: Perlinger, 1981), p. 21.

[3]Thomas H. Holloway, "Punishment in 19th-Century Rio de Janeiro: Judicial Action as Police Practice," in Aguirre and Buffington, eds., *Reconstructing Criminality.*

[4]See Terry Rugeley, "The Caste War: Rural Insurgency in Nineteenth-Century Yucatán," in Daniel Castro, ed., *Revolution and Revolutionaries in Latin America* (Wilmington, DE: SR Books, 1999); and Ricardo D. Salvatore, "The Crimes of 'Paysanos' in Mid-Nineteenth-Century Buenos Aires," in Aguirre and Buffington, eds., *Reconstructing Criminality.*

Rosas. Judas burnings, for example, were converted into political rallies of a sort. Judases, papier-mâché effigies, personified the enemies and evils that threatened the regime in an era of shifting, changing, convoluted politics.

In creating a popular following, Rosas, with the collaboration of his wife, Encarnación, skillfully used the "federal look" and the color red associated with his name to establish political unity. The federal look was a dress code, imposed by law and enforced by the police. It centered on a red badge or ribbon, worn on the left side over the heart, that bore both the profile of Rosas and the inscription "Long Live the Federalists!" The look also included a red hatband, its width specified by law; for men a suitable military mustache and long sideburns; and the undefined, but rigidly enforced, military bearing.[5]

Red, Rosas pointed out, was the color of San Baltasar, the African among the three kings who traveled to the manger of the Christ child. The symbolic reference to Baltasar appealed to many blacks among the Argentine population. In addition, Rosas made San Baltasar's Day a national holiday. Rosas used popular religion to make maintenance of the regime a holy cause. Festivities included "decorated houses, cannon volleys, processions with [Rosas's] portrait, a rosary of poems written for the occasion, and a commemorative carriage pulled by members of the Sociedad Popular Restauradora,"[6] Rosas's political organization. Thus, he became the hero of a political and moral confrontation, framed in the language of independence and aided by the imagery of Catholicism, which helped legitimize his rule. The Rosas party was particularly fond of parading the caudillo's portrait and sponsoring Judas burnings.

These practices brought Rosas popularity, including black support, and, in some ways, succeeded too well. The *Unitarios* (Liberals), his opponents, blamed blacks and rural mestizos for keeping him in power and forcing Liberal leaders into exile in Uruguay and Chile. The Unitarios, as a result, were determined to prevent anyone from using what they regarded as demagoguery with the allegedly overly susceptible lower classes of blacks and mestizos. Their solution was to flood Argentina with European immigrants. The Liberal slogan "To govern is to populate" was part of an anti-indigenous and anti-black campaign that went beyond simple racial and ethnic hostility. It became an effort to eliminate the latter's political significance and undermine popular support for caudillo leaders.

Rosas was not the only great caudillo in the early nineteenth century. Others included Antonio López de Santa Anna, who was in and out of power from 1830 to 1854 in Mexico and mastered the techniques of mobilizing followers to confront both internal and external threats. Thus, Santa Anna rallied troops to fight the Texans (1835), the French (1837), the United States (1846–1848), and the Liberals on numerous occasions. After his last campaign, he was forced into exile by the Liberals who then brought Benito Juárez to power in the 1850s.

Although both Rosas and Santa Anna combined positive and negative attributes and managed to hold their countries together, other caudillos did not achieve their stature or their success. Among these was the succession of brutal

---

[5]Glenn Avent, "Encarnación Ezcurra de Rosas," manuscript, May 1, 1998.

[6]See Salvatore, "Crimes of 'Paysanos,'" pp. 9, 15, 33.

leaders of Bolivia, including Mariano Melgarejo and Manuel Isidoro Belzú. Others, despite their use of violence, achieved success in the material development of their countries. In these circumstances, the popular masses, especially rural peasants and Indians, were treated as obstacles to progress.

In Ecuador, the independence wars caused residents in the Sierra to abandon their towns and flee to the countryside to avoid military conscription—which often meant service in Peru—and escape forced cash, crop, and livestock loans. A decline of the highland economy followed, a condition that lasted for much of the nineteenth century, accompanied by a recession in textile workshops (the leading colonial enterprise) and the deterioration of transportation routes. The deurbanization process was further accentuated by a series of epidemics, earthquakes, and volcanic eruptions during the nineteenth century.[7]

It was under these circumstances that the caudillo Gabriel García Moreno took the first steps in the creation of the nation of Ecuador. He engineered the successful construction of a wagon road from Guayaquil to Quito, opened technical schools, and promoted practical arts and sciences. The medical school was reorganized to stress the importance of laboratories and clinics and to incorporate teaching surgery, including the use of chloroform, antiseptics, and Listerine. These achievements represented the practical side of García Moreno's scheme to create national unity; on the emotional side, he attempted to establish a state commitment to Roman Catholicism. His plans included a request to have Ecuador annexed by the Vatican, which the pope refused, but he did succeed in having Ecuador dedicated to the Sacred Heart of Jesus Christ. His was just one of the more unusual efforts to mobilize popular loyalty to caudillo leaders and establish a commitment to the new nations after independence.

## LIBERAL REGIMES AND REVOLUTIONARY ERAS, CA. 1850–1929

The Liberal regimes that emerged about midcentury sponsored programs to enable more men to participate in the political system, in part to reduce the ability of caudillos to mobilize extensive followings. These Liberal efforts organized support without the dangers of mass mobilization. Latin American efforts resulted in social campaigns to preempt class revolts.

Liberal programs at midcentury focused exclusively on most, but not all, adult males. The policies derived their intellectual character from the ideology of the Enlightenment and the general anticlericalism of rationalism. Later in the century, Liberals relied on popularized Darwinism and Comtian arguments to rationalize their programs. They seized the initiative from the Church; in the words of the

---

[7]A. Kim Clark, *"The Redemptive Work": Railway and Nation in Ecuador, 1895–1930* (Wilmington, DE: SR Books, 1998), pp. 38, 39, n. 7.

Ecuadorian Minister of Public Instruction, "How can we expect the enlighten-ment of the people, if we confide the diffusion of light to those who have fought without rest to maintain the empire of shadows?"[8] At the same time, Liberals stressed what they saw as the social benefits of property, moral redemption through work, and the developmental attributes of capitalism. In simple terms, Liberals found their inspiration and their goals in images of male citizens and steam power.

These liberal images challenged the previous symbols promoted by the Church of long-suffering Christians and their preordained lives. The Liberals sought to create literate, property-owning, sober, and hard-working citizens, economically self-sufficient and politically self-reliant, who would stand ever ready to take up arms to defend their country. This ideal citizen was in sharp contrast to the stalwart Christian who endured whatever life doled out for the promise of a reward in the afterlife, who was satisfied with his social status inherited at birth, and who was content to be a subject of the ruler, not a citizen of the country. Moreover, the Liberal citizen was empowered by steam; steam meant progress, development, and, ultimately, profits for investors. Most often, however, it was actually the country's few entrepreneurs who were empowered by the railroad or the steamship.

The Liberal campaign in Colombia is a good example of the expression of the policies in the region. The Liberals seized power in 1849 and immediately attempted to implement their party's tenets. Economic policies led to a significant reduction in tariffs, the elimination of monopolies on tobacco and *aguardiente* (a raw alcoholic beverage), and the abolition of sales taxes. The Liberals also passed laws that attempted to integrate most of the male population into the body politic. The Liberals believed this initiative required both restricting the actions of the Church and broadening the areas of participation for individuals. As a result, Colombian Liberals separated church and state, expelled the Jesuits, closed monasteries, and restricted Church influence in the activities of everyday life. The definition of citizenship became more inclusive with laws that abolished slavery and extended suffrage to all males over 21 years of age. Voting became more meaningful as the laws called for the direct election of governors. These laws, once confirmed through civil war (1859–1862), created the "Radical Olympus" that survived until 1886.

During this same period, Mexican Liberals overthrew the archcaudillo Antonio López de Santa Anna (1855), created a new constitution (1857), and then fought to defend it in the Wars of the Reform (1858–1861) and against the French intervention (1861–1867). Led by Benito Juárez, the Liberals introduced new programs at the local and district levels. They separated church and state; established a civil registry; abolished personal services, at least in theory; provided for the popular election of village mayors and *jefes políticos;* created a locally recruited and commanded militia; and encouraged free, secular public schools.

---

[8]Clark, *"Redemptive Work,"* p. 68.

Courtesy of the Latin America Library at Tulane University.

Civic rituals and brass bands, such as this band from Puerto Cortés, Honduras, were important elements of state building throughout the hemisphere as often weak governments attempted to project their control over society.

This movement developed from the plans of educated and largely urban leaders who acted as patriarchs for the chiefly rural, often Indian, and usually reluctant individuals who favored the predominance of the clergy and traditional leaders. Resistance in Mexico's villages sprang from opposition to forced military recruitment, loans, and labor levies; local and district authorities resisted the imposition of outsiders as leaders; local militias resisted the intrusion of outside commanders; and village notables and parish clergy struggled to maintain their control of community and district politics and their personal social status.[9] The friction between national programs and local practices created opportunities for bosses or "fixers," called *caciques,* who worked to satisfy both national and local constituencies and, in doing so, made themselves indispensable to both. Although it appears national leaders made some strides toward forging a national cultural and political system, in local communities leaders selectively adopted tax, land, militia, or education reforms that strengthened rather than replaced local practices. Nevertheless, the Liberals strove to create a society in which men had equal standing before the law and lived by a common set of rights and obligations.

The desire to create a more egalitarian society in Peru drove Ramón Castilla to divert some of the tremendous wealth produced by the *guano* (bird dung used

---

[9] Guy P. C. Thomson, *Patriotism, Politics, and Popular Liberalism in Nineteenth-Century Mexico: Juan Francisco Lucas and Puebla Sierra, 1854–1917* (Wilmington, DE: SR Books, 1999), p. 125.

as fertilizer) bonanza to national construction and educational projects. A veteran of the Battle of Ayacucho (1824), which liberated Peru from Spanish forces, Castilla twice served as president, 1845–1851 and 1855–1862. He utilized some of the huge profits from exporting guano to Europe and the United States to undertake national projects. By diverting profits from private individuals, Castilla financed the construction of the "English" railroad connecting Lima and its port of Callao. He also contracted with Melchor Charón for a 500-light gas lighting system in central Lima. This system quickly expanded to other public and private buildings. Castilla made a tremendous impact as he directed social reforms. Notably, he abolished African and Afro-Peruvian slavery and ended Indian head taxes, although the latter returned following the disastrous loss to the Chileans in the War of the Pacific. Forced labor did not end, however. In fact, it expanded with the arrival of contract Chinese workers beginning in 1849.

Ecuador's liberal era began in 1895 and lasted until about 1930, although in political terms the Liberals held sway only until 1925. Consolidation of the Liberal project occurred from 1900 to 1910. This period focused on the railroad as an instrument to create physical integration and national consciousness. The promoters of the railroad initiated a program of social and moral reforms. Liberals saw the railroad as the key to their project. For example, the Liberal congress by law utilized the railroad to facilitate the circulation of ideas by setting low rates for shipping newsprint, permitting vendors to ride free when selling newspapers, and allowing newspaper enterprises free use of the railroad's telegraph lines for up to 200 words daily. Unlike the Liberals in Juarista Mexico, who had a plan to incorporate the indigenous population into the nation, Ecuador's Liberals promoted the universalizing goal of all Ecuadorians as equal before the state, but made no attempt to put the goal into practice. Different treatment for indigenous people was institutionalized in practices, some reaching back to the colonial period, such as forced labor recruitment for public projects, including municipal public works, and especially building and maintaining roads. This policy changed in 1918 with the Agrarian Development Law, which compelled all male inhabitants of localities to work or pay for a substitute.

Ecuadorian Liberals promoted their programs through the National Agricultural Society. At the society's first national congress in Quito, in 1922, the delegates discussed formulating legislation to distribute communal lands among indigenous villagers, reduce vagrancy, provide education, foster the habit of saving among Indians, and prohibit overspending by sponsors of religious fiestas and bullfights. Above all, the delegates found a near panacea in their campaign to improve civil participation by regulating drinking among indigenous peoples.[10]

In the second half of the nineteenth century, Liberals throughout Latin America adopted Auguste Comte's philosophy. Mexico's Liberals of the Porfirio Díaz era (1876–1910) established Positivist programs, although their plans for a Positivist calendar failed. None of the Comtian disciples carried their infatuation with the Frenchman's ideas to the extreme of the Brazilians. Only the Brazilians

---

[10]Clark, *"Redemptive Work,"* pp. 48, 76, 88, 90, 94–95, 191–192.

established a Positivist church. Moreover, when they established the Brazilian Republic in 1889, they went so far as to place Comte's slogan "Order and Progress" on the national flag.[11] Nevertheless, despite Brazilian excesses, the Mexicans pushed Comtian ideas to the limit in practice.

Historians have ignored an unorganized, but potentially powerful pressure group that existed throughout Latin America during these years and demanded recognition in politics, economics, and society from the Comtian leaders. Discharged veterans of foreign wars and internal military campaigns populated the region and demanded their interests be considered by national governments. In the name of the Fatherland, lower class peasants and workers had been conscripted, trained, and sent into battle against each other in civil wars, and against foreigners, hostile indigenous groups, and militant followers of self-proclaimed messiahs. Some, as victors in battle—Chileans after the War of the Pacific, Brazilians after the War of the Triple Alliance, and Mexicans after ending the French occupation—felt entitled to recognition and reward; others—the Peruvians after the War of the Pacific—sought some salve for the scars of defeat. For the most part, these veterans had learned the value of organization and discipline. They knew that powerful people congregated in the capital cities, where jobs and entertainment also existed in the greatest abundance. Veterans flocked to the cities, where they represented a potential political force. These men left their mark. In Brazil, for example, during the Canudos Rebellion, the army constructed flimsy encampments on a hill called *favela,* which with time became the term for Rio's urban slums. In Mexico, veterans seized power in 1876, and under General and President Porfirio Díaz they ruled the nation. Whether these veterans went to the cities or returned home to the countryside, they had experienced national service, an obligation that carried with it material rewards and the expectation that certain individual rights would be recognized and protected.

Comtian politics and economics, dismissive social programs that drew on social Darwinism, as well as liberalism's ideological hostility to the army, conflicted with the tradition of military service. The Mexican Revolution (1910–1920), the most widespread and ferocious national upheaval in Latin American history, resulted when the masses demanded a role in national life. The violence, often senseless and vicious, reflected the crosscutting interests of the revolutionaries and their leaders. Old resentments and expectations of soldiers and veterans played a major role in the violence, which consumed money and energy in its political aftermath. Some demanded land; others community control over politics, taxes, and military service; and still others wanted limits on foreign exploitation of natural resources (mines, factories, and fields) and human resources (Mexican workers and consumers). Each faction had a leader, none more charismatic than Emiliano Zapata and Pancho Villa, who have become part of the national folklore. Both died violently as the rebels went about killing

---

[11]For discussion of a classic film version of this society, see James D. Henderson, "*Gabriela: An Evocation of Elite Culture in Early Twentieth-Century Latin America,*" in Donald F. Stevens, ed., *Based on a True Story: Latin American History at the Movies* (Wilmington, DE: SR Books, 1998), pp. 256, 260.

perhaps as many as one of every seven Mexicans; estimates range from a total of 50,000 to 200,000 deaths.

Out of this fiesta of death came the Mexican Constitution of 1917, which committed the national regime to restrict the involvement of the Catholic Church in daily life, distribute lands to those who worked them, recognize and protect the rights of workers, and educate the population. Each constitutional objective resulted in a dramatic national campaign that local Mexicans molded to their own needs.

One goal of Liberal reformers throughout the region was to create standard practices and policies at local government levels. This effort to design common administrative practices failed. It took the Great Depression to compel national leaders to redefine the relationship between local and national government. Liberal politics, free-trade economics, and government support, but not regulation of the economy, all collapsed under the weight of contradictions that became apparent during the world depression.

## HEYDAY OF THE NATION-STATE, 1930 TO THE 1980S

The Great Depression collided with Latin American governments like an iceberg with wooden sailing ships; not one Latin American regime escaped unscathed, and most countries saw the collapse of the central administration and the creation of entirely new forms of government. The general solution was to fall back on the nationalism that had been forged during the nineteenth century. Everywhere in the hemisphere, leaders gave extraordinary powers to the central government, redefining the relationship between national and local government in taxes, services, and responsibilities. These nation-states assumed authority over activities previously left to private individuals, religious charities, foreign investors, municipal councils, and state governments. The education campaign in Mexico is a good example. The 1917 revolutionary constitution mandated that employers establish schools for their workers and, in isolated locations, their families. Mexican states were responsible for enforcing compliance with this provision. In early 1930, as part of the redefinition of central government and regional authority, the federal government placed control of these so-called Article 123 schools under the Ministry of Public Education. The central government also acted to expand the role of teachers as federal agents. Teachers assumed responsibility for promoting national popular culture and political mobilization for both the official party and the national government.[12]

Inspired by economic crisis, ideological assumptions, and political opportunities, leaders empowered the national government with new sources of income, new responsibilities for society, and new sources of political support through mass politics. For the next half century, politicians remained fascinated with the centralized state; it

---

[12]Mary Kay Vaughan, *Negotiating Revolutionary Culture: Mexico (1930–1940)* (Tucson: University of Arizona Press, 1998), pp. 7, 14.

seemed to be the only institution capable of bringing social stability, economic growth, and political permanence. Confidence in the central government came from politicians of all political positions and from activists of all backgrounds (see the Profile, "Patron of Populism: Victor Pizarro Rubio," on page 57).

During the 50 years of the Leviathan state, civilian, military, revolutionary, counterrevolutionary, quasi-democratic, totalitarian dictatorial, and mutant combination regimes governed. To sustain its authority, in some cases, the state created a governing party apparatus, such as the Institutional Revolutionary Party (PRI) in Mexico, or a personalistic ruler, such as Castro in Cuba; and in other cases, such as Chile, it created an exaggerated fear of the Left, or in the case of blue-collar workers in Argentina, a social myth. Examples of nation–states range from Vargas's Brazil, Perón's Argentina, and Castro's Cuba to Acción Democrática in Venezuela, military Peru, and Pinochet's Chile. Despite their differences in composition and goals, these regimes shared three common traits: use of the mass media to mobilize support; focus on the popular classes to either organize or regulate them, or both; and reliance on specialists, especially military officers and well-educated administrators, known as technocrats.

## Brazil and Vargas

Brazil's experience during the regime of Getúlio Vargas (1930–1954) illustrates a central government response to world depression through populist political organization. The collapse of the world commodities market left mountains of unsold coffee beans; exporters, owners, and pickers saw incomes plummet and faced the approaching reality of depravation. The government's unwillingness to tackle the crisis, followed by its ineffectual efforts at placing a floor under the collapsing economy, resulted in a wildly corrupt presidential election. When Julio Prestes, the unpopular candidate of the old coffee producers and the São Paulo state oligarchy who were blamed for the national crisis, eked out a victory, Vargas and his followers seized power by a preemptive *coup d'état*.

Vargas's program called for putting Brazil and Brazilians first: putting the nation before the interests of São Paulo and Minas Gerais, two states that previously had alternated the presidency; putting the national interests before the demands of the foreign investors whose loans in 1930 required one-third of the national budget in interest payments alone; and putting the national political concerns before the narrow interests of the established coffee producers. Vargas initiated an economic development campaign to reduce reliance on the export of coffee, sugar, and cotton and the import of food and consumer goods; a program of national responsibility for social issues such as education, welfare, and workers' rights; and a plan for incorporating the Brazilian masses, especially urban workers and residents, into politics.

To legitimatize his authority, Vargas turned to a romantic nationalism in which public culture served as the bond of nationality. In doing so, he promoted the vibrant Afro-Brazilian culture that had emerged by 1900 and that was chiefly associated with the migration of Bahians to Rio. To expand his political base, Vargas relied on the ward heelers, the *cabos eleitorais,* who worked the growing urban slums to mobilize black, poor, and immigrant city-dwellers. At first, Vargas ignored the *samba* schools, but his policies changed as he realized their political

| **P R O F I L E** Patron of Populism: Víctor Pizarro Rubio |
| --- |

Young Peruvians in Chachapoyas, during the last months of 1929, began to slip out of town after midnight to meet at the grave of Víctor Pizarro Rubio. They chose to meet in the cemetery in the predawn hours to escape detection, and they chose the grave to honor the daring—if not the politics—of Pizarro Rubio, as they organized a populist movement.

Víctor Pizarro Rubio was the son of the dominant family in the town's fractious elite. His father was a *compadre* of the dictator Augusto Leguía, who supported the family in the town and arranged for Víctor to receive a scholarship to the national military academy. Later, the dictator arranged another scholarship for additional studies at a French naval institute. The family had great expectations that this education would result in Víctor's receiving a military or political position from which he could help solidify the Pizarro Rubio position of power in Chachapoyas.

But the move to Lima, a city in the throes of economic, social, and cultural change from 1910 to 1920, transformed him. In this caldron of hope, ideology, and recognition of the need for change in the nation, Víctor became a communist. Once he arrived in Paris, he deserted the naval institute and traveled to the Soviet Union. He participated in the Third International in 1921, then returned to South America—to Uruguay—as an organizer for the party. Several years later he returned to Lima and continued his organizational efforts in his native country. In 1927 Lima policemen ended his work when they beat him so badly that because of his severely damaged kidneys he had only a short time to live. At this point, he returned to Chachapoyas, but his family refused to recognize him and he was reduced to living in a shack on the edge of town, where for the last months of his life he gave lectures on communism to anyone who would listen.

Young people from the town were deeply moved by his courage to challenge the town's elite oligarchy. But those who met at his grave in 1929 and after ignored communism and turned to the populism of the Alianza Popular Revolucionaria Americana (the APRA), which successfully overthrew the town elites in 1930.

SOURCE: Based on David Nugent's unpublished essay, "Freeing 'the People' to Make the Nation." See also his *Modernity at the Edge of Empire: State, Individual, and Nation in the Northern Peruvian Andes* (Stanford: Stanford University Press, 1997).

potential. Vargas learned from Rio's populist mayor, Pedro Ernesto, who had launched reforms in health, education, and welfare and had mobilized support beginning in 1932 by funding the carnival celebration through subsidies to many large and small carnival clubs, including samba clubs. Vargas soon extended official recognition for the first time to these essentially Afro-Brazilian groups, although rigid governmental censorship policies prevented other organizations from entering satirical floats in carnival parades. The first carnival float competition, in 1932, had 19 samba school participants. Vargas's rules required that the clubs adopt themes based on national historical events and personalities. This rule was given force in 1939, when the government disqualified a school that chose Snow White and the Seven Dwarfs as its theme. The participation of the samba schools in carnival demonstrated Vargas's desire to incorporate the Afro-Brazilian population into his nationalistic ideology and orchestrate their political participation. The result of Vargas's practice to use cultural expressions to forge political support was a new description of Afro-Brazilians as hard-working citizens and creators of an authentic national musical form—the samba.

Recognition of the contributions of Afro-Brazilians and other workers to national society reflected the Vargas regime's goal of "making the revolution before the people do" and of co-opting those social groups that represented a revolutionary potential. Thus, rather than improving conditions in the slums (the *favelas*), the regime promoted the idea that the slum-dweller (the *favelado*) was an accepted and equal partner in society. One part of this verbal deception was the campaign of racial democracy.

The urban masses did not mindlessly accept politically motivated programs; rather, they mastered the lessons of interest-group politics. Samba school leaders learned to use the political system, and obtained annual funds, prizes, and prestige for their members. The change can be seen in the system of awarding prizes for the best performance. Rather than selecting the winner based on the most applause from the audience, several schools insisted on using judges versed in "literature, music and poetry."

Social programs became the special interest of Vargas's wife, Darcy. The samba's integration into national life was evident during World War II when Darcy invited the leading samba schools to present a benefit performance to finance Rio de Janeiro's canteen for the armed forces. By the time Vargas lost control of the government in 1945, he had overseen the amalgamation of the government and mass organizations, such as samba groups. Relying on a culture that stressed popular and folkloric traditions, Vargas and other Latin American leaders turned away from a program to civilize the nation in favor of a campaign to nationalize the people.

## Argentina and the Peróns

A cabal of Argentine colonels including Juan Perón seized power in 1943, initiating a period in which Perón, joined shortly by his new wife, Eva Duarte de Perón, directly ruled Argentina until 1958 and influenced the government until 1973. Vestiges of the impact of the Peronist party are evident in Argentine politics even today. To foster self-esteem and preempt any revolutionary challenges, Perón's rise to power and his construction of the nation–state relied on the myth of the downtrodden blue-collar worker, the *descamisado* (shirtless), to mobilize urban workers, as well as effective use of mass media, including radio, movies, and spectacles, none greater than the first Pan American Games. To ensure order during the celebrations marking the centennial of independence, the Peróns also transformed the federal district (Buenos Aires) police into a national constabulary to represent their interests and counterbalance the military police, which had acquired expanded powers as early as 1916. These rival police forces remain problematic for Argentina's civilian government.

Juan Perón, with the assistance of his wife, built the regime on the concept of social change and nationalism without social revolution. He controlled and co-opted the urban working class by creating an umbrella labor organization, the General Confederation of Workers (CGT), and the Eva Perón Social Welfare Foundation to assist, in particular, poor urban women and children. The regime provided increased wages, benefits, and holidays for workers, and improved housing and health care for women and children, including distribution of milk. By nationalizing foreign-owned industries, such as the railroads and urban transit systems, Perón provided jobs. Even more ingenious was Perón's scheme to use booming agricultural exports to pay for industrial expansion and social benefits.

The Argentine Institute for the Promotion of Trade (IAPI) served as the marketing arm for agriculture. Producers had to sell their goods at a fixed price to the IAPI, which in turn sold them abroad at a substantial profit. This plan worked because of the tremendous demand for food products in Europe at the end of World War II. Subsequently, the U.S. Marshall Plan to fund Western Europe's recovery from the war through moderate pricing of these goods.

Evita's successes as the beloved intercessor of the poor for her husband's regime and the symbol of feminine beauty drove her to more extravagant claims and campaigns: self-portrayal as the world's most perfect figure, and a trip to Spain with the expectation of international fanfare, which never materialized. Obsessed by the desire for success and celebrity, Eva Perón died of cancer at the age of 32.

Perón's efforts to make Evita a secular saint included mummifying her body and placing it on display at the offices of the CGT. Angered by Perón's attempts to idolize Eva, Church leaders began to recognize the distance between the Church and the regime when Perón decreed the legalization of divorce and legal recognition of illegitimate children. The final break between the Church and the government occurred when Perón began flaunting his teenage mistresses around the presidential residence and the capital city's social gathering places. Eventually a military coup overturned the regime and Perón fled. While in Panama on the way to Europe, he collected a dancer, whom he later married. Evita's body disappeared, its whereabouts a mystery and a political issue for the next decade. The military junta that took power discovered that driving Perón into exile did not end his influence, and Peronism remained a major force in national politics.

Despite the damage his policies inflicted and the deep political divisions created during his presidency, Perón and his new wife returned to Argentina. In 1973, he was reelected president, and she, the new vice president. Unfortunately, he died in office, plunging the nation back into chaos. Devastated and frustrated student radicals, along with middle-class and university-educated Argentines, sought a solution to what had been an aborted social revolution starting with the populist Hipólito Irigoyen who twice served as president (1916–1922 and 1928–1930). Terror and counterterror by the military, called the Dirty War, represented the price of failure. The disastrous defeat of the army in the Falklands (or Malvinas) War discredited it to such an extent that the military had no option but to relinquish power, opening the way for the emergence of a democratic middle-class regime that, nevertheless, continued to labor under its populist past and the trauma of the Dirty War.

## Cuba and Castro

When Fidel Castro and his band of bearded rebels seized control of Cuba in January 1959, a klaxon sounded throughout the Americas. It signaled the hope for widespread social justice and economic change that inspired Castro's 26 of

July Movement and that would set in motion similar movements from Quebec to southern South America. Castro's revolution represented patriotism, frustrated since 1898 by the political intervention of the United States; reformism, motivated by the corruption of the dictator Fulgencio Batista and the presence of foreign organized criminals; and nationalism, especially in economic matters. Revulsion with the Batista government on the part of the populace made the military campaign from 1956 to 1959 less difficult than the rebels had anticipated. But once in power, Castro faced problems more serious than he had imagined.

Castro's Cuba became the eye of the hurricane during the Cold War. Quarantine by the State Department and attempted annihilation by the Central Intelligence Agency (CIA) failed. The political and economic boycott initiated by the government of President Dwight Eisenhower soon led to a planned invasion, under the auspices of the CIA and with the approval of President John F. Kennedy. The failure of both, most dramatically the invasion at the Bay of Pigs (1961), humiliated policymakers in Washington, D.C., and propelled Cuban rebels to a position of leadership in the Third World. The Soviet Union provided economic and military aid, but also discovered that Fidel Castro had no intention of turning Cuba into a Caribbean Poland.

Although developments on the international front, defeating the United States and obtaining loans and markets from the Soviet countries, went smoothly for the first several years, domestic programs lurched along, partly because of the trial-and-error approach of young Cuban leaders and partly because of the insistence on ideological purity. Che Guevara, an Argentine of mediocre abilities beyond self-promotion, increasingly became a Communist Party tub-thumper and a noisy distraction, but Fidel faced real, practical economic and political problems of government. Castro eventually encouraged Guevara to pursue his schemes to lead a worldwide revolution and sent him first to Africa and then to Bolivia.

At one point, Fidel announced to the Cuban people that domestic problems demonstrated that "it is easier to make a revolution than it is to make a revolution work." Programs of economic diversification, which enjoyed some initial success and reduced the dependence on sugar, soon foundered. By the mid-1960s Cubans resumed their efforts to achieve monster sugar harvests; Castro called for a 10-million-ton *zafra* (harvest) in 1970. With economic difficulties mounting in the 1970s, critics emerged from within Cuba and among former Communist supporters, but the regime's accomplishments should not be minimized. Castro's programs brought education to the young; widespread improvements in nutrition, even with food rationing; an end to public racial prejudice, although personal prejudice continued; and general equality for women, with the notable exception of high-ranking military positions, industrial management, and the fishing industry. The future, Castro made clear, lies with the nation's children— they have learned to read. This is his monument.

Nevertheless, Castro in the 1990s became a tired vestige of Cuba's age of revolution. The regime lacked imagination and received only grudging, declining international support. Yet Fidel held on, although he showed little interest in planning for the nation's political future or making sweeping economic adjustments.

## Peru and the Generals

Peruvian generals seized control of the central government in 1968 to institute more nationalistic policies. Led by Juan Velasco Alvarado, the generals immediately initiated a program that restricted the activities of multinational businesses in Peru and offered greater opportunities for economic and social mobility to the urban and rural poor. The military's actions, both its seizure of power and its policies, were precipitated by an agreement, called the Act of Talara, between the government of President Fernando Balaúnde Terry and the International Petroleum Company (IPC), a subsidiary of Standard Oil of New Jersey. The agreement returned title to oil properties to Peru, but left a major refinery in the company's hands. Rumors charged that a secret codicil provided extremely favorable currency arrangements for the company. These rumors split Balaúnde's party and opened the door for the candidate of the opposition party, *Alianza Popular Revolucionaria Americana* (APRA), to win the 1969 presidential election. APRA and the military were avowed enemies. The generals decided to act for two additional reasons: the slow pace of the national reform movement under Balaúnde and his refusal to allow the military to assist in this program for national regeneration. The officers, highly educated, disciplined, motivated, and keenly conscious of the needs of the marginal population, especially rural inhabitants and Indians, believed they had a role to play in creating a new Peru.

General Juan Velasco Alvarado headed the ruling military junta. Six days after seizing power, he canceled the Act of Talara and nationalized IPC properties, signaling the beginning of a series of initiatives to make Peru more autonomous, less dependent on foreign corporations and U.S. political leadership, and more responsive to the needs of its workers in the fields and factories. Among other decrees, the military asserted a claim to territorial waters extending up to 200 miles offshore. As a result of this action, the Peruvian navy captured and fined numerous American tuna fishermen; a planned visit by Nelson Rockefeller to Peru was canceled; and the number of cultural and economic agreements with Soviet bloc nations increased.

The military junta used the authority of the nation–state to begin a series of domestic programs for agrarian and industrial reform. With the highly praised June 1969 Agrarian Reform Law (decree 17716), the military attempted to use the power of the government to raise the standard of living of the disadvantaged, enlarge the national market, and provide the capital necessary to spur industrialism. The reform struck first at the huge coastal sugar estates, turning them into worker cooperatives and paying previous owners in cash and 20- and 30-year bonds. In the highlands, after a sputtering attempt to create small individual farms, the reform began to create cooperative estates. Ultimately 76 percent of expropriated Andean properties were redistributed as cooperatives and the remainder as small farms. The enthusiasm for remaking rural Peru grew from the developmentalist conviction that agriculture should feed the nation at reasonable prices and that land reform should help finance industrial development. These aspects of the national development program along with the subterfuges of estate owners to escape expropriation combined to inhibit the program's success.

This land reform law together with the new General Law of Industries (1970) aimed to weaken the power of foreign interests and mobilize resources for rapid industrialization. The industrial law offered incentives for increased investment in manufacturing, wherein the nation-state assumed responsibility for basic industries, including petrochemicals, fish meal, fertilizer, cement, and paper manufacturing. Individual capitalists could undertake these activities if they signed contracts that stipulated when the industry would be transferred to the government. To stimulate productivity and investment in industry, the regime offered generous tax incentives to all manufacturing firms except those producing superfluous luxury goods. The law also required companies to pay 10 percent of net profits before taxes as cash bonuses to workers and reinvest an additional 15 percent of net in the company to be paid to the workers as shares. The military government also took control of water resources and nationalized the banking, insurance, and telephone systems. The regime inaugurated its control of the mining industry through two state corporations, Minoperu and Centrominperu.[13]

In carrying out its economic program, the military junta established martial law, restricted freedom of the press, and eliminated all community autonomy, thus turning over authority to the central government. Specifically, the new municipal decree replaced the locally elected municipal councils with officials appointed by the central government. The developmentalist goals relied on the central government, made a revolution from above, and left no opportunity for local involvement in decision making, even in such matters as crop selection on agricultural cooperatives. This top-heavy organization eventually toppled under its own bureaucratic weight.

The social concerns of the members of Velasco's junta were most evident in the decree to assist domestic workers. This law provided a minimum salary of $1 per week, social security, guaranteed holidays, and severance pay. The army also created the National System for Support and Social Mobilization to establish ties between workers, peasants, and the government. This plan relied on a corporate state structure to ensure social harmony.

The officers' motives for seizing power and drawing up their administrative strategy came from their tradition as the guardians of national government and a command-wide concern with social issues that had developed in the 1950s and 1960s. The latter attitude had developed as a result of several factors: (1) Many Peruvian officers had emerged from the lower and middle classes and retained a concern for their neighbors and relatives. (2) In the 1960s these men participated in counterinsurgency and civic action campaigns in the Andes and had become acquainted with the "Other Peru"—the rural, poor, and indigenous marginal population. (3) The curriculum at the command school (*Centro de Altos Militares*), attended by all promising young officers, included courses in socially relevant issues such as agrarian reform and developmental economics. These courses stressed the need for central planning and, following recommendations of the United Nations Economic Commission for Latin America, the role of the central government in national development. (4) The officers had regular contact with several highly motivated civilians, notably Augusto Zimmerman, editor of *El*

---

[13]*Toronto Globe and Mail*, September 14, 1970.

*Comercio,* and Alberto Ruiz Eldridge, dean of Lima's Bar Association, who were both committed to social reform. These military officers intended to preempt the social programs that had contributed to the popularity of Leftist politicians.

The general population initially did not react to the military reformist government with the same enthusiasm as the officers. This lukewarm feeling changed in the summer of 1969 when the Peruvian national soccer team qualified for the 1970 World Cup in Mexico City by tying the Argentine team in a match played in Buenos Aires. Velasco dispatched air force jets to escort the players home. A crowd of 100,000 met the players and threw 10 tons of confetti on them as they were taken in procession to the national palace. Receiving the players, Velasco said their victory signaled the rebirth of Peru and smelled of oil and agrarian reform. The military junta capitalized on the burst of nationalism from the athletic success.

The unanimity of support for reform under military direction did not last long. The military revolution foundered on several impediments, among them the top-down structure of the program and the numbers of marginal people left outside the reforms. For example, the landless highland people did not benefit as estates were turned over to workers on the property, and many urban migrants in the ramshackle suburbs of Lima and other towns did not fit into the communities receiving aid and attention under the reforms. The fatal blow to the Velasco revolution came from the combination of two factors: The state became the major investor in economic development; it mortgaged its potential resources— the prospect of oil in the Amazon basin and the profits from expected high world mineral prices. Peru became the largest borrower in the Third World in 1973, with loans of $734 million. Within two years, the collapse of the world's minerals market and the failure to make major oil strikes threw the national economy into chaos. Economic collapse brought an end to the revolutionary program and the Velasco regime. Although Velasco's more conservative and free-market successor, General Francesco Morales Bermúdez, would trumpet the "Second Phase" of the revolution, his administration retreated on all reform fronts. With the election of 1980, the army again withdrew from direct politics. Velasco's regime demonstrated the nonideological pragmatism of many Latin American military technocrats, or what has been aptly called the politics of antipolitics.

## DEMOCRATIZATION AND LOCAL REGIMES, 1980 TO THE PRESENT

The democratization of Latin American regimes that began in the "Lost Decade" of the 1980s responded to four general trends: (1) the growing disillusionment with repressive, and increasingly ineffectual military regimes; (2) the increasing recognition that national central planning projects for reform, modernization, economic growth, and social improvements were not working; (3) the abrupt collapse of socialist states, breaking up along the fault lines caused by popular, community-based organizations, such as Solidarity in Poland, and ethnocultural groups, such as Ukrainians; and (4) the vitality of grass roots civic organizations created out of necessity in Latin America's burgeoning cities to meet the crises of shelter, food, health care, and national disasters, or the lack of public services created by the adoption of so-called Neoliberal economic programs. In Latin America, Leviathan national, usually military, governments began to give way to more politically responsive civilian regimes. These new governments shared characteristics that included a more democratic selection of leaders, revitalized municipal governments, and Neoliberal economic policies that included the privatization of state agencies. The latter movement to remove the government from the economy has reached beyond state-run enterprises, such as airlines and petroleum corporations, to activities traditionally regarded as government responsibilities, such as garbage collection. These changes have occurred both in practice and in principle, with new legislation and constitutional amendments to create the legal context for them.

Nevertheless, the adoption of Neoliberal national policies should not obscure the post-World War II pattern of local self-help communities that ignored national agencies because of their corruption or ineptitude, or both. These changes in Latin America created space for experimentation and development through grass roots organizations that sprang up in response to the daily crises confronting the resident poor and the new emigrants to Latin America's booming cities. As national regimes proved increasingly incapable of or unwilling to enforce the laws, government institutions were either overwhelmed and, therefore, unable to resolve the ordinary problems of the people, or the regime remained unwilling to do so. Marginal people had only themselves to turn to. The origins of this bootstrapping activity reached back, at least in Brazil, to groups known as Friends of the Neighborhood Societies that were common in the years 1945 to 1964.[14] Soon other volunteer groups, known as Christian Base Communities, began to appear under Church auspices. Responding to the call for social action that emanated from Vatican II, these communities had widespread success in Brazil and Central America in helping meet the needs of disadvantaged city-dwellers through informal means. The staggering population expansion of Lima, followed by Peru's economic disintegration, gave impetus to mushrooming community groups, such as soup kitchens and health and housing groups. Cultural expressions of these organizations of neighbors, especially in music using either traditional instruments in the Andes or rock-and-roll patterns elsewhere, often served as surrogates for political action in opposition to entrenched regimes. This was particularly the case in Chile under the oppressive Pinochet military dictatorship. Other innovative, informal methods using the mass media have also appeared to serve the everyday needs of Latin American peoples. In La Paz, Bolivia, Carlos Palenque, known as *El Compadre,* used his *Radio y Televisión Popular* program to resolve people's basic problems. These radio programs provide an alternative, more efficient system of justice through *La Tribuna del Pueblo* (the people's court), whereas other shows deal with issues such as wife abuse and missing children.[15]

---

[14]Gil Shidlo, "Local Urban Elections in Democratic Brazil," in Henry A. Dietz and Gil Shidlo, eds., *Urban Elections in Democratic Latin America* (Wilmington, DE: SR Books, 1998), pp. 64–68.

[15]Eduardo A. Gamarra, "Municipal Elections in Bolivia," in Dietz and Shidlo, eds., *Urban Elections,* pp. 21–62.

*Super Barrio,* a caped crusader, appeared in Mexico City after the 1985 earthquake to help bring justice to the city's disadvantaged residents. And, in another instance, Mexican women in Ciénega de Chapala, Michoacán, organized to challenge the administrator of the corrupt and inefficient local water system.[16] The informal community organizations have drawn in populations previously left outside of or abandoned by politics. No better illustration of this movement exists than the movement in Argentina, Chile, and other countries of the mothers and relatives of the disappeared.

With the transition from military regimes, these programs have assisted in the creation of democratic local government. This shift has involved the revitalization of municipal government through new legislation. Thus, the new Brazilian constitution of 1988 provided for municipal political and economic autonomy. This change was followed by expanded legislation regulating local elections in 1992. Colombian president Belisario Betancur (1982–1986) pushed through the legislature a reform package that provided for decentralization of the political system, including popular election of city mayors, shifting sales tax revenue to the localities, and local involvement in providing local services, such as utilities.[17]

Mexico's ruling PRI officials initiated reforms in 1977 and 1986 that expanded proportional representation and extended it to both the state and municipal administrative levels. Each state congress determined the proportional distribution plan for the state and its municipalities. In some cases, voters choose a mayor and council, with nominal representation for participating parties; in others, voters create the council with seats based on the proportion of votes. Peruvian elections for local officials, although tried as a brief experiment after World War I, occurred for the first time with regularity after 1980.[18]

Venezuela's congress created the legal environment for local elections in 1989 with the Organic Law of Municipalities and Voter's Rights Law, which established for the first time the direct election of governors, mayors, council members, and the parish councils (city neighborhood councils).[19]

The privatization of urban services can be seen most clearly in the Dominican Republic. There the city council transferred water delivery to the Santo Domingo Water and Sewer Corporation, transportation to private hands, and garbage collection, on a neighborhood basis, to different companies, including the British contractor Attwoods Dominicana. The capital city's government remained in charge of fire service, cemetery administration, and some cultural activities.[20]

This same move to privatization of services occurred in regimes undergoing transition from revolutionary to more open politics and Neoliberal economics.

---

[16]See John Gledhill, *Power and Its Disguises: Anthropological Perspectives on Politics* (London: Pluto, 1994).

[17]Shidlo, "Brazil," and Gary Hoskin, "Urban Electoral Behavior in Colombia," in Dietz and Shidlo, eds., *Urban Elections,* pp. 64–68; 91–116.

[18]Dietz, "Urban Elections in Peru, 1980–1995," in Dietz and Shidlo, eds., *Urban Elections,* pp. 199–224.

[19]Angel E. Alvarez, "Venezuelan Local and National Elections, 1958–1995," in Dietz and Shidlo, eds., *Urban Elections,* pp. 243–278.

[20]Christopher Mitchell, "Urban Elections in the Dominican Republic, 1962–1994," in Dietz and Shidlo, eds., *Urban Elections,* pp. 117–140.

The Nicaraguan government of Violeta Chamorro, for example, which came to power in the wake of the Sandinista revolutionary government, moved against the Nicaraguan Social Security and Social Welfare Institute. The actions that "basically privatized" the ministry can be illustrated by the nature of the Nicaraguan Fund for Children and the Family, the successor to the Sandinista Family and Child Welfare Department of the Ministry of Social Welfare. This new agency was responsible for setting standards and allocating funds to nongovernmental agencies concerned with children and families rather than directly providing services. The directors of the agency intended to have all services handled by the private sector within two to four years.[21] In Greater Buenos Aires, as a result of deregulation and privatization, two electrical utility companies serve the metropolis and neither is able to provide continuous power.[22]

Two worrisome developments threaten the revitalized municipal regimes throughout Latin America. First, in some cities voter apathy is on the rise, demonstrated by casting blank ballots and abstention. This trend may be explained in part by voter exhaustion from the recent surfeit of elections, but it may also reflect popular disenchantment with corrupt politicians and bureaucracies and greater confidence in the ability of informal, unofficial agencies to meet individual and family needs. Second, the economic crises during the "Lost Decade" of the 1980s prompted governmental leaders to shift to Neoliberal economic policies. This change often reflected the coercive influence of the World Bank and the Inter-American Development Bank, which required austere economic programs in return for loans and investment credits. Economic hardship resulted. Under these circumstances, women became especially resourceful in eking out a living through microenterprises, operating through the informal economy. In Bolivia, for example, many observers believe that the microenterprises, an estimated 55 percent of the economically active population in 1992 in La Paz, were primarily responsible for the improvements in the quality of health care, nutrition, housing, and clothing. The majority of those engaged in microenterprises are vendors, who sell all sorts of things, including family-made noisemakers for fiestas. Others operate small meat shops or neighborhood stores.

Cutbacks as a result of Neoliberal programs reduced or eliminated government-supplied services that many people had come to take for granted. Teachers went on strike against Neoliberal cuts in education budgets, for example, in Nicaragua, Haiti, Colombia, and Bolivia in 1995. They protested the loss of job security; a demotion in professional standing, like being redefined in Bolivia as superior technicians; and the lack of adequate financing for educating the nation's population. Efforts to break up teachers' unions were common.

Still, an unexpected development has occurred. The emergence of local community social projects directed by nongovernmental self-help groups, such as soup kitchens and day-care centers, has convinced many that the local community is better equipped than the central government to administer social services. This

---

[21]Karen Kampwrith, "Social Policy," in Thomas W. Walker, ed., *Nicaragua in the 1990s* (Wilmington, DE: SR Books, 1998), pp. 6–7.

[22]Peter A. Calvert, "Urban Electoral Politics in Argentina," in Dietz and Shidlo, eds., *Urban Elections*, pp. 2–20.

Courtesy of the Latin America Library at Tulane University.

Modified indigenous forms of local governance functioned under Spanish rule and continue to do so today. Here a group of town elders in Cuzco, Peru, pose in ceremonial dress. Indian cultural practices have shown a remarkable resiliency, and today at the dawn of the twenty-first century, indigenous organizations in several regions have become politically important.

acknowledgment comes just as Neoliberal economic policies are being promoted by conservative national leaders and representatives of international agencies intent on reducing governmental control and financing of many services. These civic and economic policies have encouraged political campaigns at the local level. Nowhere has this focus on local politics been more dramatic than in Mexico, where opposition politicians from the Left and the Right have eroded control of the official ruling party, the PRI. In 1997, for example, Cuauhtémoc Cárdenas, the opposition candidate, was elected mayor of Mexico City.

The issue that continues to confront Latin American government is how to integrate the masses into politics. The progress of the opposition groups in Mexico in challenging the ruling party's dominance suggests that the goal of mass political participation can best be achieved by first building on the tradition of self-help and community trust at the local level.

# 3

# Traditional Economies

This chapter considers the development of Latin American economies from the nineteenth century through the world depression of 1929–1930. The chapter explains three interlocking themes: (1) the identification of prosperity with the control of labor and property, (2) the emergence in the nineteenth century of an exchange economy based on the export of raw materials (minerals, coffee, bananas, and sugar) and the import of manufactured items as well as luxury goods (fashions, pianos, and champagne) and capital goods (machinery and tools), and (3) the introduction of technology. Boom economies based on products such as rubber in Brazil and Bolivia characterized Latin America during this era. World War I delivered a blow to this export-import economy and the world depression of 1929–1930 destroyed it.

The evolving Latin American economy resulted from several interrelated social and psychological factors, only some of which have been identified or fully understood. Culture was one of the most important because it determined the value of consumer goods and the nature of productive behavior. Trade developed in response to needs, such as those for food or raw materials, and desires, such as a taste for the exotic, for example, Chinese silks or Indian spices. These motives drove trade across oceans. Agricultural and artisanal skills determined the production of goods for subsistence and for exchange. The desire for raw materials or the search for markets determined the range of trade. Increasing economic specialization stimulated interdependency, and in Europe it promoted the concept of wealth based on the ownership of real property, the manipulation of labor, and the control of capital.

Poor roads, sometimes only deeply eroded trails, hampered development of the nineteenth century Brazilian mining industry. Here a mule train loaded with ore prepares to make the difficult and costly trek to a coastal smelter. Labor-intensive activity supported by low-wage labor hindered the modernization of Latin American economies.

## BRAZIL'S ECONOMY IN THE
## NINETEENTH CENTURY

After Brazil's smooth transition to an independent empire (see Chapter 2), coffee production underpinned modernization over the course of the nineteenth century. First planted in the Amazon basin with beans allegedly smuggled out of French Guiana in the 1720s, coffee was at first only marginally successful. In 1731, growers in São Luis do Maranhão exported the first commercial shipment to the Lisbon market. Coffee cultivation moved southward, taking advantage of the more suitable soil in south-central Brazil. Rio de Janeiro's first coffee export shipment in 1779 signaled the modest beginning of what would become a major new economic cycle. After the 1808 arrival of the Portuguese monarchy in Brazil, officials stimulated coffee production by distributing seedlings and making land available to potential growers. By 1828, they were putting 26,703 tons of coffee on the international market. Two-thirds of Brazil's exports consisted of coffee by 1889. Brazilian coffee, without serious competition, dominated the world market.

Coffee *fazendas* covered large expanses of land. One plantation in the province of Minas Gerais covered 64 square miles and functioned as an integrated economic unit, raising its own cattle and growing its own cotton, sugar, and foodstuffs; it relied on the labor of some 700 slaves. Coffee production required new land every 15 years. A hollow frontier emerged as the industry abandoned exhausted land and moved farther west. Clearing new land, planting the saplings, and tending them for five years before they produced their first crop required a substantial capital investment. Trees, planted in rows up and down the hillsides, resulted in severe erosion, and coffee growing depleted the soil. Moreover, transportation networks had to be constantly expanded westward. The combination of predictable future expenses and a current profitable cash flow prompted coffee planters to invest surplus capital in industry with the intention of withdrawing funds when needed to develop new coffee land. Thus São Paulo, the provincial capital of the most important coffee region, became a light manufacturing and railroad repair center, laying the foundation for its dominant industrial position in twentieth-century Brazil.

Coffee gave Brazil a favorable balance of trade in the 1860s, more than offsetting rising imports. British merchants dominated Brazil's trade until the 1870s, when U.S. consumers absorbed over 50 percent of coffee exports. Planters became the economic and political elite of the empire of dom Pedro II. The emperor recognized them in 1841, when he elevated the first planter to the nobility as the Baron do Piraí. He was the first of many so honored.

Beyond coffee, transportation and communications drew Brazil into the world system. Railway construction coupled with telegraph lines facilitated economic development. Baron Mauá, Brazil's foremost entrepreneur, built the first line in 1854 to link Rio de Janeiro with the imperial summer resort of Petrópolis. Thirty-five years later some 6,000 miles had been laid, mostly in the coffee region. By 1900, some 15,316 kilometers of track reached out from Rio. Telegraph lines linked the then capital with the northern province of Pará in 1886, symbolically tying together the north and south. Telegraph lines also connected Brazil with the rest of the world. A submarine cable linked Rio with Europe in 1874, followed shortly by a connection with Montevideo in 1876 and with Buenos Aires in 1883. The Royal English Mail Line in 1851 provided steamship service to Europe. Steamships entered local service in 1869, making possible reliable coastal transportation for both cargo and passengers.

The exhilaration of modernization was marred by the existence of slavery. Humane Brazilians recognized its inherent inhumanity; entrepreneurs acknowledged it represented an archaic labor system; politicians responded to international pressure; and slave owners wanted compensation and a new form of cheap labor. Moreover, international consumers questioned the morality of purchasing slave-produced products. British abolitionists, economists, traders, and manufacturers all pushed for an end to the slave system. They argued the practical case that free laborers became consumers creating profits for producers. Pressure to end slavery became overwhelming. In 1850, the emperor, prodded by the British navy, prohibited the importation of slaves signaling the eventual demise of slavery. Brazilian politicians and officials moved reluctantly toward abolition. The long overdue end came in 1888, when Princess Isabella signed the Golden Law, abolishing slavery. (The emperor, at the time, was out of the country.)

The Golden Law forced the country to modernize its labor system. Coffee growers and other planters contracted a workforce of ex-slaves and European immigrants. To everyone's surprise and relief, coffee resumed its expansion within three years of abolition by relying on sharecropping and wages to attract sufficient workers. The successful transition to free labor represented Brazil's most significant economic achievement in the nineteenth century.

The transformation of society caused by modernization gradually gained momentum. In 1850, children attending school numbered 170,000, whereas some 5.5 million Brazilians over the age of 5 could not read or write (out of a population of approximately 7 million). Although law schools provided the elite with some traditional polish, army engineering schools offered the only technical instruction. Not until the 1890s did two civilian engineering schools in São Paulo and other professional schools begin to offer technical and professional training. Industry became ever more important after 1889 introducing new values and attitudes. Floriano Peixoto, the second president following the 1889 overthrow of the Brazilian empire, viewed industrial expansion as essential for increased social mobility, national strength, and security. In 1892, he pushed tariffs up 30 to 60 percent. Congress meanwhile exempted machinery, tools, and luxuries from duties. The government devised a loan program to benefit industry. As the finance minister observed, the program demonstrated that the state had entered a new phase of protectionism and now preferred industry to agriculture.

## THE SPANISH-AMERICAN ECONOMY IN THE NINETEENTH CENTURY

Economic development in the Spanish-American republics differed from that in Brazil due to several factors. The struggle for independence from Spain had precipitated civil wars in various parts of the empire. Death, destruction of property, abandoned and flooded mines, and insurgency mixed with banditry plunged Spanish America into economic chaos. Carefully developed wealth evaporated with a suddenness that shattered all confidence in the future. Although large areas of South America and marginal areas of Central America had been spared, the economic core in Peru and Mexico had been torn apart. Tax revenues dropped to pitiful levels with a disastrous impact on the economy and the government's ability to secure life, property, and the movement of goods. On the eve of independence, the Mexican treasury collected some 39 million pesos, an amount that sank to less than 5.5 million pesos by 1823. It required more than half a century for Mexico to regain pre-independence levels of revenue. Foreign loans barely kept the new Spanish-American republics afloat, often creating crushing debts rather than restoring the economy. Inevitable defaults complicated foreign investment and made it difficult to obtain further credit. Recovery occurred in a checkered pattern; some regions were able to make a reasonable comeback by the 1830s, whereas others languished until after midcentury. Financial and economic uncertainty made the political situation unstable. Only after Latin America painfully restructured its economy to fit the needs of the industrialized countries of Europe and the United States did a measure of fiscal and political stability emerge.

The new international economy centered in the North Atlantic required adjustments in Latin America. Imports of high-value items no longer predominated.

Inexpensive, relatively well-made items for everyday use now flooded the domestic market, competing with local production and cutting profit margins for the merchant community. Free trade, a banner carried aggressively into the hemisphere by Great Britain and supported by other commercial nations, including the United States, initiated massive changes within Latin America. Pragmatic acceptance of economic liberalism by the majority of the elite provided the internal pressure for economic change.

The transition proved difficult. In Peru, a flood of British textiles and hardware, French clothes and wines, and American flour, cottons, and sundries arrived in the mid 1820s. Fearful merchants, seeing disaster for themselves and domestic producers, went on strike in August 1834. They shuttered shops and marched through the streets demanding tariff protection. It took time, but in 1838 they succeeded in installing a nationalist and protectionist regime. By the mid 1850s they lost control, when *guano* exports, primarily to Britain, created a free-trade elite group that dominated the economy.

In a similar fashion, the interior of Argentina had prospered during the colonial period by supplying the mines of Peru with all types of artisan goods from saddle blankets to clothing, much of it produced by women. The introduction of inexpensive foreign manufactured items after independence plunged the region into depression. Coastal Argentina, advantageously situated to dominate the export-import trade, emerged as the economic center of the new nation. As late as the 1890s, Mexican textile manufacturers estimated that foreign competitors could undersell them by as much as 10 percent. The new economic reality could be highly profitable for those who focused on exporting raw materials, but domestic manufacturers faced difficult, often unbeatable competition. Export liberalism swept from Argentina to Mexico as the old economic order crumbled.

## TECHNOLOGY AND THE EXPORT ECONOMY

Railroads signaled the coming of a new economic era. The rails opened new lands for plantation agriculture and extraction of raw materials. A 30-mile stretch from Havana to Güines completed in 1838 gave Cuba, still a lingering remnant of Spain's American empire until 1989, the first rail line in Latin America. Chile inaugurated its first railway in 1852, and five years later Argentina built a rail line. Bolivian tin, mined at high elevations in the Andes, made its way to world markets on a Pacific railway. Mexico, during the regime of General Santa Anna (1853–1855), negotiated contracts for a rail link from Veracruz to Mexico City and on to the Pacific coast. With the growing interest in the United States to develop the Asian trade, Mexico hoped that a railway across the Isthmus of Tehuantepec would transform that region into the crossroads of the world. Only 810 miles separated the isthmus from the mouth of the Mississippi and access to the North American river system and its connection with the manufacturing heartland of the United States. The dream endured, but in the end the Tehuantepec railway could not compete once the Panama Canal opened in 1914.

On the eve of the Mexican Revolution of 1910, the country had some 15,000 miles of track connected with the American rail net at the border towns of Laredo, El Paso, and Nogales. In Venezuela, President Antonio Guzmán Blanco (1828–1899) imposed order, restructured the economy, and rebuilt Caracas in what he believed to be the modern manner. Exports financed new port facilities, but the centerpiece of his regime was the system of railways.

In Central America, technology created an export economy. Railways on the western slope facilitated coffee exports with an effective network by the 1880s. On the Caribbean side, rail construction required a substantial investment and, in the absence of commercially viable commodities, immediate return on capital could not be expected. Consequently, the Costa Rican government used land grants to entice the American engineer Henry Meiggs in 1871 to construct a line from San José to Puerto Limón. Meiggs turned the project over to two nephews, Minor Cooper Keith and Henry Meiggs Keith. Even before completion of the line in 1890, Minor Keith shipped small quantities of bananas from Puerto Limón to New Orleans. By 1885 half a million bunches a year went to the United States. Trunk lines branching off the main line opened up additional land for banana cultivation. Keith's company merged in 1899 with a Boston-based banana importer to form the United Fruit Company. The now giant company expanded throughout Central America, building rail lines into promising areas. The International Railways of Central America (IRCA), owned by the fruit company, delivered bananas to the company's "Great White Fleet." United Fruit steamships dominated trade on the Caribbean coast. By 1910 radio communication made it possible to monitor market conditions closely, and in 1913 a subsidiary, Tropical Radio Telegraph, provided Central America with a communications network. Two other American fruit companies, Standard Fruit and Steamship and Cuyamel Fruit, also entered the region. Large stretches of foreign-owned plantations led to use of the derogatory term "Banana Republics" to refer to the export-dominated Central American republics.

Colombian banana production, in a similar fashion, followed the rails. José Manual González Bermúdez shipped bananas to New York City in 1889. Unfortunately, they arrived overripe and could not be sold. Colombian planters without sufficient capital could not finance both production and marketing. Foreign capitalists able to raise significant investment funds, armed with a good grasp of the needs of the market, and knowledgeable about useful technology soon became the dominant force in the industry. United Fruit owned some 250,000 acres in Colombia, Costa Rica, Cuba, the Dominican Republic, Honduras, and Nicaragua. The company operated 117 miles of track, 300 freight cars and 17 locomotives, and 41 steamships, in addition to docks, storage, and communications facilities. Radio telegraph made it possible to fine-tune supply and demand. When "scarce" came over the wires, all bananas would be accepted, but when "abundance" was reported, independent producers found it difficult to get the company to accept their fruit. Prices rose and fell with the clattering of the telegraph key. United Fruit's ability to deploy financial resources as well as the latest technology gave the company an overwhelming advantage.

Argentina provides another example of the role of technology in creating an export economy, but without the same level of foreign domination as in Central

Beginning around 1900, foreign banana companies invested heavily in modern technology, purchasing steamships, establishing railways, and setting up radio telegraph equipment to aid their marketing strategies. They often appeared to have more power than weak Central American governments, giving rise to the derogatory term, "Banana Republic."

America. Railways and the new refrigerator ships for shipping frozen beef, first used in 1876, represented high technology, whereas low-technology barbed wire made modern cattle breeding possible. By 1900, the country had 278 refrigerator ships carrying chilled and frozen beef to Great Britain. In addition, some 2.25 million tons of Argentine wheat entered the world market. Who could doubt that the country had become a modern cornucopia—shipping beef, wheat, and wool—thanks to the inventiveness of a brilliant century and the pull of foreign markets.

## MOBILIZING CAPITAL

Foreign and domestic banks appeared throughout Latin America to facilitate imports, service the international export trade, and handle the banking needs of foreign investors. Brazil in 1845 had only a single bank, but by the end of the next decade 12 new financial institutions had been established. In 1862, the first foreign commercial bank, the Bank of London and Brazil, opened for business.

That same year, the Bank of London and the River Plate began operation in Argentina. The London Bank of Mexico and South America, capitalized with 1 million pounds, provided Mexico City with its first modern commercial bank in 1864. It issued banknotes, provided debt and discount services, dispatched silver to England, and became a highly profitable endeavor.

French, Italian, Portuguese, Spanish, German, and American banks opened throughout the hemisphere. Whether domestically or foreign controlled, banks tended to cluster in important export regions. Thus Torreón, the heart of the Mexican cotton area of Laguna, had 10 branch banks. Banks initially established by foreign investors could become rooted in a particular country. For example, in Mexico the *Banco Nacional Mexicano,* a branch of the Franco-Egyptian Bank, opened in 1882, issued banknotes and established branches and agencies throughout the country. A group of Spanish merchants formed the *Banco Mercantil Mexicano,* which merged with Banco Nacional Mexicano to form the *Banco Nacional de México.* Colombia's first commercial bank began servicing customers in 1870, and four years later Guatemala also had a commercial institution. In Argentina, a group of cattlemen founded the *Banco Popular Argentino* in 1887. Another bank, *El Hogar Argentino* (1889), mixed profit with social policy by specializing in lending to those interested in purchasing family-sized farms. The largest private domestic bank, *Banco de la Provincia de Buenos Aires,* issued paper money until the financial crisis of 1872 resulted in the establishment of the Banco Nacional to regulate currency. After the War of the Pacific, Peru reestablished its financial structure on a sounder footing. The Bank of London and Peru and several other banks were formed with Peruvian capital. The Italian community formed the *Banco Italiano* in 1889; it soon became the country's largest commercial bank and changed its name to *Banco de Crédito* in 1941 as a consequence of World War II.

Regional banks constituted a secondary financial tier. Small regional banks, usually controlled by local families, tended to be used as personal investment vehicles. Family members and those closely connected with them could expect favorable credit terms and an understanding collection policy. Despite the expansion in the latter half of the century, the financial network remained inadequate. Individual banks often proved to be short-lived.

Irineu Evangelista de Sousa, subsequently honored with the title of Baron of Mauá by Emperor Pedro II of Brazil, understood the uses of money and credit. Nevertheless, his different banks, including the Bank of Mauá and MacGregor, all failed to thrive. Undercapitalization, insufficient liquidity, inexperienced managers, and a host of minor and major difficulties hampered the banks. Mauá's own career ended in bankruptcy.

A large part of the problem in Brazil and elsewhere in Latin America stemmed from inadequate or incomplete commercial codes. Brazil's commercial code of 1850, for example, recognized land as property but not financial instruments such as stocks, debentures, bank accounts, and other intangibles. Nor did the code indicate clearly how banks could recover debts other than those secured by land. These murky procedures made debt recovery difficult. Thus, only the most financially solid individuals secured bank loans. Investment loans needed by developers could come only from more daring individuals or foreign sources.

## PROSPERITY AND ITS STRAINS

Export prosperity can be seen in trade statistics. In the last decade of the century, Latin American exports exceeded $1 billion annually. In the 14-year period between 1870 and 1884, exports jumped approximately 43 percent. Each year seemed to set new records, although for individual countries a boom could be followed by a bust if commodity prices collapsed for an export item. Five countries—Argentina, Brazil, Chile, Cuba, and Mexico—supplied the bulk of Latin America's exports. Nevertheless, smaller export economies also experienced large increases. Because Latin America's economy relied on primary products for the industrialized nations, inter-American trade hardly existed. These economies in large measure competed against each other. In 1902, a group of Mexican entrepreneurs, seeking an outlet for their products, decided to investigate whether Brazil might provide a market. Their visit to Brazil illustrated the problem. They first had to travel to New York, then England, before they could book passage to South America. Without direct steamship connections, the dream of Mexico–Brazil trade was an impossible fantasy. Even neighboring countries had little they could offer each other that they themselves did not produce, nor could their nascent industrialization absorb a significant amount of raw materials from other Latin American republics.

Foreign investment, attracted by the profitability of primary products and the need to develop an infrastructure to get products to ports, totaled $8.5 billion by 1914—$5 billion from Americans, with investments totaling some $1.6 billion concentrated in Mexico and the Caribbean. France invested $1.7 billion and Germany around $1 billion. Argentina, Brazil, and Mexico received the largest percentage of such investments. Along with foreign capital came expansion of production made possible by the march of technology introduced and often owned and operated by foreigners (see the Profile, "Clemente Jacques," on page 77). Telegraph networks constructed by British and American firms, railways, and electric utilities built and operated by foreign technicians provided the infrastructure that made expansion possible. The dangers of overproduction seemed a distant possibility in a rapidly modernizing world.

Nevertheless, at the turn of the century Latin America encountered increasingly saturated markets for many of its primary exports. Expansion of commercial agriculture, improved technology in the fields and mines, better transportation, and rapid communication all contributed to changing the balance between supply and demand. Moreover, unanticipated competition from African and Asian producers undercut the hemisphere's monopoly on many tropical and subtropical products. Price instability, along with downward pressure on export profits, created uncertainty and had a negative impact on society and the state. Prosperity became an economic roller coaster subject to sudden descents, creating ruin and suffering, only to rise abruptly, beginning the process once again.

Technology altered the ratio between labor and capital, contracting rather than expanding the number of jobs and reducing workers' wages. Wealth associated with modernization appeared to flow along with the region's material assets out of Latin America and into the hands of foreign investors. In Chile, copper production experienced major technological changes, becoming capital-intensive

---

**P R O F I L E**     Clemente Jacques

Clemente Jacques—whose name is immediately recognized today across Mexico and the southwestern United States in connection with a brand of bottled jalapeño peppers—was an immigrant entrepreneur who personifies the dynamic economic opportunities in late nineteenth-century Mexico. Despite the odds against him, he successfully developed an enterprise with both domestic and foreign markets. Jacques left France for Mexico in 1880, and by 1887 he had established a business producing corks for the bottling industry. He soon diversified the bulk of his activities into food processing. His products included olives; olive oil; sauces, including mole; chilies; beans; fruit juices and jams; and honey. As part of his business, he continued to produce corks and diversified into lumber. He also determined that it was cheaper to buy a print shop than it was to contract for labels and advertising. Nevertheless, he specialized in Mexican foods and worked diligently to create a domestic market for processed foods and an international market for Mexican items. Hoping to promote exports, he exhibited his products at several world's fairs. At the exhibitions in Chicago (1893) and St. Louis (1904), he won several gold medals. As a promotion, he printed decks of playing cards to advertise his jalapeños to attendees.

Printing playing cards quickly became a major industry for him. He produced both Spanish and American (poker-style) decks of cards. He soon recognized the growing domestic market for table games in Mexico, so he added a line of *juego de oca* (a board game similar to Chutes and Ladders) and *lotería* (a traditional game similar to bingo that used figures rather than numbers). As one of his trademarks, Jacques used *el gallo* (the cock), the national image of his native France. Under this trademark, he copyrighted the images of his lotería game in 1913. The characters he included were based on social types (such as the drunk, the lady, the gentleman) with whom he was familiar in the state of Campeche, Mexico. This game has become extremely popular and the images are widely recognized.

---

as workers were replaced by efficient machines. Technology made it possible to increase production steadily throughout the twentieth century. American capital, through the Anaconda and Kennecott corporations, dominated the industry. Abundant production in Chile and elsewhere made for unsettling price instability. Copper prices fluctuated as much as 1,000 percent within months. Copper contributed approximately 50 percent of Chile's exports in 1956, providing 20 percent of the government's revenues. Price volatility made economic planning impossible. Commodity markets appeared to govern Chile's everyday existence. Copper companies became the focal point of resentment and the object of nationalist reaction. In a similar fashion, foreign capital dominated the Mexican mining industry, with the United States accounting for 60 percent of all investments. Foreigners played a major role in producing, shipping, fabricating, and consuming minerals. Copper, lead, zinc, gold, and silver provided the bulk of Mexico's exports from the latter half of the nineteenth century until the disruptions caused by the Mexican Revolution of 1910.

In sharp contrast, Bolivian tin entrepreneurs competed successfully with foreign interests for control of the industry. European, American, and Chilean capitalists lost out to Bolivian tin barons who dominated mining by the 1920s. Simón I. Patiño, Bolivia's foremost entrepreneur, joined forces with American tin consumers to take control of the world's largest tin refinery, a British company in Liverpool, in 1916.

Patiño and his partners established a high degree of control over the overseas market, and he remained the major primary producer of ore in Bolivia.

In Brazil, foreign capital specialized in public utilities, but the coffee industry remained almost completely in Brazilian hands. Agricultural production in Argentina likewise remained under domestic control despite a significant number of Anglo-Argentines involved in cattle raising. Processing and marketing, however, soon fell into the hands of foreigners, giving them the ability to set prices of live cattle. Frozen meat export became a British monopoly. In 1907 Swift and Company, the largest meat packer in the United States, bought the largest freezing plant in Argentina. Several years later the National Packing Company, a joint venture of Swift, Armour, and Morris, purchased an Argentine-owned operation in La Blanca. Chicago-based packing companies controlled more than half of all frozen beef exported from Argentina by 1910. In this case, alarmed British interests attempted to form an anti-American alliance with Argentine nationalists directed against the Chicago beef trusts.

Regardless of the actual ownership of productive enterprises, Latin Americans appeared to be hostages of foreign commodity markets and the ebb and flow of foreign exchange. Even a relatively well-balanced export economy of commercial agriculture, minerals, and cattle exports could do little to offset a drop in demand caused by a recession in the United States or Europe. Latin American economies followed the fortunes of their markets, often enduring an across-the-board decline in the case of a generalized economic contraction. In specific industries, over-production or technological change caused a drop in demand for a crucial export. The classic example of boom and bust occurred in the latex or rubber industry in the Amazon basin.

The waterproof qualities of latex had been observed long before Europeans arrived in the hemisphere. The sticky substance could be obtained from a variety of New World plants and trees; the Amazon region, however, contained the largest concentration of rubber trees. Europeans experimented with latex, including novelty items such as coated boots for the amusement of the royal family in Lisbon. The instability of latex limited its utility until technology transformed it into an industrial product. Impregnating textiles with rubber, developed in 1823, created a minor market in Europe that expanded greatly with the development of vulcanization in 1840. Vulcanization created usable rubber. Quickly, producers made waterproof clothing and balloon tires for bicycles, creating a craze for two-wheelers, and belts for industry. These items combined to create a market that expanded once the automobile appeared, with its demand for rubber tires and tubes and other parts.

Vulcanized rubber caused boom times in the Amazon. In 1853, Belém, at the north of the Amazon river system, already exported 2,500 tons of natural rubber; and by the early 1900s, rubber made up one-third of Brazil's exports. Peru's Amazon region also experienced the rubber boom. Iquitos, Peru's outpost on the Amazon river system, grew into a substantial city, as did Brazil's Manaus, at the confluence of the Negro and Amazon rivers. Both cities enjoyed direct steamship connections with Europe. All the trappings of civilization poured into the Amazon forest in a frenzy of conspicuous consumption by the newly rich rubber barons.

*Courtesy of the Latin America Library at Tulane University.*

American meat packers, including Armour, moved aggressively into Argentina in the early decades of the twentieth century. They succeeded in effectively using their marketing network to set prices for live cattle and chilled and frozen beef, and displaced many Argentine and British packing companies.

The Amazon's rubber industry depended on collecting sap from trees scattered throughout the forest. Susceptible to disease, rubber trees could not be profitably grown on plantations. Unfortunately for the rubber barons, British smugglers took seeds out of the region, nurtured them in the greenhouses of Kew Gardens to develop a disease-resistant strain, and then introduced the trees into their colony of Malaya. Plantation rubber quickly drove down prices and ended the Amazon's once profitable monopoly. Industrial technology made the boom and agricultural technology abruptly ended it.

General recessions could be devastating to the Latin American economies. The worldwide financial panic of 1907 disrupted markets and plunged dependent primary product economies into despair. Mexico's economy hovered on the edge of collapse. A credit crisis (1907–1908) caused banks to call in loans, destroying property values and wiping out working capital. Commercial agriculture faltered and mining halted, exports dropped sharply, commodity prices fell, and imports plunged some 34 percent. The 1907 crisis jeopardized both the economic and political structure as the poor and unemployed desperately sought to survive. Although other factors contributed, the economic shock played a significant role in precipitating the Mexican Revolution of 1910.

Brazil relied on Great Britain, Germany, and the United States as its major markets, making the country exceedingly vulnerable to overseas conditions. More-over, weather could undercut Brazil's market. Overexpansion by coffee fazendas and good growing conditions resulted in 20 million sacks of coffee in 1906, of which only 12 or 13 million could be sold. In succeeding years, adverse weather reduced harvests and drove prices up but encouraged more growers to enter the market. When the Great Depression of 1929–1930 spread across the world, coffee prices fell from 22.5 cents to 8 cents per pound. Brazilians burned surplus coffee or dumped it into the ocean. The few barter agreements traded coffee for items the country did not need. Bartered coffee tended to be resold, further depressing the world market. Recovery over the decade of the 1930s appeared modest.

Brazil's coffee exports in 1940 did not equal what they had been 30 years earlier. Although Brazil had controlled 75 percent of the coffee market in 1900, a fatal combination of economic blows and competition from hemispheric growers (in Colombia, the Caribbean, Central America, and Mexico) and African producers forced Brazil to concede its once dominant position. By 1978, Brazilian producers supplied only 18 percent of the market.

## REEVALUATING THE EXPORT ECONOMY

The Great Depression convinced Latin American politicians and economists that their political and economic stability required industrialization. The state needed to direct development in a planned, rational manner both to absorb primary materials and to ensure access to needed manufactured goods. Latin America's modest industrial base provided an initial foundation for a mixed economy. Planned industrialization differed from undirected growth in that it involved a high degree of state intervention.

Some state encouragement of industrialization and even direct involvement in the economy antedated the crisis. The Chilean government in the 1870s encouraged the secondary processing of both local and imported raw materials. Ore from Bolivia, Peru, and Argentina provided profits for the Chilean smelter industry. Raw materials brought in from Oceania sustained soap and burlap cloth production. As in colonial days, Chile dominated the wheat market in the Andean region. Commodity trade channels provided market access for some Chilean manufactured goods including items used in the mining industry.

In Uruguay, José Batlle y Ordóñez shaped a state-run economy well in advance of the great economic shocks of the twentieth century. Batlle, twice president and a dominant influence in politics for almost 30 years, injected the state into virtually all aspects of economic activity. He did so with middle-class support. His Colorado Party established control of the country in the 1860s and moved to create an educated middle-class population. Free public education and scholarships emphasized merit over class. Support for public education received a major push in the latter part of the nineteenth century from the flood of European immigrants. By 1889 Montevideo was home to 100,000, who constituted slightly less than half the capital's population. Although political opponents, with some justification, called the Colorados the "party of foreigners," it soon became the "party of the sons of foreigners" who had become middle-class citizens of the republic. Batlle sought to replace foreign businesses with Uruguayan enterprises. Displacing foreign capital appeared to be beyond the ability of individuals. Therefore, Batlle introduced state intervention through tariffs and investments. Behind a protective wall, domestic industry could be nurtured. Shielded from competition and staffed by an educated population, domestic industry provided reasonable jobs and an enviable standard of living. Lower-middle-class workers were encouraged to unionize by the state. The government adopted the eight-hour day and minimum wage legislation in 1928. The Uruguayan government also passed laws promoting gender equality in the workplace. Uruguay provides an early, singular example of state involvement in the economy. Most Latin American republics, however, turned to government-directed industrial development only with the economic collapse.

Indirect government promotion of industry, however, existed long before the depression. Governments conceded tax exemptions and tariff protection to business enterprises. The Cuauhtémoc Brewery, Mexico's first modern beer producer established in 1892, prospered behind a 75 percent protective tariff on imported bottled beer and charges that raised the cost of an imported barrel to $25 over the St. Louis price of $8. Other Mexican industries expected and received tariff protection. The higher price of domestic products constituted a development tax on the consumer.

Argentina's nascent industrialists formed the short-lived Industrial Club in 1875 to lobby the government in support of their activities. They argued that the country's comparative advantage as an agricultural producer should be complemented by industry. They pointed to the examples of the United States and Germany, countries that had used high tariffs to good advantage. The Argentine Congress responded by setting a high tariff in 1876 to protect textiles, clothing, beverages, furniture, and other items. The legislature noted its intent to nurture "infant industries," produce revenue, and help the balance of trade by reducing imports. Agricultural exporters tried to counter the demands for tariff protection. Nevertheless, the congress passed tariff bills in 1887, 1889, 1891, and 1905.

In Colombia, the Antioquia region thrived as a major gold-producing area; then the coffee boom of the 1880s provided sufficient capital for modern development. Rail lines soon tied Medellín, Antioquia's major city, with coastal ports of Cartagena, Barranquilla, Santa Marta, and Buenaventura. New machinery and advanced techniques transformed primitive local production. New industries emerged, such as manufacturing of light mining equipment and agricultural implements. An iron-works underpinned the process. Between 1902 and 1907, three textile factories opened in the Medellín region. The Compañía Colombiana de Tejidos, founded in 1907, became one of the largest corporations in Latin America. In the early 1900s, Colombia had a steel mill and cement, rubber, and chemical industries. By 1918, Medellín had become the republic's major manufacturing center. They could count on government support when needed. Medellín remained the country's industrial center until 1945, when Bogotá superseded it.

Peru's industrialists founded the National Industrial Society in 1896 to represent their interests. Electrification began to transform manufacturing as well as mining. The Peruvian government, eager to encourage use of electricity, removed import duties on electrical equipment. In Lima, gas lamps gave way to modern lighting. A reservoir in 1902 supplied hydroelectric power and, together with a fossil fuel generator, provided energy sufficient to service 8,500 customers and 1,800 public light posts. In 1910, *Empresas Eléctricas Asociadas* generated 47,400,000 kilowatt hours of power. Between 1896 and 1899, several industries including a shoe factory, a ceramics manufacturing plant, and a milk pasteurizing company began to meet local needs. Technology's ability to create jobs impressed politicians. Thus, legislators exempted typewriters from import taxes in 1903, asserting that such advanced technology would create jobs in Peruvian offices and government bureaus. That same year, automobiles also received an exemption, and by 1929 Peru had built approximately 18,000 kilometers of roads to accommodate the growing automobile traffic. Peru's early industrialization demonstrated the state's willingness to encourage development as well as its desire to create modern jobs. The government leaders responded to the demands of a still small, but growing urban working class, who relied on strikes to express their views. In 1896, 500 textile workers struck the Vitarte mill over wages and working conditions. Printers and pastry cooks also took to the streets to press their demands. In both cases, government leaders acted to satisfy the demands of the workers. Industrialization, initially linked to the internal needs of primary producers, broadened with state encouragement to supply domestic demands. First textiles, then beer, glass, cement, iron, steel, and items for everyday use, developed behind protective barriers that shielded them from cheap imports from Great Britain and the United States.

Direct government investment was scarce before the 1929–1930 depression. With the economic collapse, that abruptly changed. The solution used to pull national economies out of the depression relied on the economic activity of central governments—governments became the primary investors and entrepreneurs in national economies. The Liberal economic world envisioned by Adam Smith in his book *The Wealth of Nations* crashed, and the new world of government-directed economies emerged.

# 4

# Modern Economies

Worldwide depression in 1929–1930 pushed policymakers in Europe and the Americas into the Keynesian revolution. The new economic policies they adopted carry the name of John Maynard Keynes, who advocated government deficit spending and developmental investment. Latin American government officials used his ideas as guidelines for recovery and development programs. The Keynesian experiment ended in the 1980s, when overwhelming international debts crushed all confidence in it. On the official level, Neoliberal economics emerged, and on the unofficial level, large informal and illegal economies developed. National governments took direct control of their economies as a result of the world depression. At first, government officials responded with the traditional liberal solutions of balancing budgets and reducing expenses. These policies failed. Only when national governments adopted Keynesian programs did recovery begin. The new policies brought Latin American central governments into direct daily economic contact with the people. Government action regulated investment and expenditures; selected exports and imports; calibrated wages, prices, and profits; and, at times, created government corporations, directed their management, and marketed their products. Central regimes used representatives of the new economic agencies to bypass the intervening state and local governments and interact directly with people at the grass roots. Today, in a new century, we are witnessing another great economic swing. Latin American governments, in a reversal of this policy, have returned most state-owned corporations to private ownership. This program of privatizing national production corporations and investment agencies and decentralizing social services is called Neoliberalism. This chapter focuses on Latin American economies from the Great Depression through the emergence of Neoliberalism.

During the Keynesian era, most politicians believed government should do more than just encourage economic growth. These officials thought government should stimulate economic and national development. They devised programs to manipulate taxes, currency, domestic credit, and consumer demand. Development became the universal goal. State programs attempted several different strategies. Latin American economists developed a Keynesian initiative called import substitution. Keynes also advocated an international monetary organization to supply the credit needed to restore world trade. Latin American policymakers employed Keynesian theory to restructure the economic system.

## IMPORT SUBSTITUTION—THE FIRST STAGE, 1930–1955

The conceptual framework and the intellectual support that lent legitimacy to state intervention in Latin America rested, in large measure, on the ideas of Raúl Prebisch. As a brilliant young economist, Prebisch struggled with depression-era problems in Argentina. Confronted with dire circumstances, Argentina entered into a trade agreement with Great Britain to save its export economy. In return for a guarantee from the British not to reduce purchases of beef below the 1932 level, Argentina pledged that the money earned would be spent on British goods. The Roca-Runciman Agreement of 1933 appeared to make Argentina an economic dependent of Great Britain. Subsequent agreements emphasized the country's weak position. With little choice, Argentina agreed to British demands. Prebisch, involved in all aspects of such agreements, understood reality. He noted that agricultural prices fell more than the price of manufactured goods. As a result, Argentina had to sell 73 percent more to purchase the same amount of imports as before the economic collapse. Short-term measures, virtually on a day-to-day basis, kept Argentina afloat. With the return of a severe depression in 1937–1938, Argentina had to scramble to meet its immediate obligations. Prebisch became a convinced Keynesian.

Prebisch hoped to simplify the process of economic growth and reduce the risks of failure. An economy required access to raw materials, able workers, adequate technology, and, finally, a market. The plan had three steps: (1) identify an existing market supplied by imported goods for which the nation had raw materials; (2) train the workers; and, (3) begin domestic production. Shoes and leather goods in Argentina, petrochemicals in Venezuela and Mexico, and food processing throughout the region offered immediate possibilities. The idea was to transfer the known market for an established product from a foreign supplier to a domestic manufacturer. This way, new industries supplying consumer goods could be created at modest cost. Besides a known market, other advantages existed: used machinery bought on the world market made equipment prices affordable, and sharp currency devaluations and protective tariffs gave domestic products an advantage. Foreign-owned subsidiaries, encouraged to increase local operations, also benefited from tariff protection. The scheme did not envision the end of all imports, but simply a reduction of dependency on foreign manufactured goods.

Import substitution appeared to be an evolutionary stage of modernization. Latin America's existing industrial base had reached a point where further expansion could be expected. A certain momentum, fueled by urbanization and industrialization, already had been achieved. Governments now had to accelerate the process and strategically redirect industrial development to strengthen the national economy. Planned development aimed to reduce import dependency and establish a better, healthier balance between the export-import sector and internal industrial growth. Active state intervention quickly went far beyond tariff protection or tax exemptions to direct state ownership and investment.

During the 1930s, Brazil, Chile, and Argentina all experienced impressive increases in manufacturing. Prebisch's call for "inward development" had been answered out of necessity. In Brazil, the national currency's external buying power dropped 50 percent and income levels declined 25–30 percent, causing a 60 percent drop in imports. As a result, Brazilian manufacturers began to meet internal demand. Industrial production had dropped just under 10 percent at the start of the depression, but by 1932 it had increased 60 percent over 1929 levels. The profits of industrial production and the inability to purchase exports channeled investment into industry and away from agriculture. New industrial concerns bought second-hand equipment at bargain prices abroad, expanding the number of manufacturers. Subsidies to coffee growers helped maintain that industry, along with its sharply curtailed export income. But more important, subsidies kept income levels high, supplied the capital to invest in industry, and supported demand for domestically produced goods. Not all the country's agricultural exports struggled to the same extent as the coffee industry. Cotton, for example, continued in demand. Nevertheless, the depression encouraged shifting investments from primary export products, especially agricultural commodities, to industrial enterprises with a domestic market.

In Chile, exports dropped 87 percent from their pre-depression level. Nitrate exports collapsed as prices fell 98 percent, whereas copper prices dropped 70 percent. Economic uncertainty led to a 1932 coup and the declaration of a short-lived Socialist republic. A series of military regimes seized idle factories, nationalized banks, and took a number of other desperate measures. The army became alarmed, forced out ineffectual government officials, and scheduled a presidential election in two years. Meanwhile, trade with the United States shrank drastically, although European trade limped along with the quasi-barter arrangement through compensation trade agreements. By 1936, Germany replaced the United States as Chile's most important trading partner. Eventually, world demand for minerals recovered and improved the country's export revenues. In 1939, the government established a development agency, the *Corporación de Fomento* (CORFO), to plot strategic investments in both the public and private sectors of the Chilean economy.

Mexican officials responded to the depression in numerous ways. The government increased demand for steel and cement and created jobs with federally funded public works projects. The economy stabilized in 1932 and investment in manufacturing increased. Exports, hard hit in 1929–1930, partially recovered and thus provided some revenue for expansion and enabled the government to

Courtesy of the Latin America Library at Tulane University.

Modernization of port facilities contributed to the export boom in Latin America in the early twentieth century. Cranes, railcars, and modern warehouses made the port of Montevideo, Uruguay, an effective export-import hub.

emphasize employment. Spending on rural schools, potable water, roads, irrigation, railroads, and electrification projects provided jobs, put money into circulation, and built up the country's infrastructure. President Lázaro Cárdenas, a master at mobilizing popular support, effectively employed antibusiness rhetoric in the process of redirecting both the anger and expectations unleashed by the violence of the Mexican Revolution and the economic difficulties caused by the Great Depression. Although his speeches alarmed business to the point that they organized against him, Cárdenas was an economic pragmatist. During the financial crisis of 1937, he demonstrated his understanding of the vital importance of industry. Minister of the Treasury (*Hacienda*), Eduardo Suárez, a disciple of John Maynard Keynes, rescued the economy with the help of the U.S. government. President Franklin D. Roosevelt agreed to a one-time purchase of 35 million pesos of Mexican gold and pledged to continue regular purchases of silver. Recovery was complicated by U.S. economic difficulties and the U.S. reaction when Cárdenas decided to nationalize the petroleum industry in 1938. The impact of both developments resulted in a 50 percent drop in U.S. investments in Mexico between 1929 and 1946. Nevertheless, whatever investments occurred went into manufacturing. Cárdenas's successor,

Manuel Avila Camacho, who assumed office in 1940, created an openly pro-business environment, and the boom resulting from World War II occurred largely in the manufacturing sector.

Mexico's chemical fiber industry offered a successful model of import substitution. Initially, textile mills had imported rayon from Europe, particularly Germany, until the war cut off supply. Mexican industry had no domestic source for such fibers other than a minor rayon operation run by Italian noblemen of unpredictable business habits. Mexican officials decided to recruit a large American chemical corporation—the Celanese Corporation, headquartered in New York. Celanese synthetic fiber had a wide-open and eager market, but only if the company established a Mexican plant. The government stood ready to assist in any way possible. After extensive discussions, a new organization, Celanese Mexicana, was incorporated; the U.S. parent company owned 51.2 percent, and Mexican investors, the rest. Ocotlán, Jalisco, became the site of a new Celanese chemical plant. After interviewing the entire graduating class of 25 chemists at the National University of Mexico, the company hired 12 and sent them to the United States for further training. These graduates became the core of the technical staff. Celanese Mexicana constituted a near-perfect import-substitution model. It attracted new capital, introduced modern technology, trained national citizens in advanced techniques, provided well-paying jobs in an impoverished town, and supplied an existing market. The managers and the technicians were Mexican, and only a handful of foreigners were involved in any operation. A decade after its establishment, most observers recognized the company as Mexican, operated by and largely owned by Mexicans.

Not all Latin American republics in 1930 had reached an economic level that justified moving to import substitution. In Ecuador, then still a rural country, most of the population had access to food and shelter through subsistence agriculture. Nevertheless, the government had to respond in some way to the Great Depression. Political instability complicated economic planning. Ill-conceived protectionist tariffs severely reduced customs revenues and failed to stimulate domestic manufacturing. Inflation, fueled by deficit spending and forced loans from the central bank, eventually led the government to seek out Mexican economist Manuel Gómez Morín. He advised restructuring the Ecuadorian economy through a system of national development banks to supply credit to enterprises whose functions appeared most useful. Even with deficit spending, the results proved meager. In Ecuador, efforts to promote import substitution did not bring about development and wasted capital resources needed for recovery.

## IMPORT SUBSTITUTION—THE LATER STAGE, 1955–1970

The first stage of import substitution ended with a decided thump in 1955 with the end of the Korean War. Wartime demand for primary exports fell, pulling much of Latin America into a recession. Mexico devalued the peso 50 percent as it faced a balance-of-payments crisis. Brazilian coffee prices dropped some 30 percent, and inflation appeared on the verge of surging out of control. Nowhere in Latin America could imports fueled by wartime profits be sustained at the Korean War level.

Moreover, national corporations created in the first wave of import substitution encountered a variety of problems after the Korean War. These companies discovered unhappy consumers and declining profits. A company that possessed a monopoly market never needed a sales force or strategy. State-owned companies discovered that they had bruised a lot of consumers. Many private concerns had confused tax concessions with profits. When the concessions ended, company profits plummeted. Celanese Mexicana paid 3 million pesos in taxes in 1958, the last year of its concession; the next year, it had to pay 22 million pesos in taxes.[1] The 19 million additional pesos came from profits.

The time for a modified economic strategy had arrived. Countries faced large-scale capital drain, a result of the import of high priced consumer durables, particularly automobiles. The solution seemed obvious—build up capital and foster intermediate manufacturing. Expanding employment also required a new approach. First-stage import substitution, behind its protective tariff walls, had caught up with domestic demand, which had reached the point of stagnation. Moreover, all the ills of this semi-monopolistic system had become obvious— high prices, inferior quality, disregard for consumer preferences, and little interest in developing new markets. Latin American industry, under existing conditions, threatened to retard development. Planners then launched second-stage import substitution, which required large investments in machinery and higher levels of technology, both of which could be acquired from transnational corporations eager to expand into underdeveloped markets. Governments, using various inducements from subsidies to tariffs, brought foreign companies into their domestic economies.

Government planners felt a sense of urgency as they recognized that stagnant markets, inefficient production, and poor capital allocation threatened the hard-earned advances of the previous three decades. Mexican President Adolfo Ruiz Cortines (1952–1958), faced with inflation, insufficient tax revenues, and balance-of-payment deficits, understood the need to make rapid adjustments. In the private sector, Celanese Mexicana provided a sober example of the problems. Celanese faced customer backlash for years of forcing consumers to accept what the company had available, regardless of the color or gauge of the fibers.

Like Mexico, other countries had to make a rapid transition. Brazilian President Juscelino Kubitschek assumed power in 1956, promising "50 years of progress in 5." On his second day in office, he shifted Brazil to second-stage import substitution with a rush as he created a National Development Council and a "Program of Targets" to set objectives for both private and state investment. Kubitschek used private domestic capital, direct foreign investment, and government-guaranteed loans to fuel his mad dash to development. The president's

---

[1] Richard W. Hall, *Putting Down Roots: Twenty-Five Years of Celanese in Mexico* (New York: Vantage Press, 1969), pp. 42–43.

imagination and determination have as their monument the long-dreamed-of national capital city. Congress approved the project during Kubitschek's first year in office. The city, to be called Brasília and to be built in the interior state of Goiás, became a focal point of national pride and the country's integrating economic force. Work began in 1957 on a 24-hour/day, 7-day/week schedule that continued until the city was inaugurated as the new capital in April 1960.

Construction created jobs for workers from unskilled laborers to professionals. Once built, the city required new highways in all directions to connect Brasília with the nation it ruled. Kubitschek's government built approximately 11,000 miles of roads. It required 1,400 miles of highway to reach Belém in the north, 1,060 miles of roads to Fortaleza in the northeast, and connecting links to existing roadways throughout the east and south of the nation. The government decided that the cars, trucks, and buses on these new roads had to be manufactured in Brazil. The administration pressed automobile companies to begin production in Brazil, and by 1962, the country had become the world's seventh-largest producer. Brazilian-made cars satisfied the domestic market and were exported to several Latin American countries. Kubitschek also promoted hydroelectric power. His program increased production almost 60 percent and launched construction of the massive Furnas project and the Três Marias dam. When Kubitschek's term ended, he had directed a 33 percent expansion of Brazil's industrial base, from automobiles to high-priced consumer durables.

Kubitschek used everybody's money—domestic, foreign, borrowed, and taxed—and printed whatever additional funds seemed necessary. Paper currency in circulation jumped more than 300 percent by the end of his term. Many government planners believed that inflation constituted a useful developmental tool because it forced people to spend rapidly before their money lost value. Brazilians struggled with massive foreign debts and double-digit inflation. Nevertheless, the nation had outstripped the rest of Latin America in the race to develop an advanced industrial base. Incredibly, Kubitschek had delivered the promised 50 years of progress in 5.

In contrast, the effort to move Argentina into second-stage import substitution stalled amid the populist confusion in the aftermath of the collapse of Juan Perón's regime in 1955. Nearly everyone understood the need to upgrade Argentina's industrial capacity, but attracting the necessary capital through direct foreign investment had long been a touchy subject in Argentina. Yet domestic capital alone could not get the country moving again after a decade of Peronist mismanagement. Argentina desperately needed foreign capital but had to find a way to make it acceptable to populist political leaders. As a consequence, government policy swerved back and forth from a search for foreign investors to fear of foreign domination. Arturo Frondizi personified this ambivalence. Three years before becoming president, he was a vigorous opponent of any foreign involvement in the petroleum industry. Shortly after taking office, he argued, "It does not matter where capital originates . . . if it serves national ends." To attract foreign business, the government wrote new legislation that required companies to promise they would not damage domestic industries. This left investors free to remit profits and repatriate capital as they desired. The government offered special tax advantages to those who reinvested profits in Argentina or built factories in the interior. Frondizi concluded a deal with private oil companies to expand production and enter the retail market. His plan aimed to save the country some $300 million annually in energy imports.

Like Kubitschek's strategy in Brazil, Frondizi's plan required a massive inflow of capital to take care of balance-of-payments problems. But Frondizi did not adopt Kubitschek's frenetic pace and failed to instill investor confidence. His project collapsed in 1962 and Argentina skidded into economic decline. Capital flight, unofficially estimated at some $2.5 billion, threw thousands out of work and resulted in widespread bankruptcies. The nationalist program, moreover, cost vast sums of money in compensation for broken contracts with foreigners and government-inflicted damages. Lacking sufficient foreign investments, the government resorted to foreign loans. By 1972 the foreign debt, owed mostly to U.S. creditors, consumed more than one-third of Argentina's export income.

Government officials used money obtained from foreign loans for political purposes, whereas most of the remainder went to poorly managed, inefficient, and wasteful state-owned enterprises. These companies absorbed 42 percent of the $3.2 billion debt. State industries, managed by political cronies, hired workers who had few duties beyond loyalty to the regime. Political support replaced production as the goal of state-owned industries. Even more damaging, government economic policies discouraged private entrepreneurs and tended to politicize all economic decisions in both the private and public sectors. Argentine entrepreneurs, constrained by politics, could not operate creatively or freely. Consequently, they could be bought out cheaply by foreign companies with the political influence to force the government to make accommodations. Between 1962 and 1968, 39 major businesses, including 9 banks and 4 cigarette manufacturers, sold out to foreign investors. Renault, for example, purchased the Argentine automobile plant, and foreigners bought a host of other medium-technology enterprises. By 1972, multinational subsidiaries operated 17 of Argentina's 20 major export industries. Nevertheless, foreign companies miscalculated the intensity of Argentine nationalism. Growing hostility toward foreign capitalists resulted in onerous regulations that eventually drove them to withdraw their capital. Domestic entrepreneurs, however, had a difficult time sending their money out of the country and soon faced business closures and bankruptcies. Juan Perón's return in March 1977 brought further economic contraction. Life became increasingly grim with price controls, inflation, corruption, graft, and politically inspired labor slowdowns and strikes. A predictable sequence followed: economic collapse, political chaos, and military coup.

## THE POPULIST TEMPTATION

Latin American populism developed a recognizable economic pattern. Populist regimes in Argentina, Brazil, Chile, Mexico, Peru, and Nicaragua all relied on state activism with the goals of full incorporation of labor into national life, accelerated industrialization, and redistribution measures to meet social and economic needs. Maldistribution of wealth creates social pressures difficult to deal with in the short term. Anxious to avoid class conflict, politicians turn from idealistic rhetoric, to political mobilization, to economic populism.

Populist economic experimentation generally proceeds through several phases. First, programs increase employment and real wages, holding down inflation. Government planners satisfy consumer demand by drawing on current inventories and financing imports with existing foreign exchange, monetary reserves, or suspension of foreign obligations. After depletion of material and financial reserves, a second stage occurs as price adjustments and exchange restrictions become necessary in the face of increased budget deficits. Wage and price subsidies eventually result in runaway inflation, capital flight, growing use of barter, and falling tax revenues. In the third phase, desperate governments allow prices to rise and reduce real wages to levels that workers perceive to be worse than before. The remaining capitalists flee, leaving labor and a bitter middle class behind. Collapsed populist experiments often end in overthrow of the government by the military. The relatively painless process of horizontal or first-stage import substitution did not prepare policymakers or the public for the stresses that accompanied vertical or second-stage import substitution programs, nor, in the 1990s, for the Neoliberalism that followed. Economic shocks laid the groundwork for desperate measures.

## DEBT CRISIS IN THE 1980S

Latin America's maldistribution of wealth made it difficult to expand consumption beyond a certain point. Correcting this inequitable distribution required long-term, expensive structural changes, such as improving access to and quality of both education and public health programs. Such programs required mobilizing a social consensus across class lines without slipping into yet another populist experiment. As a result of small, slowly emerging consumer demand, most surplus production of high-value products of national industries had to find foreign markets. Industrial production outstripped the ability of the domestic economy to absorb it. Measures to increase domestic consumption risked creating more inflation as well as depleting foreign exchange reserves as industrialists imported machinery and materials to meet artificial demands. Promoting exports expanded employment opportunities and provided external funds that could be used to address problems that accompanied income disparity. Such a long-range, rational, and restrained program demanded a high level of social cooperation and discipline.

One threat to rational economic development came from transnational companies. Domestic manufacturers, whose products were often of poor quality and design, had difficulty developing export markets in competition with transnational companies. Planners tried various programs to protect national enterprises and regulate transnational corporations. The Mexicanization law of 1973, for example, required national participation in, or even majority control of, foreign companies operating in Mexico. Brazil, in contrast, used other devices, such as requiring the use of local materials. As early as 1962, Brazil insisted on 99 percent local content by weight in the assembly of passenger cars, although its automobile industry remained totally foreign owned. Other measures were tried to counterbalance profit remittances and the effects of imported capital. In this way, Brazilians earned a trade surplus of $300 million from an automobile industry worth $700 million. Unfortunately, taxes and export incentives made the calculation much less rosy. Transnational companies received from 15 to 20 cents from the government for every dollar exported. Moreover, many exports were simply intracompany sales. Three-fourths of Brazil's exports and four-fifths of Mexico's exports fell into this category. Pinto automobile engines produced in Brazil, for example, had only one customer, the parent company, Ford Motor Company.

Setting up state-owned, high-technology companies with the potential to enter the regional export market produced mixed results. Brazil's state-owned Cobra Corporation, created to produce minicomputers, failed disastrously. Excluding International Business Machines (IBM) from Brazil in order to help Cobra appealed to nationalists but, in the end, wasted resources and retarded the development of industries dependent on computer technology. In the end, transnational companies often dominated local production and determined the export market. Export promotion transformed to varying degrees Latin America's position in the international division of labor. Yet, although the region seemed to move to a higher economic level, it remained dependent on the economic cycles of the major industrial countries.

## THE PETROBUST

Sharply increased energy prices caused an economic slowdown in the industrialized world in the early 1980s. Weak demand for commodities resulted in lower export prices for Latin American products. Reduced revenues unbalanced budgets, forcing governments to shift operating costs to loan revenues. Ironically, at the moment of greatest need, international banks, with more petrodollars than they knew what to do with, stepped forward. Although Venezuela was itself a major petroleum exporter and a beneficiary of OPEC's predatory pricing, it rushed into the loan market. Mexico, following the 1978 discovery of vast new oil reserves, began reckless spending in anticipation of a seemingly unlimited flow of petrodollars. Counting unhatched chickens, Mexicans could not spend or borrow quickly enough. In many Latin American countries a large percentage of the loan proceeds went to pay the high cost of oil imports. Brazil, for example, spent approximately $8 billion on oil imports annually including interest and amortization payments.

Pressure to recycle petrodollars made bankers eager to lend money with few conditions, although they preferred to lend to the most developed countries— Argentina, Brazil, Chile, Colombia, Mexico, and Venezuela. With the exception of Costa Rica, Panama, and Uruguay, the smaller republics depended less on bank loans. Colombia, traditionally more conservative, preferred more solid sources of capital. Consequently, when the bottom fell out, Colombia continued to meet its obligations.

Latin America's combined debt, in defiance of prudence, increased between 1979 and 1982 from $184 billion to $314 billion. A consumer frenzy doubled imports, leading to massive deficits. Capital flight soon followed as business lost confidence in public policy and feared currency devaluations. Export-to-debt ratios soon reached unsustainable levels, and it all came crashing down as oil prices peaked in 1982 and then fell rapidly. Staggering foreign debts and unmanageable balance-of-payments deficits drove Mexico to the point of default. Mexico once again became a supplicant for help from the U.S. government. At the same time, what subsequently would be called the "tequila effect," pushed all of Latin America into crisis.

Latin American governments proved unable to service bank loans and incapable of restraining skyrocketing interest rates. Foreign and domestic confidence disappeared. The crisis soon threatened to bring down several North American banks. Eighteen banks in the United States and Canada held loans totaling $70 billion in plummeting Latin American economies. Citicorp alone had $10 billion at risk. Such a grave threat to the hemisphere's economy elicited a rapid reaction from U.S. government officials, who coordinated the response of lenders hoping to avoid damaging the international financial system and avert economic collapse in Latin America. Debtor nations, particularly Mexico, cooperated in the belief that the crisis involved liquidity, not long-term insolvency. Rescheduling debt payments, reducing interest rates, and negotiating bridge loans, all under the watchful eye of the International Monetary Fund (IMF) and the World Bank, brought the immediate danger under control. A phase-out program allowed minor lenders to move out of the secondary debt market. This simplified negotiations. Debt-equity swaps, loans exchanged for physical assets, acceptance of local currency in place of dollars, and even payment of debts with environmental preserves created the illusion of progress in resolving the problem. Nevertheless, the flow of capital out of Latin America in the form of interest payments, profit remittances, and capital flight continued. Those with large or small savings, insofar as possible, used foreign bank accounts to preserve their assets. Shocks, such as the decision of the Mexican government to convert dollar-denominated accounts into pesos following the nationalization of the banking system in 1982, reverberated throughout Latin America. In 1983 alone an estimated $12.1 billion fled from Argentina, Brazil, Chile, Mexico, and Venezuela.

In 1985, the United States announced the Baker Plan, which called for $30 billion in new loans to help relieve the debt burden. The Baker Plan had a greater psychological than financial impact. Governments sold discounted bonds or printed money in order to purchase the foreign exchange to service their external debt. As a result, internal debt rose rapidly and currency values fell. Argentina and Brazil eventually defaulted partially on their national debt. By the mid-1980s, inflation throughout the region soared to new heights. The 1980s earned the title "the lost decade," as many observers predicted Latin Americans would have to choose between debt and democracy.

Latin American governments, facing hard and often unpopular decisions, turned to foreign advisors. "Technocratization" provided the political cover needed for decisions already made by the governing elite. Chile, after the fall of Salvador

Allende, brought in the "Chicago boys"—a group of economists, most of whom had been trained at the University of Chicago. Economists Milton Friedman and Arnold Harberger functioned as sages for the Chicago boys. The group called its policy for Chile "the seven modernizations": (1) revision of labor legislation, (2) transformation of the social security system, (3) privatization of health care, (4) municipalization of education, (5) internationalization of agriculture, (6) reformation of the judiciary, and (7) decentralization of national government. Ideological excess marred the experiment when the Chicago boys facilitated both the economic and sociopolitical restructuring of Chile by the dictatorial and repressive regime of Augusto Pinochet.

In Bolivia, President Víctor Paz Estenssoro announced his New Economic Policy on August 29, 1985, and within 10 days the country's hyperinflation came to an abrupt halt. When the New Economic Policy faltered at the beginning of the following year, Paz turned to Harvard economist Jeffrey Sachs. To the financial community, the appointment signaled Bolivia's unwavering commitment to economic reforms. Sachs succeeded in renegotiating repayments with major creditors, the so-called Paris Club, including an arrangement to repurchase half of Bolivia's debt at 11 cents on the dollar. His efforts convinced the international financial community that it could not expect total repayment of the Latin American debt. He changed the negotiations from rescheduling payments to debt reductions. Sachs became the latest money doctor in Latin America, and as a concession to the circumstances of the 1980s, admirers called him "Dr. Debt."

The U.S. government's Brady Plan of 1989 also aimed at debt reduction. Although a crushing debt burden remained, the worst was over for Latin America and the international banking system. High interest rates and record returns on consumer credit in the United States made it possible for banks to write off a large part of their Latin American loan portfolios and return to both profit and stability.

## ILLEGAL ECONOMIES

Illegal drug production and distribution became an important part of the international economic system by the 1980s. Colombia, with substantial foreign currency flows from the drug industry, maintained imports at only a slightly lower rate during the 1980s. By 1986, Bolivia was able to surpass its previous import level. Money laundering, reexport of goods, and transshipments of illegal drugs helped prop up the economies of Panama, Costa Rica, Guatemala, and Mexico. The drug traffic produced vast sums of money, but the total retained value to Colombia in the 1980s is estimated to have been less than a quarter of legal exports. In the same decade, other drug-exporting countries such as Bolivia and Peru probably retained somewhat less. In the 1990s, the elimination of restrictions on dollar accounts encouraged the flow of drug money into the region. In Colombia, legalized dollar accounts after 1990 caused rising inflation. Efforts to control inflation, including restricting the national money supply, raised the value of the Colombian peso, increased production costs, and lowered demand for Colombian products. Declining legal exports and increasing drug money resulted in a disastrous new economic dependency. By the 1990s, the economic distortions of the drug industry had become increasingly difficult to deal with throughout Latin America. Legal exports remained crucial for long-term economic and political survival.

## NEOLIBERALISM

Out of the trials of the "lost decade" of the 1980s, a new economic model emerged. Latin American nations had to compete with other countries in a capital-scarce world in order to stimulate renewed growth, as well as to meet debt demands. Liberalization of trade and exports of higher value manufactured goods became the priority. Trade liberalization would reduce costs and, along with the region's lower labor and raw materials prices, could provide an advantage. Inefficient state enterprises that had soaked up large amounts of capital also came under pressure. Returning state-owned industries to private ownership became desirable. Privatization freed capital frozen in state industries, which governments could then invest in further development. Privatization also shifted the cost of modernization to the purchaser. Telephone companies, energy firms, and petrochemical corporations appeared to be prime candidates for privatization. As early as the mid-1980s Neoliberal Chile and Ecuador reduced tariffs, eliminated quotas, and lowered import-export customs duties. Bolivia moved toward a single, uniform tariff in 1985, and that same year Mexico reexamined its quota system and lowered tariffs. Such polices were adopted by most of Latin America. To avoid the risk of trade barriers being raised against Latin American exports, the countries that had not joined the General Agreement on Trade and Tariffs (GATT) applied for membership. Many had to restructure their trade policies to conform to GATT requirements. Mexico and Venezuela abolished the licensing systems used to control imports in order to enter GATT.

Critics of the new economic thinking correctly identified it as Neoliberalism—essentially nineteenth-century liberalism adjusted to technology, global markets, and relentless capital flows. Unfortunately, critics presented no acceptable alternatives as country after country accepted the need to conform to market forces (see Figure 4.1, which shows annual economic growth in Latin America and in three major economies). Neoliberalism represented a reversal of historical proportions. It required an extreme economic strategy—restructuring of the domestic economy to mesh with the perceived global reality. Existing economies, as well as the social structures dependent upon them, might or might not survive as determined by the international market rather than by national politics. Although Latin American governments did not sweep away all state controls and regulations, the philosophical underpinnings had changed dramatically. Neoliberalism assumed that whatever resulted from the process would be economically viable as well as politically and socially acceptable. Philosophically it represented a backing away on the part of the

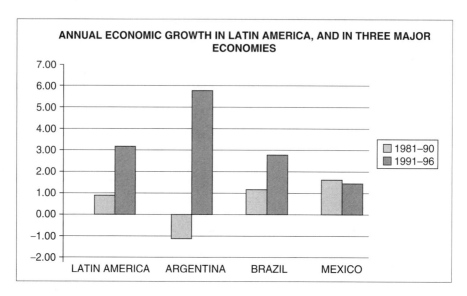

**FIGURE 4.1**

SOURCE: U.N. Economic Commission for Latin America and the Caribbean.

government from its responsibility to cushion or modify the impact of economic forces on its people. Being left behind in a global economic race preoccupied government officials.

Establishing free trade agreements, stimulated by the example of the European Common Market (now the European Union) as well as the fear that the world might evolve into competing trade blocs, became an objective. Mexico successfully pressed for the North American Free Trade Agreement (NAFTA), and Chile and many other Latin American countries declared their desire to be included. Interregional agreements emerged, such as the Southern Common Market (MERCOSUR), which required Argentina, Brazil, Uruguay, and Paraguay to set up a free trade zone with common external tariffs. The Andean Pact as well as the Central American Economic Community (CEC) sought to revitalize regional trade. Numerous bilateral agreements were seen as steps toward some larger trade zone, perhaps embracing the entire hemisphere.

## TOURISM

Tourism became increasingly important as planners saw it as a low-cost revenue source that involved marketing scenery and the local culture. A relatively small industry in the 1950s, by the 1990s tourism produced an estimated $10 to $12 billion annually. In both Mexico and Argentina, tourism accounted for some 20 percent of export earnings. Other republics had lower percentages, but smaller countries closer to the U.S. and European markets tended to be highly dependent on the industry. An estimated 2.3 million Latin Americans were employed directly by the tourist industry in 1996. It is not clear that tourism, from an economic standpoint, makes a permanent contribution to the host country. Some experts argue that profits are drained back to the developed economies. Tourism may supply cash flow, provide employment, and stimulate small feeder businesses; but beyond that, its contribution to the economy may be more supposed than real.

The tourist industry requires extensive, expensive investments including modern state-of-the-art comforts; splashy hotels and airports; and, more mundane but costly, efficient water and sewage systems. Constant upgrading of facilities and widespread advertising—ranging from television, newspapers, and slick magazines to the lowly billboard on the interstate highway—have high costs in tourist markets. Self-contained tourism, such as that promoted by Club Med, is even more expensive for developers and draws heavily on imported resources with prepaid packages payable abroad. Under these arrangements little foreign exchange passes through local hands. Tourism tends to create enclaves surrounded by the native economy, which functions virtually independently from the tourist center in its midst. This dual economy insulates the locals from price inflation, but only in large countries. Small islands, the so-called busboy nations, have been caught in an economic squeeze of price competition for limited resources in which locals with low wages lose out. The exchange of tourists, just as the balance of trade, can be positive or negative. In short, tourism's economic contribution depends on what, where, and how governments structure the industry. It represents an unpredictable capital flow and its economic contribution is unclear.

## A NEW SHOT OF TEQUILA

Mexican President Carlos Salinas de Gortari campaigned successfully to convince the United States and Canada to establish a free trade zone in North America. Suddenly, it seemed that Mexico had become a partner in a new economic arena. A flood of direct foreign investments, joint ventures, and purchases of Mexican stocks fed the hope. President Salinas became a leading candidate to head the newly established World Trade Organization. Wal-Mart, Sam's Club, and other American retailers flooded into Mexico in anticipation of a consumer boom. Banks issued credit cards with abandon, as private sector credit increased from 19 percent of gross domestic product (GDP) in December 1990 to 43 percent when the crisis hit. Plastic money stimulated consumer spending. Mexican companies rushed to modernize plants and equipment to compete within the NAFTA zone. The sense of a new economic era spread to all parts of Latin America as stockbrokers and investment counselors talked of emerging markets.

Reality returned only after the damage had been done. In Mexico, violence-marred political succession, followed by a mishandled devaluation of the peso, ended post-NAFTA euphoria. Capital flows reversed suddenly, a change caused by the abruptness of electronic transfers and the nervousness of traders hedging their bets. The new Mexican crisis occurred in December 1994 with a general withdrawal of investment capital from all Latin American markets. Brazil and Argentina declared that their economies were different from that of Mexico. They feared the "tequila effect" might take a toll throughout Latin America.

Mexico paid a frightful price for its economic miscalculation. A massive and unpopular loan from the United States, secured by Mexican petroleum revenues, fended off the total collapse of the economy, and possibly the government. Stabilization schemes forced a severe economic contraction, high unemployment, falling wages, and rising prices. Fortunately, the rest of Latin America, after several tense months, survived the Mexican collapse, although Argentina lost $8 billion, the equivalent of 18 percent of its bank deposits. Nevertheless, world investors lost much of their enthusiasm for Latin America's emerging markets.

## EXPLAINING ECONOMIC DISAPPOINTMENT

Latin America's economic progress, from independence in the early nineteenth century to the present, has been disappointing. The initial promise, based on abundant natural resources and sufficient labor, has not been realized. Why has the region not yet achieved self-sustaining economic stability and elevated the standard of living of its people? Explanations often sound more like excuses. Yet, there has been substantial progress, including the creation of a significant middle class and the expansion of industry. Predictability and fiscal stability, however, continue to elude Latin America in general.

Recurring cycles from boom to bust, with developmental optimism to debt and default, capital flight, and populist rage, are often followed by returns to austere economic orthodoxy. Latin America appears helpless in the face of commodity prices in distant markets and recession abroad. Fickle capital flows in and out, often leaving little behind except economic desperation. Moreover, the intervals between disasters appear to be shortening. Just what leads to stable development is difficult to identify. André Gunder Frank, proponent of the dependency theory, which posited the draining of wealth and resources toward the industrial center and left Latin America on the undeveloped periphery, admitted after some 30 years, "I don't really know [what determines development;] nobody really knows. . . ."[2] Nevertheless, some factors that have hindered the region's economic progress can be identified.

Latin American industrial and commercial concerns remain closely tied to family interests. Movement from family control toward depersonalized stock ownership has been slow to spread to small- and medium-sized companies—often the enterprises with the most potential for growth in any economy. Family control makes it difficult to raise expansion capital in the stock market. Indeed, expansion, and hence loss of control, may be seen as undesirable. By choosing to

---

[2] *LAcc News* (Florida International University), 13, no. 2 (Fall 1993/Winter 1994), p. 3.

remain a manageable, family-sized enterprise, a business forgoes access to venture capital. Family obligations and financial needs tend to expand in tandem with profits, leaving little for business expansion. The major goal becomes conserving the business for the next generation. Responsibility for family welfare, including the next generation, acts to restrain risk taking.

Latin American industrialists sharply separate their business and personal lives. Spouse, friends, and subordinate family members typically know little about an individual's business activities. In a similar fashion, clients, suppliers, business associates, and acquaintances rarely enter an executive's personal life. Subordinates seldom challenge their superiors, even when they are convinced that a mistake has been made, nor do they feel free to make suggestions. Opinions must be offered carefully and only when clearly solicited. Latin American firms developed certain practices that explain their reluctance to engage in vertical integration, that is, manufacturing all the necessary parts for their products. For example, the Mexican manufacturing industry must import 91.2 percent of the components for the items they manufacture. Even the modern furniture industry, as distinct from traditional artisan production, imports 32.3 percent of its component parts. The lack of vertical integration undercuts profitability because of the need to import high-priced parts for their export products. Technology must be purchased abroad. Moreover, sophisticated consumers, motivated by suggestive television programming and product commercials, demand the latest in design and technology, which keeps pressure on Latin American manufacturers to import the needed innovations almost immediately or lose their market.

Latin America tends to inherit old technology. Thus, it has moved into mass production, whereas more advanced economies have shifted to computer-controlled industrial production. Customized production to exploit small and varied demands and quick product-line changes make it possible for advanced economies to expand their markets and meet demands as they occur. Large corporations increasingly coordinate information, financial resources, distribution, and market development. So-called offshore production, such as the assembly plants in northern Mexico or hand-sewn baseballs in Haiti or the Dominican Republic—both labor-intensive tasks—squeeze profit from old technology because of various cost advantages, including low wages, that are not necessarily permanent.

Bilateral trade agreements and the formation of economic zones have yet to overcome nationalistic and economic barriers, and it is not clear that regional arrangements will survive if NAFTA expands. Intraregional trade faces distribution difficulties. For example, Brazil's Amazonian free trade zone in Manaus attracted Brazilian and multinational companies that collectively produced some $10 billion worth of goods. The hope is to export Manaus's production to Venezuela, Colombia, Ecuador, Peru, and Central America. Nevertheless, in 1994, Manaus exported twice as much to Singapore as it did to Venezuela. Ninety-five percent of its production entered Brazil's domestic market. The problem for Venezuelan trade is a 375-mile gap in the paved road. Once the road connection is made, it is still a four-day haul to Caribbean ports. Demand continues to be problematic. Brazil's neighbors are intent on manufacturing the same items Brazil wants to export.

Investment in research and product development remains low in Latin America. Only three countries invest more than $10 per person in science and technology. Brazil invests $20 per capita, followed by Costa Rica at almost $15, and then by Argentina at just slightly less. Given the general level of expenditure throughout Latin America, it is not surprising that the region has been unable to generate or absorb world-class science. Latin American universities have approximately 100,000 scientists, many trained abroad, and most work in a climate of generalized adversity. A lack of basic resources, scant project start-up funds, and limited access to the latest information pose major obstacles. Subscriptions to scientific journals often are beyond the means of university libraries and individuals. Mexican subscriptions to *Science* went from 196 to 96 between 1978 and 1987, in Brazil from 203 to 81, and in Venezuela from 89 to 18. Academic isolation and meager funding make it almost impossible to keep up with developments in Europe, Asia, or the United States. A mere 1 percent of science literature comes from Latin America. *Chemical Abstracts,* the most important reference source for research chemists, abstracted a scant 0.4 percent of its entries (1993) from Spanish-language publications—the same percentage as that from South Korea alone. Articles abstracted from Portuguese constituted an even smaller percentage, even though Brazil is the eighth-largest market economy and the world's fifth-largest nation. Of course, some Latin American scientists use English rather than their native language in order to communicate with a larger audience. Nevertheless, these figures indicate the restricted ability to conduct research. Moreover, the latest scientific equipment is expensive, fragile, often heavily taxed, and, given the almost complete absence of manufacturer's technical support, often cannot be repaired. Under the circumstances, breakthrough science is difficult. Weak, almost nonexistent ties exist between university researchers and industry, and few projects move from the laboratory to commercial production. In contrast, all the newly industrialized Asian countries made substantial investments in science and technology. In South Korea, for example, investment went from 0.3 percent in 1970 to 2 percent in 1988.

The absence of capital needed to finance product research and development and open new markets is directly related to family-controlled enterprises and their unwillingness to take risks. More than 50 Latin American companies are listed on the New York Stock Exchange and others are traded over the counter in the United States, but most Latin American firms must raise money locally. Brazil's Rio de Janeiro Stock Exchange and the larger São Paulo exchange list over 500 companies. Mexico, Argentina, and Peru each have stock markets with about 200 listed companies. Yet, many family-controlled firms, although listed, barely trade. For example, in Argentina fewer than 100 listed stocks are traded more than once a month, whereas a third are not bought or sold that often. In Brazil, 10 stocks account for 80 percent of the trading volume. Stock market indexes rise and fall on a narrow number of companies. Capital flows in and out of Latin America often reflect interest rates in the United States, not conditions in Latin America. Consequently, Latin American stock markets provide only marginal help in raising capital. Business contractions, in the absence of sufficient capital, exaggerate the impact of economic cycles. The rise and fall of the gross domestic product (GDP), varying inflation rates, and sudden changes in consumption and investments have negative consequences. They immediately affect living standards, income distribution, and consumption. If such volatility could be controlled, as it is in major industrialized countries, living standards for the bottom 7 percent of the population would improve significantly.

Other negative elements include excessive regulation, incredibly high taxes, and the bewildering assortment of licenses needed to engage in business. These factors all reinforce the underground economy. Consider the experience of René González, who managed two medium-sized printing businesses, one in Tijuana, Mexico, and the other across the border in San Diego, California. In the United States, he needed the services of a part-time accountant; in Mexico he employed three workers to assemble the necessary documentation and an accountant to steer it through the various government agencies. A 1995 study discovered that Mexico required 26 procedures involving 107 regulatory requirements, and 312 days to embark upon small-scale manufacturing. A retail shop required 294 days to open legally. Both types of businesses required from $4,500 to $5,200 for the process. Excessive details and confusing legal language provide ample opportunities for petty graft. Payoffs to inspectors and clerks constitute ongoing business expenses. Efforts of various Latin American governments to eliminate regulatory hurdles have met with only limited success.

Regulatory and credit obstacles retard business formation and restrict employment opportunities. Despite such barriers, a significant number of workers have found jobs in microenterprises. The figures range from a high of 80 percent in Peru to 33 percent in Uruguay. Even in Brazil, Latin America's industrial powerhouse, 50 percent of the workforce is employed in small-scale enterprises. If microbusinesses were relieved of the burdens imposed by high taxes and a hostile regulatory maze, and had reasonable access to credit, they could absorb more workers and underpin strong economic expansion.

Unfortunately, small-scale entrepreneurs often find it easier to stay in the informal or underground economy. Taxi networks that keep many large cities moving provide one example. By functioning in the informal economy, they avoid high taxes; most, however, remain small in order to avoid calling undue attention to their activities. Their illegal status requires them to bribe officials and the local police. Raising capital to purchase new equipment proves difficult, and existing assets cannot be mortgaged for business reasons. Money lenders, rather than legitimate financial institutions, service the underground economy at high interest rates. Rarely can underground businesses provide the foundation for a flourishing legal enterprise. Poverty and income inequality play a major role in any explanation of the region's economic history (see Figure 4.2, which illustrates the comparative income share of the population by world regions in the 1990s). Maldistribution of wealth had reduced the number and quality of consumers. Weak internal markets cannot be relied on to help carry an export industry through rough periods of slack overseas demand. And Latin America does not have a significant savings pool to finance new ventures or carry industry when necessary. Severe contractions, in the absence of adequate credit, further deepen even temporary downturns.

In contrast to other emerging economies, most Latin American republics do not have sufficient funds to finance their own projects, nor is significant regional

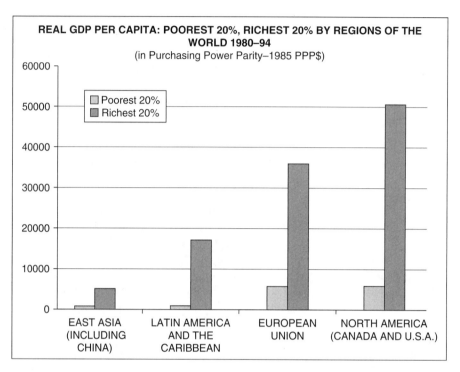

**FIGURE 4.2**

SOURCE: UNDP—Human Development Report, 1997.

funding available. Small to medium-sized businesses in Argentina in 1996 paid 3 to 4 percent interest monthly, despite an annual inflation rate of 3.4 percent. Moreover, they had to supply collateral equivalent to two or three times the amount borrowed. In effect, the lender would not assume any risk, and only those who do not need credit get it. Almost total risk aversion acts to choke off all but the most conservative expansion. Lack of strong trade and industrial ties between Latin American republics discouraged the development of regional financial resources.

Efforts to provide small-scale entrepreneurs with access to credit are still in the experimental stage, and the amount of financing available is limited. One promising development is the growth of Alternative Trading Organizations (ATO). These nonprofit organizations, developed in Europe in the 1970s, have spread to Latin America. ATOs provide credit to small-scale producers; set up direct export-marketing management, bypassing local middlemen; and offer business advice. Mexican coffee farmers in Oaxaca, who previously struggled to survive, posted $5 million in export sales with the help of an ATO and are now entering the domestic market. To guarantee a fair price and steady market, ATOs help identify markets and provide technical knowledge that small-scale producers frequently lack. For example, in 1996 an ATO helped establish a plantain chip industry in Costa Rica. Small organizations, such as the Mennonite Church's

Courtesy of Eladio Ortiz, *El Financiero International Edition,* March 23–29, 1998, p. 13.

Carlos Slim epitomizes the success-ful, dynamism, and thoroughly modern Latin American entrepre-neur. The richest man in Mexico, and perhaps in all of Latin America, his ability to mobilize investment capital is important to the Mexican economy and the general well-being of the country. He symbolizes also the poor distribution of wealth in Latin America that hinders the development of a strong internal market economy.

Peacecraft in Albuquerque, New Mexico, market high-quality goods made by Latin American Indian artisans, such as handwoven pine-needle baskets. These small ATOs make a difference locally and often spawn complementary self-help projects. Nevertheless, such nonprofit, socially responsible efforts do not change the basic economy. It remains to be seen whether they will eventually do more than make life better for the fortunate few.

Concentration of wealth contributes to the volatility of capital. Well-to-do Latin Americans safeguard their assets abroad to protect themselves from arbi-trary government policies and inflation. Half of Argentina's banks in 1996 were owned by public entities. Latin America's largest bank, *Banco do Brasil,* remains government owned. Seizure of assets, forced conversion of dollar-denominated deposits, or substitution of government bonds for demand deposits have occurred frequently enough to make depositors wary. All these factors explain the low percentage of bank deposits relative to the GDP. In 1994, deposits relative to GDP amounted to about 30 percent in Mexico, Venezuela, and Chile, and to a mere 18 percent in Argentina and Peru. For Colombia and Brazil, at the top, the figure was over 30 percent. This compares to 90 percent in Britain, 70 percent in Germany, and 55 percent in the United States.

Insuring the soundness of individual banks, difficult even in more advanced economies, poses another problem. In 1995, banks collapsed in Argentina, Brazil, Mexico, and Venezuela. In an effort to address the problem of regulating banks, 350 financial experts, central bankers, and Latin American treasury officials met at the Inter-American Development Bank in Washington, D.C. Aristóbulo de Juan, a former general manager of *Banco de España,* noted the widespread use of doctored balance sheets and paper capitalization to project a strong position, whereas in fact banks often were insolvent. Because of the Mexican crisis, the IMF proposed greater surveillance of central banks and government fiscal policies, which depends on timely, accurate, and honest economic statistics. In a veiled warning to treasury officials throughout the world, IMF Managing Director, Michael Camdessus, called the Mexican collapse the "first crisis of the twenty-first century," implying that the lessons must be heeded to avoid similar events elsewhere. As the Asian financial crisis of 1997–1998 made clear, these lessons were learned the hard way.[3]

Government-owned banks posed serious macroeconomic problems in the 1990s. The São Paulo state bank, *Banespa,* was used to finance expensive political projects and government operations. The state's debt was rolled over and seldom repaid. By the end of 1995, São Paulo owed the bank $15.5 billion or nine times the institution's net worth. State and municipal governments throughout Brazil have borrowed an estimated $140 billion, a sum far beyond their ability or intention to repay. Brazil's central bank bailed out state banks by issuing more paper money to cover their accounts, and the cycle started over again. Banespa and other publicly held institutions encourage mismanagement, corruption, and inflation. Even private banks have been drawn into political lending.

Private financial organizations have found it necessary and profitable to cater to political needs even if this required riding on a tiger's back. Brazilian privately owned *Banco Nacional* required a $5 billion government bailout in 1996 after a decade of politically motivated operations. President Fernando Henrique Cardoso, galvanized by possible political damage to himself, members of the government involved in dubious financial dealings with banks, and even his immediate family, who are rumored to be implicated, arranged the bailout. Then, to avoid a legislative investigation, he hammered out a deal with important politicians that required the government to assume $3.3 billion of bank debt incurred by the city of São Paulo; constructed a $36 million canal in the state of Paraíba; poured $30 million into road work and rural electrification in the state of Rondônia; and finally, allowed a senator from Goiás to name Brazil's principal mining official. The exact cost of the bailout will never be established. It demonstrated the extent to which banks can direct public monies into investments and developments whose main objectives may be political or to enrich those involved in public contracts. Meanwhile, Brazilian banks fail to perform the role of combining savings and surplus capital, responsibly providing credit and building bank assets that can serve the country and its people into the future.

Monetary difficulties, sometimes those of a country's own making as well as those beyond its control, can result in a sudden devaluation, sometimes accompanied by a change in the name of the national monetary unit. Attempts to stabilize the currency require using precious foreign reserves to fight off speculators. To counter inflation fears, in 1996, Argentina required that each peso be backed by one U.S. dollar of foreign reserves. In effect, the central bank cannot print paper money without necessary backing. In a complementary move the same year, Argentina's central bank arranged for international banks to guarantee emergency loans in the event of a future crisis; its return was an annual commitment fee of 0.3 percent of the amount. Chase Manhattan in New York agreed to supply $1.5 billion of a projected cushion of $5 billion. Behind this innovative arrangement, the IMF remains as a crisis lender of last resort. The Argentine

---

[3] *IMF Survey* (September 1995), pp. 1–2.

| **PROFILE**    Daniel Keith Ludwig's Adventure |
|---|

For every successful entrepreneur, at least 10 failures can be identified. Both successes and failures tend to be spectacular. Daniel Keith Ludwig's Jari Company in the Amazon offers an example. A shadowy, seldom seen, and extremely secretive American billionaire, Ludwig has been likened to the reclusive Howard Hughes. Ludwig purchased land near the confluence of the Amazon and Jari rivers in 1967 in the belief that the impending communications revolution would create a worldwide paper shortage and high profits for paper- and forest-product companies. The Jari Company staked its future on what appeared to be a miracle tree from India. The fast-growing gmelina tree was expected to grow at least 10 feet in as many months, providing large amounts of wood pulp. Ludwig invested $1.1 billion between 1967 and 1982 to create a vast plantation on his Connecticut-sized property; a company town (Monte Dourado), eventually with a population of 30,000; water and sewage facilities; a modern hospital, schools, airports, and roads. He outfitted his company with the latest machinery and technology.

His investment failed. He never investigated the Brazilian reality. The scarcity of skilled labor able to utilize modern technology quickly became a major obstacle. Symbolic of the massive planning failure were several hundred Caterpillar tractors that sank into the soft rain-forest soil, where they serve as stationary monuments to inappropriate technology.

Ludwig assumed that because he purchased his holdings from the government, he held clear title. In fact, conflicting titles and competing claims have plagued Brazilian property owners since colonial days. As a result, counterclaims periodically brought the company's operations to a standstill. Ludwig also did not grasp the importance of Brazilian nationalism. His obsessive secrecy led to rumors that the company worked hidden gold mines with slave labor. Nationalists claimed that his plantation represented a private country within a country. Stories circulated that U.S. Marines trained in Ludwig's enclave, suggesting that he had a military force at his disposal. Ludwig assumed that the government, as promised, would take over responsibility for maintaining the infrastructure—roads, airports, and the town itself. It came as a shock to him that the government had no intention of using its own limited resources to do so. Adding to Ludwig's woes, the gmelina trees failed to flourish and had to be removed and replaced with pine and eucalyptus trees. By 1982, a thoroughly defeated Ludwig sold out for $280 million to a Brazilian consortium organized by the government. Given his massive business miscalculations, planning failures, and political and social missteps, he was lucky to escape.

arrangement required internal financial discipline and strict avoidance of politically motivated spending. Unfortunately, it did not restrict floating foreign debt: an omission that proved fatal.


## THE ARGENTINE COLLAPSE OF 2000–2001

The acceptance by politicians of hard currency debt at market rates, without attention to debt repayment, created a debt bubble. Argentina's commitment to convertible currency, allegedly because they had finally conquered the old economic problems, convinced many investors to continue to lend money with rollover loans, new short-term loans, and other devices that put off repayment and kept things afloat until they began to fall apart. The fact that it did so at one time, kept alive the hope that the IMF would make things right. The world's largest (to date) default of $141 billion in 2001–2002 ended the fantasy.

Postmortem analysis exposed the irresponsibility and mistakes of banks, international financial institutions, brokerage houses, pension managers, and politicians. Argentina failed to make comprehensive structural reforms. Partial reforms created an optimism that became speculation, but did not create a balanced economy able to effectively use foreign debt. Letting go of optimism, even when the signs turned mixed, occurred reluctantly and over a considerable period. In the slow-motion economic collapse on the way to its dreadful finale in 2001, the government failed to take proactive measures, other than pressing the IMF for more loans. The people, now reduced to poverty and unemployment and unsure of their ability to recover, reacted with anger. A collapse of the state appeared to be a possibility. A rapid series of brief presidencies finally stabilized with the election of President Kitchner in 2003. It will be years before Argentina returns to normal.

# 5

# Peoples

The leaders of the independence movements (1808 to 1824), for the most part, aimed to create societies of self-disciplined and hardworking individuals. Achieving this goal required reforms to end slavery of blacks and eliminate both head taxes and labor levies on Indians. José de San Martín (southern South America), Simón Bolívar (northern South America), and Vicente Guerrero (Mexico) attempted such reforms. Their goals were frustrated, at first, when plantation and hacienda owners devised a debt peonage system whereby they loaned money to workers who could never repay it, thus binding them to their jobs. This labor system continued into the twentieth century. These leaders feared the unleashing of race wars, part of the legacy of slavery, exemplified by the Haitian slave revolt and the independence of Haiti. They saw danger lurking in the lower classes, especially when they comprised racially distinct peoples—blacks in Brazil, Indians in Mexico and Peru—and multiracial mixtures, such as *gauchos* in Argentina. Consequently, both liberals and conservatives attempted to devise national programs that would restrict the political influence of the so-called dangerous classes, the lower social orders, and reduce the threat they represented to national society. During the nineteenth century, leaders initiated three major campaigns to reform the people: (1) an Enlightenment-inspired plan to require self-discipline and education and, in the process, promote individualism; (2) a program to remake the population by attracting European immigrants and assimilating indigenous peoples into national cultures modeled on Europe; and (3) a policy to champion nationalism and create a modern elite and middle-class identity in sharp contrast to what was perceived as the behavior of the general population. These campaigns worked differently in each nation, but everywhere they went by the name of modernization.

Both economic changes and Enlightenment reforms, occurring roughly over the century from 1750 to 1850, had the enduring effect of promoting individualism and reinforcing elite dominance in politics, particularly in Liberal programs. Promoting individualism, moreover, tended to encourage nuclear, rather than extended, families. The Enlightenment brought numerous reforms to the Spanish and Portuguese imperial governments and created new policies for government administration and finance regulation. Even the Church felt the influence of Enlightenment ideas regarding practical knowledge, specifically, demonstrable cause-and-effect relationships over simple faith. Taken together, these reforms called for an expanded role for the individual in society.

The Bourbon reformers in Spain and their successors in the New World agreed on government decrees that demanded self-discipline. Laws against such crude behavior as defecating and urinating in public and new city codes requiring the construction of privies for all private buildings reflected the influence of Enlightenment ideas about regulating individuals and their bodies. Other reforms increased restrictions on drinking establishments to curtail drunkenness, scrutinized street behavior to create greater social order, and encouraged education to promote literacy. One reform effort called for constructing new cemeteries outside the town limits. The reformers had several goals—improve public health, tame grandiose social displays by local elites at funerals, and replace mysterious notions about the dead with no-nonsense realism. The practice of burying the dead in churchyards and under church floors created health hazards the reformers wanted to eliminate. Powerful families used gravesites in the church as places for an ostentatious display of their social status. Finally, a mystical relationship existed between the living and the dead, which reformers interpreted as a religious superstition that hindered the acceptance of modern empirical explanations of life. Moving the cemeteries out of town seemed to accomplish all three goals. An opposition group, including many women, challenged the new policy. The reform proponents broadened the scope of the campaign, and charged that women were too emotional to participate in major decisions and too religious to escape the influence of their parish priests. Both of these stereotypes became tenets of nineteenth-century Liberalism in its campaign for modernization.[1] Eventually, officials moved the cemeteries out of town.

This social campaign was accompanied by a parallel economic program. New demands grouped together under the label of modernization distorted the economy. Powerful industrial countries, increasingly eager to open up markets and purchase primary raw materials of a seemingly endless variety, demanded accommodations from Latin Americans. The Latin American elites understood

---

[1] Pamela Voekel, "Scent and Sensibility: Pungency and Piety in the Making of the *Gente Sensata,* Mexico 1640–1859" (Ph.D. diss., University of Texas, 1997).

that if their newly independent nations hoped to survive, they must adjust to the new international reality. Failure raised the specter of becoming dependencies or colonies of industrial powers, or even losing territory to more powerful neighbors.

A panicky sense of urgency infused both conservative and liberal elites with the energy to confront the external demands of the nineteenth century. Latin America had become economically and politically vulnerable. The international powers, especially Great Britain and the United States, introduced new rules that had a major impact on how people worked, how they conducted themselves, where and how they lived, how much they would be paid, what they could consume, and how wealth would be distributed. The modernizing elites saw no alternative to a social, cultural, and economic transformation. In human terms, they hoped to modernize the national population by creating a work ethic of regular hours, imparting technical skills, implanting new values among all classes, and fixing responsibility on individuals. The modernizers interpreted any opposition to their schemes as backward behavior and determined to eliminate it. Even when setbacks occurred, the direction seemed clear. These national leaders never envisioned losing control over the process of modernization. Their confidence rested on their social status, economic success, and political authority. They presumed the right to command and the obligation of the lower classes to obey. They expected that as the benefits of change trickled down, self-interest would broaden and accelerate the entire process. They failed to foresee the open-ended nature of complex modern societies. Transformation represented only the start of a chain reaction, a series of modifications that could not be controlled, stopped, or, in the end, directed. Individual self-interest became the driving force.

Determining how to join the modern world required a new national vision and resulted in the second great campaign of the nineteenth century to re-create the Latin American people. This plan turned to European immigration to fulfill two alleged needs: occupy the wide-open spaces and biologically absorb the black and indigenous populations. Moreover, the planners believed Europeans would introduce new values and technology. In the name of progress, new national leaders sought to transform or extinguish the rural lower classes and minority peoples. Domingo Sarmiento (1811–1888), intellectual, educator, and eventually president of Argentina (1868–1874), embodied all aspects of the assault. In his classic work *Civilization and Barbarism: The Life of Juan Facundo Quiroga* (1845), he posited a series of simple dichotomies. The city of Buenos Aires represented civilization, whereas the countryside of the *pampas* stood for barbarism. Those who dressed like Europeans and lived a European lifestyle obeyed laws, accepted government, and supported the idea that progress stood for the modern world; whereas the gauchos, inhabitants of the pampas, and others who allegedly obeyed only their primitive instincts lived a backward existence. Two worlds existed—"one Spanish, European, and cultivated" and the other "barbarous, American, and almost wholly of native growth." While Sarmiento was Argentina's representative to the United States (1865–1868), he asked the American educator Horace Mann to recruit Wisconsin schoolmarms to help transform the people of the pampas as they had supposedly done in the American Wild West. Eventually, some 65 teachers arrived in Argentina to make civilized beings out of uncouth frontier children. In the same vein, Anglophile Juan Bautista Alberdi urged the transformation of Indians into laborers like those in England because, he believed, the Indian had no place in Argentine politics or society.

The Argentine dream of a new people became a partial reality as 5.5 million Europeans arrived between 1857 and 1924. By 1881, the British represented 36 percent of all immigrants, 9 percent of the entire population. They brought new attitudes and technology with them. Robert Bruce, a Scottish immigrant, introduced milk-pasteurizing equipment and produced the country's first butter for the domestic market. Improved cattle- and sheep-breeding methods upgraded the quality of meat and wool. Such technology, although economically beneficial reinforced the country's role as an exporter of agricultural products.

Foreigners found it relatively easy to make an impact on the economy with improvements that to them verged on common sense. Consequently, they developed an ill-concealed contempt for the natives. Their cultural arrogance and economic displacement of natives occasionally flared into violence. In 1856, Colonel Silvio Olivieri, a former Italian army officer who founded New Rome, Argentina, as a quasi-military agricultural colony, imprisoned 16 locals, setting off a revolt that ended in his own murder. The most famous xenophobic reaction in Argentina occurred on New Year's Day, 1872. A messianic healer, respectfully called *Médico Dios* or *Tata Dios,* espoused a mixture of folk Catholicism, herbal medicine, and mystical redemption that promised to rescue native Argentines from the calamity of modernization. Encouraged by one of his disciples, a group of gauchos rampaged through the largely immigrant-controlled town of Tandil, leaving 17 dead. Native inhabitants searched for scapegoats, whereas the elites did their best to accelerate change.

In their attempt to transform the native population as an instant step to progress, governments used statistical evidence in their pursuit of immigration. Benjamin Vicuña MacKenna, secretary of the Chilean Immigration Commission and himself an example of what the government hoped to accomplish, presented a report in 1854 suggesting what national groups should be sought. According to the report, the best immigrants would come from Germany. If Germans could not be persuaded to immigrate, then the second best would be Swiss and other northern Europeans. Allegedly, unlike other Europeans, they completely cut their ties with the old country. In comparison, the British, steeped in cultural pride, made excellent settlers but preferred English-speaking Australia and the United States. The report asserted that the self-absorbed, vain, and emotional French made the worst immigrants. As showy birds of passage, they searched for pleasure and fortune only to return to their nest even more swollen and smug. Spaniards rated only slightly better, haughty and unable to forget that America once belonged to them.

Other republics generally agreed with these preferences. In Mexico, the government's desire to alter the composition of the people and expand the sparse settlements, particularly in the north, made immigration policy a national issue as early as 1823. Subsequently, the colonization director estimated that the republic needed to increase its population from 7 million in 1850 to some 70 million. Mexico failed to attract European immigrants in any sizable number partly because of its proximity to the United States.

The search for immigrants in Brazil took on a different character because it required the end of slavery, which finally occurred in 1888. Former slaves, and by association all lower-class workers, were considered deficient in the skills and aptitude necessary to modernize the country. The abolition of slavery in 1888, followed a year later by the collapse of the Brazilian monarchy and the establishment of the first republic, added to the feeling of a new beginning. It was thought that foreign immigration, psychologically detached from the former servile and monarchical systems, would bring skills from modernizing Europe, reinforce the elites' desire to whiten the population, and help build a new Brazil.

In reality, most European immigrants had not completed the transition from peasant to worker in their home countries. Many came from rural southern Europe, where they had been displaced by modernization, and brought no industrial experience with them. Europeans with highly marketable skills tended to move about within Western Europe, often to Germany or Belgium, rather than choose an uncertain future in Latin America. Brazil, for example, in contrast to Argentina, did not attract British immigrants, who possessed a high degree of modern agricultural expertise as well as some industrial experience.

Industry, the symbol of modernization, first utilized native-born labor. The census of 1872 recorded that slaves made up 11.1 percent of Brazil's industrial workers. Brazilian labor also sustained coffee production, augmented by foreign workers who found it difficult to adjust to a system designed psychologically as well as structurally for slave labor. Immigrants who signed indenture contracts found that the contracts could be sold to another planter. Technically, the debt transferred and the individual merely followed the debt. Moreover, the employment law of 1837 required a discharged worker to pay his entire debt or be dispatched to work it off on public projects. Abandoning employment caused any debt owed to double. On completion of a contract, an immigrant received a certificate much like that of a freed slave. Without such a certificate an individual could not seek other legal employment.

Eventually, the Brazilian government offered free passage to immigrants in order to end the practice whereby plantation owners paid the fare and assumed they had purchased the worker. Subsidized transportation attracted entire families, and the low wages forced men, women, and children into the labor pool. Immigrant workers might find work because of the preference for European labor, but it did not translate into higher wages. Subsidized transportation for immigrants continued until 1927. After a slow start, Brazil received some 125,500 immigrants annually between 1891 and 1900. Rio de Janeiro's population, between the 1870s and the 1920s, went from one-fifth to one-third foreigners. Immigrants flooded into Argentina, Chile, Uruguay, and Brazil, but elsewhere they came only in sparse numbers.

The by-products of modernization, especially increased access to education and exposure to mass media, created greater popular demand for political participation, social programs, and consumer goods. The rise of popular movements expanded opportunities for women, who often became leaders of these new organizations, especially those that focused on meeting the material needs of the family. For example, during the period of teacher unrest in Mexico in the 1980s, women teachers comprised the majority of those who participated in sit-ins, marches, and the meetings to demand more resources.

## THE FAMILY AT MIDCENTURY

The extended family of the colonial era began to erode during the 50 years after independence. Immigration attracted individuals and sometimes their immediate families, but not their extended families. When they arrived in Argentina, Brazil, or some other Latin American country, the demands of making a living put additional stress on the family. In the cities, family members went off to different jobs and worked long hours. Even children had to earn money. Often the youngsters spent most of their time in the streets, selling small items or running errands and finding some time to play with friends.

The extended family also became a victim of Liberal political campaigns to promote the individual, eliminate communal economic activity, and reduce the influence of the Church in daily life. Generally, Liberals such as the Mexican Miguel Lerdo de Tejada saw the individual—politically independent and economically self-sufficient—as the building block of society. Their political reform campaigns focused on promoting the individual by eliminating communal and Church landholdings. Liberal efforts to separate church and state also diminished the importance of the extended family and promoted individualism. The Mexican laws contained in the 1857 Constitution established the civil registry as the mandatory and legal basis for certifying births, marriages, and deaths. The Church sacraments of baptism, marriage, and last rites became only matters of individual choice. Powerful social bonds created through the participation of godparents in these religious ceremonies also declined. The civil registries required witnesses, but, unlike godparents, they did not assume moral responsibility for the child, the married couple, or the survivors of the deceased. The extended family at midcentury remained strong in the countryside and among the urban elites. Elsewhere, it had dramatically waned.

Overall, Liberals believed they could regenerate Indian peoples, for example, by forcing them into a competitive society. Replacing communal landholdings with private property would set the stage for development. The lower classes, held to a new standard of conduct, would be forced to accept the discipline needed to modernize. These nineteenth-century elites luxuriated in the belief that they had devised a procedure that eventually would benefit the national community, no matter how harsh the transformation might be for the backward classes.

Liberal programs did not go unchallenged. Revolts, often devoid of ideology, erupted throughout the nineteenth century. In Yucatán, Mexico, Mayan Indians, hard pressed by the demands of commercial agriculture, engaged in ongoing warfare between 1847 and 1855 with sporadic outbursts lingering for much of the century. The *Cruzob,* as the Mayan rebels called themselves, revived ancient religious beliefs, integrated some Catholic forms, and rallied Indians against change. Angry peasants in northeast Brazil succeeded in derailing government modernization plans. The Quebra-Quilo revolt (1874–1875), actually a series of riots, destroyed official records and, through violence, discouraged commercial agricultural development, thus delaying economic restructuring in the region for several decades.

An Andean myth reflected the fear of those suddenly confronted by progress. The story revolved around the imagined existence of Pistaco, a tall, pale foreigner who drank milk and carried a sharp knife on his nocturnal rambles in the mountains in search of hapless victims. He looked for unfortunate travelers whom he could butcher and render into grease to lubricate machines. Previously isolated Indians reacted to the apparent commercialization of everything as outsiders scoured the Andes in search of marketable resources. Banditry became an endemic problem throughout Latin America as various companies and individuals attempted to exploit the human and natural resources of the region.

Attempts to find a middle ground between unrestrained progress and the old ways received little support from the elites. In Guatemala, Rafael Carrera, a lower-class *mestizo* who ruled the country from 1839 to 1865, understood the problem. He came to power as a result of a reactionary Indian revolt. Although Carrera did not reject change, he believed it should occur at a more acceptable

Courtesy of the Latin America Library at Tulane University.

Children in Latin America have long played and worked in the streets selling newspapers, running errands, and engaging in other minor economic activities. These Mexican children, photographed playing marbles in about 1860, remained part of a family unlike today's largely abandoned street children. Uncontrolled

pace than the city-centered elite demanded. As president, he attempted to ensure that the government represented all the people by Indianizing the army and the bureaucracy. In Bolivia, Manuel Belzu brought urban workers and *campesinos* (rural inhabitants) into a political alliance in 1848 against what he called the selfish elite. In a similar fashion, Juan Manuel de Rosas established a populist government in Argentina. Rosas discouraged foreign economic penetration and distrusted European intentions as well as cultural pretensions. With the support of Brazil and Uruguay, the Argentine elites finally forced him into exile in 1852, throwing open the gates to modernization (see Chapter 2, Politics, for more discussion of these developments and leaders).

Courtesy of the Latin America Library at Tulane University.

Attired in the latest European fashions, an upper-class Peruvian extended family posed for this photograph in about 1860. Only a few background features offer clues to the physical location. This group would not have been out of place in England or France, reflecting their almost slavish desire to appear European and thus modern.

By the last decades of the nineteenth century, Latin Americans had become a diverse people. From the viewpoint of race, ethnicity, class, and nationality, the region was populated by people grouped in families to form a human mosaic. The diversity of Latin America fascinated foreigners. In Europe at the end of the eighteenth century, a market developed for paintings of Latin American peoples, especially paintings depicting the intermingling of different races and ethnicities. These images, called caste paintings, generally showed family portraits. The popularity of these visual presentations continued into the nineteenth century. Once photography became common, photographs replaced the caste paintings as curiosity about the peoples of Latin America increased. Meanwhile, around 1870, a major change occurred, which began to reshape the way individuals defined their relationship to societies throughout Latin America.

About 1870, at least some Latin Americans began to change the way they saw themselves and their societies. This resulted in the emergence of the individual on one level and the self-conscious creation of classes on another. In the last decades of the nineteenth century, the economic elites and the growing middle class struggled to define themselves. Their efforts had three dimensions: (1) an individual ambition to identify with the cosmopolitan practices called modern life, (2) a desire to promote national uniqueness, and (3) a campaign to draw a contrast between themselves and the lower social groups. Making a distinction between other peoples and themselves, elites described the inappropriate behavior of Indians, blacks, immigrants, peasants, and the poor. National leaders established campaigns "to civilize" and make them model citizens.

In the twentieth century, government leaders, recognizing the untapped political potential of marginal peoples, developed new programs to instill in the masses a sense of nationalism that became the basis for populist politics (see Chapter 2 for a discussion of this development). Moreover, in the twentieth century, new channels developed for social mobility, especially for aspiring individuals to reach the middle class through professional careers that required specialized training. From among these various professions, including medicine, architecture, and law, we have selected professional military officers to illustrate this development. Additionally, these channels were forced to open wider to accommodate not only socially mobile men, but also ambitious, talented women. Advancement for both men and women rested on the recognition of their merits as individuals. In this section, we discuss increased opportunities, in professional careers and in political participation, not for extended families or social groups, but for the individual.

## THE SEARCH FOR COSMOPOLITAN SOCIETY

From about 1870 to the Depression of 1929, European styles and manners captivated Latin America's elites and the ambitious, although small, middle class. Eager to join the cosmopolitan society of Europe and North America, Latin Americans responded to the "allure of the foreign" and indulged in the new culture of consumption. These *Belle Epoque* elites sought out the latest in foreign styles in home furnishings, clothing, hygiene and health products, and leisure activities. Department stores, newly established by French companies in Mexico and Argentina and by local entrepreneurs in Brazil and Chile, offered imported goods and created a place where women could circulate freely in public. Tastes in food, etiquette, entertainment, home design and decor, and clothing followed foreign, especially French, models. Cosmopolitan Latin Americans expected that their consumption of modern goods and their participation in progressive activities would serve as a model of behavior to reform the working class, the marginal groups, and ultimately the nation.

The elites, relying on education, law enforcement programs, and themselves as examples, intended to refine the behavior of the masses and raise them to what the elites regarded as an acceptable level of civilization. These social reformers dismissed recreational activities such as cockfights, horsemanship contests, and bullfights as crude and even barbaric, and turned to bicycling, tennis, roller-skating, cricket, and baseball. Meanwhile, they planned to curtail the scandalous behavior of the lower classes, especially gambling, heavy drinking, and frequenting brothels, by offering literacy classes and physical fitness training and instilling good work habits.

Setting the correct tone with the general population proved difficult. Nevertheless, the elites held fast to their justification for remodeling the people. Their rationale rested on a combination of economic Liberalism and Comtian Positivism, with a strong dose of popular Darwinism. Both Liberals and Positivists argued against governmental disruption of natural processes. Liberals believed in the market, which could function properly only if left alone by government. Positivists adopted the philosophy of social progress, formulated by the father of sociology, the Frenchman Auguste Comte. Comte maintained that inevitable social improvement could be accelerated by governments that adopted his ideas of science and kept their hands off natural progress. He also suggested that this improvement would be slowed by regimes that indulged in assistance to the weak. Above all, Positivism, with its scientific-sounding theories, encouraged its followers to be morally lazy. Citing adherence to Comte's notions, government officials and social elites could turn their backs on poor, ignorant, and rural peoples. The latter had to become progressive, productive members of society. The elites believed this program would soon raise their nation to the same cultural level as Europe.

## NEW VIEWS OF IMMIGRATION

Many national elites who adopted this campaign to civilize the population changed their view of immigration. Rather than national savior, they saw immigration as social danger. In Argentina especially, the elites feared that immigration would destroy their cultural uniqueness. A reaction set in, including a cry for recognition of national identity. Yet the old society, with its distinctive social types, was gone; only romantic notions of the lost society remained. In Argentina, the once despised gaucho became the hero of national folklore and the symbol of the nation. The poet and historian Leopoldo Lugones in 1913 asserted that the gaucho's legacy had been absorbed into the collective mentality of the people despite a tidal wave of immigrants who had changed the composition of the population. Carlos Octavio Bunge boldly suggested that the gaucho provided the embryonic roots of national identity.

Previously blanket support for immigration now moved in the opposite direction. Juan Bialet Massé, commissioned by the Argentine government to study the productivity of foreign and native-born workers, concluded that natives performed better. The writer Enrique Larreta disdainfully commented, "true talent does not migrate . . . the wave washes up only the most insignificant fish." The search for authentic, unique national roots also turned to the city. Argentines identified with both the music and the dance called the *tango,* which represented the soul of Argentine urban culture. Initially, the lyrics and movements of the tango proved too vulgar and explicit for national elites. Only when it became the rage in Parisian cosmopolitan society did the tango become acceptable to Buenos Aires high society and become, like the gaucho, another expression of Argentine nationalism.


## THE MIDDLE CLASS

Simultaneously with the introduction of elite social reform programs, the middle sectors of Latin American societies determined to distinguish themselves from the masses, especially by identifying behavior characteristic of civilized people. During the late nineteenth century, the middle class became a dynamic group that commanded greater status and more resources. A social system based on economic status had emerged during the colonial centuries; it grew stronger as the new republics swept away archaic social institutions, such as the nobility, powerful extended families, and guilds. The economic imperative expanded as independent Latin America entered more completely into the worldwide market economy. Demand for technicians, managers, educated professionals, commission agents, and others able to comprehend increasingly complex interconnections with distant and changing markets spurred the expansion of the middle class. The growth pace of the managerial class varied greatly from one region to another and from country to country. As a class, they developed certain characteristics. Whether salaried or self-employed, they did not possess a high degree of social and economic security, but depended on professional skills, advanced education, and economic development for their continued well-being. In percentage terms, the managerial class remained a small part of the total population.

The growth of the middle class in Argentina coincided with the rise of Buenos Aires and the increase in foreign immigration. Before the 1880s, the population was divided into a socially acceptable class and a poor laboring class. European laborers and others with ambition and talent struggled to move into the middle class, stimulated by opportunities resulting from industrial development, commercial agriculture, and urban growth. An immigrant could abandon heavy manual labor and with three weeks' salary purchase a flock of sheep. A generation or two later the family might be accepted into the elite. The *Club del Progreso,* the Jockey Club, and the *Círculo de Armas,* all exclusive gathering spots, soon listed members with English, Irish, Basque, French, Italian, and German names. Even if fortune failed to carry a family into the elite sector, many families joined the middle class. By the early decades of the twentieth century, Argentina appeared to be a middle-class nation in the making. Few recognized that, although it seemed well defined, the middle class had little political power and a scant sense of unity.

Hard work, innate genius, and a little luck enabled individuals to move into the middle class and even to skyrocket into the new elite stratum. Success stories

---

**PROFILE**    Carlos—One of Bogotá's Street Kids

Carlos is a survivor—just barely. Born into an impoverished Bogotá slum family, he experienced hunger, neglect, and physical violence in bitter proportions. His illiterate father, a man defeated by life, sought bravado and a fleeting measure of self-respect in alcohol. Drinking bouts usually ended with beating his hungry children. Finally abandoned by his family, Carlos undertook his own survival as a *gamín*, a street child. He lived by his wits and a sly hand. He slept in doorways along Bogotá's fashionable Twelfth Street, comforted by sniffing a container of glue and relying on the security of a sharp knife. Older gamínes preyed upon the younger children. Some police also abused them. At age 11, Carlos made a semiopportunistic decision to join Father Javier's program for street children. Father Javier offered food, a secure place to sleep, and minor medical attention. This program allowed Carlos to consider new options. He could return to the street or he could enter the program in earnest. Only those able to call on unexpected sources of self-motivation and discipline survive this program. Carlos had to demonstrate his willingness to give up drugs and petty crime. Eventually, he became one of the 500 former gamínes attending the high school at Father Javier's center. Elected mayor of the self-governing student community, Carlos enforced the rules and provided peer guidance. The program gave him a sense of control over his life.

Thanks to the program and his own resources, Carlos became an accomplished student. An avid reader of philosophy and literature, he learned to play the piano with a preference for Beethoven and Mozart. Carlos also played modern jazz on the saxophone and folk music on the guitar. In many ways, he serves as an example of a life rescued. Although Father Javier's program can make only a dent in the problem of street children in Colombia, it is a showcase of possibilities to help them.

SOURCE: Michael Shafter, "Majito and Carlos Alberto: The Gamín Legacy," in William H. Beezley and Judith Ewell, eds., *The Human Tradition in Latin America* (Wilmington: Scholarly Resources, 1987), pp. 275--282.

---

reported tales of individuals who created personal fortunes, not families who claimed noble titles. Simón I. Patiño, for example, born in 1860 to a modest artisan family in Bolivia's Cochabamba valley, became one of the world's richest men. After struggling to finish secondary school, he learned the mining business as an apprentice to equipment importers, then purchased a tin mine. In 1900, he struck one of the richest veins in history, bought out the competition, and by 1910 controlled 50 percent of Bolivia's tin production. Patiño eventually extended his financial empire to Europe and moved there to manage his vast holdings; he continued to dominate Bolivian tin mining until his death in the 1940s. Patiño left Cochabamba far behind to become a major international capitalist.

In Mexico, several individuals took advantage of opportunities to achieve both economic and social success. In Chihuahua, Luis Terrazas, a butcher in the 1850s, went into large-scale cattle ranching, then built textile mills, a flour mill, and a brewery, and eventually started insurance companies. These enterprises assured that the Terrazas family would dominate this northern state. Only the revolution of 1910 ended the family's economic control of Chihuahua. Traditionally, elite families had used marriage as a base upon which to build economic success, and occasionally this strategy still worked. The alliance of the Garza and Sada families through marriage led to the founding of the Cuauhtémoc brewery in 1892 and eventually to the formation of the Monterrey Industrial Group, a financial and manufacturing empire that remains a dominant economic and social force in contemporary Mexico. The expansion of capitalist enterprises in the three decades from 1870 to 1900 created tremendous opportunities for many Latin Americans to move into the middle class.

Business was not the only route to middle-class life, however. Many people obtained a technical education, leading to occupations that provided solid middle-class status. Those who reached the middle class lived comfortably and expected to offer the same advantages to their children. As central governments assumed greater social responsibilities, often taking over duties reformers had stripped from the Church, the number of available professional positions increased. For example, civil registries, instead of parish priests, now recorded births, marriages, and deaths. Between 1876 and 1910 the Mexican bureaucracy grew some 900 percent. An estimated 70 percent of educated professionals depended directly on government employment, contracts, or concessions.

During the last decades of the nineteenth century, middle-class people became increasingly self-conscious and determined to define themselves as distinct from the lower elements. To some extent, their self-consciousness reflected advertising campaigns directed at them as part of the effort to create a consumer society. The middle class learned to desire goods purchased by elites in the new department stores. The creation of both individual desire and choice affected the family as well. With less frequent use of the dowry and the declining influence of the extended family, romance often replaced parental negotiation in the selection of marriage partners. Moreover, without dowries and other contractual requirements before marriage, young couples increasingly asked for proofs of love from each other, which ranged from small gifts to sexual favors.

Spokesmen for the middle classes also worked out their identity in contrast to the lower classes. They claimed that the middle classes were hardworking, self-disciplined, moral, sober, and orderly. These traits distinguished them from members of the lower classes who took a casual approach to work, held a whimsical attitude toward life, and generally behaved in an immoral and drunken fashion. Once the middle class had clearly defined these traits, they joined national campaigns to bring order to the lower classes through strict rules of behavior that would eliminate, or at least regulate, vice, particularly excessive drinking, gambling, and prostitution. They supported statutes to promote healthy habits through vagrancy laws, curfews, and, if necessary, rehabilitation, and imposed sentences in new penal institutions in an effort to teach individual discipline.

The definition of middle-class values and the introduction of legal reforms to regulate vices attributed to the lower classes brought a greater sense of security to the middle class. But economic downturns, often the result of world market cycles or global politics, caused severe dislocations. The Argentine economic collapse of 1890, for example, forced a hard-pressed government to borrow funds

Courtesy of Champion Latin American Collection, Tucson, Arizona.

Tokens such as this photograph served as proof of love for courting couples. Other gifts might include religious medallions, handkerchiefs, locks of hair, and sometimes sexual intimacies as the ultimate proof. This image reveals the way this swain wanted to be thought of by his sweetheart. The photograph represents the growth of romantic love and the decline of economic considerations, including dowries.

at high interest rates, issue excessive amounts of paper money, and hope the country would survive inflation. Finally, adverse socioeconomic conditions impelled a fearful middle class to take action. *La Noventa,* a revolt supported by contingents of the army and navy, sputtered to life. A middle-class political party, the *Unión Cívica Radical,* led by the indifferently educated but dogged Hipólito Irigoyen, emerged. Irigoyen, a former teacher, minor bureaucrat, spiritualist, and apprentice lawyer, provided austere, messianic leadership. Interested in neither money nor conventional behavior, he appeared unmoved by everything except power and politics. Strong rhetoric and growing militancy eventually convinced the elites that the middle class had to be accommodated to prevent a revolution.

As a consequence, a new election law of 1912, called the Sáenz Peña reform, provided for a secret ballot, suffrage for males over 18 years of age, and honest elections. Irigoyen claimed the presidency in 1916.

Although the Argentine elites shared political power with this reform, they retained economic control. The compromise proved to be unstable, disruptive and, in the end, unworkable. The Sáenz Peña reform and the frustrating period of political opportunism, corruption, and demagoguery it created led to an army coup in 1930. The worldwide depression added more urgency to the issue of national integration. Unfortunately, the army delivered the nation back into the hands of the oligarchy, who now believed that electoral reform had been a major mistake.

## THE WORKERS

The changes made both deliberately and accidentally by the elites and the middle classes greatly affected all sectors of society in Latin America. Workers found themselves in a quickly changing world. Many were migrants who had come from foreign countries or rural communities and who were living in a city for the first time. The strangeness of the urban environment was compounded by social pressures from the elites and the middle classes. Workers faced a difficult transition characterized by the uncertainty of change. New work disciplines, displacement from community lands, and the assault on old customs created a deep sense of anxiety. The fruits of modernization, evident everywhere, did not seem to reach them or compensate them for what they had lost. As a consequence, some workers began to seek alternate visions of the future.

Workers rejected the reformers' notions that much of what they did was immoral, wasteful, and irrational. Nevertheless, the lower classes responded to the pressures of the workplace and transformed themselves accordingly. Yet, social resentment, aggravated by the uneven distribution of the benefits of modernization, simmered just below the surface. The transformation of self-sufficient rural folk into either modern urban or commercial agricultural workers could not be accomplished overnight, nor without stress on the society.

Various forms of working-class activism emerged, from the relatively moderate mutualists, who advocated self-help, to the dogmatic anarchists, who called for the total destruction of economic and government institutions. Within broad movements, splinter groups, ranging from the pragmatic and moderate to the idealistic and radical, emerged.

Some workers found a powerful tool in literacy, often required to perform modern tasks. The expansion of literacy made it possible to disseminate political ideas. Broadsheets distributed in the mines, factories, and plantations offered new possibilities to workers. Cheap, inexpensive newssheets filled with amusing caricatures of the elites and middle-class managers circulated widely. Sarcasm and humor could be used to reduce reformers to a more realistic and humble size. Ironically, Italian and Spanish socialists and anarchists were among the many immigrants who came to Latin America in the nineteenth century.

Anarchism in particular caused concern. Its emphasis on dismantling the state and abolishing property aimed a dagger at the heart of nineteenth-century Liberalism. The tendency within anarchism to support violence—bombings, assassinations, and other forms of direct action—provided governments with ample rationale to curb working-class militancy. Nevertheless, the difficulties faced by workers could not be overlooked. In Mexico, Andrés Molina Enríquez, an elite Yucatecan, warned that without significant changes in the treatment of workers, anarchists and other radicals would eventually threaten modernization. In a similar fashion, Wistano Luis Orozco, a member of Mexico's still small and dependent middle class, attacked the concentration of wealth that led to a degraded working class.

The most comprehensive defense of the working class came from the Roman Catholic Church. Pope Leo XIII issued the encyclical *Rerum Novarum* in 1893, which directed Catholics to extend social assistance to the working class. The pontiff condemned child labor, excessive work hours, and abuse of women in the workplace. He defended the right of workers to organize unions and bargain for better wages and working conditions, but he rejected radicalism. Although dismissed by many as white communism, *Rerum Novarum* provided religious legitimacy for working-class demands. Economic and social justice could no longer be dismissed. Workers became a class increasingly able to insist on being accommodated in some fashion. Spokesmen for Liberalism still dominated economics and set national political agendas from Mexico to Tierra del Fuego, but now they faced the competing forces they had inspired through modernization.

## THE PROFESSIONAL MILITARY

The late nineteenth century in Latin America witnessed the rise of many professions that opened doors to the middle class. People sought new, specialized training in architecture, civil and hydraulic engineering, law, medicine, and the military. Military training probably offered social mobility to more individuals than any of these careers through World War II.

Military officers represented a distinct group, characterized by esprit de corps and internal discipline. Above all, they were sworn to defend the nation, its honor, and its constitution. These responsibilities occasionally meant confrontations with foreign armies, but more often they meant conflict with what the officers perceived as internal threats. The army's acceptance of these special responsibilities provided a rationale for political action and, on occasion, direct involvement in governing the nation.

Armed conflicts in the nineteenth century over unresolved border disputes, competition over natural resources, and threats from foreign powers left little doubt that Latin American nations required professional armies. Conflict began in the era of independence when Brazil seized control of the disputed eastern bank of the Río de la Plata. This resulted in the inconclusive Emperor's War (1825–1828) with Argentina, which ended only when the British intervened and created the buffer state of Uruguay. The United States–Mexican War (1846–1848) ended when the Americans detached Mexico's northern territories, amounting to 50 percent of the nation, including what is today the U.S. Southwest. The War of the Triple Alliance (1864–1870) pitted Paraguay against Brazil and its allies, Argentina and Uruguay. After a bitter struggle, the Brazilians defeated the Paraguayans, who endured occupation and territorial loss. Less than a decade after the War of the Triple Alliance, Chile soundly defeated both Peru and Bolivia in the War of the Pacific (1879–1883). Chileans took Bolivia's seacoast, occupied Peru's capital, and seized the Peruvian nitrate fields in the Atacama Desert. Later, Bolivia endured further territorial losses when Brazilians occupied rubber-tree-rich Acre province in 1903.

These wars persuaded government leaders of the need for a well-trained officer corps and resulted in efforts to improve military instruction. The educational campaign to create professional soldiers, in turn, offered social mobility to the young men from the lower social orders who were recruited to be officers. Of course, in the development of this new training program, national leaders turned to Europe for military instructors, just as they did for consumer goods. In 1873, the Guatemalan government brought in three Spanish military engineers to establish its new professional military school. The Chileans, seeking to professionalize their army in 1885, contracted Captain Emil Körner, an experienced Prussian artillery officer, to reorganize military training. Körner, with an established reputation in military education at the School of Artillery and Engineering in Berlin, introduced the latest training and fashions. Chile's army and riot police, the *Carabineros,* still have a distinctly Germanic look. The Peruvians brought a French mission in 1896, and the following year the new military academy in Lima enrolled its first students. Argentina employed Colonel Alfredo Arent and a cadre of German officers in 1899. By the turn of the century, most Latin American republics had attempted to improve the professional level of the military through instruction and the exchange of officers. Although usually European officers served as instructors, Chile did dispatch training missions to Colombia and El Salvador. After World War II a significant number of Latin American army officers received training in the United States at the School of the Americas and the armed forces academies, including West Point.

The notion of an educated and trained officer corps, with advancement based on individual merit, has become deeply ingrained in the Latin American military. This pattern created a strong tie between the middle class and the army. Brazil's Advanced War College (*Escola Superior de Guerra*), established in 1949, brought together promising officers and prominent civilians. Academics, economists, writers, industrialists, both local and national politicians, and even clerics attended classes with young officers, bringing the soldiers into the national elite. Mexico expanded military education dramatically with the opening of the National Defense College (*Colegio de Defensa Nacional*) in 1981 to award master's degrees. Graduation from the college became a requirement for those who aspired to general rank or a position within the Ministry of Defense.

The development of professional armies had major social consequences throughout Latin America. The skills needed for a modern military could be supplied only through the creation of merit-based jobs with middle-class status. Recruits were drawn from lower and middle social groups rather than from the elites, thus creating a channel for upward mobility. Although first-generation officers might have a tenuous hold on middle-class status, their children easily claimed membership and married within that class. Professionalization of the officer corps also made the military less attractive to the elites. For example, the Chilean army, even before the War of the Pacific, had lost most of its attraction for the elites because of the number of common officers. The navy, traditionally popular with upper-class families, increasingly lost favor as it too became professionalized. Middle-class junior officers became senior military leaders by the early twentieth century, consolidating their hold on the institution.

An example of the military as a channel for social mobility comes from the career of Luis Carlos Prestes (1898–1990), who played a major role in creating the Revolution of 1930 in Brazil and who later served as the leader of the Brazilian Communist Party. Luis's father, a captain, died and left behind five children and an inadequate pension. Luis, the only son, entered a military preparatory school in Rio de Janeiro at age 11 on a scholarship offered by the Ministry of War to needy military sons. His mother gave lessons in music and French and took in sewing. She barely clung to lower-middle-class respectability until the young Prestes graduated first in his class from the military academy and secured the family's social status.

Army officers assumed that hard work, coupled with professional dedication, entitled them to social respect. Their personal struggles often took on heroic and virtuous overtones. Thus, General Humberto Castelo Branco, on retiring from the Brazilian army and in preparation for becoming president after the military coup of 1964, made a point of the fact that his father, "a modest old soldier," had guided his own education in various military schools. As further proof of his middle-class virtues, Castelo Branco listed his financial assets at that moment as a three-year-old Aero-Willys car (an inexpensive subcompact automobile); an apartment in Rio de Janeiro, paid for in part with his wife's inheritance and monthly installments over 10 years; a house destined to go to his children following his wife's death; a few shares of stock in Brazilian companies (a subtle suggestion that he was an economic nationalist); and a cemetery plot. There could be little doubt that the imposed military leader possessed solid middle-class virtues grounded in hard work, thrift, honesty, and family.

Army officers shared with the middle class a strong faith in education and its ability to confer social status. A recent program of the Mexican army incorporated selected noncommissioned personnel into the officer corps, in effect lifting them into the middle class. The program also revealed some of the consequences of social mobility. Although the Mexican army provided sufficient social guidance for the new officers, their wives could not function in the somewhat snooty circles of officers' wives. Reluctantly, the army canceled its program to promote promising enlisted men to the officer ranks. In Bolivia, students can enter the military academy once they reach secondary school age. High school students can enroll in the second year of the military academy. Completion of the academy's program is equivalent to two years of university training. From that point, the curriculum in advanced military schools shifts from military subjects to academic courses, including philosophy, political economy, and sociology. Graduation from the Command and General Staff School in Cochabamba, followed in due course by graduation from the School of Advanced Military Studies, offers the prospect of advancement to the upper levels of the officer corps. Education reinforces social cohesion in the army, forming a technocratic elite with strong middle-class values.

With few exceptions, military officers during the twentieth century have become suspicious of politics and politicians. Officers tend to equate politics with populism and, often, demagoguery. Expenditures to cultivate political support often are perceived as damaging to the country's orderly development. Democratic procedures are not highly valued by those in the hierarchical, disciplined military life. Officers emphasize order, obedience to superiors, and loyalty—traits that are decidedly secondary in importance for politicians, who must serve their constituents. Officers have turned to authoritarian regimes not out of naïveté, but a deeply ingrained belief in the chain of command. Whenever civilian politicians seem out of control, officers turn to authoritarian regimes to restore order. Moreover, in times of crises, a panicky middle class often is tempted to call upon the military for help. At such times, the combination forms an almost irresistible antidemocratic force. Nevertheless, the fickle nature of middle-class support has disappointed many military officers turned political rescuers. Chilean General Carlos Ibáñez, who carried out a series of middle-class reforms in the late 1920s, had to resign following a strike mounted by the middle class in 1931.

Salvador Allende provides an example of the military's impatience with the democratic process. Elected president of Chile in 1970 due to a split in the majority Christian Democrat Party, Allende attempted to move Chile to the socialist left. He eventually faced a hostile alliance among the middle class, the elites, and the army determined to bring his experiment to an end. On September 11, 1973, Chilean air force planes bombed the presidential palace, and Allende died defending his position. A repressive military regime led by President Augusto Pinochet purged the left, reversed radical measures initiated by Allende, and held the country political hostage. Reluctant acceptance of authoritarianism and its harsh measures rested upon the regime's promise of national economic deliverance. Pinochet's successful economic programs enabled him to continue in office until the election of 1980 returned the country to democratic rule. By then the middle class had withdrawn its support. Nevertheless, General Pinochet remained in charge of the army and ignored requests for his resignation. The Chilean military illustrates the institution's readiness to intervene as well as its long-range political limitations.

Pinochet's dictatorship and the dirty wars (so-called because the military and police murdered opponents to the regime) carried out by the military in several Latin American countries in the 1970s should not obscure the important channel of social mobility provided by the army. The Peruvian army in the 1950s is a good example. Junior officers, of lower-middle-class and rural origin, eagerly embraced the concept of civic responsibility taught in the advanced training classes, often given by U.S. military instructors. These young officers initiated major civic action programs—road construction, sanitation works, and public health campaigns—in the Andean region, which helped them forge a bond with the desperately poor

This postcard, distributed during the bloody Chaco War (1932–1935), conveyed the message that the Bolivian government had the situation under control. In fact, Bolivia lost the war and most of the Chaco to a victorious Paraguay, bringing down the Bolivian government. The struggle over resources reemphasized the need for a professional officer corps. For the middle class throughout Latin America, the army provided an important channel of social mobility.

peoples of the Andes. These junior officers led the 1968 military revolution determined to alleviate poverty in Peru (see Chapter 2, Politics).

Other professions have also opened up to members of the lower middle class, who somehow acquired the necessary education, but none to the extent that the military did.

## MODERNIZING WOMANHOOD

Increasing demands for talented, skilled individuals ultimately created opportunities for women, beginning in the nineteenth century. As a result, the social, civic, and legal status of women began to change as the government shifted in the late colonial era from a religious to an economic basis of authority. Some eighteenth-century reformers believed that women should be encouraged to utilize all their productive talents and, moreover, that excluding women hurt the economy. Spain's most important proponent of Enlightened ideas, Benito Feiyóo, wrote in his *Defensa de las Muyeres* (Defense of Women) that women must be allowed to succeed. Another major Enlightenment figure, the Count of Campomanes, complained about the idleness of women imposed by social attitudes and senseless regulation. Despite the efforts of eighteenth-century reformers, social attitudes trailed far behind. Nevertheless, a rough correlation between economic progress and the need to improve the status of women had been established.

In the nineteenth century, economic change further altered the status of women. Values and social attitudes that had caused women to be excluded from certain activities were progressively modified. For example, in 1827 a Brazilian law opened primary schools to female students, but only in gender-segregated classes; its unintended effect was to create teaching positions for educated women. Teaching represented a respectable occupation with at least semiprofessional status. By 1872 women made up one-third of Rio de Janeiro's teachers, and by 1920 three-fourths. In 1879, Brazilian higher education opened its doors to women and progressively broadened the opportunities available to them.

Literacy resulted in the establishment of journals and newspapers directed by and aimed at women. In 1852 Joana Paula Manso de Noronha, an Argentine-Brazilian, created the *Journal das Senhoras* (Women's Journal), which lasted only a short time. Another Brazilian journal, *O Bello Sexo* (The Beautiful Sex), resulted in the formation of a group that met weekly to discuss the paper's contents. Among other efforts, *O Sexo Feminino* (The Feminine Sex), published in Minas Gerais by Francisca Diniz, advocated women's rights as a necessary part of the gigantic steps of progress.

Many Latin American women looked to the United States as a model. A rapidly developing modern nation, the United States seemed to offer women more economic and social opportunities than Europe did. Thus, Brazilian students attending Cornell University advocated in the student newspaper the admission of women to higher education institutions in Brazil. The women's rights newspaper *O Domingo* (Sunday) reprinted the article with approval. Midcentury Brazilians avidly followed the academic progress of Maria Augusta Generosa, who attended medical school in New York. Emperor Pedro II graciously contributed financial assistance during the course of her studies. Dr. Generosa returned in triumph to establish a medical practice devoted to women and children. She inspired other women to follow her example, although not until 1887 did a woman, Rita Lobato, receive a medical degree in Brazil. Chile permitted women to earn professional degrees as early as 1877. As a result, in 1866 Eloísa Díaz became the first woman to earn a Latin American medical degree. Six years later Matilde Throup became the first female lawyer in Chile and Latin America.

Books and magazines encouraged women to broaden their horizons, especially through education. In the 1830s, Patrona Rosenda de Siera published the magazine *La Aljaba* (The Tremor) in Buenos Aires, advocating that women be schooled along European lines. She maintained that educated women would be more effective, less frivolous wives and mothers. Subsequently, in 1852 Rosa Guerra's magazine, *La Camelia,* promoted education as a means of making women fit companions for educated males. She later established *La Educación,*

A black street vendor, photographed in about 1880, is dressed in an embroidered blouse, African shawl, several necklaces of worked silver and gold, rings, and amulets. Women dominated street vending in Bahia, Brazil, into the early twentieth century. Their dress mirrored their economic and social successes. Such women, while all but ignored by elite women reformers, participated in the process of modernizing women's roles on a day-to-day basis. Many lower-class women throughout Latin America have assumed leadership posts within their communities.

another magazine filled with material for women and translated from French and English. Guerra pressed on with her campaign to educate women through newspapers, novels, and a children's book titled *Julia y su Educación* (Julia and Her Education).

Some prominent men, particularly those influenced by European and North American ideas, supported greater opportunities for women. They believed that in modern nations women must participate fully in society, economics, and politics. One of the most ardent supporters of change in the role of women was Domingo F. Sarmiento. While in exile in Chile during the 1830s and 1840s, he advised women to delay marrying until they had obtained their education. He believed that it was in the national interest for women to be educated and eventually participate fully in public life. Later, as governor of Buenos Aires province, he pushed through reforms giving educated women limited suffrage. Sarmiento placed women in important governmental posts, usually within the education ministry.

Many advocates of women's education tried to blend traditional roles with new needs rather than press for radical change. Thus, the noted Puerto Rican writer Eugenio María de Hostos suggested that women needed an education in order to develop in a psychologically healthy fashion that would make them better mothers and wives. In effect, everyone stood to gain as a result of a woman's education. In Mexico, the wife of President Porfirio Díaz, Carmen Romero Rubio de Díaz, symbolized change in the status of women. As the president's young second wife, she projected an image of freshness and modernity.

Well educated, fluent in English, and with a lively, intelligent mind, doña Carmen suggested the unlimited opportunities that awaited the modern woman.

Characteristically, during the early stages of the process, elite upper-class women often led the way with the encouragement of their families and politicians who believed that economic modernization required corresponding social change.

At this time, the women's movement functioned as part of the modernization effort promoted by the elites. A number of nineteenth-century Mexican modernizers married foreign women, thus indicating by their personal action their desire for a partner able to function far beyond the domestic sphere. Professionally trained women, here and there, became active in business. The Honduran Nina Luisa studied photography in Havana in the 1850s, for example, and returned to establish a studio in Tegucigalpa. In addition to a seemingly continuous stream of "first" female professionals, women made publicly recognized intellectual contributions. Gabriela Mistral, a young schoolteacher, won the 1914 Chilean poetry contest, and 31 years later became the first Latin American, male or female, to receive the Nobel Prize for literature. Brazil had its own trailblazer, attractive and daring 20-year-old aviatrix Anesia Pinheiro Machado, who took to the air in 1922 and lived long enough to hold the world's oldest pilot's license. The celebrity status of women such as these obscured the plight of their less prominent sisters, who struggled in silence within the broader process of urban industrialization and technological innovation.

Working-class women labored along with their children, husbands, and other household members, out of sheer necessity. A Brazilian textile union estimated in 1913 that a family of four required twice the amount earned by the highest paid male factory worker to meet its needs. Unexpected events—illness, layoffs, or wage reductions—plunged the family into disaster. Food intake, never excessive even under normal conditions, could easily drop to a cup of coffee and a crust of bread. Unionization of female workers in a surplus labor market proved difficult. Workingwomen often held jobs characterized by high turnover, making union organizing problematic. Moreover, many union leaders shared the traditional notion that women should remain in the home, but they recognized that necessity forced these women into factory work. Union men believed the solution was to increase male wages so women could remain at home. Such an attitude made the issue of equal pay for equal work secondary to increasing male compensation.

Some anarchists and socialists, although not all, proved more sympathetic. The Second Socialist Congress of 1902 supported equal pay, political and judicial equality, and the extension of the vote to women. Many anarchists in pursuit of ideological purity supported equality across the board, including the notion of free love. Some anarchist women accepted and practiced sexual freedom, but it appealed more to predatory males. Such self-indulgent radicalism constituted an attack on the family and disregarded the single mother's struggle to survive. Most women understood that love might be free, but the social and economic consequences of it certainly were not. This became an obstacle to women's participation in the anarchist movement. Anarchist Giovanni Rossi, lamenting the rejection of free love, proposed buying Indian girls, free of bourgeois influence, to participate in a new anarchist settlement.

A high point in establishing the legitimacy of working-class demands came with the papal encyclical *Rerum Novarum* (1893), which provided a moral basis for fair wages and reasonable working conditions throughout the Catholic world. Nevertheless, the papal pronouncement undercut the demands of women workers. The pope declared that biology intended women to remain at home attending to their families, whereas the responsibility to provide financial support rested on the men. Bialet Massé, author of an Argentine government survey of the workplace, noted that "work for women is unacceptable except for the misfortune of destiny. . . ." Nevertheless, Massé supported the idea of equal pay on the grounds of basic fairness. Ambivalence toward the notion of women in the workplace encompassed sympathy, fear of competition, and worry about the impact on the family—a combination of concerns that acted to impede efforts to confront the exhausting demands of poverty and the reality of work.

Legislation reflected social ambivalence. The Mexican civil codes of 1870 and 1884 altered the patriarchal basis of the family. The *patria potestad,* formerly reserved for males, now passed to the widow or separated mother and included legal recognition of equal responsibility for care of children. A woman would have the right, at age 21, to manage her own property, enter into contracts, and marry without paternal permission. The Civil Code of 1870 provided for legal separation based on a couple's own wishes, thereby disregarding religious restrictions on family dissolution. Although the code recognized the importance of compatibility in marriage, it still prohibited actual divorce and therefore remarriage. The dowry, already slipping into disuse, was dropped as a legal prerequisite for marriage. Perhaps more important, the code abolished the guarantee of equal sharing of property among surviving children. The cumulative effect of such changes left women unprotected, subordinate to the social reality of male economic dominance, and dependent on manipulative skills. Such legal modification had little impact or relevance for the lower classes, where poverty eclipsed all issues, including gender.

Argentines legislated restrictions in 1907 on a woman's workday, limiting work hours, mandating rest periods, establishing the right to infant care, and prohibiting women from engaging in dangerous and unhealthy work. The province of Santa Fe, following the allegedly progressive lead of Buenos Aires, forbade employment of women in 36 industries, including chemicals, liquor, and certain types of textile manufacturing. Legislators asserted that their efforts protected the vulnerable and weaker sex. Such legislation represented a cultural reaction to economic and technological developments and at the same time shored up traditional values in defiance of the emerging economic reality. Exclusion, justified as protection, provided for a male monopoly of certain types of work. The considerable physical demands gave men a gender monopoly in mining and to a large extent in agriculture and manufacturing. Nevertheless, continual modernization of machines, notably in textiles, and the replacement of steam power with electricity progressively decreased the demand for physical strength. Thus, lower wages, coupled with less taxing machinery, made increased use of female workers feasible. Gender-based wages also made women more attractive to employers eager to reduce costs. The shift away from the emphasis on

This well-to-do *campesino* (rural) family was photographed on their way to Cuernavaca, Mexico, in 1904, on the eve of the Mexican Revolution. The burro both extended and limited the distance rural inhabitants traveled and in effect defined their world.

physical strength favored women over the long term and introduced gender competition for jobs.

The emergence of white-collar jobs also opened up semiprofessional positions for women. In the 1880s, Buenos Aires relied on a few secretarial schools to supply female clerical workers. Women attended a Crafters and Service Institute to learn dress design, glove making, lace fabrication, and bookbinding, as well as laundering and ironing. A coeducational commercial high school, opened in 1912, trained women for more responsible positions in banking and business. Professionalization of health care led to the establishment of a nursing school in 1886. The tendency to view female labor as marginal, despite the fact that women constituted 22 percent of the labor force by 1914 and an even greater percentage of low-paid workers, impeded the expansion of educational opportunities for women.

Upward mobility through education developed slowly. In Argentina, a National Girls High School, established in 1905, prepared young women for entrance into the national university. By 1910, 25 female university graduates had entered the professions. The reputation of the Girls High School attracted talented students but accommodated only a small enrollment. Nevertheless, the growing number of women professionals demonstrated the social utility of female education. Foreign visitors, such as the Italian educator Maria Montessori, who lectured at the Girls High School as well as at the university and elsewhere, added international support for the education of women.

Social change, impelled by economic change, inevitably had an impact on women's status and modes of behavior. Women who went too far beyond acceptable limits became vulnerable to charges of plotting to overturn gender roles. The Mexican newspaper *Excelsior* (1925) published a cartoon showing a very masculinized woman ensconced in what had previously been the male head of household's easy chair, cigar in hand, reading the financial pages of a newspaper. Ragged, weeping children fruitlessly pleaded for attention while the woman's husband cowered in the kitchen. The 1920s—*los años locos,* the crazy years, in Argentina—constituted a new stage for women. Radio broke the isolation of women across space and individual circumstances as it sought to capture a broad audience in the effort to market all sorts of new products and services. Tango music, previously associated with aggressive male dominance, disposable women, drinking, and casual attitudes toward respectable society in general, underwent a process of gentrification as it wafted across the airwaves. Radio began the process of a unisex modification of culture as "Women cut their hair, supposedly tried to be men, smoked, drank whiskey and wore pants." According to the lyrics of a popular 1924 tango, *La mina del Ford* (The Skirt with a Ford), the modern woman wanted material rewards, "an apartment with a balcony, gas heat, waxed floors, carpets, beds with mattresses, and a maid to announce 'Madam, the Ford is here.'" Few in fact could afford such a lifestyle. The tango's words captured, in exaggerated fashion, women's desire for a modern life free of the domestic drudgery associated with traditional ways and archaic attitudes. Thanks to radio, the message fell on distant ears across the land and even beyond national borders.

In Mexico, leaders and politicians used radio to broadcast a message of change. The widely held perception that women tended to be politically conservative and Catholic, and thus only marginally committed to the Mexican Revolution of 1910, motivated revolutionary leaders to develop mass media tools. President Lázaro Cárdenas established a federal department of press and publicity. Radio XEFO, the ruling party's station, coordinated propaganda efforts to enlist women in the movement for change. A symbolic high point came when the broadcast of independence day ceremonies in Mexico City (September 15, 1938) reached a national radio audience for the first time. Literacy campaigns further broadened lower-class and rural women's perspectives and suggested that the old ways had chained them to a poverty of mind and body. Reading programs elevated female literacy from 24 percent in 1910 to 42 percent in 1940. Technology played an important role in altering women's lives, and propaganda encouraged them to utilize it.

Technological advances altered the traditional gender balance of time and task within the family. A simple, yet profound, change involved the *metate,* the grinding stone used by Mexican women to grind the corn used to prepare the *masa* from which tortillas are formed. The arrival of large grinding machines now made it possible to prepare enough masa for the entire community. Although women lined up early in the morning to purchase the fresh masa, the time and effort devoted to food preparation had been reduced significantly. Stoves replaced charcoal fires and lifted the work surface off the ground, much to the physical relief of the cook. Better distribution of water, with the introduction of pumps, eased the daily chore of providing water for the family. Freedom from mundane tasks allowed women to focus on other types of modern work and contemplate becoming involved in the broader sociopolitical life of the region and nation far beyond their traditional space. Women had always played an important role in village life, often aggressively defending the well-being of their community and family. Modern conditions now moved them from reaction to initiating desirable changes. Working in the context of urban poverty and drawing upon their local experience, women established an array of community organizations. Consumer cooperatives, *favela* and *barrio* associations, and self-help and personal improvement groups came to depend on women as members as well as leaders. The various organizations applied political pressure at virtually all levels of the government.

## THE WOMEN'S SUFFRAGE MOVEMENT

The conviction that modernization required a significant degree of gender equality made the issue of women's participation in politics a topic of public discussion. Those involved in the women's suffrage movement understood that eventually equality must be political as well as economic and social. Nevertheless, because of historical and perceptual factors, the drive for the vote in Latin America lacked the emotional intensity of similar movements in Europe and the United States. Everyone understood that male suffrage historically had a marginal impact on who ruled and how. Political corruption, blatant disregard for constitutional requirements overturning electoral results, and outright seizure of the government often made male suffrage a mere formality. Its existence, however, served to reinforce the idea that politics functioned as a male preserve. Thus, Julieta Lanteri-Renshaw ran for the Argentine congress in 1919 to make the point that the lack of the franchise denied the full adulthood of women.

Many feminists accepted the notion that women in general, especially lower-class women, held conservative values incompatible with the needs of modernization. To extend the vote to such women might be counterprogressive. Indeed, when Ecuador became the first Latin American nation to enfranchise women in 1929, it did so under a conservative government. The Brazilian feminist Bertha Lutz had a little more faith in the mixture of women and politics and promoted suffrage as a means of accomplishing legislative reforms.

A 1922 women's conference in Baltimore, Maryland, well attended by Latin Americans, supported women's suffrage throughout the hemisphere. In Havana a National Women's Congress met in 1923, and representatives from 31 women's groups participated. Another Cuban congress two years later called for social equality and equal pay for equal work, among other objectives. As a result of the Baltimore meeting, a number of new organizations formed under the umbrella of the newly established Pan American Association for the Advancement of Women. Bertha Lutz, fresh from the conference, established the Brazilian Federation for the Advancement of Women, which in turn sponsored the Brazilian Female Suffrage Alliance, directed by the wives of prominent politicians. The Federation actively supported the International Labor Organization's recommendation on the status of female workers and passed a resolution condemning the inferior position of women in the competition for industrial and agricultural salaries. Lutz's efforts laid the groundwork for the eventual extension of the vote to Brazilian women in 1932. The battle, however, was far from won. Lutz failed to win national office in the 1933 elections, in which women voted for the first time. Only one woman was elected. Carlota Pereira de Queiroz, from an elite São Paulo family, relied on family connections to win office. Elections in 1934 and 1935 proved more encouraging, particularly at the state level. In 1936, Lutz, elected as an alternate, became a deputy upon the death of the incumbent. Unfortunately, the establishment of the *Estado Novo* (New State) in 1937, following a coup, ended political participation in general. Women lost most of the gains they had made in the previous decade. In 1940, a discouraged Lutz wrote to U.S. feminist leader Carrie Chapman Catt and said that Brazilian women had failed to "hold all that was conquered."

Although the women's suffrage drive constituted an elite movement, psychologically the struggle for gender equality involved all women. Literacy, radio, and, beginning in the 1960s, television broadened expectations and inadvertently provided political expertise and skills across class lines. Urbanization created concentrated populations and facilitated the dissemination of information by the media. *Fotonovelas,* which combined still photography with balloon captions, posed problem scenarios and suggested possible solutions to life's everyday dramas. Although comic books provided a higher level of fantasy than other forms of print media, they frequently emphasized ideal contrasts between good and evil, often involving authority figures gone bad. Newspapers and scandal sheets made the point that politicians, the rich and wellborn, had feet of clay and very human vices. The elites lost their monopoly over the definition of how and why things are—the lower classes believed themselves competent to assist in creating social realities within which they would play a part.

# 6

# Religions

Religious beliefs and practices have framed much of the everyday lives of Latin Americans since prehistoric times. The great indigenous cultures had religious structures that guided economic and social activities. The European conquerors came to the Americas as crusaders to convert the peoples they encountered, or used the goal of conversion as a justification for their imperial and personal economic ambitions. Their success can be seen in the fact that in Latin America today the majority identify themselves as Roman Catholics, and Catholicism, despite tremendous inroads by Evangelical Protestants, expanding Jewish groups, and reconstituted African faiths, remains the defining context of daily life. Roman Catholicism marks architecture, language, holidays, domestic life, and hopes for the future, despite the official separation of church and state throughout the region.

## THE CHURCH AND INDEPENDENT STATES

Competition between the church and state in Europe emerged as monarchies consolidated their power and drew away from Rome. Eventually, the Vatican and European monarchs established working agreements. In the New World, Rome allowed both the Spanish and the Portuguese to nominate bishops and decide which papal pronouncements would be allowed to go into effect in their possessions, as well as collect the tithe to meet the expense of the Church in the Americas. This arrangement began to unravel in the eighteenth century as the Enlightenment led to a more secular approach to politics, society, and church-state relations. The Church, mindful of the political shift, responded by attempting to withdraw from an arrangement that subordinated clerics to state officials. After independence, the Church challenged the use of colonial prerogatives by the independent states. Many argued for a larger role for the Church in daily life, whereas the liberals wanted to exclude the Church as much as possible. Conflicting views hardened into categorical divisions with scant give and take. Politicians and citizens in Latin America thought in absolute terms about good and evil. Their insistence on imposing moral absolutes on political divisions made compromise impossible, a circumstance played out time and again through violence.

Categorical politics suffused with the language and symbols of religion can be identified throughout the political history of the region: from the regime of Juan Manuel Rosas (1829–1852) to the military's Dirty War (1970–1983) in Argentina; from the campaign against the Counselor at Canudos to the grassroots politics of *samba* clubs and Christian Base Communities in Brazil; from the nineteenth-century raging of caudillos (Gabriel García Moreno in Ecuador and Antonio Guzmán Blanco in Venezuela) to the twentieth-century pronouncements of revolutionaries (the Tupamaros in Uruguay, Montoneros in Argentina) and death squads. Politics provided a forum for imposing categorical judgments, not for compromise.

Political corruption also became widespread. Branded by their opponents as guilty of embezzlement for draining public revenues, politicians rarely convinced anyone they were honest. Whatever peculation occurred, it rarely reached the levels of the charges made by those who identified nothing but evil in the previous regime. Such moral absolutes encouraged corruption; found guilty in the public forum, many felt it only fair to profit after the charges were already made against them. Corruption received, if not approval, at least acquiescence from the general public, as did the moral failures of individual priests. Believers did not hold the Church responsible for the transgressions of its priests, who, after all, were only human. Politicians, too, were viewed not as social avatars, but only fallible individuals. In this way, vernacular religion carried with it a pattern for politics. Tolerance for personal failings on the part of politicians opened the way for periodic moral crusades against graft, corruption, and peculation in public life that matched the campaigns to reinvigorate the Church. Official relations between church and state affected the formal religious practices at the higher social levels.

Catholicism, with its pantheon of saints, belief in the Trinity, and copious apparitions of the Virgin, provided a matrix that local people modified through community practices. Theological flexibility at the bottom contrasted sharply with rigid formalism at the top political and social levels. The universe of saints, relics, and miracles expanded to reach local holy persons who became living expressions of devotion, charity, modesty, and abnegation. Parishes and shrines preserved the material remains and possessions of these sainted persons and combined them with relics and mementos from pilgrimages and international shrines and the proofs of miracles. Miraculous occurrences framed folklore and parables, cautionary and hortatory tales for the young, and telling gossip for the older members of the community.

Liberal leaders in Latin American republics determined to remove the Church from practices they believed needed the supervision of civic officials, particularly education; charity; governmental affairs, such as public marriage, birth, and death registers; justice, abolishing separate Church courts; and economic enterprises, such as loans and agricultural and urban rental properties. Church leaders responded. Pope Pius IX directed Mexican Catholics, under threat of excommunication, to reject Mexico's Liberal Constitution of 1857, which opened the way for religious tolerance by remaining silent on making Roman Catholicism the official church. The War of the Reform (1858–1861) followed. The pope continued his assault on Liberalism in the *Syllabus of Errors* of 1864, in which he censured rationalism for its connection to progress and Liberalism. He forbade a series of individual liberties and described freedom of religion and the press and the separation of church and state as depraved, false, perverse, and detestable opinions. His statements inspired strident forces in Colombia, who squared off over the church–state question. The Liberals tried to establish freedom of religion and create other reforms, a move that led to sporadic but vicious civil war during the 1860s. The Liberal–Conservative struggle in Ecuador resulted in the assassination of the deeply religious president, Gabriel García Moreno, attacks on his Liberal successor, and arguments about the meaning of the eruption of the volcano Cotopaxi in 1877. The question was whether God prompted the eruption because of the Liberal attack on the Church or because churchmen had closed churches and withheld sacraments from the people.

Although these bitter struggles predominated in the capital cities and in national politics, community practices continued. Conservatives and most Liberals continued to recognize the patron saints of towns and neighborhoods. Foreign travelers noted the prevalence of festivals in honor of these local saints. Elizabeth Agassiz, visiting west of Manaus in the Amazon basin in 1865, reported on community celebrations, "festas are celebrated at different sitios in turn, the saint of the day being carried, with all his ornaments, candles, bouquets, . . . to the house where the ceremony is to take place, and where all the people of the village congregate. Sometimes the festa lasts for several days, and is accompanied with processions, music and dances in the evening."[1]

In local communities, hybrid mixtures of religious practices and parallel beliefs emerged. The Church hierarchy chose to ignore them or praise them as adaptations that helped propagate the faith. During the early nineteenth century, Afro-Catholic vernacular faiths emerged, and Indian–Catholic admixtures appeared. Essential in these vernacular religions was participation through confession, devotion to saints or the cross, and appearances in processions or possession by spirits. The participatory occasions—festivals, processions, pilgrimages, and possessions—provided not only the opportunity to engage with divine powers and display faith but also the occasion to mock political, Church, and social leaders and reverse the registers of life—sex, power, ethnicity, and age—by turning the world upside down. The overriding organization of these events reflected broader community interests.[2] Often the festive or carnivalesque references were so narrowly local that the criticism implicit in these weapons of the weak and the deeply satisfying satirical humor eluded later spectators, especially because they generally had to rely on written accounts. Nevertheless, on occasion these aspects leap out, in

---

[1] June E. Hahner, ed., *Women through Women's Eyes: Latin American Women in Nineteenth-Century Travel Accounts* (Wilmington, DE: SR Books, 1998), p. 139.

[2] See David Guss, *"Indianness" and the Construction of Ethnicity in the Day of the Monkey,* University of Maryland Latin American Studies Center Series, no. 9 (1995).

Courtesy of the Latin America Library at Tulane University.

Catholic symbols, rites, and relics, real or imagined, form an important element of popular religion. Here an alleged tooth of St. Dominic is displayed in appropriate splendor for Mexican believers.

spirit possessions, mock epitaphs and confessions, and last testaments. Too often the largely inexplicable but crucial elements in these celebrations remained unrecorded, brushed aside as failures to do it properly, and therefore evidence of the backwardness of local people.

The vernacular character of these approaches to everyday life found expression in the personal nature of home altars. A family's assemblage usually appeared to be Roman Catholic, but included personal additions that often made this claim little more than a hopeful assertion. Four categories of items customarily appeared in each altar grouping: flowers, lithographs, crosses, and personal miscellany. Besides their intrinsic semiotics, the flowers possessed a lexicon of color and scent. Later in the nineteenth century, photographs of family members held an honored place. Beyond crucifixes, none of these items, including cross designs or patterns, had exclusive Catholic significance. The personal items included images of saints or the

Virgin, palm work, small glasses of water, candles, relics of pilgrimages and personal miracles, and mementos of deceased family members.

Home altars had two roles. Some were for everyday devotion, and others were prepared especially for certain holiday seasons. A description of a home altar from Valparaíso, Chile, in 1822 comes from Lady Calcott, wife of the captain of a visiting British man-of-war, who told of a visit to a typical home:

> On a table in a corner, under a glass case, I saw a little religious baby work—a waxen Jesus an inch long, sprawls on a waxen Virgin's knee, surrounded by Joseph, the oxen and asses, all of the same goodly material, decorated with moss and sea shells. Near this, I observed a pot of beautiful flowers, and two pretty-shaped silver utensils, which I at first took for implements of worship and then for inkstands, but I discovered that one was a little censer for burning pastile, with which the young women perfume their handkerchiefs and mantos [cloak], and the other the vase for holding the infusion of the herb of Paraguay, commonly called mate [sic], so universally drank or rather sucked here.

In early 1880, another traveler, Amie Sampson Poole, praised an altar, "a blaze of flowers and tinsel," made especially for the Christmas holidays by one of her maids in Guanajuato, Mexico. After describing the beautiful candles, hung with "wreaths of little white wax bells," and "two little coloured glasses" filled with holy water, she added, "At the very top of the altar—and it was a high erection—was a large looking-glass, in front of which stood a little wax figure of the Virgin, crowned with gold and dressed in a splendid blue silk robe, embroidered in gold and silver."[3]

Vernacular Catholicism, or popular religion, also affected the communities' fabricated environment in many ways beyond the obvious temples of worship. Until the secular movements took hold in the mid-nineteenth century, the streets bore (and many still do) the names of saints, martyrs, and holy events. Thus in the words of Mariano Cuevas, an ordained priest and Mexican historian, "Our streets were God's streets." Religion also had an impact on architecture. Cuevas continued, "the cross crowned the entryways of our buildings; devout niches dedicated to a particular saint—so typical—each with its own little lantern, adorned our corners." Outside of town, Cuevas romanticized, "our fields were God's, their best flowers were for the church altars and their newly harvested wheat stalks were the classic decoration for home altars to Our Lady of Sorrows." Of course, the language contained sayings and parables with religious references. Cuevas noted that Mexicanisms had the mark of the Church: "'Whatever souls may come'; 'What a miracle to see you again!'; 'Those Saint Peter left'; 'It's as soon as a dance at Chalma'; 'Don't break the fast at fifteen minutes to midnight.'" And, of course, the same comments could be made for Colombia, Peru, Guatemala, or Cuba and the languages of those nations. Even the social hierarchy could be identified with,

---

[3]Hahner, ed., *Women through Women's Eyes*, p. 29; "A Resident [Amie Sampson Poole]," *Mexicans at Home in the Interior* [Guanajuato] (London: Chapman and Hall, Ltd., 1884), pp. 96–97.

or at least became associated with, certain practices the Church regarded as venial sins. Thus it was widely held that "among Indians, drunkenness seemed to dominate; among Blacks and Mulattoes, robbery and superstition; among mestizos, libertine propensities, untrustworthiness, and theft; among creoles, gambling; and among Spaniards, greed."[4]

As the end of the nineteenth century approached, Latin America experienced a growing encounter with the products of the industrial and scientific revolutions; vernacular versions of faith instilled the principle that some aspects of life are irreconcilable. Quite properly, good and evil cannot be reconciled. A corollary added that some challenges, improved technology notwithstanding, prove insolvable for men and women alone. To this way of thinking, many promises of progress sound hollow or irrelevant or misguided. What observers have dismissed as ignorant traditional resistance to change was instead the belief that change did not and could not work.

In between modern and traditional societies, individuals emerged who acted as bridges between the two communities, the two systems of knowledge, and the two ways of life. Some of these individuals were considered city fools, the Duke of Roca Negras in Caracas and Nicolás Zúñiga y Miranda in Mexico City, for example; others developed followings as folk saints. Representative of the latter was Miguel Perdomo Neira, a folk healer (also called an empiric or *curandero*) in the 1860s and 1870s, who claimed he cured illnesses and performed operations in over 1,290 Andean villages and towns of southern Colombia and Ecuador. In the year 1872 alone, he reportedly treated some 1,200 persons in Bogotá. His widespread popularity grew from reports that he used herbal potions that enabled him to perform minor surgery without causing pain, swelling, or excessive bleeding. He generally charged nothing for his services, explaining that healing was his Christian obligation. Disputes erupted when Perdomo and his followers challenged university-trained doctors, medical students, and hospital workers, who regarded him as a quack. The clash between the two sides represented the division between Hispanic medicine, which was a blend of Catholic healing beliefs and the balance of bodily fluids with the beliefs of indigenous peoples, Africans, or both; and that of rationalist, scientific medicine, or biomedicine.

Apparently Perdomo had something of a reputation as a healer before the Colombian civil war (1859–1862) because he was assigned to the field hospital of the Conservative, pro-Church forces. Following the Liberal victory, he sought refuge in an indigenous community in Caquetá, where he learned the medical secrets of the Indians, especially their use of medicinal herbs. His medical practice, combining this knowledge with the Catholic framework of healing, was reflected in the decision to name his hacienda San Juan de Díos, for the patron saint of the ill and hospitals. He left Caquetá after two or three years and began to travel the northern Andes to provide health care to the needy.

Perdomo's emergence as a folk saint exemplified the common connection between healers and sainthood, which continued after his death in 1874 during an

---

[4]Cuevas is cited in Mills and Taylor, pp. 355–357.

epidemic in Guayaquil. Most early saints were sanctified as martyrs; but during the medieval years, the majority of saints earned their status through charitable works. The healing power of the saints continued at their shrines. Perdomo and other folk saints had an ambiguous character. Writing in *La Ilustración,* May 7, 1872, Maria Madiedo reported that opinion about Perdomo was sharply divided. "For some, Perdomo was a wise man, a wizard, a man of providence, or perhaps a demi-god. Others ridiculed these sentiments, claiming that he was nothing more than a demonic, audacious charlatan."[5] This difference of opinion characterized the attitudes toward many folk saints of popular religion.

Vernacular Catholicism also suggested, or provided, organization and activities for those who challenged the emerging state regimes. In the great rebellions—Tupac Amaru in the Andes in the 1780s, the Mayan Caste Wars of Yucatán in the 1840s, and the rebellion of the backlanders of Brazil in the 1880s—religious forms prevailed. Among the Maya, the early leaders in the struggle named their own priest. This individual was "equipped with a device for pressing out hosts [communion wafers]; they also used captured creole priests to provide religious service for their troops. Their movement, the Speaking Cross, was the culmination of a process which used religion as an instrument for popular mobilization."[6]

The era of Enlightened demands for change both within and without the Church did not end with a clear-cut victory for either side. Both the representatives of Caesar and Church learned how to live, albeit often uneasily, with each other.

## COMPETITION WITH CAPITALISM: MARXISM AND REVOLUTION, 1891–1962

The papal encyclical on capital and labor, *Rerum Novarum,* issued by Pope Leo XIII in 1892, represents a change of paradigm just short in magnitude of the Galilean recognition that the Earth circled the Sun rather than the reverse. Resisting the homogenizing forces of industrialization, urbanization, and modernization, the pope declared divine support for local variations of society and the Church to replace the insistence on a uniform Christendom (although in practice, as we have seen, vernacular practices had existed for centuries). This papal decree allowed for numerous Church-sponsored labor unions across Europe; mutual associations of workers in Mexico, Argentina, and elsewhere; and even political parties. None in Latin America, however, experienced the success of those in Germany, until after World War II, when successful Christian Democratic parties emerged in Venezuela, Costa Rica, and Chile.

---

[5] Sowell, "Miguel Perdomo Neira," pp. 1–3.

[6] Terry Rugeley, "The Caste War: Rural Insurgency in Nineteenth-Century Yucatán," in Daniel Castro, ed., *Revolution and Revolutionaries in Latin America* (Wilmington, DE: SR Books, forthcoming).

In these circumstances that began in the 1890s, the Church advocated a new evangelization campaign, better training for priests, and greater concern for the poor. Nevertheless, as this operation began, space remained for a number of popular saints who received national, even international, publicity. In Mexico, Santa Teresa of Caborca in northwestern Chihuahua became a rallying symbol of rebellion against the agents of modernization in the region. In Venezuela, José Gregorio Hernández, from the Andean state of Trujillo, combined Christian piety with European medical and scientific training to epitomize what the Church represented in this new age. His tragic death in a bizarre Caracas streetcar accident expressed for many the negative side of modernization. San Gregorio, as a folk saint, is reported to have healed people, even to have performed surgery. On occasion, stories report that holy water with curative powers seeps from his tomb. Vendors outside churches and in curanderos' shops sell prayer cards with his image. Moreover, as his popularity has increased, his image has appeared on murals, on home altars, and adorning automobiles. In Colombia, the healing cult has taken on more spiritualistic ramifications, such as in Brother Walter's Puerto Tejada *Centro Hospitalario de José Gregario,* where he calls upon doctors' spirits to guide him in his surgical procedures. Indian healers in Putumayo also use José Gregorio's curative powers.[7] Venezuelan Church leaders promoted his sanctification and his popularity as a holy man. San Gregorio has a large following today in Venezuela, Colombia, and Ecuador, especially Guayaquil. His image and prayer can be purchased throughout the Andes, including Peru, and even in the southwestern region of the United States.

At the turn of the century, several well-known individuals incorporated the practice of using intercessors in secular activities. Carmen Romero Rubio, for example, developed the role of Mexican First Lady as intercessor between the people and President Porfirio Díaz. Petitioners asked her to intercede with the president on their behalf for pensions or army pay or pardons. The pattern she initiated reached its apogee in Argentina, where Evita, in melodramatic fashion, emerged as the intercessor between the people and her husband, President Juan Perón. She created the Eva Perón Foundation, which sponsored orphanages, hospitals, and sports programs in addition to the social programs available in the capital city. She delivered sewing machines to poor women, brought help to the needy, and provided comfort to the distressed. María Delgado de Odría, wife of Peruvian president Manuel Odría, imitated Eva Perón in the 1950s when she made frequent and highly publicized visits to the slums of Lima, the capital city, where she distributed food and money. Journalists reported, "Her hands open, sincere, friendly, extend toward the suffering poor of Lima," thus calling to mind numerous religious icons of vernacular religion.

The actions of Carmen, Evita, and María drew on a tradition dating to the early colonial era: the appeal to intercessors for solutions to personal problems and crises. The relationship between the individual and the intercessor was based on

---

[7]Sowell, "Miguel Perdomo Neira," chapter 4, p. 14.

offering assistance and comfort in exchange for devotion. This practice, resting on mutual obligations in personal relationships, carried over to secular affairs.

During the two decades from 1890 to 1910, great emphasis was placed on the well-being of family and children through national public hygiene departments (especially in Argentina), charitable welfare campaigns (in Mexico), and international meetings of the Pan American Union. Although some saw the family as the template for larger social organizations in Latin America, in fact, vernacular religion organized the family, dictated politics, and regulated religion. Various national and international campaigns attempted to enact reforms and provide assistance to women and children, but they did not challenge the popularly held views, derived from the Church, of the roles of father, mother, and child.

Populism in the twentieth century often relied on political intercessors. Mexican president Lázaro Cárdenas became known as *Tata* (a diminutive of father) because he listened to individuals relate their problems, one after another, the way a priest heard confessions. Once he became president, Cárdenas set aside certain hours on a regular basis for Mexicans to send him telegrams, free of charge, to request assistance or ask for expressions of comfort.

In a similar fashion, Peruvian political leaders drew on this tradition of intercessors from popular religion. Luis Sánchez Cerro appealed to the masses in Peru. When he campaigned for president in 1931, he played on his ethnicity—a dark-skinned *mestizo*—to emphasize common origins. Identifying with the masses and the poor made him approachable; voters sought out his campaign headquarters to speak with him in person and perhaps request small favors. He acted as the usual patron—or more specifically as the *padre protector* (protective father)—who secured their daily bread. Raúl Haya de la Torre, leader of the extremely important APRA political movement, appealed not to street vendors and day laborers but to organized workers in the same era. He styled himself as the "Father of Workers" and "Father of APRA" in reference to the family religious template, God the Father and the Mother Church. Fernando Belaúnde Terry used populist techniques based on popular religion in his 1962 campaign. He toured the nation *pueblo por pueblo* and in the Andes he reported, "in the cold of the highlands I once again donned with pride my Huaraz poncho, with the same solemnity as a priest would don his sacred vestments to recite a prayer for the past, present and future of Peru."[8]

Mexican popular religion has been the subject of much study, epitomized in Octavio Paz's classic *The Labyrinth of Solitude,* which relies for much of its analysis on the discussion of *guadalupanism* (the importance of the Virgin of Guadalupe) in national life. The prevalence of the Virgin in Mexican popular religion is evident in all forms of media. Representations of the Virgin of Guadalupe are prominent in high art, popular art and handicrafts, and the body art of both individuals (tattoos) and automobiles (on hoods and trunk lids). In popular music, Fernando Rosas had a World War II hit record, whose A side was titled *"Traigo mi .45"* and

---

[8]These examples from Peru are taken from Steve J. Stein, unpublished essay, "Populism in Peru."

Courtesy of Champion Latin American Collection, Tucson, Arizona.

Juan Soldado (idiomatically translated as GI Joe) was killed trying to escape after being convicted of murder in Tijuana, Baja California de Norte in February of 1938. How he became a folk saint raises intriguing questions about popular religion and culture. A poor enlisted soldier and murderer in life, who after death heals the sick and comforts the wretched, offers the hope of redemption to everyone.

B side *"Corrido de los bravucones,"* in which he called on all Mexicans to unite under Guadalupe's banner to defeat the nation's enemies.

When faced with difficult circumstances, many people in Mexico and throughout the region turned to popular religion, and still do, when neither education nor experience were of any help. One situation, common to many Mexicans, was crossing the border into the United States without documents. This undertaking has resulted in new expressions of popular religion. Many preparing to cross the Rio Grande first offer a prayer to the *Virgen de Los Lagos,* and if successful, make a votive offering to record the miracle of her assistance. Farther west, many who cross from Tijuana into California call on the assistance of Juan Soldado—GI Joe (Juan Castillo Morales), a folk saint whose grave has become a shrine. Stranger still, the drug traffickers operating along the southwestern border of the United States have adopted as their patron saint the popular outlaw Jesús Malverde.

Health has remained a major area in which popular religion has influenced the community in Latin America. A powerful healing cult, for example, surrounds the Costa Rican doctor Ricardo Moreno Cañas, who was assassinated in 1938 by a disenchanted patient. Spiritualists have incorporated Moreno Cañas into their ceremonies, and his image is sold along with those of other popular saints.[9] In northern Mexico, an active healing cult developed around the spiritualist healer José Fidencio Sintora Constantino, *El Niño Fidencio,* who practiced

---

[9]Sowell, "Miguel Perdomo Neira," p. 15.

his healing arts in Espinoza, Nuevo León, in the 1920s and 1930s. Most of his cures involved herbs and humoral treatments, but he also performed minor surgery. These healing cults attend primarily to the physical aspects of healing. The African *Bataque* cults of Brazil, however, envisioned health somewhat more broadly. The curative aspects of Bataque address the broad array of problems that affect the quality of life for Brazil's mostly black urban poor, not just their illnesses. The Bataque medium might seek to redress the trauma of family strife, alcoholism, the loss of employment, or problems with a boyfriend or girlfriend.

Popular religion is manifested in civil–religious hierarchies, popular religious festivals, dances and dramas, and in healing. The hierarchy of graduated religious and civil offices, often called the *cargo* system, requires the officeholder to carry out the duties of the office and assume the associated expenses as well. These systems of civic and religious responsibility are the subject of numerous anthropological studies of Mexican villages.

Elements of popular religion are incorporated into many forms of popular art, such as drama, dance, and oral humor. Ritual joking, for example, can give instructions in proper morality. But perhaps the most prevalent medium for displaying the icons, symbols, and relics of popular religion is handicrafts—from primitive sheepskin paintings in Ecuador (the Tigua art) to papier-mâché figures called the "big bellies" (*panzones*) of Corpus Christi in Puebla, Mexico, and carnival masks in Bolivia. Perhaps no image is more pervasive in Latin America, and certainly not in Mexico, than the Virgin of Guadalupe. She adorns shirts, decals, tattoos, and auto gearshift knobs.

*Rerum Novarum's* greatest impact probably came in the training and encouragement it gave to younger priests and religious leaders who came of age late in the nineteenth and early twentieth centuries. They worked in various countries for Catholic social action programs created to respond to local community needs. These men and women were indistinguishable, for example, from those young men and women trained to turn the Mexican Revolution's rhetoric into revolutionary programs in the 1920s and 1930s. The only difference between the two groups, both deeply committed to local social change, was their position on the role of the Church. The result in Mexico was the three-year civil-religious war called the Cristero Rebellion (1926–1929). The social action programs inspired by *Rerum Novarum* constituted the local Catholic community's response to both Marxist organizers and popular revolutionaries.

## THE SPLINTERING OF THE CHURCH, 1962 TO THE PRESENT

The Cold War era witnessed a series of challenges in Latin America: increasing poverty; declining social justice; and the demand for human rights, expressed as campaigns for civil rights, indigenous rights, black rights, and women's rights. Revolutionary programs and reform campaigns, ranging from Communist-inspired guerrilla movements, U.S.-supported reform governments, and Church-inspired Christian democratic parties, all pursued in different ways reforms that would improve the lives of the people of Latin America. A new direction in the official role of the Catholic Church came with the meeting of Church leaders called the Second Vatican Council, or Vatican II, convened by Pope John XXIII in October 1962. The delegates, including more than 2,000 bishops, focused on two socially progressive themes: expanding the participation of lay Catholics in Church activities and developing Church programs to benefit the least privileged members of society. Regional meetings in Medellín, Colombia (1968), and Puebla, Mexico (1979), focused specifically on these themes in Latin America.

Vatican II and subsequent meetings inspired the widespread creation of Christian Base Communities (CBC), which from one perspective represented the renewal of local vernacular religious groups. The dynamic leadership for most CBCs came from the laity, who responded to the needs and concerns of their local community. Moreover, the CBCs worked to reestablish a community built on face-to-face relationships rather than idealized and imagined associations— horizontal alliances of class and generation and vertical affiliations of ethnicity and gender. Personal interaction and participation in self-help programs formed the basis of the CBC programs.

The CBCs developed unique vernacular programs for social change and practice of the faith because of the absence of priests. Thus María Ferreira dos Santos, who led a CBC in São Paulo, could speak of Christ as "liberator of the poor and oppressed" who encouraged the poor to challenge socioeconomic oppression in Brazil.[10] The shortage of priests remained—as it has since the Iberians' arrival in the Western Hemisphere—a major reason for the persistence of popular religion. In 1978, for example, there was only one priest for every 5,000 Catholics in Latin America, whereas in Europe the ratio was one priest for every 800 Catholics. Thus members of religious brotherhoods (*cofradías* and *hermandades* in Spanish America; *irmandades* in Brazil) and *beatas* and *beatos* (holy women and holy men) continue their active role in shaping the religious practices of local communities. Each vernacular expression of popular Catholicism has its own preoccupation with daily needs, health, and death, and its own practices, such as prayer to favorite saints and *promesas* or *mandas* (promises made to God or a saint in order to gain some favor). The formal rites and sacraments, such as the Eucharist, confirmation, or even baptism and last rites, receive less emphasis than the personal relationship with saints. Extra-sacramental rituals include the pilgrimage, praying to saints, carrying images of the Virgin to visit other churches, and taking saints to the fields.

Since early 1960, with the explosive growth of cities and the widespread availability of both radio and television, popular religion has appeared in both old and new, but recognizable, forms. Folk saints who grapple with the problems of everyday life continue to appear (see the Profile, "Sarita—The People's Saint," on

---

[10]See Warren E. Hewitt, "María Ferreira dos Santos [a pseudonym]," in William H. Beezley and Judith Ewell, eds., *The Human Tradition in Latin America: The Twentieth Century* (Wilmington, DE: SR Books, 1987), pp. 245–257.

**PROFILE**  Sarita—The People's Saint

Stevedores in Lima's port of Callao, beginning early in the twentieth century, first sought out the common grave in the Baquijano cemetery as the burial place of saintly individuals capable of performing miracles. Soon other marginal persons, such as prostitutes, peddlers, and others desperate for aid, came to pray for help from several folk saints buried there. They appealed to the "Little Unknown Soldier," Sister María, Isabelita, and Brother Ceferino. All these cults have been subsumed since 1970 in the devotion to Sarita.

Sara Colonia Zambrano was born in 1914 in the poorest neighborhood of the Andean town of Huaraz. Her father, a carpenter, soon took the family to Lima in search of better living conditions. The move allowed Sara to attend the Catholic elementary school, Santa Teresita, where she learned to read, write, and sketch. After three years, she had to leave school to return to Huaraz to be with her ill mother. Following her mother's death, Sara's family returned to Lima, where they lived in several poor neighborhoods, and finally settled in Callao. The extended family was extremely religious, and aunts were regarded as practically nuns. The family's house held a collection of holy images, especially of Sara's patron, San Martín de Porras, whom she considered the saint of the humble. She devoted herself to work as a domestic and a vegetable vendor, to the care of her younger sisters and brothers, and, especially, to prayer. She had a reputation in her community as a person willing to share with others in need. Sara died from malaria in 1940 at the age of 26. She received only the most basic burial in a common grave in the Baquijano cemetery. Months passed before her father could mark the spot with a simple cross.

Still, a cult developed around her. At first, family and neighbors came to her burial site. Then, a Señora Zoila began popularizing devotion to Sarita as the first among the holy spirits in the cemetery. Longshoremen, prostitutes, petty criminals, homosexuals, abandoned mothers, housewives, the unemployed, small merchants, and bus and taxi drivers—all came to the site to ask for assistance. Since 1970, the cult has grown dramatically. Those devoted to Sarita have contributed money, materials, and labor to build a small chapel in the style of the functional homes in the marginal neighborhoods. Since its construction, the chapel has been covered with votive candles and flowers, and vendors sell amulets and pictures of the little saint. The walls of the chapel are covered with signs giving thanks for miracles performed by Sarita. A sampling of the petitions and thanks to Sarita reveals that men most often request her aid in business or work-related issues, followed by health concerns. Women also seek her aid with work and health issues, generally not for themselves but for their children, parents, or other loved ones.

The Roman Catholic Church does not recognize Sarita. Nevertheless, those who come to her shrine emphasize that she was humble, pure, and charitable, and shared willingly with those more needy than she. Thus, she represents the virtues most valued by those who come to the chapel, and because of her origins, she is accessible to believers, who say that, after all, she too was poor and Peruvian.

SOURCE: Ana María Quiroz, "Cuando Dios dijo que no, Sarita dijo quien sabe," and Gonzálo Portocarrero, "Un mediodía con Sarita," in Gonzálo Portocarrero, ed., *Los nuevos limeños: Sueños, fervores y caminos en el mundo popular* (Lima: Taller de Estudios de Las Mentalidades Populares [TEMPO], 1993), pp. 143–160, 177–183.

page 148). During the Dirty War in Argentina, when the commanding military officers decided to torture and then murder everyone opposed to their way of thinking, two major cults emerged to offer some solace and hope to the people. The devotion to Antonio Gil of Corrientes province and to La Difunta Correa throughout the nation zoomed in popularity. Folklorist Kathleen Figgen concluded, "Because all of the normal channels for talking about the political situation in the country were blocked, these two cults became symbolic idioms for expressing resistance and protest."[11] The military had essentially banned people from congregating during these years, but did give their approval to pilgrimages. Thus, each year some 800,000 young Argentines walked the 43 miles from Buenos Aires to the shrine of the Virgin in Luján.

Besides these traditional forms, popular religion also found outlets in the new media, including *telenovelas,* the extremely popular television soap operas. Telenovelas often incorporate aspects of popular religious ritual and mix it with sexual and violent content. The struggle remains that between good and evil.

The cultural encounter in what today is Latin America initiated a unique political attitude. Scholars have examined the process by which regimes, following the French and Russian revolutions, for example, acquired popular legitimacy by transferring sacrality from both Church and dynastic institutions to new political regimes. In a similar manner, Spanish evangelization early in the conquest of the New World also transferred sacrality to governing institutions leaving the myriad emerging communities to create their own variety of popular religion.

The significance of this occurrence is evident in two enduring habits. The first is a forgiving attitude toward institutions, matched by an understanding but accusatory approach to individuals. There were bad priests, but they were bad because of human frailties. They did not damage the expectations and practices of the Mother Church. This attitude was evident during the colonial period, a time characterized by respect and fealty to the institutions of the monarchy, even when the people held nothing but contempt for the individual who was king. Fixing responsibility on the person but not the institution has led to the survival of governing institutions long beyond their utility. Willingness to maintain institutions despite the personal failings of their leaders has given the former a certain brittleness, so when rejection of the system finally comes, the people demand a complete replacement rather than repair. In this system, compromise—the key to politics—means capitulation.

The second major aspect of popular religion is its vernacular character—it reflected the character of each local community. This aspect often resulted in unique practices, at times combining indigenous and African practices, at other times masking nearly full-scale continuation of these activities, but still calling them Catholic.

Thus, examining Latin American culture, it should be clear that vernacular religion, that is, local variants of Catholicism, serve as much more than a coping strategy. Individuals use their understanding of the relationship between the everyday and the divine and their confidence in the supernatural (the essence of faith) to guide their actions, move them to endure hardship, and compel them to make sacrifices. Although local religion offers defensive mechanisms ranging from prayer to the manipulation of saints to oaths and curses, it also creates a reality—an everyday world in which the individual and the community function.

The bonds that hold the community together include religion, as well as family, gender, place, and occupation. But it must be kept in mind that the reference to

---

[11]Kathleen L. Figgen, "Miracles and Promises: Popular Religious Cultures and Saints in Argentina" (Ph.D. diss., Indiana University, 1990), p. 4.

The feast of Corpus Christi in honor of the Eucharist remains a popular religious festival throughout Latin America. Religious icons are removed from churches and paraded through the streets. Individuals vie for the honor of bearing the images. This celebration occurred in Cuzco, Peru, in 1934. While on the surface such festivals appear to be Catholic ceremonies, they often incorporate local popular religious beliefs and vary from one region to another.

religion means vernacular, local religion, which includes local holy places, community miracles, divine intervention stories, and neighborhood holy men and women. Relics brought back from pilgrimages, of course, form part of the community's material connection to the hereafter. The interpretive flexibility of local religion could, and often did, provide a means of liberation. The vernacular religion enables individuals to make a leap of faith: they could believe change was possible, a revolution might succeed, they could own land, they could find the good life by staying put in the community, or they could find the good life by moving to the city. Finally, and perhaps most important, popular religion forms the glue (or matrix) of local knowledge. This paradigmatic guide to life, customs, relationships, community, and beliefs, which we call culture, is indelibly shaped by local religious understanding. Clifford Geertz's discussion of eye movement—was it a flirtatious wink, a conspiratorial signal, or an involuntary tic?—can be answered only in local terms that in Latin America rely heavily on popular religion.

Other popular belief systems have appeared along with vernacular Catholicism. Spiritualism, covert Judaism, and recently, Evangelical Protestantism, all thrive in Latin America. Although these significant systems of belief and behavior are beyond the scope of this chapter, they merit the readers' consideration. A widely told Mexican anecdote sums up popular religion as a set of habits, customs, and attitudes. A traveler, the story goes, once said to a Mexican he had just met, "It appears that most Mexicans believe in the Catholic faith, but don't practice it." The Mexican responded, "On the contrary, we Mexicans all practice the Catholic religion. But only a few of us believe in it."

Emergent vernacular religion formed patterns of behavior in everyday life. Foremost among these, popular Catholicism was a personal kind of faith. The individual had a personal relationship with the divine, from which emerged habits that extended to work, social, and political relations. Said another way, personal ties superseded group—ethnic, class, or gender—definitions. The individual soon developed a web of personal relationships, such as coparentage (*compadrazgo*) and client-patron ties, based on mutual obligations. This personal relationship provided the foundation for political, economic, and social relations and mirrored the relationship between the individual and his or her patron saint. Consider, for example, the popular anecdote about a Mexican villager and a special saint. Of course, the individual kept an image of the saint on the home altar, prayed before the image, and made special offerings such as flowers and food—and later, in the nineteenth century, liquor and cigarettes. In times of unexpected success, the believer acknowledged the saint's assistance. In time of need, to cure illness, for example, the believer expected the saint's assistance. If the saint's efforts proved ineffectual or slow in coming, the image might be removed from the altar and placed in a dark corner or stood on its head to remind the saint of his or her obligation and to discipline the image for failing to keep the bargain. Ultimately, if the saint utterly failed to assist the believer, the image would be replaced with that of another, more reliable holy figure. This practice was reflected in the exercise of mutual obligations between worker and owner, leader and follower, friend and friend. Whether it was the debt-peonage system, the *caciquismo* system, or the social network, an exchange of responsibilities on each side was implicit in these variations of the client-patron system based on the model of vernacular Catholicism.

Throughout Latin America, and almost certainly throughout the Andean highlands, the individual and the saint or other spirits were viewed as nearly equals. Only in the Judeo–Christian religions do believers hold deities in such high esteem that they separate divinity and humanity.[12,13] In other religions and

---

[12]See liner notes, *Festival of Early Latin American Music,* Roger Wagner Chorale and the Sinfonia Chamber Orchestra (El Dorado/UCLA Latin American Center), USR 7746.

[13]Olivia Harris, "'The Coming of the White People': Reflections on the Mythologization of History in Latin America," *Bulletin of Latin American Research* 14:1 (1995), pp. 9–24.

local variants, gods may be treated almost as equals, worshiped, feared, bargained with, ridiculed, even abused. Often analogies appear between human and divine authorities; in the Andes certain mountain deities are identified as lawyers, priests, and policemen. This suggests that analogous behavior toward these authorities is practiced with the deities as well, especially the kind of resistance or efforts at manipulation called the "weapons of the weak."[14] Thus we should expect that these weapons were exercised or rehearsed in relationships between individuals and personal saints. Consequently, rather than abstract descriptions of behavior based on sermons or Bible stories, Latin Americans had the enduring experience of practicing actual behavior with community or family-owned holy images.

These images of saints and virgins helped motivate Martin Luther, John Calvin, and other Protestants, who viewed them as idols, to break with the Roman Catholic Church. The Protestant Reformation in turn inspired Catholic leaders to clarify the role of images and saints in their faith. The Council of Trent (1556–1563) defined these local saints and images:

> Images of Christ, the virgin mother of God, and the other saints should be set up and kept, particularly in churches, and that due honour and reverence is owed to them, not because some divinity or power is believed to lie in them as reason for the cult, or because anything is to be expected from them . . . , but because the honour showed to them is referred to the original which they represent. . . . [T]he faithful are instructed and strengthened by commemorating and frequently recalling the articles of our faith through the expression in pictures or other likenesses . . . , which is a help to uneducated people.[15]

These images found a home in local churches that served as the vital center of each locality. In small community chapels across colonial Latin America, the most valuable and valued public art was the *retablo,* the main altarpiece. The altarpiece represented the life of Christ and the lives of saints in common images. The altarpiece at Huejotzingo, Mexico, for example,

> was the main expression of colonial ideology in Spanish America before the eighteenth century and provided some of the concrete symbols for social order and authority that appear repeatedly in other kinds of records. The altarpiece suggests both hierarchical order and mediated authority, much as power in colonial Spanish America frequently was exercised by appointment and entreaties were made through inter-mediaries. On the altarpiece, saints stand between the viewer and God, inviting appeals for intercession.

---

[14]James C. Scott, *Weapons of the Weak: Everyday Forms of Peasant Resistance* (New Haven: Yale University Press, 1985).

[15]Kenneth Mills and William B. Taylor, *Colonial Spanish America: A Documentary History* (Wilmington, DE: SR Books, 1998), pp. 274–275.

As the Council of Trent recommended, "It is a good and beneficial thing to invoke them [the saints] and to have recourse to their prayers and helpful assistance to obtain blessings from God through his Son our Lord Jesus Christ."[16] Thus decorations, such as altarpieces in the local church, created the material and spiritual center of community identity. Statues of Christ, Mary, and the saints, as well as altarpieces and other decorations, formed a collage of direct and mnemonic references to the faith. (A modification of this practice appeared in twentieth-century Mexico, when revolutionaries turned to the use of murals in civic buildings to depict the country's secular history.) The community identified with and took pride in the parish church's collection of miraculous virgins or holy relics capable of healing and helping believers.

Appearances of the Virgin or one of the saints resulted in the creation of local shrines. In modern-day Colombia, the Virgin of Chiquinquira forms an integral part of popular Catholicism. To guard its home in the 1550s, a family in Boyacá placed a wooden tablet with the painted image of the Virgin of the Rosary between images of Saint Anthony of Padua and Saint Andrew. Time eventually dulled the luster of the painting, but on December 26, 1586, a servant girl saw the Virgin cause the tablet to rise into the air, glow, and regain its splendor. The Virgin remained suspended for several days. The image was credited with performing several healings, and even more in the years that followed, including ending an epidemic in 1588 in Tunja. These powers earned the Virgin widespread acclaim and brought countless pilgrims to see her in Boyacá. The Virgin has increased in stature over the years, served as a national symbol after independence, and in 1919 was named patroness of Colombia.[17,18,19] The cultivation of folk saints and observations of the Virgin continue to be common experiences throughout Latin America.

---

[16]Mills and Taylor, *Colonial Spanish America*, pp. 274, 278.

[17]David Sowell, "Miguel Perdomo Neira: Healing, Ideology, and Power in the Nineteenth-Century Andes" (manuscript), chapter 1, p. 13.

[18]See Pamela Voekel, "Sensibility and Piety in the Making of the Veracruz Gente Sensata, 1780–1810," in William H. Beezley and Linda Curcio-Nagy, *Latin American Popular Culture: An Introduction* (Wilmington, DE: SR Books), forthcoming.

[19]The celebration of Mexican Independence Day, which begins on September 15 with an evening fiesta and continues on September 16, has overshadowed the commemoration of the Virgin of Dolores. In the town of Dolores Hidalgo, and throughout much of the state, observance of the saint's day now takes place in January.

# 7

# Cultures

Cultures have important functions, economic and social ramifications, and esthetic values that add quality to life in all societies. Only an artificial distinction divides what is often called "popular" and "elite" or high cultures. People across society are influenced and shaped by culture wittingly or not, as voters, consumers, and citizens. Their individual choices form an integral part of the overall cultural matrix. The varieties of culture are almost limitless. Here we are able to suggest a small sampling only. Cultural differences define Brazilians, Mexicans, and Costa Ricans, while at the same indicating shared elements of general Latin American as well as Western European cultures. Cultural filters—used to praise or mock cultural practices, whether they be *lucha libre* wrestling, opera, or literary works—serve to provide social or class identity. Different forms of culture provide enjoyment in the lives of people. One Brazilian who danced in Rio de Janeiro's annual carnival expressed this point when she reflected on the year-round preparations: "The samba was our family, our Sunday stroll, our movies, our lover. It was all we really knew of happiness."[1]

Four eras can be identified in the evolution of Latin America's cultures:

1. The Patriotic–Liberal Era (1820–1870). Immediately after independence, patriotic leaders had to consolidate political support and unify the nation. Imitating the French revolutionaries, the new national leaders created symbols, spaces, and celebrations, as well as a new national calendar. During this period—the first 50 years after independence—conservatives and liberals throughout the hemisphere struggled against each other to determine the nature of the new societies. Often their controversies centered on the role of the Roman Catholic Church in public and political affairs. As they contested the issue of religion, both groups fostered new aspects of culture.

---

[1]Neida of the Mangueira Samba School in *O Globo,* April 1, 1978, p. 35, cited in Alison Raphael, "Samba and Social Control: Popular Culture and Racial Democracy in Rio de Janeiro" (Ph.D. diss., Columbia University, 1980), p. 20.

2.  The Belle Epoque (1870–1920). During the era from 1870 until the end of World War I, coinciding with efforts to promote national uniqueness, new media communicated culture. The introduction of broadsheets, inexpensive newspapers, photography, silent films, and phonography resulted in expanded ways of expressing culture.

3.  World War Society (1920–1960). After World War I through the early years of the Cold War, Latin America experienced the rise of mass media including new print forms, radio, and sound films that redefined and reaffirmed culture as well as modified it. In several Latin American countries, the media explosion resulted in the so-called Golden Age of radio, recorded music, and movies.

4.  Contemporary Society (1960 to the present). Television in the last four decades has added a new media dimension. Radio, however, remains the most influential force in culture, particularly because it broadcasts music, the most pervasive of all cultural forms. Contemporary society is witnessing the beginning of the computer medium for culture as well. Nevertheless, although the medium changes, the forms and the concerns in culture remain the same.

## THE PATRIOTIC–LIBERAL ERA (1820–1870)

Following the wars of independence, the new republics and empires (Brazil and initially in Mexico) organized and displayed different aspects of regional culture in civic and religious holiday festivals, almanacs, and itinerant puppet theater. The need to define what it meant to be an Argentine, a Brazilian, or a member of other newly independent nations required the fashioning of unique cultural roots while retaining acceptable European colonial elements.

### Festivals

Independence brought political and economic autonomy to most of the former Spanish and Portuguese colonies in the Western Hemisphere. It provided an opportunity to make social changes and create new cultural attitudes to form unique national identities. Each new nation built upon its heritage of Iberian culture, Roman Catholicism, indigenous tradition, and African survivals.

Creating new celebrations to foster nationalism in many cases meant the appropriation of religious and royal celebrations and symbols for national purposes. Patriotic leaders intended to establish national values. Patriotic committees used national holidays to teach lessons about history, values, and heroes to the general public; reinforce lessons taught in the new public schools; and echo the common knowledge of the veterans of the independence campaigns. These efforts required new holidays, new symbols, and new uses of public spaces. Royalism and religion both came under attack, because in the thinking of many patriots, neither the political (Spanish or Portuguese) heritage nor the Roman Catholic Church could serve to bind the nation together. Other patriots argued that either the cultural heritage (language, political structure, and social hierarchy), the religious traditions (of the Roman Catholic Church), or both had to serve as the foundation of the new nations. The founding leaders argued over what could and could not form part of the definition of an Argentine, a Mexican, or a Colombian.

Each new government, in the process of this debate, revised its holiday calendar to honor patriotic heroes and independence days. Argentina, for example, created new visual symbols, including coins, colors on the flag, and images in celebrations; new audio symbols with the composition of new music; and new written materials. Streets and plazas received new designations, as the names of patriots replaced those of saints. Argentines chose some symbols that had their origin in the previous regime. The light blue and white that eventually became the colors of the Argentine flag, despite apocryphal stories, had Bourbon antecedents. Argentine nationalists noted that these colors represented the Virgin of Luján, the patroness of Argentina, thus identifying as well with the colonial religious heritage.

New authorities also moved to make the medium of exchange—money—a form of national expression. Argentines drew imagery from coins minted by the Dutch after the Netherlands was freed from Spanish rule. Thus, the Argentines adopted as national images the Phrygian cap, the symbol of liberty on the Dutch coins; the two clasped hands taken from the Dutch sign of the Sea Beggars; and the sun with 32 rays, another Dutch and Christian symbol adopted during the Dutch struggle against Spain. On a more common level of usage, matchbox labels carried the new icons of independence.[2] Celebrations initiated by new patriotic leaders retained the form of colonial festivals, as new leaders subtly claimed legitimacy through continuity. San Martín Day, November 11, continued to celebrate the patron of Buenos Aires, as it had since 1580.

The new independence days showed a variety of influences. Mexicans debated the proper day to celebrate—Padre Hidalgo's call for independence, September 16, 1810, or Agustín Iturbide's entry into Mexico City, September 27, 1820—and experimented with the proper form of the holiday. The 1825 celebration scheduled fireworks on the eve of the holiday—and on the day itself, a grand procession, patriotic orations, a slave emancipation, and patriotic allegories performed in the Alameda and the city's theaters.[3] Of these events, freeing slaves enabled the celebration's organizers to give real character to the rituals of independence.[4] This practice continued until 1829, when President Vicente Guerrero

---

[2]The Dutch struggle to drive out the Spanish and free their nation from Hapsburg control inspired these symbols. The common enemy—the Spanish throne—resulted in Argentine and other Latin American usage of these images. Henry Ph.Vogel, "Elements of Nation-building in Argentina: Buenos Aires, 1810–1828" (Ph.D. diss., University of Florida, 1987). See also William Rowe and Vivian Schelling, *Memory and Modernity: Popular Culture in Latin America* (New York: Verso, 1991), p. 25.

[3]"Como se celebró la primera vez el aniversario de la independencia," *El Nacional,* September 16, 1893, reprinted in *Boletín Oficial del Consejo Superior de Gobierno del Distrito Federal,* 13, no. 22 (September 14, 1909).

[4]Here we are following Richard Warren, although our interpretation varies slightly. Richard Warren, "The Construction of Independence Day, 1821–1864," unpublished paper presented at "Mexico in the Nineteenth Century: A Symposium in Honor of Nettie Lee Benson," April 15, 1994.

announced the emancipation of all slaves on independence day.[5] After the abolition of slavery, the organizing committee demonstrated the meaning of independence through acts of charity to fellow Mexicans—cash allotments to disabled or destitute veterans or to the surviving families of those who died in the independence struggle; a special meal for prisoners; and, commonly, clothing for poor children.

Corpus Christi remained the most important religious holiday. Just as in colonial festivals, the celebrations included cannon salutes; fireworks; illumination of buildings, streets, and plazas; attendance by the high and mighty; music, dancing, eating, drinking; and often bullfights. The obvious difference came in funding. The colonial authorities had provided more financial support than could a hesitant Church or the impoverished newly independent governments.

Other informal celebrations continued and became more important. Festivals such as carnival were not spontaneous festivities, nor were they sanctioned or formally organized. These carnivalesque occasions allowed for role reversals. Nowhere did carnival become more important than in Brazil, especially in the then capital city of Rio de Janeiro. The carnival festivities drew on the dance-and-drum traditions preserved as a cultural memory before slavery. For black Brazilians, family *samba*[6] parties provided in many cases one of the few pleasures available.

## Almanacs

The revised annual cycle of holiday festivals circulated to the public through the publication of cheap almanacs. These volumes, some as many as 250 pages long, listed the major civic and religious holidays, indicated the appropriate celebration, and contained a wealth of additional information. The latter included astrological predictions and astronomical phenomena (comets, eclipses, and the transit of planets through the night skies), travelers' assistance for the major cities (dancing and fencing masters), lists of curiosities, and commentary on events. Almanacs identified Church holidays, marking the Holy Days of Obligation, which required attendance at mass for the entire population; days of obligation for non-Indians (a category that existed throughout the century in Mexico and the Andes); and fasting days. Moreover, the holiday list included civic festivals and often explained why the person or event was being honored. In this way, lessons of civic virtue and about national heroes received widespread distribution.

The almanacs contained images that illustrated the landscape or gave features to national heroes. These images resulted from the introduction of lithography in Latin America, the most visual medium in the nineteenth century. Alois Senefelder

---

[5]Michael P. Costeloe, "The Junta Patriotica and the Celebration of Independence in Mexico City, 1825–1855," in *Viva Mexico! Viva Independencia: Independence Day Celebrations in Mexico, 1821 to c. 1940*, edited by William H. Beezley and David R. Lorey (Wilmington, DE: SR Books, 1999), pp. 5–6.

[6]The first song to be officially identified as a samba was "Pelo Telefone." The mulatto composer Donga (Ernesto dos Santos), from Rio, registered it with the National Library in 1917.

Fireworks have long provided much to the excitement during religious and civic celebrations. Here a street vendor, photographed in about 1860, is surrounded by several potential customers. Such celebrations, then as now, are major popular cultural events and often include bullfights, puppet shows, and other popular diversions.

had invented the process in 1798, and lithographs quickly appealed to people who could not afford paintings. Prints and lithographs found their way into ordinary homes through books, albums, almanacs, newspapers and magazines, and particularly broadsheets.[7]

The broadsheet had many antecedents in Latin America, dating back to clay stamps of both the Aztec and Inca worlds and wood engraving introduced in the colonies in 1539 by the Italian Giovanni Paolo. Better known as Juan Pablos, he opened the first print shop in the New World and began producing playing cards—extremely popular, even though they were declared illegal—from wooden engraving plates. After 1598, several printers imported copper plates from Spain, Flanders, Italy, and Germany for books, religious images, portraits, coats of arms, maps, rural scenes, obituaries, and allegories. In 1781, Jerónimo Antonio Gil established Mexico's first school of engraving in La Casa de Moneda, and two years later it became the Academy of San Carlos. Claudio Linati introduced

---

[7]José N. Iturriaga, *Litografía y grabado en el México del siglo XIX* (Mexico: N.p. 1993), vol. 1, pp. 9, 10, 12.

lithography to Mexico in 1826. His first lithograph—a women's fashions plate—appeared in the newspaper *El Iris* on February 4, 1826; on July 12 Linati's disciple, Oaxacan José Gracida, published an image of patriot Miguel Hidalgo in the same newspaper.[8]

Fernando Leal, after surveying the printing of images, concluded that "lithography is unquestionably the most characteristic art [form] of the 19th century." It focused on naturalistic themes, portrayed events of daily life, and exalted historical episodes involving the struggle for independence. Because lithographs could be duplicated easily, they quickly reached a mass audience. In 1836, J. Rocha and Carlos Fournier opened the first commercial lithography shop in Mexico City. By mid-century, shops also opened in the provinces in Toluca, Guadalajara, Puebla, Mazatlán, San Luis Potosí, Michoacán, and Aguascalientes (the last shop, belonging to Trinidad Pedrozo, was where José Guadalupe Posada, an artist who produced popular engravings in the late nineteenth century, began his career). The most conspicuous engravings of the nineteenth century appeared first in books and albums. Beginning in the last years of the 1830s, they could be found in magazines, serial stories in newspapers, almanacs, and calendars.[9] Political caricatures became common newspaper features in the second half of the nineteenth century, particularly in the 1860s and 1870s when the struggles between Liberals and Conservatives and other political factions reached a boiling point.

Lithographs depicting life in Latin America came into vogue throughout Europe. José Luciano Castañeda served as the engraver on the three archaeological expeditions of the Spanish dragoon Captain Guillermo Dupaix (1805–1808). His lithographs appeared in the 1830 edition of *Antiquities of Mexico,* under the patronage of Lord Kingsborough, and their widespread popularity inspired other engravers in Europe. German Karl Nebel produced *Viaje pintoresco y arqueológico sobre la parte más interesante de la República Mexicana, en los años transcurridos desde 1829 hasta 1834, "Observaciones" de Alejandro de Humboldt* (1840). He took some artistic liberties, such as "inventing" a statue symbolizing peace and liberty for the central plaza in Aguascalientes, Mexico, to replace the one representing the Spanish king that patriots pulled down during the struggle for independence. Another German, Johann Moritz Ruegendas, produced typical scenes of Mexico during the 1830s. Italian Pedro Gualdi, who traveled with an opera company as its set director, found time to produce a book of lithographs called *Monumentos de México.*

These Mexican examples are representative of the widespread printing of lithographs throughout the region. For an Andean perspective, Wilson Hallo's *Imágenes del Ecuador del siglo XIX* illustrates the same pattern of popular daily scenes and categories of social and ethnic types.[10] Lithography as an art form

---

[8] Claudio Linati, *Trajes civiles, militares y religiosos de México (1818)* (México: UNAM-Instituto de Investigaciones Estéticas, 1956), pp. 14, 15.

[9] Fernando Leal "The Mexican Lithograph in the 19th Century," *Artes de México* 14, año IV, vol. III (1986), pp. 6, 15, 16, 17. Leal was talking about Mexico, but his comments can be applied to all of Latin America.

[10] Quito: Ediciones del Sol; Madrid: Espasa-Calpe, 1981.

declined with the growing use of photography, photolithography, and photoen-graving after 1880. Its decline affected almanacs as well.

## Puppet Theater

Entertainment during the nineteenth century often combined political com-mentary, local customs, and melodramatic tales. Certainly these elements defined the performances of itinerant puppet theater, a widely popular amusement of the time. This diversion can be traced to Spain.[11] On his 1524 campaign to subdue Honduras, Hernán Cortés, the conqueror of Mexico, counted a puppeteer among the members of his expedition. In many Spanish colonial areas, puppet theater arrived before other European-styled theatrical performances, but their everyday nature meant that only tantalizing elusive references to them remain. For example, sixteenth-century reports exist of a Spanish woman giving puppet shows in Lima during the Convent of St. Francis's festival for the martyrs in Japan. Traces exist of the popularity of puppet shows in Mexico City, where the Comptroller of Hospitals and Theaters ordered that actors and dancers could no longer participate in the more popular puppet performances because the late nights kept them from successfully performing their theater roles. Inquisition records contain more on this diversion. Certainly by independence, numerous small puppet companies existed in the principal capitals—Mexico City and Lima—and scattered references show that they wandered through remote parts of southern South America (Argentina, Uruguay, and Chile). Mexican traveling shows may well have journeyed across the Gulf of Mexico and up the Mississippi River into Spanish Louisiana.

Puppets became especially popular during the nineteenth century. In Spanish America, puppets served a didactic purpose, entertaining spectators while teaching them the prevailing values. Thus, in Ecuador, puppets gave ecclesiastical lessons as they had during the colonial era by performing sketches of religious festivals, including the Passion of Holy Week and the miracles of the saints. Visual continuity between the puppets and religious images was possible because the same artisans (santeros, or "makers of saints") produced both sets of figures.

Puppet shows often had a political nature and featured stock characters of national culture. The performances could become bawdy, even scandalous, as the puppeteers exercised license in language and political criticism not allowed to regular citizens. In Brazil, puppeteers gave performances regularly at local markets and fairs.[12] The outstanding example of these troupes was the Rosete Aranda family in Mexico. This family came from the town of Huamantla, Tlaxcala. Their

---

[11]Small figures that could be manipulated by strings or on sticks existed in some pre-Columbian cultures; we know for certain that the indigenous peoples in both present-day Mexico and Peru had them. See Roberto Lago, *Teatro guiñol mexicano* (Mexico: Federación Editorial Mexicana, 1987), pp. 38–41, for an account of pre-Columbian puppets in Campeche, Mexico.

[12]Marion Oettinger, Jr., *The Folk Art of Latin America: Visiones del Pueblo* (New York: Dutton Studio Books, 1992), pp. 56–57.

success resulted in annual tours across the republic. They specialized in representations of regional life, national holidays, and Mexican politics. Their marionettes created widely known stock characters such as Vale Coyote, a campesino whose speeches expressed the hopes of rural people; and Doña Pascarroncita Mastuerzo de Verdegay Panza de Res y Gay Verde, a high-society woman who sang the widely known "Coplas de Don Simón" in each performance. The Rosete Aranda company remained active until 1958.[13]

Of course, other entertainments from the colonial period continued. Bullfights and cockfights remained popular, although theater generally declined during the first half of the nineteenth century. European music groups, especially opera companies, made regular concert tours to Latin America. These became annual visits in the late nineteenth century.

## THE BELLE EPOQUE (1870–1920)

During the time known as the Belle Epoque, roughly from 1870 until 1920, Latin Americans witnessed a rise of urban centers, an introduction of new forms of media, and an elaboration of new popular symbols. In the general rush to appear modern, Latin American elites adopted the leisure activities of the wealthy classes from Europe and the United States. This desire to emulate the foreign upper classes resulted in the introduction of soccer and baseball. Soccer spread throughout the hemisphere, and baseball achieved popularity in the Caribbean islands and along the coast—including coastal Mexico, Nicaragua, and Venezuela—and attracted all classes. Various fads also came and went. Of these, the bicycling craze endured throughout Latin America for two decades (1890–1910). Upper-class riders dressed for an English hunt and rode out into the countryside. The safety bicycle—with two wheels of equal size and pneumatic tires—became the emblem of the modern lifestyle from Mexico to Argentina. These elites lived urban, modern lives, but rushed out to the countryside (once considered the site of barbarism) on their bicycles to find peace and solitude. The new media reported on these and other new cultural developments, including the series of world and national fairs and expositions; the rise of photo magazines and the penny press; the invention of sound retrieval and transmission systems, including the telegraph, telephone, and phonograph.

### World Fairs

The Universal Exposition in Paris in 1889 provided the first major occasion for Latin American nations to display their resources and peoples before an

---

[13]Paul McPharlin, *The Puppet Theatre in America: A History* (New York: Harper & Brothers, 1949), pp. 6, 7, 70, 71, 73, 77, 78; Catalog of the Museo Nacional del Títere (Huamantla, Tlaxcala, n.d.).

Courtesy of Museo del Banco Central de Reserva de Perú.

Bicycles represented modernization in its most personal terms. Two wheelers with pneumatic tires offered a safe mode of transportation and recreation for these cyclists in turn-of-the-century Lima, Peru. Once regarded as barbarous and savage, the countryside became a tranquil and serene location for cycling excursions.

international audience. For Argentina, this exposition provided the opportunity to attract both entrepreneurs eager to invest in modernization projects and prospective immigrants hoping to find a new home in a sparsely populated region of great natural resources. The Argentine and other Latin American pavilions stood together—Mexico's and Argentina's buildings, next to each other, looked across a narrow walkway to Brazil's pavilion—in the shadow of the newly constructed Eiffel Tower. The Ecuadorian exhibit stood at the base of the tower itself. The Latin American exhibits featured natural resources, agricultural products, and representations of the country's national size, implying open spaces for growth. The Argentines attracted attention with their display of frozen beef, which the organizers hoped would demonstrate national technological capacity and create an export market for meat. The Uruguayans also featured huge canisters of conserved beef in the main salon of their pavilion. Latin American nations were well represented at other world and hemispheric fairs and expositions both in Europe and the United States.[14]

---

[14]See Ingrid E. Fey, "Peddling the Pampas: Argentina at the Universal Exposition of 1889," in William H. Beezley and Linda Curcio-Nagy, eds., *Latin American Popular Culture: An Introduction* (Wilmington, DE: SR Books, 1999).

## Print Media

New technology allowed the development of cheaper printing methods for chapbooks and newspapers. In Buenos Aires, the new printing technology made possible the publication of booklets for the new urban market. Upper-class critics denigrated this fiction, describing it as stories about drunks and criminals written in the language of the slums and prisons. But these booklets were published in runs of tens of thousands, whereas serious literature appeared in only thousand-copy print runs. Some of these novels, such as *Juan Moreira* by Eduardo Gutiérrez, appeared first as serials in newspapers and then in book form. As a so-called *gaucho malo* figure, Juan Moreira, a well-known folk figure, appeared in other forms, including pantomime, circus, and carnival performances. Books about him tapped a widely recognized cultural personality.[15]

During the era of Porfirio Díaz, a vigorous culture flourished, especially in broadsheets. Antonio Vanegas Arroyo and Ildefonso T. Orellana both began publishing penny booklets for children's or puppet plays. Vanegas Arroyo's chapbooks had a competitive edge because the covers featured engravings by the master of the art, José Guadalupe Posada. Posada relied on modern printing techniques, but created images that had the appearance of familiar old-style woodcuts. Produced on short notice, these broadsheets, with both prose and verse, reported on sensational crimes, natural disasters, melodramatic love affairs, and tragic events in everyday lives. They constituted a penny press of human interest stories, not public events of civic life. Vanegas Arroyo and Posada dominated this market.

Posada produced several bodies of engravings, including religious prints, social stereotypes portrayed as skeletons (called *calaveras*), crime sheets, and embellished printed versions of corridos (Mexican narrative folk ballads). In the religious images of Christ, Mary, the saints, and the apostles, he used pictorial conventions reaching back to the Middle Ages and commonly seen in the statues and paintings of Roman Catholic churches. The calaveras, printed on cheap paper, often dyed with cheap vegetable colors, and lettered in type set by hand, were sold not only in the capital but also across the nation. Above all, Posada spoke for the urban underdogs and presented their viewpoint. Through his images he gave voice to their rural roots and to the traditional morality of the Roman Catholic Church. His works applauded urban criminals and scofflaws who embarrassed the established regime. He represented the capital's lower-class subculture with its own concerns, outlooks, and ways of solving problems. Posada achieved his greatest success in representations of sensational events. He never moralized, appealing instead to the morality of traditional folk religion.

More than half of Posada's broadsides (2,000 plates are known to be extant) deal with the world of crime. The driving force in choice of subject was the publisher Vanegas Arroyo's determination to print what he knew would sell. Ordinary Mexicans must have been fascinated by sensational crimes. They had little interest in the sorts of misdemeanors—drunkenness, fighting, and robbery—that represented the most common cause for arrest in Mexico City or in crimes committed by the

---

[15]Rowe and Schelling, *Memory and Modernity,* pp. 33–34.

upper class. More often, the broadsheets told stories of domestic violence, grue-some murders, and fiendish rapes.

These broadsheets satisfied curiosity about how far people were willing to go when driven by hatred or desire, when forced to endure captivity, or when faced with death. The sheets allowed people to compare themselves with the persons depicted who were "praised, condemned, enraged, subjected or victimized." While some people found answers to the meaning of life in literature, art, religion, drama, mythology, or grand opera, others turned to stories of sensational crime. Violent forms of emotion often appeared as storms or lightning and earthquakes. The broadsheets in their own way supported traditional morality, often drawing directly from Catholic teachings.

Many of these broadsheets clearly show the influence of oral traditions, offering folkloric tales about horrible punishments awaiting those who violate the natural order (such as murdering one's parents or children). The broadsheets became popular because they gave people something to talk about and reinforced traditional morality. Some dealt with rural life, recalling home and memories of local *valientes;* others depicted strongman heroes popular among urban migrants. Posada and Vanegas Arroyo also presented accounts of bandits, both to satisfy curiosity about them and to present a moral exhortation.

Police and penal institutions appear in another set of broadsheets. These concerned prison conditions, administration of justice, and, especially popular, executions. Miguel Macedo, who later became head of the Federal District penitentiary, reported that between 1891 and 1895, Mexico City had an average of 12,171 crimes a year and an average of 11,097 arrests. Of those arrested, 45.1 percent were deemed to be drunk when taken into custody, 61 percent were unemployed, and 83 percent were illiterate. Thus, in the overwhelming majority of cases, at least three of these four adjectives could describe the suspect: unemployed, illiterate, drunk, and disorderly. Macedo blamed this situation on the immorality of the lower classes.

The broadsheets also covered bullfighting, promoting popular matadors, reporting gorings, and providing details of scandalous events associated with the bullfight. Of all the matadors, the most popular was Rodolfo Gaona, once a shoe-factory worker in the provinces who later became the toast of Mexico City.

As for the rich and high-society Mexicans in Posada's work, they were portrayed as lacking in moral virtue and tempted by greed and envy. Nevertheless, these broadsheets aimed their ridicule not at upper-class individuals and governing officials (perhaps exercising self-censorship), but rather at the emerging middle group of office workers, lawyers, and bureaucrats, who had not completely escaped their traditional origins. Posada used the stock character Don Chepito Mariguano Charrascay Rascarrabias, probably based loosely on Honoré Daumier's caricature named Robert Macaire, to represent this group. Don Chepito's actions lampooned these pretentious upstarts.[16]

---

[16]See Patrick Frank, *Posada's Broadsheets: Mexican Popular Imagery, 1890–1910* (Albu-querque: University of New Mexico Press, 1998).

Newspapers, magazines, and books became the first modern cultural medium readily and inexpensively available. Although an impressive number of colonial and early independence papers met the needs of merchants and enlightened bureaucrats, the modern print era begins for most of Latin America in the latter half of the nineteenth century. Specialized publications emerged as countries modernized and became more complex. Perhaps the best, but certainly not the only example is Argentina, where the print media closely tracked economic development and the march of technology. Publications between 1880 and 1887 revealed modern Latin America. In Argentina the *Revista Argentina de Ganadería* (Argentine Animal Husbandry Magazine, 1880) appeared the same year as the English-language *Argentine Live-Stock and Agricultural Review.* The following year, the *Anales de la Sociedad Rural* and the English-language *Buenos Aires Herald* joined a list that indicated the growing importance of Anglo-Argentine trade and agricultural exports. Weekly magazines such as the *Consejero del Hogar* (1903) and *Mundo Argentino* (1911) offered advice on modern living. Early film photo-journals, such as *Cinema Chat, Héroes del Cine,* and *Hogar y Cine,* infused culture with Hollywood dreams. The public had a wide choice of general interest and specialized papers and magazines to shape their views and expectations of the modern world.

The publishing industry grew out of the newspaper business. Books were usually printed on poor-quality paper and inexpensive, made for an avid book trade. Issues of immediate concern could be explored at length. Works published by Latin American presses dealing with literature, history, psychology, politics, philosophy, and medicine, among other subjects, met strong demand by readers from Mexico to Argentina.

## Later Puppet Theater

Posada's sketches and the booklets of puppet plays featured folk characters and typical activities from throughout the republic, all its town squares and well-known districts. Toy puppets worked by a string or two were found in many town markets, so that children and amateurs could emulate the professional puppeteers using Posada and Vanegas Arroyo's little books.

During this era in Peru, *ño* (a title meaning less than señor) Valdivieso developed a puppetry repertory that became well known. His characters included Chocolatito, the Faint-Hearted Soldier, the Little Ghost that grew taller and taller during the performance of "The Haunted House," and Padre del Sermón, who was given to pronouncing precepts and Latin jargon. His puppets reportedly gave a running commentary on Peruvian manners and morals. On at least one occasion, his puppet show resulted in a jail sentence for Valdivieso.

In southern South America, puppets abounded. Argentine puppet theater featured the black character Francisco Pancho and a collection of foreign immigrants. Newspaper boys in Montevideo, Uruguay, attracted customers with puppet shows that experienced a kind of golden age in the 1890s. The flood of Italian immigrants to these countries and to Brazil in the second half of the century included puppeteers, so that Italian-style marionettes became predominant.[17]

## Celebrations and Costumbrismo

Carnival remained the major popular celebration in Brazil. During this era the festivities closely mirrored the nation's social stratification. Three types of carnival groups existed: the Grandes Sociedades for the upper class, the Ranchos dos Reis for the middle class, and the Blocos de Sujo for the poor. The Grandes Sociedades appeared first in 1855 as a masked marching group, with bands and floats, called *carros críticos,* that made humorous criticism of current events. By 1907, these groups also commissioned songs with satirical political overtones, on topics such as the high cost of living and corruption in government. These high-society groups provided an organization for expressing views on political issues, such as abolition in Brazil. The Ranchos, organizations of families that originated in Bahia and soon became factory groups in the cities, chose themes based on history and culture. The Blocos de Sujo, loosely translated as the "dirty group," who could not afford lavish costumes, paraded in bathing suits, sandals, straw hats, or whatever they had to wear.

The most notable development during the Belle Epoque witnessed the appearance of the romantic, nationalistic notions that have been labeled *costumbrismo.* Deeply ingrained in this new sense of nationalism was "aristocratic racism." The elites rejected Latin American identity as second-class European culture and instead traced their ancestry to historical Indian (especially Aztec or Inca) aristocracy, in a kind of archaeological patriotism. The visual representations of Indians in Ecuador during this period, for example, were produced by four painters: Rafael Sals, Agustín Guerrero, Rafael Troya, and Joaquín Pinto. Costumbrismo also appeared in other artistic forms, such as music and literature.

Costumbrismo influences in music broke with the general nineteenth-century pattern of the performance of European opera, often with visiting European performers. In the last quarter of the nineteenth century, composers wrote national operas incorporating indigenous themes. Placing national culture into a European context while struggling to suggest uniqueness depended on adapting old-world forms, but with a slight, but important twist that connected Latin Americans with Western European civilization. Manners, language, literature, and music created transatlantic bonds as well as national uniqueness. In Colombia, for example, José María Ponce de León wrote national music, including *Sinfonía sobre temas colombianos,* that incorporated folk-dance themes such as the nation's most popular dance, the *pasillo.* In a similar fashion, Francisco Hargreaves composed his *Aires nacionales* (1880) for the piano, drawing on traditional songs and dances as did Alberto Williams in his monumental *Aires de la pampa* at the turn of the nineteenth century and his *Primera Sonata Argentina,* Opus 74, for the piano in 1917. Songs and dance melodies classically arranged by Julian Aguirre (1868–1924) opened the way for the *tango* songs of Carlos Gardel. Itinerant theatre troupes, the *zarzuelas criollas,* presented gaucho dramas complete with folk dances and music.

---

[17]McPharlin, *Puppet Theatre,* pp. 238–258.

A distinct literature emerged, often centered on the gaucho. José Fernández's (1834–1886) epic poem, *El Gaucho Martín Fierro* (published in 1872 and 1879), chronicled the gaucho's heroic passing into history. Eduardo Gutiérrez's (1853–1890) semifictional *Juan Moreira* depicted the gaucho's life as a lost but valiant struggle against progress—making the point that the country, although unique, had also embraced civilization. Dramatization of *Juan Moreira* marked the beginning of a distinctive Argentine theater, although European operas also remained popular.

Anciento Ortega's *Guatimozín* (the last Aztec emperor) in Mexico and Carlo Enrique Pasta's *Atahualpa* (the Inca emperor captured and executed by the Spaniards) in Peru, suggested the nobility of the hemisphere's indigenous inhabitants. Musical nationalism added national character to European forms, infusing indigenous elements and genres that in turn influenced their own and European perceptions of the New World.

Developments in music can be seen clearly in the compositions of the Mexican "Group of Six," which was also known as *Los Francesistas*. These young musicians—Felipe Villanueva, Ricardo Castro, Gustavo E. Campa, Juan Hernández Acevedo, Ignacio Quezadas, and Carlos J. Meneses—rejected Italian opera, the elite music of the previous generation. They turned to costumbrista traditions, French composers, and the works of Bach, Chopin, and Liszt. Villanueva, from a small village now renamed for him in Mexico state, typifies this group. A child of a large and poor family, he sought musical instruction where he could find it. The parish organist, his cousin, supplied piano lessons; and a member of the village band, another cousin, taught him violin. His father sent him to the National Conservatory, but the other students from elite families drove the poor, rural youth from the school. Nevertheless, he continued to study music, playing violin in theater orchestras, paying for occasional lessons, and attending concert and opera performances at the Gran Teatro Nacional whenever he could. With other young musicians, he formed the Group of Six and began composing. Villanueva expressed his patriotism by writing several collections of dances and contra dances based on criollo musical expressions. Typical of these pieces were his *danzas humorísticas,* which simultaneously used two different rhythmic schemes. The ambiguity created by both double and triple metric systems was common in Mexican music, especially in theater music. By the 1880s, the music of Villanueva and the Group of Six had become popular among Mexicans.

Elite musical fans soon began attending performances and salons with the musicians. At one gathering in the home of Villanueva, Benito Juárez Maza, son of the great president, asked him to write a composition. Villanueva agreed, on the condition it be dedicated to the president's memory, and composed *Lamento: a la memoria del patricio Benito Juárez*. A funeral march, it served as an ironic rejoinder to Franz Liszt's *Funeral March in Memory of Maximilian, Emperor of Mexico* (1867). With this piece and many others, by the 1890s the Francesistas had become the musical expression of Mexico, showing again the complex relationship and circular nature of cultural forms.[18]

---

[18]"Recital: Felipe Villanueva," pianist Eva María Zuk, Serie Siglo XIX, vol. 1/DDD/ INBA/Instituto Mexiquense de Cultura/Difusión Cultural UNAM/CENIDIM.

Costumbrismo's creation of romantic nationalism included promotion of Indian nobility, exhibits in museums, works of art, performance of music, and photography extended to landscapes as well, with the "invention" of costumbrista geography.


## WORLD WAR SOCIETY (1920–1960)

During the era of the two world wars, cultures became increasingly urban phenomena, especially with respect to subject matter. The contemporary Mexican pundit Carlos Monsiváis identified five main sources of Mexican urban culture: film, prints by José Guadalupe Posada, the political theater (a kind of music hall variety program), the comic strip, and the musical style associated with Agustín Lara and José Alfredo Jiménez that transformed traditional rural songs into three-minute record tracks. Monsiváis could have added to the last source the requirements for broadcast on the radio.[19]


### Radio

Radio emerged in the years after World War I as the most important of the mass media, and it continues to be so today in Latin America. Over the past 70 years, radio has had an overwhelming influence on culture. By 1990 radio coverage approached 100 percent of the region, with 164 million radio receivers in 1991; that is, 1 for every 2.7 inhabitants in Latin America.[20] Programming has been shaped by consumer demand for programs that reflect prevailing cultures.

Radio came to Latin America largely through the efforts of U.S. corporations that were seeking a market for their broadcasting and receiving equipment. Nevertheless, U.S. radio promoters had no role in the first Latin American radio broadcast. On August 27, 1920, four eager Argentine radio amateurs broadcasted Wagner's *Parsifal* to some 20 home receivers in Buenos Aires. This amateur effort aside, U.S. representatives quickly appeared throughout the hemisphere. Both U.S. corporations and American government agents campaigned for American dominance of hemispheric communications. These grand designs for the spread of radio coincided with local efforts in various nations. Latin American listeners, both actual and prospective, were eager for radio and pressed for access to broadcasts.

Argentine interest in radio blossomed. By 1923, the nation had three stations transmitting regular programming of news and music, including daily broadcasts of entire operas. These stations included Radio Sud América, a branch of the U.S. company Radio Corporation of America (RCA), originally established as a way to market RCA receivers in South America. American-made equipment became

[19]Rowe and Schelling, *Memory and Modernity,* p. 100.

[20]Elizabeth Fox, "Latin American Broadcasting," in Leslie Bethell, ed., *The Cambridge History of Latin America,* vol. 10: *Latin America Since 1930: Ideas, Culture and Society* (Cambridge: Cambridge University Press, 1995), p. 521.

the most popular; but the local model, the Pekam, could also be found throughout the Southern Cone.

The first broadcast occurred in Argentina, but regular radio broadcasting in South America first appeared in Brazil as a consequence of the 1922 celebration of the centennial of independence. Initially, government regulations severely limited private ownership of radio receiving and broadcasting equipment. As part of the centennial celebration, Brazil hosted an international exposition in Rio de Janeiro that included representatives of the U.S. mass-media industries. U.S. film distributors shipped hundreds of recent movies to Brazil and helped finance the construction of several theaters in which to show them. U.S. government films drew small audiences, but the theaters overflowed when Hollywood feature films were shown. American radio companies exhibited their products at the celebration in displays that showed the pleasures of listening to the radio at home. Moreover, Westinghouse Corporation installed equipment on Corcovado, the mountain where the famous statue of Christ (*Cristo Redentor*) stands today, and broadcasted daily from loudspeakers around the exhibition grounds. Radio so impressed centennial officials that both Westinghouse and Western Electric received grand prizes. In what was a good public relations and marketing decision, Westinghouse left its broadcasting station behind at the conclusion of the exhibition. Radio fever spread throughout Rio; using unauthorized receivers, people as far away as São Paulo were able to hear the broadcasts.

American companies began exporting receivers to Brazil in 1922, where merchants stockpiled them while waiting for a change in the regulations that would permit their sale. The government encouraged individual efforts by issuing licenses to radio club members. As a result, clubs spread quickly across Brazil. Finally, in November 1924, submitting to the inevitable, Brazil's president eliminated government restrictions on ownership of radios and established guidelines for the operation of transmitters. Besides enjoying Brazilian stations, listeners could also tune in to other broadcasts, especially the shortwave transmissions of Westinghouse's Pittsburgh, Pennsylvania, station, KDKA.

In addition to its function as a communications medium, radio became an advertising medium. Companies promoted automobiles, phonograph records, motion pictures, cigarettes, clothing, and furniture. Such opportunities drew American advertising agencies to Brazil in the late 1920s and subsequently to other republics. Uruguayans listened to both Buenos Aires and the southern Brazilian stations. Soon, Uruguay launched its own transmitters, and by 1930 Montevideo alone had more than 19.

Radio spread rapidly throughout the continent. Uruguayan stations became the first in South America to begin using transcription discs. Developed in the United States in 1930, the discs held 15 minutes of programming on each side and were widely used for continuing dramatic radio series, such as soap operas, detective shows, and adventure tales. Both Bolivia and Paraguay had low-wattage transmitters in their capital cities. Chile developed uniquely national broadcasting because the Andes mountains and the Atacama Desert isolated the country from other outlets. Although the Peruvian government gave the Marconi interests a broadcasting monopoly from Italy in 1920, it soon broke down and radio developed

slowly there. Venezuela also tried to establish a national monopoly on broadcasting to protect government transmissions from being heard. But by 1924 the
Venezuelans had changed their position, and consumer radio began. In Ecuador,
radio emerged only in the 1930s. Colombians faced geographical problems
because of the mountainous terrain and tropical conditions, but two stations
began operations in Bogotá in 1929 and 1930.

Radio came to Mexico in 1921, when Constanto de Tarnara, an American-
trained electrician, established a transmitter on the U.S. model. His efforts
inspired several imitators in the Federal District during the next two years, and by
the middle of the decade the country's other large cities, including Guadalajara,
Veracruz, Mazatlán, and Chihuahua, had broadcasting stations. Radio mania
resulted in ownership of 100,000 receivers, and listeners were able to hear 30
stations by 1930 (for an unusual early use of radio in Mexico, see the Profile,
"Mexican Beauty Queen, 1928," on pages 171).

Two patterns emerged in the Caribbean region, where independent nations
followed American trends. The island colonies obtained receivers but did not
have transmitters until the 1930s, when they followed European models. Cuba,
where International Telephone and Telegraph introduced broadcasting in the
early 1920s, showed the most rapid growth. In Haiti, a U.S. naval officer
supervised the government-owned station. Families of U.S. troops owned most of
the receivers. American phonograph records were the most popular programming. In cooperation with the Haitian government, the station broadcasted some
educational programs in Creole.

Central America's low standard of living impeded the growth of radio.
Nevertheless, Honduras, Guatemala, El Salvador, Nicaragua, Costa Rica, and
Panama tended to adopt American broadcasting patterns. In this region, Costa
Rica led the way. The U.S. Navy's security concerns in Panama limited civilian
access to radio there. Under growing pressure, in 1923 the United States and
Panama permitted the ownership of receivers, and the Navy began regular
broadcasts. In 1925, Panamanians obtained their own transmitter.

Radio provided a medium for the communication of traditional cultural
forms, especially music, and it also brought changes to them. An example of the
technological impact on form is the case of Mexican mariachi music in 1930.
Emilio Azcárraga, the organizing force behind Mexican radio, felt that the traditional *mariachi* group (an all-string ensemble) had too little volume for radio. He
wanted a richer, fuller sound; he preferred the mixed mariachi bands with
trumpets, which originated after 1862 with the introduction of valve wind
instruments when French troops invaded Mexico. Today a band of five brass and
string instruments is regarded as the traditional mariachi.[21] Likewise, when
Brazilians began broadcasting the samba in the early 1930s, they played a softer,
gentler samba in which lyrics prevailed over the beat of the earlier, hotter, more
rhythmic *batucada* of Afro-Brazilians.[22] Carlos Gardel sang tango songs in

---

[21]Claes af. Geijerstam, *Popular Music in Mexico* (Albuquerque: University of New Mexico
Press, 1976), pp. 41–42, 44.

[22]Raphael, "Samba and Social Control," p. 63.

**PROFILE**     Mexican Beauty Queen, 1928

María Teresa de Landa lived a life that twice captured the attention of the Mexican public. From a collateral wing of an old wealthy family, her middle-class parents encouraged her education and career plans. She entered the dental school at the National University. Attractive and popular, María was chosen by her classmates to represent the school in the contest sponsored by the newspaper *El Excelsior* to select a Miss Mexico. The first round consisted of newspaper interviews and public appearances in swimsuits in the Toluca public gardens. Mexicans voted by mailing in coupons from the newspaper to elect the finalists.

María Teresa reached the finals. Despite her parents' mortification, she gave additional interviews, paraded in her swimsuit, and persuaded the judges that she indeed was Miss Mexico. As the winner, she became a contestant in an international pageant in Galveston, Texas, and from capital city merchants she won a collection of gifts—called a dowry—for the beauty queen. As the Galveston event approached, the pageant's sponsors learned that a group of European contestants would stop in Veracruz on their way to Texas. The sponsors decided to invite these women to come to the capital for a parade of welcome. The beauty queens agreed to participate—and the procession had a surprise conclusion when Charles Lindbergh, who had made the first solo airplane crossing of the Atlantic and was visiting Mexico, also appeared in the parade.

Returning from Galveston, María Teresa briefly resumed her studies. During these weeks, she was courted by General Moisés Vidal Corro of Veracruz. He eventually persuaded her to leave school, marry him in a private ceremony, and move to Veracruz. The marriage almost immediately turned strange when the general restricted her to the house and refused to let her see newspapers. Nevertheless, she eventually came upon a local newspaper in which the social pages discussed her husband and his wife and family. When María Teresa confronted her bigamist husband, she first threatened suicide, but his satirical response persuaded her to turn the pistol on the general and shoot him to death. The murder led to a sensational trial in Mexico City in popular court, where jurors were chosen by lot. The public avidly followed testimony as the *autoviuda* (self-made widow) sat in the courtroom, an elegant, somber, wronged beauty queen. The proceedings revealed that the general had faked the civil marriage; the religious service had been performed by his brother, a former priest. Public attention climaxed on the last day, when the Mexican distributor of RCA Victor radio receivers seized the opportunity and placed radio speakers around the city, so that enraptured Mexicans could listen to the marathon 13 hours of testimony as the trial concluded. The judge and jury reached a popular decision, finding María Teresa innocent. The autoviuda then disappeared from public view.

In fact, she returned to school and became a teacher. Ultimately, she became an inspector of government schools in the Federal District. Her life—model student, beauty queen, self-made widow, and schoolteacher—represented the range of new, baffling, and challenging roles for women in revolutionary Mexico.

SOURCE: Víctor Macías, "Murderous Beauty: Politics and Gender in Revolutionary Mexico" (manuscript); Michele J. Mericle, "Imagings at the Judas Tree: The Pardon Tales of Miss Mexico" (Unpub. master's thesis, University of Arizona, 2003).

Argentina on Radio Excelsior, Radio Razón, and other networks. His records, recorded in Argentina and Europe, made it possible to enjoy Gardel throughout the world.

Beginning in the 1930s, radio producers developed several successful programs. The radio melodrama proved an extremely popular program—one that would eventually appear on television. These serials, usually broadcast five days a week with story lines lasting up to a year, first appeared in Cuba and were produced by the Colgate-Palmolive company, which had financed the broadcast of popular soap operas in the United States. Other successful programs included live musical performances, sporting events, and talk shows.

The widespread adoption of radio and its communications potential resulted in the organization of the Inter-American Association of Broadcasting (IAAB) in 1946. Emilio Azcárraga, owner of XEW, touted as "The Voice of Latin America from Mexico," and connected to the National Broadcasting Company and the Columbia Broadcasting System of the United States, the Canadian Broadcasting Company, and companies in Cuba, chaired the inaugural session. The IAAB focused on the principles of freedom of information and soon received recognition from both the United Nations and the Organization of American States.[23]

Radio contributed substantially to the creation of the imagined community that constituted national identity, and it provided a powerful medium for the promotion of populism. One of the first national leaders to grasp the power of radio was Mexico's President Lázaro Cárdenas. During his 6-year presidential administration, he distributed a radio receiver to every agricultural and workers' community in the nation, so that people could listen to educational and political programs broadcast on stations operated by the national educational department and the official political party.

## Cultural Nationalism

Forces besides technology drove the rise and development of cultural forms. In Cuba, nationalists reacting to U.S. meddling in the island's affairs under the Platt Amendment to the Cuban constitution turned to cultural nationalism. They rejected both an exclusive Spanish heritage as well as one derived from North American mores. During the first three decades of the twentieth century, Cubans revived African and some Chinese components mixed with the Spanish influences to create unique Cuban literature, music, dance, and visual arts. The emphasis on a multiethnic national legacy was a deliberate reaction to both Spanish and U.S. efforts to influence Cuban society. Nevertheless, elites still promoted a Eurocentric version of Cuban nationalism.

Cuba's validation of its African cultural heritage paralleled similar movements as Latin American intellectuals rediscovered the indigenous and African elements in their national cultures. In Haiti, Venezuela, and Brazil, nationalists gave new emphasis to their African heritage, and similar campaigns to recognize the Indian components of national culture occurred in Mexico and Peru.

Cubans turned to the "pure poetry movement," which included depictions of Afro-Cuban dances, music, religion, and folktales that enhanced the picturesque character of the work. Poetry in the *Negrismo* style followed in 1928 with

---

[23]Juan M. Durán, "Biography of Emilio Azcarraza Milmo" (undated, unpublished), State Historical Society of Wisconsin, Archives Division, Mss 8AF/7.

"La Rumba" by José Tallet. This poetry used African words for rhythmic effect and utilized, at first, the concepts of African primitivism developed by European intellectuals and artists such as Pablo Picasso. Afro-Cubans soon altered the character of this style so that it revealed the social and economic racism on the island. Nicolás Guillén became the foremost exponent of this poetic style.

Music was transmitted widely in the twentieth century through live performances, radio broadcasts, and phonograph recordings. Throughout Latin America, the musical heritage, despite costumbrismo, continued to draw on the study and performance of European music. As early as 1866, Cubans had established the Society of Classical Music, and their counterparts in Santiago de Cuba formed the Beethoven Society in 1872. Slavery added its influence in Afro-Cuban religion, music, dance, and cuisine. Such influence manifested itself during the nineteenth century in the *danzón, bolero, danza,* and *contra-danza,* which originated from *santería* and *ñañiquismo* religious ceremonies. These dance forms evolved into the popular *rumba-cubana* and *conga* dances that, early in the twentieth century, moved from the Afro-Cuban neighborhoods to the cabarets of Havana and Santiago de Cuba.

In Brazil, at the end of the 1920s, the first samba school appeared in Rio; others quickly followed based on the membership of the Ranchos and Blocos de Sujo. The idea of calling it a school came from the neighborhood of Estácio de Sá, where there existed a teacher training school. The sambistas decided they were the professors of samba and so took the name, much to the disdain of middle- and upper-class Brazilians. The samba schools appropriated the carnival celebration as the focus of their activities.

Musical trends across the region became more patriotic in the 1920s and 1930s with the appearance of musical nationalism, a theme that continued through World War II. Musical nationalism reflected, in part, the flourishing of the national conservatories created at the end of the nineteenth century, the music curricula offered in universities, the construction or reconstruction of opera houses and concert halls at the turn of the century, and the organization of national symphony orchestras in several countries in the 1930s.

Musical nationalism reached its apogee in the 1920s. Mexican composer Carlos Chávez evoked pre-Columbian themes as part of the revolutionary program of Indianism. He and his followers incorporated into their works indigenous rhythms, melodies, and instruments. His *Sinfonía India* typifies these compositions. Chávez enjoyed national prominence as director and conductor of the Orquesta Sinfónica de México and as director of the National Conservatory. The indigenous cultures also influenced the music of the Andean regions. Ecuadorian and Peruvian composers found inspiration in rhythms and instruments of indigenous peoples, while Bolivian composers continued in the European Romantic style with the addition of folk-music elements.

Africa had a deep and significant influence on music in Latin America. In Cuba, Afro-Cuban rhythms and methods inspired the national music. Venezuela had a rich Caribbean heritage that, of course, included a distinct West African influence. Venezuelan composers Vicente Emilio Sojo and Juan Bautista Plaza drew on folk dances such as *jorovo.* Only later did the Afro-Venezuelan influence appear in formal compositions.

Sound recordings first appeared in Latin America in the 1890s and featured national music. In Argentina, the first records (1893) featured *Aires de la Pampa,* traditional dances. The major expression of Argentine musical nationalism came from composer Alberto Ginastera, who built on the *gaucho* tradition, including sung and recited portions of the national epic, *Martín Fierro.* In Brazil, Heitor Villa-Lobos occupied a similar position. He combined his experience with popular urban strolling serenaders with avant-garde European techniques.

The international competition to sell both phonographs and recordings resulted in campaigns as early as the 1890s by both Thomas Edison's U.S. company and the English company BMI to record Latin American music groups and market the records. This recording activity did not have widespread success until the 1920s and 1930s, when the *mambo* and, above all, the tango became popular.

After World War II, a movement toward musical cosmopolitanism swept the hemisphere. Of course, crosscurrents to the nationalism of the previous four to five decades had existed, but now the rejection of nationalistic themes reached full force in avant-garde compositions, featuring serialism and atonality. Some of these compositions captured moments of great import; others chose as their themes the achievements of prominent leaders. Examples include José Ardévol's celebration of the Cuban triumph at the Bay of Pigs in *La Victoria de la Playa Girón* and *Che Comandante.* Meanwhile, under the influence of Paolo Guarnieri, Argentina experienced a musical renaissance. Universities and the Latin American Center for Advanced Musical Studies at the DiTelli Institute offered musical instruction under Guarnieri's direction. Avant-garde Brazilian music emerged in 1960, particularly in the compositions emanating from the Salvador Seminários Livres de Música in Bahia.

A powerful trend in Latin American music has been the appearance, since 1950, of urban, commercial music, distributed widely on the radio and through the sale of records, cassettes, compact discs, and recently computer downloads. This music can be traced to European salon dances, popular among the elite, especially the waltz in the nineteenth century. Cuban dance music such as the *habanera,* the bolero, the rumba, the conga, and the mambo added elements of Afro-Cuban polyrhythms and syncopation.

In Mexico, the *jarabe* (a music and dance form) can easily be transformed into a fast-tempo waltz, such as "Cielito Lindo." Miguel Lerdo de Tejada (1869–1941) became the first popular composer to use lyrics in the modified jarabe form. Mexican music (*canción romántica mexicana*) found its expression in Lerdo de Tejada's 1901 "Perjura." Influenced by Cuban boleros, Mexican romantic music was popularized in the 1920s through sound films. Phonograph companies (the Victor Talking Machine Company opened a Mexican factory in 1935) made the music popular throughout Latin America.

The most popular interpreter and composer of this genre was Agustín Lara, best known for his song "Granada." Known as the "Minstrel of the Nation," Lara personified the new mass cultural forms of recorded music, radio, and movies. His songs reflected the changing identity and consciousness of a society becoming increasingly urban and modern. Their popularity came from the focus on the

Courtesy of the Latin America Library at Tulane University.

Music, perhaps more than any cultural expression except cuisine, represents national identity in Latin America. Cuban mambo, Argentine tango, Brazilian samba, and Mexican ranchera are all readily recognized national musical styles. Bands, often sponsored by municipal authorities, linked officials to the popular classes. They performed in the main square on Sundays and on holidays for all to enjoy.

social underdogs (such as prostitutes) in language that borrowed heavily from both the widely known liturgical forms of music and modernist poetry. His romantic tunes expressed sentimental nostalgia for rural Mexico. (Argentine singer Carlos Gardel captured these same sentiments, set to different rhythms with different instrumentation, in the tangos.) Lara, beginning as a house pianist in a bordello, learned popular styles that he combined to create his "cosmopolitan" style. He soon began performing on Mexico City radio station XEQ. He also started writing music for the movies, first in 1931 for *Santa,* creating the style known as *cabaretara,* or dance-hall films. The movies and music served as cautionary tales or morality plays for young women migrating from the countryside to the capital city. These sentiments found expression in such songs as "Mujer," "Perdida," and "Amor de Mis Amores." Radio, records, and the movies gave Lara a loyal following that persisted, even when new music (such as rock and roll) appeared. In 1970, when he died, his funeral drew thousands of fans, who followed his cortège through the streets of Mexico City.[24]

---

[24]See Andrew Grant Wood's forthcoming biography, *The Intimate Hour: The Life and Music of Agustín Lara* (Wilmington, DE: SR Books).

From South America has come the most popular and enduring dance form in Latin America, the *cumbia*. It originated as an Afro-Panamanian and Caribbean-coastal Colombian dance. Some of the more sensual male movements have been lost in its urban form, but the music remains unchanged. Somewhat related is the urban popular music called *chichi* developed by Peruvian young people in the 1960s and 1970s, which combines Caribbean and Afro-Peruvian dance rhythms with Andean melodic style.

In Argentina and Uruguay, the tango, which began as a scandalous dance of bawdy houses, became an expression of popular cultural nationalism. Its greatest interpreter remains Carlos Gardel (1887–1935), still popular long after his death in an airplane crash. He made the dance and music a form of social and political expression. Among the many examples of tango, a favorite is "Adiós Muchachos," by Julio César Sanders. The tango enjoyed a major revival in the 1960s and 1970s.

In Brazil, carnival sparked the development by the 1920s of the samba. The first record of this form, "Pelo Telefone" by Ernesto dos Santos (known as Donga), was made in 1917, and samba quickly spread to the favelas and particularly to the samba schools that paraded during carnival. In the mid-1950s the *bossa nova,* followed later by the *tropicália* form of music and poetry performances, swept Brazil. During the 1950s and 1960s, the popularity of North American music increased dramatically in Brazil. U.S. companies and their subsidiaries produced half the record labels in the 1950s. Disk jockeys received cash (payola) from record companies to play more and more U.S. rock-and-roll music, although its popularity was superseded for two weeks each year by carnival and samba. The visit of the French ambassador to one of the samba schools in 1955 gave the needed European cultural approval of the music, so that it became acceptable to upper-class Brazilians.[25]

No discussion of music in Latin America would be complete without mention of protest songs. In virtually every Latin American nation, songs have been used to examine sociopolitical questions, or simply for social protest. Beginning in the 1960s, Chileans prompted an entire genre of protest songs, called the *Nueva Canción.* The Chileans gave musical form to demands for social revolution. The *Nueva Trova* style in Cuba and the folk music, or *peña* style music, of the Andes typified protest music. Easily accessible in the United States is Caribbean calypso music, some of which was sanitized and popularized by Bing Crosby, the Andrews Sisters, and Harry Belafonte. Calypso developed as political and social commentaries by such Trinidad and Tobago artists as Atilla the Hun (Raymond Quevedo), the Mighty Sparrow, and the Mighty Lion.[26]

---

[25]Raphael, "Samba and Social Control," *passim.*

[26]This discussion is based on the excellent essay by Gerard H. Béhague, "Latin American Music, c. 1920–c. 1980," in Leslie Bethell, ed., *The Cambridge History of Latin America,* vol. 10: *Latin America Since 1930: Ideas, Culture and Society* (Cambridge: Cambridge University Press, 1995), pp. 307–364. See also his "Popular Music," in Harold E. Hinds Jr., and Charles M. Tatum, eds., *Handbook of Latin American Culture* (Westport, CT: Greenwood Press, 1985), pp. 3–38; Graham E. L. Holton, "Oil, Race, and Calypso in Trinidad and Tobago," in William H. Beezley and Linda Curcio-Nagy, eds., *Latin American Popular Culture: An Introduction* (Wilmington, DE: SR Books, 1999).

Although in context these were protest songs, both American and British production companies recorded them or recorded "cover" versions by their own artists as entertainment. Sold throughout Europe and in the United States, the protest was lost to the popularity of rhythm.

## Movies

Motion pictures vie with music for the attention of the population in Latin America even today. The year 1896 brought the movies to the region. C. F. Bon Bernard and Gabriel Veyre, agents of the French Lumière brothers, showed President Porfirio Díaz and his family *The Arrival of the Train* and *The Arrival of the Czar.* The representatives soon offered the films in public showings. Bernard and Veyre began to make films in Mexico, especially of President Díaz. More agents from the same company arrived that year with projectors to show films in Argentina and Brazil. Veyre went to Cuba and established regular film showings in early 1897.

Cinema exploded in popularity over the next two decades. Even small towns soon had theaters. By 1902 Mexico had some 300 cinemas, while resourceful entrepreneurs moved into the countryside projecting their films in cafés, village halls, or on the walls of their own tents. Many of the earliest films portrayed the dangers of city life in melodramas, such as the Mexican film *Santa,* based on Federico Gamboa's 1903 novel. In a reversal of the civilization (city) and barbarism (countryside) arguments of Domingo Sarmiento of the nineteenth century, the village became the reservoir of virtue and values and the city the site of immorality, danger, and destruction of national traditions. These early silent films drew on a variety of influences, including Hollywood, theater melodrama, and itinerant vaudeville troupes. Few movies of this silent era reached memorable status, except for the Brazilian film *Limite,* made in 1929 by Mario Peixoto. In 1988, critics voted it the best Brazilian film of all time.

Adding sound to movies initially resulted in the production of multiple versions of the same film in different languages, because the technology did not allow mixing of dubbed sound tracks. Latin American stars appeared in Spanish-language films. Carlos Gardel, Xavier Cugat, and Lupita Tovar were among the most notables to make the journey to California or to Paris, where Paramount opened facilities to make non-English-language films. These films suffered many liabilities, not the least of which was the absence of popular Hollywood personalities. Only a few performers, such as Carlos Gardel, had the star power to make these movies profitable.

In the mid-1930s Brazil, Argentina, and Mexico, with large domestic audiences, began producing their own "talkies." Most of the early actors and production personnel had some experience in Hollywood, so these films were technically and artistically very good. Outstanding Mexican examples include *Santa, El Prisionero Trece,* and *Allá en el Rancho Grande,* which featured the quintessential singing *charro* (cowboy) who became popular throughout the hemisphere.

All three domestic film industries achieved box office success in the production of musicals. Mexican sound films, after some experimentation, found enduring stars in three performers: Jorge Negrete, as a charro, sang nostalgic ranch songs; Agustín Lara represented urban amorality as a nightclub crooner; and Pedro

Infante gave voice to the urban dispossessed. Argentine cinema required no period of trial and error. The Paramount films starring Carlos Gardel were immensely popular and were quickly imitated by domestic film companies. The 600 or so movie houses featured Hollywood productions unless they could get a tango flick, such as the extremely popular *Los Muchachos de Antes No Usaban Gomina* (*Back Then Boys Didn't Use Hair Cream*). Brazilian talking films also built on the national musical heritage of both comic theater and carnival. Bringing musicians already established as radio and recording stars to the screen ensured movie success. Carmen Miranda, for example, made more than 300 records and then made five films before being lured to the United States in 1939.

Both Mexican and Argentine films became so successful that they developed an export market in other Spanish-speaking regions, including the southwestern United States. Of these three national cinema industries, only Mexican companies expanded during the 1940s. Brazilian experience, especially that of the Vera Cruz company, demonstrated that the market could not support extensive and expensive production. Argentina, meanwhile, endured boycotts; for example, the United States responded to Argentina's neutral position in World War II by cutting off the supply of raw film stock.

Movies remained widely popular from 1940 to 1970. The 1940s were the golden decade of filmmaking in Mexico. The U.S. government, as part of its Good Neighbor Policy through Nelson Rockefeller's Office of the Coordinator of Inter-American Affairs, provided access to raw film stock and other raw materials as well as technical assistance during World War II. Government financial support through Banco Cinematográfico underpinned production costs. By 1949 the Mexican film industry enjoyed a 25 percent share of the domestic market, and its films were exported widely. Mexican movie stars—Cantinflas, Jorge Negrete, Tin-Tan, Pedro Infante, Dolores del Río, María Félix, Pedro Armendáriz, and Niñón Sevilla—had fans throughout the hemisphere. In the 1950s and 1960s, Mexican theatergoers flocked to films starring masked wrestlers, especially El Santo (who made 21 films), while Argentines preferred glimpses of Isabel Sarli's body in sex comedies.

The New Cinema and the Brazilian version, Cinema Novo, of the 1960s received great encouragement from the general excitement generated by the Cuban revolution. The result was the emergence of filmmakers committed to linking their work with the ideologies of change that were sweeping the hemisphere. New Cinema produced its greatest successes in Cuba, Chile, and Bolivia. Representative films, respectively, were *Memorias del Subdesarrollo* (*Memories of Underdevelopment*), *El Chacal de Nahueltoro* (*The Jackal of Nahueltoro*), and *Yawar Malku* (*Blood of the Condor*). Near the middle of the 1970s the wave of military coups and the unleashing of the military's "dirty war" against radical intellectuals and leftist politicians in several nations for the most part brought an end to New Cinema.

Movie production remained strong for a time in Mexico, Brazil, and Cuba until Neoliberal economic policies cut government financial backing. Argentina's film industry made a dramatic recovery following the return to democratic government in 1983, highlighted by an Oscar for best foreign film awarded to *La Historia Oficial* in 1986. In Mexico, the state has been heavily involved in the movie industry since 1970. The government took control of the industry, hoping to re-create a sense of nationalism after the massacre at Tlatelolco (1968) and to restore the quality of the national cinema. On taking office in 1970, President Luis Echeverría initiated a major government program to support the film industry. Initially, young directors were encouraged to address social and political issues; but they exercised self-censorship, fully aware that three topics remained off limits: certain religious themes, especially the Virgin of Guadalupe, the military, and the presidency. This self-censorship can be seen clearly in the transfer of written materials to the screen, such as the award-winning screenplay about the appearance of the Virgin, *Nuevo Mundo,* which became a lackluster film of the same name.

Official control of the industry generally damaged the integrity of the films and their directors. President Carlos Salinas (1988–1994) sold much of the film industry to private concerns. Beginning in 1990, censorship restrictions were loosened, allowing for the showing of *Rojo Amanecer,* a film about the massacre of 1968, and *La Sombra del Caudillo,* a searing account of the process of presidential succession, which had been banned for over 20 years. In general, despite difficulties of production and funding, cinema audiences remained large, especially in Mexico, Brazil, and Argentina.[27]

## Comic Books

Comic books have constituted one of the most popular cultural forms in Latin America, especially in urban centers, during the twentieth century. Translations of U.S. comic strips arrived as early as 1902 in Mexico, with the first Mexican cartoon—*Don Lupito* by Andrés Audoffred—appearing the following year. Both Argentine and Brazilian newspapers began publishing translated and national cartoons by 1912. A great burst of creativity in the comic industry occurred in the late 1920s.

Many regard the 1920s to the early 1950s as the heyday of comics. Mexico's first comic book, *Paquín (Frankie),* appeared in 1934 and was quickly followed by a host of others. In Argentina, Dante Quintero's *Patorugú* told the story of an Indian of the pampas, akin to *Popeye,* and his encounters with urban Buenos Aires. *Patorugú* appeared first in the newspapers and in 1935 as a comic magazine. Brazilians welcomed the publication of weekly color tabloid comics, called *Suplemento Juvenil,* by the newspaper *A Nação.* The first comic book, *Gibi Mensual (Monthly Comic),* appeared in 1934.

This era ended in the early 1950s with a wave of censorship campaigns and a decline in creativity. The only notable innovation after this time was the pocket-size comic book developed in Mexico by Manuel de Landa. The most popular of these was *Lágrimas, Risas y Amor (Tears, Laughter, and Love).* By the early 1960s,

---

[27]See John King, "Latin American Cinema," in Leslie Bethell, ed., *The Cambridge History of Latin America,* vol. 10: *Latin America Since 1930: Ideas, Culture and Society* (Cambridge: Cambridge University Press, 1995), pp. 455–518; David R. Maciel, "Cinema and the State in Contemporary Mexico, 1970–1991: A Study in the Politics of Culture," in David R. Maciel and Joanne Hershfield, eds., *Mexico's Cinema: A Century of Wondrous Films and Filmmakers, 1896–1996* (Wilmington, DE: SR Books, forthcoming).

Argentine Joaquín Salvador Lanado had created *Malfalda,* about a precocious young girl who commented on middle-class life. The comic strip became a hemispheric sensation. The Brazilian counterpart was the series of Mónica books of Maurício de Sousa. Melodramatic stories also appeared in comic book form and were called *fotonovelas* (photo novels).[28]

## CONTEMPORARY SOCIETY
## (1960 TO THE PRESENT)

### Television

Television came to Latin America in the 1950s. Despite the increased role of state enterprises, the new broadcasting companies were privately held. The Mexican government named a committee to evaluate private (as in the United States) and public (as in England) ownership before deciding on the former. Television built on the successful programming patterns of radio and relied heavily on popular personalities from the movies. It quickly created new celebrities and new forms, such as the combination variety and game show in the 1950s. The emergence of videotape in the 1960s resulted in a rush of imported foreign, especially U.S., programs. Then in the 1970s, Brazil, Mexico, Venezuela, and Colombia developed their own production companies and soon began exporting programs on videotape to the rest of the region.

Radio has remained a powerful medium throughout the hemisphere. Today local radio broadcasts have become increasingly important for the preservation of indigenous languages and campaigning for ethnic politics; but the most important programming, especially in Mexico, has relied on music shows, sports events (especially soccer and boxing), comedies, and above all, serial melodramas. All of these programs appeared in pioneer television. Radio soap operas became *tele-novelas.* In Mexico the first series, *Angeles de la Calle* (*Street Angels*), appeared weekly in 1951, followed in 1957 by *Senda Prohibida* (*Forbidden Path*), with installments five times a week. Mexico soon became the leader in this style of program and remains so today. The Mexican telenovela tends to be romantic and melodramatic. Brazilian telenovelas lean toward more social realism and, occasionally, feature a discussion of social issues. The Colombian programs generally have a preference for historical themes. Despite the huge popularity of these serials, for a single program they finish second to soccer championships in both Mexico and Brazil. Telenovelas have a mass appeal that since their origin has cut across class, gender, and ethnic lines. In Mexico, like the extremely successful comic book stories, the telenovelas often represent the clash of traditional or rural values with contemporary, especially urban, ones. These programs reached a so-called golden age (1982 to 1986) with classics such as *Tú o Nadie* and *La Cuna de Los*

---

[28]Harold E. Hinds Jr., "Comics," *Handbook of Latin American Culture,* pp. 81–86.

*Lobos.* These Mexican serials even became successful in Europe, where *Simplemente María* nearly brought Moscow to a complete stop each afternoon, and in other parts of the world, including both China and Arab countries. The popularity of these melodramas reached new levels in the entire hemisphere including the United States with *Beti, La Fea* (the tale of how unattractive Betty transforms herself into a supermodel). Recently Televisa (Mexico's most powerful network) and TV Globo (Brazil's television giant) reached an agreement for joint production of telenovelas. Televisa also provides telenovelas to Univision, the largest Spanish-language network in the United States.

Variety shows also appeared with characteristics unique to Latin America. These shows from their beginnings have been broadcast live, with a charismatic host (called the *animador*) and a studio audience. The archetype remains the 6-hour Mexican *Siempre en Domingo* (*Always on Sunday*) with Raúl Velasco, who directs the corny games, popular music, slapstick comedy, and amateur performances.

Generally television in Latin America suffers from two weaknesses: its news coverage and programming for children. Self-censorship has been the major limitation on news reporting. (For example, in Mexico, reporting on the Zapatista Liberation Army's rebellion in Chiapas resulted in widespread debate over prejudicial coverage.) That television did not host a debate among presidential candidates in Mexico until 1994 also illustrates the shortcomings of television news programming. Children's programming continues to rely on imported shows, with translations, and on poorly produced local ones. The Spanish-American programs lack creativity and, like the government-supported documentaries, attract only a small audience. The exception has been the Brazilian children's variety program, hosted by Xuxa, which attracted such a widespread and enthusiastic audience that efforts have begun to export the program in Spanish translation to the rest of the region, including the United States. Xuxa, a sexy blond, attracted adult viewers along with children. The success of the Brazilian program reflects the size (both in budget and number of viewers) of TV Globo, the world's fourth-largest network, behind the three major U.S. television networks.[29]

## Personal Computers and the Internet

The Internet, the worldwide network of interconnected computer networks, has a growing impact on Latin American cultures. The scientific, government, and business communities used the Internet for communication purposes as early as the 1960s; but it was not until the 1990s, with the arrival of the World Wide Web, that the Internet became a part of everyday life in many corners of the world. The World Wide Web is the part of the Internet that combines text, color, sound, graphics, animation, video, interactivity, and ways to jump (via links) from place

---

[29]See the entries on radio, television, and telenovelas in *Encyclopedia of Latin American History and Culture* (New York: Charles Scribner's Sons, 1996), vol. II: 238–239; vol. IV: 528–529; and the entry on telenovelas and television in the *Encyclopedia of Mexico: History, Society & Culture* (Chicago: Fitzroy Dearborn Publishers, 1997), pp. 1395–1396, 1397–1400; Celeste Gonzalez, "The Early Decades of Mexican Television" (Ph.D. dissertation, University of Arizona, forthcoming).

to place. Individuals with personal computers may connect to the Internet by means of a modem and telephone line or satellite. Once connected, users have an array of information resources at their disposal and may communicate and exchange ideas and information with people and computers around the world.

Latin American government agencies, banks, and large businesses began using computers in the 1960s. By the 1980s personal computers were on the market, and individuals and small businesses began purchasing them in large numbers. More than a dozen computer manufacturers had established plants in Mexico in the late 1970s under Mexican majority ownership, although in some cases, Mexican interests controlled only production and distribution of hardware and software. The Brazilians tried to develop their own computer hardware industry in the 1970s. Efforts by such firms such as Computadores e Sistemas Brasileiros, S.A. (COBRA) and the Brazilian government to manufacture computers, printers, and peripherals and to develop software limped along until the Brazilian government lifted restrictions on the importation of foreign products and components in 1992.

Although computers are widely available in Latin America, connecting to and communicating via the Internet has been constrained by unreliable power sources, shaky telephone service, minimal technical support and services, and the high cost of access. Nevertheless, these problems have not impeded the spread of personal computers. In 1993 there were 13 computers per 1,000 residents in Mexico, 6 in Brazil, and 2 in Guatemala, compared to 265 in the United States.

Developing the infrastructure to support widespread Internet access has been a slow process. By the early 1990s several countries—notably Mexico, Argentina, Peru, Brazil, Costa Rica, and Chile—had established Internet hosts (computers that enable other computers to connect to the Internet). The Organization of American States in 1991 established its Hemisphere Wide Inter-University Scientific and Technological Information Network throughout Latin America and the Caribbean. By 1994, some 600 private networks throughout Latin America had been connected to the Internet. As a result, the national telephone companies in Argentina, Colombia, and Costa Rica (and the alternative telephone company in the Dominican Republic, Tricom) offer Internet services.[30]

Perhaps the best example of the Internet's impact on Latin American culture and contemporary events are the communiqués from Sub-Comandante Marcos and the Zapatista National Liberation Army about the rebellion in the Mexican state of Chiapas—widely circulated on the Internet before wire service stories reached the mainstream news media.

The Mexican government of President Vicente Fox became the North American leader in the development of educational computer systems. Fox announced the creation of *e-Mexico* to provide the Internet to all Mexicans in the country and in the United States over the next 20 years. This campaign includes the goal of opening 10,000 community centers with free computer and Internet access, with at least one in every municipality and several in the southwestern United States. As of April 2005 the government has opened over 7,200 centers,

---

[30] *Encyclopedia of Latin American History and Culture*, vol. II: 238–239.

## Internet Access in Latin America

covering every state in Mexico, and 69 centers in 18 of the states in the United States. The *e-Mexico* program, with information and instructions on its website in Spanish, Maya, Mazahua, English, and French, has four main categories of programs: e-Aprendizaje, focusing on providing Internet educational programs; e-Salud, offering information and accessing to health care and social services; e-Economia, accelerating development of digital markets, with both producers and consumers; and e-Gobierno, providing information on government services (and it eventually may allow for voting in national elections). The *e-Mexico* program also provides a portal called e-Migrantes containing critical information on migrant rights, remittances, and legal requirements.

## Soccer

Of all the popular cultural manifestations in Latin America, nothing rivals soccer matches or ties this region to the rest of the globe more securely than does the World Cup. Pelé, a Brazilian, is considered the greatest soccer player of all time. Brazil is the only country to have won four World Cup championships.

The psychological importance of soccer varies by class, gender, and region; but its hold on Latin American men is virtually total. Incidents, both amusing and tragic, demonstrate how seriously fans take the game. A hapless member of the 1994 Colombian team who inadvertently scored a goal against his own side in World Cup competition was shot to death in the streets of Medellín. Mexico's 2–1 loss to Germany in 1998 sparked rioting in Mexico City. In Paris, a drunk, bitterly disappointed Mexican fan urinated on the perpetual flame commemorating the unknown soldiers of World War I, extinguishing the flame that had burned under the Arc de Triomphe since 1929. Luis Hernández, who scored Mexico's only point against Germany, apologized for the loss and insisted that Mexico had nothing to be ashamed of—many soccer fans agreed.

Soccer is actually a relatively new sport in Latin America. Its popularity is linked closely to urbanization. Initially, throughout the region the game was associated with foreigners, the elite youths who studied abroad, and European modernization. With the rapid growth of cities, soccer soon became an important part of urban culture. For the lower classes, soccer provides a means to achieve dignity and affords a sense of participation in the broader society and the nation itself. Of all Latin American countries, Brazil appears to have the most fervent attachment to the game and provides the best example of the culture of soccer.

## The Culture of Soccer in Brazil

Charles Miller, an Englishman born in Brazil, introduced soccer there in 1894 after returning from school in England. The São Paulo Athletic Club, originally organized to promote cricket, became the first group to sponsor a soccer team in Brazil. The game became popular among the elite and foreign community. Another Englishman, Oscar Cox, founded Rio de Janeiro's Fluminense Soccer Club.

Soccer's nearly exclusive association with high society and the foreign enclave began to weaken in 1904 when English technicians at a Rio textile mill organized the Bangu Athletic Club, subsidized by the mill. So that they would have a rival practice team, the Englishmen organized factory workers and taught them the game. Bangu unexpectedly attracted lower-class fans. Nevertheless, the elite, upper middle class, and particular ethnic groups continued to organize clubs. The Portuguese community's Club Vasco da Gama; the Atlético Mineiro, founded in 1913 by Belo Horizonte's Middle Eastern community; and the city's other club, Cruzeiro, originally organized as the Sociedad Sportiva Palestia Italia in 1923, are notable examples. Some 5,000 soccer clubs now exist; they are no longer dependent on foreigners or the elite.

Sometime around 1910, *peladas* (pickup games using rolled-up balls of cloth) became popular in lower-class neighborhoods. Out of the peladas culture emerged some spectacular lower-class players who came to the attention of the clubs. São Paulo's Corinthians, founded by British railway engineers in 1910, was one of the first organizations to recruit talented lower-class players, paying them varying amounts based on their skills. Fluminense in Rio followed reluctantly, avoiding blacks and recruiting only light-skinned players. Carlos Alberto, a mulatto, dusted himself with rice powder (*pó de arroz*) before public games. Fluminense's nickname remains po de arroz. Black clubs such as the São Geraldo Athletic Association (1910) and Cravos Vermelhos (1916) soon began to be organized. Until the late 1920s and early 1930s black soccer clubs competed only against each other, despite the by then racially mixed teams of traditional clubs.

In the 1930s radio broadcasts of major club games created a following far beyond the club's actual location; in effect, clubs developed a national constituency. By then Brazilian soccer players had international reputations, and other countries avidly recruited them. Soccer in Brazil became legally professionalized in 1933 in response to the loss of players to Italy, Argentina, and elsewhere. The Brazilian Sports Confederation (CBD) recognized players as salaried employees subject to labor laws and worker protection.

Soccer in Brazil reflects the country's class system. Paradoxically, it mixes class and racial tensions with the leveling and unifying force of Brazilian nationalism. Such seemingly contradictory impulses stem from the club structure. The clubs are owned by their dues-paying members, who in turn own the teams they sponsor. Clubs are now mainly middle-class organizations with large memberships. Rio's Flamengo has around 65,000 dues-paying members, while São Paulo's Corinthian has over 150,000. The clubs provide swimming pools, weight rooms, tennis courts, and social events along the lines of an American country club. Much of middle-class socializing is centered at the club. To play soccer for the club does not mean one is a member. Players are employees—perhaps well paid—not members entitled to vote or use the facilities of the organization.

The lower classes cannot afford to join clubs. Even if these people had the money, social barriers discourage them from becoming members. Nevertheless, their avid interest in the game has resulted in the rise of shadow organizations—fan clubs called *torcidas organizadas.* One of the easiest organizations to join, the torcida welcomes poor soccer fans as members and provides an instant sense of belonging and group solidarity. The torcida has its own president and officers and offers many benefits. These fan clubs offer a variety of services, such as assistance in finding housing; legal advice; useful information on finances, health, and education; and emergency help. Such services are important to migrants new to a complex and often intimidating urban environment. Although there are no membership fees, participation is not without expense, because members often buy banners, shirts, and other symbols of club loyalty. In general, a torcida has twice as many members as the team-sponsoring club. In São Paulo, soccer torcidas have more members than do religious groups, unions, or neighborhood associations combined. Lower-class dependency on fan clubs leads to fierce loyalty. Mafia Azul, which supports the Cruzeiro team, is a typical torcida with members in every region and city of Brazil. Fans arrive at the stadium several hours before the game to prepare elaborate demonstrations to support their team. Mafia Azul members frequently travel to other locales to attend games, staying with fans in that particular city who in effect are part of a national kinship group. Cruzeiro club members and Mafia Azul members are separated by function and class, united only in their support of the team. The former legally own and manage the team, and the latter supply the emotional spirit and unify the general public in support of the team.

The selection of a national team to compete in the World Cup brings the clubs and torcidas together in defense of Brazil's honor. The national team, not the government, represents Brazil before the world—it is a tense time for all. A win brings euphoria while a loss causes deep, divisive, and self-searching remorse. For example, the loss to Uruguay in 1950 is bitterly remembered by individuals born well after the event. Years later, in 1963, a journalist wrote:

> Friends, you all remember the shame of 1950. It was a humiliation worse than Canudos. The Uruguayan Obdulio beat our seleção with a shout and a finger in our face. Do not tell me that the seleção is only a soccer team. No. If a team enters the field with the name of Brazil, with the national anthem playing, then it is as if our nation was wearing shorts and soccer shoes.[31]

Even in victory, shame—or the merciful absence of it—is evoked. After Brazil's World Cup victory in 1970, an editorial declared that thanks to the Brazilian team, "We do not *have* to be ashamed to be Brazilians."

The combination of club involvement and lower-class players draws the classes together at least temporarily. Brazil's 1998 World Cup superstar Ronaldo, rated the world's best player, at one time could not afford bus fare to attend soccer practice. His fellow team member Ze Carlos sold watermelons in order to survive. Players like these are close to the hearts of lower-class torcida members. The 1998 competition was indeed a classic. The finals pitted Brazil against France. France represented everything Brazilians perceived themselves not to be but wished they could be—highly cultured, intellectual, and self-confident, befitting a historic center of Western civilization. In effect, the match offered Brazilians an opportunity to escape, for a moment, Brazil's partially self-imposed burden of colonial shame. As coach Mario Zagallo observed, "If we win I don't expect them to build a statue to me . . . but if we lose, they'll kill me." Unfortunately, France's 3–0 victory plunged Brazilians into despair. Soccer clearly is more than a game. On the other hand, with World Cup victory number four in 2002 in the Japan and Korea Games, Brazilians celebrated for weeks.

---

[31]For more on Brazilian fan clubs and the issue of shame and remorse, see Jerome P. Villella, "Soccer in Brazilian Society: Historical Development and Social Significance," master's thesis, Tulane University, 1995.

# 8

# Cities

Independence changed urban life and cities themselves in significant ways. Fragmentation of former colonies into new nations tended to follow the spheres of influence of cities. Political and population centers for defined regions became the hubs of new nations. At independence, the population of Mexico City exceeded 120,000, Lima 53,000, Buenos Aires 40,000, and Bogotá 30,000. Former colonial capitals assumed a leadership role within the new republics of Spanish America. Secondary cities such as Guadalajara (Mexico), Guatemala City (Guatemala), Salvador (El Salvador), Tegucigalpa (Honduras), Montevideo (Uruguay), Santiago (Chile), Caracas (Venezuela), Asunción (Paraguay), and Quito (Ecuador) dominated regional politics and challenged the abrogation of national power by the former colonial capitals. Some of these secondary urban centers succeeded in becoming the focal point of a new nation—as did Guatemala City, Montevideo, Santiago (Chile), Caracas, Asunción, and Quito. Guadalajara did not, although Mexico City greatly feared that the residents of that city might try. The splintering of Central America thrust national roles on a series of smaller cities that contested Guatemala City's attempt to control the region.

In Portuguese America, cities did not serve as the centers of new nations because of the unique manner in which Brazil became an independent empire. The transfer of the Portuguese monarchy to Rio de Janeiro (1808) strengthened the political and territorial integrity of Brazil. When the king went home to Portugal in 1821, he directed his son to stay and lead the independence movement, if one developed.

The drawing of national boundaries and the structuring of all the elements of a sovereign nation required urgent attention. Policy governing national functions such as managing international relations, negotiating trade agreements, setting tariffs, establishing a monetary system, and defending the country's borders had to be determined and implemented. Unfortunately, the economic dislocation and population displacement that accompanied the wars of independence enfeebled many formerly important cities and damaged their surrounding agricultural or mineral resources. Recovery in the devastated countryside depended on the city leaders' ability to assemble the financial and material resources necessary to reestablish order and productivity. Resources, although scarce, tended to be concentrated in the larger cities, particularly the national capital.

The social, political, economic, and physical configuration of the city changed dramatically in the nineteenth century. The change reflected, in part, the number of recognized cities. At the beginning of the century, before independence, the Spanish Constitution of 1812 directed settlements of 1,000 persons or more in Latin America to establish town councils. This requirement resulted in a rapid increase in the incorporation of towns. The notion that the city itself, the capital in particular, displayed the nation's level of progress and represented the degree of civilization of the new republics, forced governments and the elite inhabitants to examine their towns. They did not like what they saw. Primitive conditions affronted them personally and constituted a national disgrace. Indeed, in the early 1800s many Latin American cities, despite their small population in modern terms, had become nearly unlivable. They seemed congested, physically unpleasant, and socially difficult locations in which to carry on day-to-day activities. For water, people relied on inadequate municipal fountains or water carriers to meet daily needs. Haphazard garbage disposal, inadequate sewage collection, and dust or mud—depending on the season—made urban life difficult and unhealthy. The city center, with elite mansions surrounding the major government or municipal buildings, the traditional seat of political and social authority, declined in desirability and importance.

By the 1870s, the elite began to abandon the plaza mayor and their old colonial mansions and moved to the outskirts of the city, where they constructed foreign-styled homes in a more pleasant environment. They used their political and economic influence to press the municipal government for wider streets, drains, clean water, and waste disposal. The retreat of the elites reversed the colonial pattern in which social status was associated with proximity to the physical seat of power. Owners subdivided old mansions into tenements, often called *conventillos* (little convents) because of their tiny apartments, for the urban poor. The lower classes now dominated the city center while the middle and upper class established new suburbs.

The nature of the economy had a direct reflection in the cities. Profits from the export of raw materials and commodities and loans on future production financed the modernization process. Coffee, cotton, sugar, latex, lumber, copper ore, and other products had to be moved in bulk into international trade channels

Courtesy of the Latin America Library at Tulane University.

Urban transportation altered the nature of cities in Latin America creating commercial zones, displacing the mixed residential and commercial pattern of colonial times, and making suburban residential development possible. Here a tram passes in front of a colonial church in Guanjuato, Mexico, in about 1900.

as efficiently as possible. Adequate ports, roads, and railways were essential to establishing a transportation network, but Latin American governments were unable to finance their construction. Foreign investment, loans, and engineering expertise became a critical need. Urban modernization followed the European model, with the importation of European styles, tools, and public and domestic decorations including monuments, iron columns, and garden ornaments. The new city became both a goal and a propaganda tool to add substance to the illusion of incredible returns to those willing to invest. Throughout Latin America the model became Paris, reconstructed by Baron Georges-Eugène Haussman according to the inspired whims of Emperor Napoleon III. The monumental and physical beauty of the French "City of Lights" symbolized a new age of urban refinement and progress.

To Latin Americans, the new city as an expression of modern life became the important objective. Antonio Escandón, a railway promoter and member of a wealthy money-lending family in Mexico, understood the imagery of European cities. Through his efforts to encourage the physical modernization of urban space, quickly seized upon by others, the Paseo de la Reforma in Mexico City became a ceremonial boulevard lined with civic statuary. His compatriot, Ignacio Cumplido, a founder of the liberal newspaper *El Siglo XIX,* pressed for the planting of trees, following the model of the Champs Elysées. The Paseo, created by the elite, remained apart from the "old" city. Open land on all sides allowed for new modern subdivisions. In the last decade of the nineteenth century new *colonias* (neighborhoods) were established, and the Paseo was adopted as the preferred location for the mansions of Mexico's foreign colonies and its own new financiers and entrepreneurs.

The same pattern of urban modernization occurred in every major capital. As the Brazilian Eduardo Prado observed, "Without a doubt the world is Paris."[1] In Brazil, the elites slowly transformed the federal capital of Rio de Janeiro (now located in Brasília) into the *cidade maravilhosa,* the marvelous city. For most of the nineteenth century, Rio had been a crowded, unhealthy place with low buildings, which had now achieved a certain splendor. Streetcars opened up spaces for housing developments and population growth. A trio of engineers—Francisco Pereira Passos, André Gustavo Paulo de Fontin, and Francisco de Bicalho—collaborated in a relentless remodeling of Rio in the final decade of the nineteenth century. Tenements and twisting alleys were destroyed to make way for new buildings and streets. A wide boulevard, Avenida Central (later called Rio Branco Avenue), cut through the old city. New, modern buildings with three to five stories sprang up along its length. The National Library, Municipal Theater, Senate, and Fine Arts Museum anchored one end of the avenue, an area today referred to as Cinelândia. The goal was not simply a modern city, but a city that would reform Brazilians, so they would adopt the elite's commitment to "order and progress." By the 1920s, Rio had at last caught up with Buenos Aires in terms of its cosmopolitan appearance. Behind the façade of progress, older areas underwent a transition to tenements, the refuge for the poor and newcomers.

In nineteenth-century Argentina, the city beautiful represented the pinnacle of civilization. The elites, following Sarmiento (see Chapter 3), characterized the surrounding countryside as backward, even barbaric. Idealization of the city coupled

---

[1]E. Bradford Burns, *The Poverty of Progress: Latin America in the Nineteenth Century* (Berkeley: University of California Press), p. 20.

with a flood of European immigrants created a destructive campaign, pitting urban civilization and progress against the traditional and backward rural areas and their rustic inhabitants. The banner of civilization firmly planted in Buenos Aires justified urban imperialism and conquest. The so-called Conquest of the Desert (1879–1880), mounted from the city, sought to reduce the countryside and force its inhabitants to become civilized. General Julio A. Roca urged his troops to "drive out or kill the Indians of the Pampa so that the land could be turned into markets of wealth and flourishing towns in which millions of men may live rich and happy."[2]

The "mission" of the city, accepted widely throughout Latin America, required urban control of the economy as well as the nation's political and cultural life. These city people cast everything in a European model (see the Profile, "'Have You Heard from the Princess?'—The Duque de Roca Negras," page 193). To José Enrique Rodó, writing in the last decade of the nineteenth century, the "large city" appeared to be the "necessary organism of high culture."[3] Meeting such expectations, the *Teatro Solís,* Latin America's oldest opera house, opened in Montevideo in 1851. The Solís soon attracted the best European talent. The great diva Adelina Patti thrilled audiences in the gala 1888 season. That same year, soprano Romilda Pantaleoni re-created her performance as Desdemona in Verdi's *Otello* only a year after its premiere in Milan. The Teatro Solís reached a new brilliance in 1903 when the entire La Scala company, including Enrico Caruso and conductor Arturo Toscanini, arrived in Uruguay. All the Latin American capitals soon boasted their own opera house, with regular performances by touring European troupes.

National resources tended to be lavished on major cities, particularly the capital. Railroads and telegraph and telephones lines radiated out from these primary centers, creating further distance between the city and lesser and shabbier settlements and the stark backwardness of rural areas. The nation came under the control of the "national" city. By 1903 Montevideo had become the world's largest capital in proportion to the country's population. At the turn of the century, 30 percent of Uruguay's population of 900,000 lived there. People referred to Montevideo as the "Suction Pump" as it relentlessly pulled wealth and power toward itself.[4] In Brazil, one could observe the jarring contrast between the graceful modernity of Rio de Janeiro at the turn of the century and the backlands settlements and secondary cities such as Niterói, just across Guanabara Bay. Amazed visitors felt that they could move magically from modern times into the past when they left Rio for

---

[2]Burns, p. 32.

[3]José Enrique Rodó, *Ariel,* trans. Margaret Sayers Peden (Austin: University of Texas Press, 1988), p. 91.

[4]John J. Johnson, *Political Change in Latin America, The Emergence of the Middle Sectors* (Palo Alto: Stanford University Press), p. 49.

Niterói. In a similar fashion, Buenos Aires and Mendoza appeared to occupy totally different universes. The nineteenth century represented a romantic age of urban innocence. Surely, the elites believed, modern, well-planned, and beautiful cities went hand in hand with progress.

## TWENTIETH-CENTURY CITIES

Demographic growth concentrated in the city. Between 1850 and 1900 the population of Latin America doubled; over the next 40 years it doubled again, reaching 200 million by 1970. The city became the destination of a mobile rural population. Although such demographic growth historically was not unusual, in the Latin American context it presented some unique aspects. On the one hand, in Europe the agricultural and industrial revolutions had caused rural surplus population relocation. In Latin America, on the other hand, population movement induced economic changes. Urban centers became attractive to the rural peasantry despite the city's ability to offer only limited productive employment. The promise of access to education, medical attention, potable water, and other urban attractions—a sense of participating in the modern world, coupled with the undercapitalization of the rural infrastructure—drew rural inhabitants into the cities.

The new arrivals came to the cities, even though they could not be absorbed in an orderly manner. By the middle of the twentieth century, the percentage of the population residing in cities ranged widely: 79 percent in Uruguay, 64 percent in Argentina, 54 percent in Chile, and 50.3 percent (1955) in Mexico, followed closely by Colombia (36 percent), Panama (35 percent), and Peru (31 percent). Thirty years later, all had become urban republics. Brazil tipped from rural to urban in 1975. For all of Latin America, the urban-rural balance shifted in 1965, when 50.3 percent resided in cities.

Migrants strove to maintain ties with their rural villages. In a secondary city such as Oaxaca, Mexico, where rural migrants had no previous urban experience, movement back and forth was common. Even a brief return provided a sense of retaining roots. These migrants lived and worked in the city, but their souls remained in the countryside. Because many of the people retained their rural mentality, commentators before World War I often called Mexico City the world's largest village.

The population shift, although predictable, overwhelmed the ability of city planners to cope with the influx of new arrivals and strained the availability of resources. State efforts to control land use, especially fertile agricultural land close to the city, failed. An unwillingness to divert capital into rural areas, coupled with construction of transportation routes that converged on large urban centers, funneled people into the city. The population of Lima spread beyond its original limits with the opening of the Lima-Callão rail connection in 1851 and the Lima-Miraflores-Chorillos line shortly thereafter. Other rail links to Magdalena on the Pacific coast formed an urban triangle that soon attracted a sizable population.

---

**P R O F I L E**    "Have You Heard from the Princess?"—The Duque de Roca Negras

In the 1920s, the age of the flapper and the Charleston, the entire world seemed mad as change swept aside old values. In the cities, changing sex roles and public smoking and drinking by young men and women gave life intensity, but robbed it of elegance and romance. Vito Modesto Franklin came to the rescue in Venezuela. He assumed the title of *Duque de Roca Negras* (Duke of Roca Negras), an imaginary title with equally doubtful but, in his mind, direct connections with the grandees of Spain. The Duke took Caracas by storm. Dressed in a morning suit embellished with dashing colors, with top hat and cane, he seemed to be a throwback to *La Belle Époque.* The Duke's courtly manners and natural elegance contrasted sharply with contemporary life. He appeared to be on his way to the gaming tables of an imaginary Monte Carlo or bound for a fashionable royal spa.

The Duke made known his passion for beautiful women at every opportunity, loudly pledging his undying love to them at the opera, at the bullring, or in the streets. Yet, the love of his life was the exquisitely beautiful Princess Piperazina du Midi—who allegedly lived in Europe, was often the houseguest of the British royal family, passed time with the kaiser in Potsdam, Germany, and played cards with idle royalty in Cintra or Estoril. His imaginary princess wrote loving, eloquent letters to her distant lover in Venezuela. An excited Duke took great pleasure in passing along the news to any remotely suitable audience. It became customary for people to inquire politely as the Duke moved through the streets of the city, "Have you heard from the princess?" The Duque de Roca Negras generously shared the goings-on of his beloved. In a courtly manner befitting royalty, he allowed all those who chose to do so to share his truly elegant delusion. He is barely remembered today, but for a time he brought life and romance to Caracas, a city undergoing great change.

SOURCE: "Duque de Roca Negras," *Venezuela Up-to-Date* 19, no. 1 (Spring 1978), p. 22.

---

Squatter settlements, once viewed as temporary, transitional centers composed of displaced peasants, by the middle of the twentieth century had become permanent shantytowns that could not be ignored.

The Lima suburb of José Gálvez began in 1943 as a squatter settlement consisting of a few makeshift dwellings. The earthquake of 1940 had destroyed much of the existing housing in the port city of Callão. Homeless workers gradually turned to José Gálvez, where they built shelters out of cardboard, tin cans, and anything else they could find. They soon created a major new suburb on the unstable banks of the Rimac River, but within a reasonable distance of employment opportunities.

A new stage of uncontrolled urbanization arrived with the sudden creation of the neighborhood called *Ciudad de Dios* (City of God). This settlement was well planned, not by the authorities, but by the potential squatters. Home seekers formed an association whose members carefully scheduled the "invasion" for Christmas Eve 1954, a time when they expected the authorities would be celebrating. The association chose the neighborhood's name to suggest religious protection and had already lined up substantial political support. A rapid influx of

Courtesy of the Latin America Library at Tulane University.

Band members pose in front of the National Theater in San Jose, Costa Rica, around the turn of the century. Modeled along the lines of the Paris Opera House, the building opened in 1897 with an elaborate production of Goethe's *Faust.* Construction of opera houses and national theaters asserted Latin America's claims to culture and served as focal points of national pride. The early notion of the city as a beautiful center of high culture collapsed with the onset of unplanned urbanization.

people built homes of makeshift construction materials, making it difficult for property owners on the southern rim of Lima to evict them. Within months, with close to a thousand families, the permanence of the settlement was assured. Because Ciudad de Díos was located far beyond business centers and potential employers, the settlement had to create its own internal economy with little assistance from either the state or municipal governments.

Near the end of the 1950s, new neighborhoods pushed the urban sprawl of Greater Lima even farther toward the north and south. In the 1970s, squatter neighborhoods represented half the city's population. The poor used community action to address problems that the state would not. People housed themselves, created an untaxed and unregulated economy, and, in short, accomplished what the state appeared unable to do. As the Peruvian social scientist Hernando de Soto so aptly noted, the poor created another path (*El Otro Sendero*), one that bypassed ineffectual authorities and restrictive regulations and that put social rights ahead of property claims. In the process, they forced municipal politicians and national authorities to negotiate with them as a social reality. Uncontrolled urbanization undercut the moral legitimacy and prestige of the government as the lower classes began to view the state as an obstacle to meeting their needs.

The Peruvian military, on assuming power in 1968, attempted without success to regain control of urbanization through the creation of the Ministry of Housing and the National Agency for the Development of New Settlements. In 1971, these agencies seized an unoccupied area and established a zone for new "spontaneous settlements." Called Villa El Salvador, it served as an escape valve, making it possible for a time to control Greater Lima's population growth. The government warned that invasions elsewhere would not be tolerated. By May 1971, Villa El Salvador had 10,000 inhabitants; two months later there were 50,000, and by January 1973 there were 105,000. It became a separate political district in 1983 with a population of more than 350,000.

In Brazil, Rio de Janeiro after World War I attracted increasing numbers of squatters. By the early 1930s, more than 70,000 people lived in shacks, constructed wherever possible in and around the city. The French urban planner Alfredo Agache received a contract to design a wondrous city that would solve this population problem. His plan was widely admired, but totally ignored. By the time he had completed it, the slums (*favelas*) had shattered all pretense that the city could be a school of progress, and the plan collapsed under the pressure of the Great Depression.

The squatter settlement of Vila Brasil, which arose west of Rio in 1946, serves as an example. Open flatlands were soon converted into a working-class neighborhood that had 2,700 inhabitants in 1986. Once all available spaces were occupied, lots were subdivided and the number of houses continued to grow. Some owners replaced flimsy construction material with hollow block so they could add a second and even third floor, although most housing remained one story. The streets of Vila Brasil resemble those of medieval cities or the Casbah of Casablanca. Three narrow roads able to accommodate vehicles and a maze of alleyways connected the settlement's 524 or so dwellings with the outside world in 1998. Paved and lit roads and alleys, and water, electricity, and sewer lines made the settlement reasonably attractive. Vila Brasil's neighborhood association, founded in 1952, has its own building and recreational area for children. Membership dues pay the wages of a full-time secretary and support the association's social and educational programs, including an adult literacy course and nursery programs for children ages three to six.

The location of Rio's slums, in the heart of the city, has acted to keep the inhabitants engaged in the general community. Babylonia, constructed on an unstable hillside but with a breathtaking view of Guanabara Bay, provided the setting for the movie *Black Orpheus*. The community overlooks Rio de Janeiro's best beaches and the modern buildings that house the slum dwellers' more affluent neighbors. Other favelas, while not so splendidly situated, are also located near the residences of more well-to-do city dwellers. The central location, which promoted contact between the favelas and the more opulent areas of Rio, made the incorporation of favela residents (*favelados*) into politics almost natural. Lively

The uneven modernization process in Latin America sometimes grafted the latest technology onto a primitive infrastructure. Here llamas deliver fuel, food, and other items in La Paz, Bolivia. The absence of modern transportation systems restricts distribution, production, and consumption. Low labor costs help perpetuate primitive methods and do little to raise living standards for the poor.

competition for votes at the local level enabled favelados to gain access to public funds and services.

The importance of politics to favelados and vice versa became obvious with the military coup of 1964. The new military government began razing existing favelas and moving, often by force, the displaced inhabitants to large housing projects on the distant fringes of the city. In many cases, the relocated residents faced a 2-hour bus trip into the city in search of possible employment. The army succeeded in removing the most visible favelas, much to the satisfaction of the tourist and hotel industry; but in the end the cost, both financial and political, doomed the program to failure. The new housing projects, moreover, concentrated unhappy and, consequently, politically disconnected tenants.

In a similar manner, Mexico City, the world's largest city today, experienced runaway urbanization. Between 1940 and 1970, some 4.5 million Mexicans moved there. By 1975, the metropolis had 2,600 people a day arriving, spilling over the city's boundaries. A new squatter city, Ciudad Netzahualcoyotl, arose on a barren lakebed northeast of the capital. First settled in 1946, it was the fourth largest city in the country by the early 1970s. It grew with little government intervention. Newcomers found a suitable plot, built a *jacal* (hut) from available cardboard, tin cans, plastic sheets, and if they were lucky, discarded construction material scrounged from old building sites and moved in. The makeshift shelter, usually placed at the rear of the lot, would be improved slowly as more durable material could be found or purchased. Eventually the original structure would be expanded with the addition of a string of rooms advancing toward the front of the lot. The city lacked potable water, sewage disposal, paved streets, and storm drains—all the services of modern cities. The government offered little more than water trucks and minimal municipal services, along with paving some principal streets and access roads. The threats to public health were soon staggering, but only serious epidemics received state attention. During the rainy season (June to October) mud turned streets into impassable bogs, stranding residents and isolating them from jobs and emergency medical care. In the dry season the old lake bed became a source of swirling dust containing dried fecal matter that contaminated food and water and irritated the eyes and lungs. Wind-borne contamination, a major source of chronic respiratory and intestinal problems, spared no classes, reaching far beyond the limits of Ciudad Netzahualcoyotl.

Many smaller groups of squatters built shelters in nearby gullies, hidden from public view. The people of Cerrada del Cóndor squeezed into a narrow, steep strip of land in Mexico City proper. As in the Peruvian case, the government's unwillingness or inability to provide any assistance has made Mexico's poor disdainful of authority. Contact with the police, for example, always seemed to be hostile, abusive, corrupt, and exploitative. The poor have experienced similar encounters with other government agencies.

For the poor, Latin American cities constituted a harsh frontier. As urban hunters and gatherers, they scavenged an existence from the debris of city life. The garbage pickers of Cali, Colombia, provide an example. At the bottom of the city's social structure, they struggled to survive and in the process made an often overlooked economic contribution. A surprising degree of organization characterized their activity. The largest group of pickers worked at the municipal garbage dump. Some 400 to 500 people of all ages, whole families, males and females, awaited the arrival of each garbage truck. Between deliveries, they poked around searching for reusable items to sell. Each find brought a rush of fellow pickers, hoping to be as lucky. The pickers clothed themselves with well-worn castoffs and occasionally fed themselves with discarded food. The dump served as their home, livelihood, and sometimes their final resting place.

Cali had a second contingent of pickers, almost as large as that of the dump residents. They followed the route of the city's garbage trucks, staying just ahead of them to search quickly for usable items. A half dozen or so of these front-runners preceded each truck. Still another group collected paper from shops and offices. Some of the better-off pickers used carts to collect empty bottles, scrap metal, and any article that would lose value if thrown into a garbage truck. Pickers sold empty bottles to various local liquor and soda producers. Small-scale foundries depended on collected scrap as their primary raw material. Marginal plastic manufacturers, in a similar fashion, relied on the garbage pickers almost exclusively. Others picked out bones and sold them to producers of animal food. Most, but not all, of the industries in the city served by the pickers were economically fragile and could not exist without the inexpensive supply of raw materials provided from the discarded items.

## Major Urban Centers in Latin America

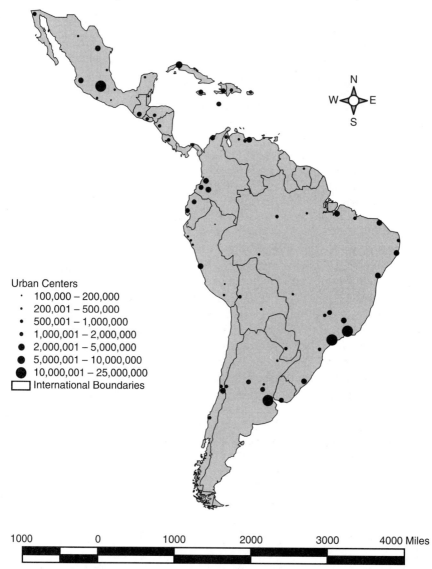

Urban Centers
- ·    100,000 – 200,000
- ·    200,001 – 500,000
- •    500,001 – 1,000,000
- ●    1,000,001 – 2,000,000
- ●    2,000,001 – 5,000,000
- ●    5,000,001 – 10,000,000
- ●    10,000,001 – 25,000,000
- ☐    International Boundaries

1000      0      1000      2000      3000      4000 Miles

Cali's pickers had little choice but to squeeze a livelihood from an activity that demanded long, exhausting hours and provided poor working conditions. They enjoyed no social esteem; yet their urban hunting-and-gathering skills enabled them to survive, if barely. The industries they served, for the most part, provided low-cost items consumed by the lower classes. The pickers represented part of the economic chain, perhaps its last link.

Life for squatters required constant innovation. They built makeshift huts, identified the closest source of reasonably clean water, ingeniously and illegally tapped into power lines for electricity, and clung to the backs of overcrowded buses for free transportation through the dangerous pathways of an urban jungle. They generated an informal economy independent of the broader, national economy, although it was not sufficient to sustain all the residents who were looking for work.

Nevertheless, the ability of illegal settlements to generate informal economic opportunities gave residents a degree of social and political independence. Established squatter settlements and their inhabitants have been incorporated into the local political structure. As a result, by the early 1990s, Rio's estimated 1 million favela dwellers exercised a decisive influence on Brazilian politics. Large favelas could not be overlooked by elected officials, who offered protection against removal, recognition of land titles, and public services such as electricity, water, and bus service in exchange for votes.

Officials in several countries soon understood that slum removal did not solve the problem of urban poverty. This recognition, coupled with pressure from international agencies to attack social problems and to oppose arbitrary removal, forced a change. In 1979, the Peruvian government accepted responsibility for urbanization, whether planned or unplanned. Brazilian cities established agencies to deal specifically with favelas. Until then, government agencies had claimed that such settlements had no legal basis for existence; therefore, from a bureaucratic standpoint they could not be serviced. Governments at least confronted the issue of the favela. Brazilian politicians still preferred to offer favors in return for votes—a practice that prevents long-range planning for general social improvements.

Trading votes for municipal services or local improvements proved a successful tactic for Vila Brasil and other slum organizations. Nevertheless, it meant bartering for inclusion within the municipality. Recognized neighborhoods did not have to bargain for services; they simply expected them to be provided. Civic expectation distinguished the full citizen from the would-be citizen of the slum. This recognition led leaders of the favela association of Vidigal to adopt a policy of pressing for improvements, but without trading their votes. Like any other citizen group, they reserved the right to vote for or against a particular politician. This marked a change in the relationship between favelados and municipal and state authorities. A high point of slum political participation came with the municipal elections of 1982. Benedita da Silva, a black, Protestant (Assembly of God) favela dweller, won a council seat in Rio de Janeiro and subsequently became the first black woman elected to Brazil's congress.

In the 1990s, drug production and distribution had a notable impact on the informal squatter economy and settlements. Trafficking in Colombia, Peru, Bolivia, and Brazil has become an occupation of choice. Large numbers of uneducated, unemployed young people anxious for work made recruiting a simple matter. Among the unemployed, indeed unemployable, few options existed. Brazil, with the largest population in Latin America, provided the most graphic example. One in four Brazilian workers earned less than the minimum wage in 1998. Millions remained on the bare margins of survival. Malnutrition and hunger characterized both urban areas and the countryside. In contrast, a young urban drug trafficker earned from $7,000 to $30,000 a year in 1998, moving from *olheiro* (lookout) to *vaporeiro* (packager) to *avião* (literally, airplane), a distributor. Slum dwellers involved in the drug business might enjoy some success, but often only briefly. Many aspiring drug lords died in a hail of bullets while attempting to move up the pyramid. Drug workers often are members of organized paramilitary groups. In Rio de Janeiro some 10,000 constitute a criminal army, able to confront a weak police force with better weapons and the latest communication equipment. Several of Brazil's states are controlled by drug lords, with reluctant toleration from officials. Rio shares political control unofficially with the Red Command and the Third Command. In 2002 an elaborate communication center operating inside a maximum security prison was able to coordinate drug-related activities worldwide.

Damage to political structures and local communities resulting from the combination of weak police forces and vast sums of drug money has reached alarming levels. In the Mexican border cities of Ciudad Juarez, Tijuana, and in small towns between, murderous battles over drugs are bloody and public. In Nuevo Laredo during 2005, *narco-traficantes* have fought battles with each other and the police and have murdered school teachers and ministers who speak out against drugs in open warfare, causing U.S. authorities to close the border temporarily. Murders of uncooperative police and military authorities make the battle a political as well as a social one. Death, drugs, and profit combine with fear and greed to rend the fabric of communities seemingly beyond anything yet experienced.

Latin American cities have become victims of the transformation of the national state from a relatively weak entity at the beginning of the nineteenth century into a centralized force in the late twentieth century. Fiscal authority has rested with the national government. The concentration of resources at the top severely restricted the independence of individual states and municipalities, which must turn to the central government for funds. The process of centralization began slowly as regional elites recognized the national government's need to collect taxes throughout the republic. In the 1930s, when the worldwide depression temporarily disrupted markets for primary products, only the national government could attempt to deal with the economic disaster, negotiate debt moratoriums, set up barter arrangements with other similarly devastated countries, and save as much of the old social structure as possible. In Brazil, for example, the regime of Getúlio Vargas worked out exchanges of coffee, including a swap for wheat with the United States, and of flying boats with Italy and pumped money into the industrial center of the city of São Paulo. Military regimes took control of several Latin American nations in an effort to rescue their economies and prevent political collapse.

In Mexico the situation differed somewhat. The Mexican Revolution of 1910 spawned regional violence that was only gradually brought under control by the new government. The impact of the Great Depression pushed the national revolutionary regime into assuming primary financial responsibility for the country. As revenue sources slowly recovered, the national regime dictated spending and investment programs, tipping the balance further to Mexico City and the national ministers. With the economic boom that began in the 1940s, tax revenue flowed into the treasury, although municipal control over revenues and expenditures was all but nonexistent. In the last decade of the twentieth century, Mexican municipalities received only 3 percent of all tax revenues—not enough to keep sewage treatment plants functioning, pave streets, maintain water systems, or perform other municipal functions. Federal revenue sharing and the collection of minimal property taxes were not enough to enable local governments to carry out municipal responsibilities. Mexican local governments cannot issue bonds. As a result, many cities owe huge debts on paper to the federal authorities, a pattern that has strengthened local dependency on the central government.

The draining of resources by the center has impoverished cities, except for the capital cities. Financially strapped municipalities, unable to pay adequate salaries to city employees, including the police, have witnessed a high level of graft. Petty corruption, from this perspective, represented a fee imposed by a service provider on the user—a tip to an official for the use of the highways, or to a bureaucrat for handling paperwork. The existence of more serious corruption, however, eroded legitimate authority and led to such outrages as improper disposal of hazardous chemicals and other dangerous activities. A direct connection has been established between environmental degradation and inadequate municipal revenues. Fiscal centralization and demographic change pushed many urban centers to the point of economic collapse. Although the Mexican case may be an extreme one, many Latin American cities drifted into a position of unbalanced dependency on the national government.

The inhabitants of impoverished towns far from the prosperous center created their own, often illegal, economies. Ciudad del Este (formerly Puerto Presidente Stroessner), Paraguay, on the border with Brazil, is one example. A city decidedly lacking in civic grandeur, with decrepit buildings and potholed streets strewn with garbage, it depended on a booming illegal trade that has made it Paraguay's wealthiest city. The town's residents generated an estimated one-third of the money in national circulation in 1996. Some 25 years ago, Ciudad del Este had no running water, sewers, or electricity. Townspeople smuggled cigarettes and American blue jeans and relied on prostitution to eke out an existence. A boom came in the 1990s, as the town's merchants sold almost the same quantity of goods as did the retailers of São Paulo, Brazil. An estimated $1 billion of illegal, tax-free merchandise a month passed through the town from Paraguay into Brazil in 1996. Some 60,000 professional shoppers, 500 buses, and 5,000 cars crossed the border from Brazil into Paraguay each Saturday. The Brazilians picked up items in demand, bribed their way back home, and delivered their tax-free goods to eager Brazilian distributors. A horde of small-time smugglers, so-called ants, earned $10 a trip in 1996 to carry items across the border to Brazil in a steady, endless stream. In addition, large-scale contraband wholesalers sent an estimated $800 million worth of goods into Brazil.

In a similar fashion, Tingo María in Peru's coca region created an illegal drug economy that supported numerous branch banks and several large imported luxury car dealerships. The owners of these automobiles had to drive them on nearly impassable streets. These examples demonstrate that impoverished inhabitants of Latin America did what was necessary to survive, regardless of the heavy price in corruption of the law, government, and individual morals; the social ravages of drugs; and the physical insecurity that often accompanies illegal activities.

The development of Latin American megacities distorted national politics. The capital city, home to a large percentage of the national population, consumed a disproportional share of the nation's resources, leaving what seemed like crumbs for the provinces. Regional antagonism toward the center held the potential for separatist movements, tax rebellions, and other forms of protest politics. No one has a solution to the continuing growth of the megacities. The Mexican government in the 1970s tried unsuccessfully to relocate some government agencies outside of the capital city. Brazilians relocated the national capital to the new city of Brasília, but it remains almost a ghost town on weekends and holidays when politicians flee to their homes in other cities. The growth of centralization and urban populations has created a political nightmare—the existence of nearly ungovernable megacities and the prospect of regional rebellion against them.

In Colombia between 1970 and 1986, a series of "civic strikes" by local citizens protested poor municipal services and the concentration of expenditures in the largest cities. The three largest cities in 1979 received 72 percent of the funds available, or six times the per capita expenditure. Pressure resulted in changes in the national constitution of 1991, which pointedly defined Colombia as a "decentralized" nation. The new constitution extended a degree of financial and political autonomy to local governments and allocated to them a greater share of revenues.

Long overdue modernization of municipal codes has been undertaken in many countries (see Chapter 2, on politics). In Peru, the 1984 code replaced laws and regulations put into effect in 1892. In 1996, El Salvador replaced local legislation dating back to the first decade of the century, and Colombia revised its 1913 code. New codes in Bolivia (1985), Nicaragua (1988), Mexico (1983), and Paraguay (1992) have redefined the relationship between municipal and national governments. In addition, in a development that promises essential funding for municipal revival, the Inter-American Development Bank and the World Bank (both of which previously preferred to deal only with national governments) have begun providing money directly to municipalities, thereby avoiding the problem of national governments burdened by staggering international debts. By the 1990s, both financial institutions had made significant loans to municipalities throughout Latin America. Moreover, to prepare municipal officials for managing these revenues, funds were given to establish training centers. As a result, in 1983 the Latin American Center for Training and Development of Local Government (CELCADEL) was established by the World Bank and is headquartered in Quito, Ecuador. An Urban Management Program was created in 1985 in cooperation with the United Nations to assist local authorities in improving their professional skills. Revitalization of smaller towns may counter the growth of megacities and reduce some of the pressure on them, but it will be a long process. Meanwhile, controlling the growth of megacities will be a difficult challenge.

Managing Latin America's great cities has demanded careful allocation of resources, such as land and water, and an aggressive road construction program. One of the best examples was the administration of Mexico's Federal District by

Ernesto P. Uruchurtu, who served as governor (mayor) from 1952 to 1966 and attempted to improve life in the city. Ultimately, he failed. Still, his programs deserve review. Uruchurtu focused on upgrading urban services in order to hold the middle class within the city. He carefully avoided creating incentives that would attract these people to the new suburbs. He devoted resources to creating parks, gardens, and well-landscaped boulevards, all maintained by a ubiquitous army of street cleaners; modern garbage trucks, and gardeners. Newspapers reported that the city's residents regarded Uruchurtu as "one of the best, if not the best, mayors [in the history] of Mexico City." He established restrictions on new housing developments, urban squatter settlements, land speculation, and excessive rents. His goal was to preserve the capital as a "livable city." He opposed the building of the subway (metro), believing that it would contribute to metropolitan sprawl. Construction and maintenance of the subway, he argued, would drain financial resources needed to address social needs and would exacerbate the problems of urban growth. He proved to be an ignored prophet. Uruchurtu ordered the razing of the *colonia* Santa Ursula, a squatter settlement. Rather than viewing his actions as an attempt to curtail unplanned urbanization, politicians who opposed him depicted him as a heartless bureaucrat who thought nothing of turning out the poor from their homes. The Chamber of Deputies censured him and forced him to resign.

A week later the new mayor announced support for the metro project, and construction began in the spring of 1967. As Uruchurtu had predicted, the metro proved to be excellent transport but compounded the city's problems. Although the metro attracted thousands of commuters, even more automobiles choked city streets than before. The pollution pouring into the air encouraged more and more residents to abandon the city for the suburbs and the illusion of escape from urban environmental degradation.

Mexico City, as of 1996, included the Federal District and 17 municipalities technically within the state of Mexico. A system of urban zones (*delegaciones*) was created to provide public services to this huge city. The delegación coordinates the delivery of services to meet the needs of its immediate area. The showcase zone, Cuauhtémoc, has undertaken revitalization of Mexico City's principal boulevard, Avenida de la Reforma, renovated the Chapultepec zoo, promoted the construction of the Four Seasons and Marquis hotels, and funded the construction of a larger national auditorium. Whether other urban zones will follow this model or devise another model to directly benefit the middle and lower classes remains to be seen.

Those who despair over the relentless growth of the Latin American city believe that the political commitment and social discipline required to stop it will never be mustered. Environmental limitations, on the other hand, may do what human beings cannot. Consider the dangerous levels of air pollution and its effects on health and life expectancy and the breakdown of public sanitation systems. The lack of potable water may be the first constraint on the growth of cities. For example, demand on the aquifer lying beneath Mexico City in the valley of Mexico exceeded the aquifer's recharge rate in 1990 by 50 to 60 percent. Additional water from the Lerma Valley aquifer and the Cutzamala river system must be utilized. Together the two sources supplied 43 percent of the city's needs.

Cutzamala water must be transported over 72 miles and lifted some 396,000 feet from one valley to another before entering the city's system.

Mexico City's water needs and demands for social services are not unique. São Paulo, Lima, Bogotá, Caracas, and other major cities face the same problems. The capitals of smaller republics with fewer resources appear even more helpless. Nicaragua's capital, Managua, accounted for 20.5 percent of the country's population in 1971 and 42.3 percent in 1991. The size of Managua's population has overwhelmed its ability to deliver adequate municipal services. No one seems to be in control. Despite these tremendous challenges, Latin Americans remain, as they have always been, city people.

## POVERTY AND MODERNIZATION

Despite the development of complex cities and societies, cultural achievements, and modern economies, the defining element for Latin America's peoples at the beginning of the twenty-first century is poverty. Disproportionate distribution of wealth, compounded by urbanization, megacities, population growth, and inadequate public health care, threatens the stability of almost all Latin American republics. State survival and the future well-being of the people are at stake. An estimated 9 out of 20 Latin Americans live in extreme poverty. Approximately 30 million, or 9 percent, have never had permanent employment, according to the International Labor Organization. Unemployment and underemployment characterize a significant percentage of the workforce. Of those who have reasonably steady jobs, many barely survive on their earnings. The International Monetary Fund estimates that 43 percent of Latin America's population is poor. The World Bank's standard for well-being requires a diet of 2,350 calories daily; access to health services for treatable illnesses, infant care, and information on nutrition and hygiene; shelter; and clean drinking water within reasonable distance of the shelter. People who fall below the level of well-being are considered poor. Poverty, though not distributed evenly across the hemisphere nor within individual republics, appears most evident in large megacities. In areas where economic growth lags well behind population increases because of high birthrates or rural-to-city migration, poverty appears to be an almost uncontrollable problem. In Ecuador, an estimated 80 percent of the population in 1993 lived at the poverty line, with about half that number in extreme misery. In the countryside, 91 percent lived in poverty with well over half in misery. Such figures help explain the movement into cities where life is, marginally, better. In absolute numbers, out of a total population of some 11.5 million (1995), 9 million Ecuadorians are poor; of that number, 5 million barely live above the poverty line.

Poverty implies no social status, and although correctly viewed as a problem by the state, municipal authorities, and international agencies, its symptoms often are dealt with in inappropriate ways. The most vulnerable of the poor, and the next marginal generation—the children—are victimized in economic and social terms (see the Profile in Chapter 5, "Carlos—One of Bogotá's Street Kids"). The majority of urban children work in the informal economy as shoeshine boys, car guards, windshield cleaners, vendors of all types, prostitutes, and drug dealers. They take up any activity that promises to help them survive. The United Nations Children's Fund estimated (1990) that some 7.5 million children between the ages of 10 and 17 work in Brazilian streets. Most of the children return home at night; a much smaller number sleep where they can. Street children, viewed as actual or potential criminals, are treated as human pests. Private death squads hired to clean up a neighborhood—the so-called *grupos de extermínio*—are often made up of off-duty policemen, operating with few restraints. "Final Justice" (*Justicia Final*), a well-known death squad in Rio de Janeiro headed by a former military police-man, perceives itself as engaged in the useful and socially acceptable task of eliminating criminals. Between 1988 and 1991, the government recorded 5,644 juvenile murders. Many killings go unrecorded. Society tacitly, and sometimes openly, approves of extrajudicial murder. An overloaded, often corrupt judicial system cannot control the widespread vigilante activity of the death squads, which operate in virtually every Brazilian city.

Street children, abandoned by the state and sometimes by their impoverished families, demonstrate admirable organizational skills, joining loosely knit groups and occasionally developing mutual support networks and sharing their meager resources. In Cali, Colombia, street children view their condition in social and economic terms that are accurate in a broad sense, and they respond in rational, if not approved, fashion to a harsh reality. Guatemala's 5,000 (1993) street children function in a similar manner, in constant fear of violence. Even in Costa Rica, a country with a more humane reputation, police and vigilante violence directed against street children has become a problem.

A small group of children are abandoned during the course of poverty-driven migration northward to the United States. It may be assumed that in all cities on the illegal immigration routes, small groups of foreign street children are also present. The growing problem of socially abandoned children brings into ques-tion the nature of progress and change in Latin America.

Meanwhile, as the average age in the cities grows younger, the median age in rural villages grows older. The young go to the city or to another country, especially the United States. The older folks stay home in the countryside, where all the rural problems eventually become compounded by the difficulties of old age. The graying countryside is now becoming a new problem for Latin American governments.

Migration from the countryside to the city, and from both countryside and city to foreign countries, disrupts families. Only young men search for work in foreign agriculture, and only young women seek work as domestics in the city or some neighboring country. Certainly the remittances that come home to the elderly or the single-parent families help to maintain the family unit, but it is a new family, characterized by often-absent members. The long-term effect of this pattern remains to be seen. Surely, any pattern of abandoning children in the cities and elders in the countryside weakens and, in some instances, shatters families. This situation in turn becomes a great threat to social stability, and therefore to political stability, in Latin America.

## Population Density

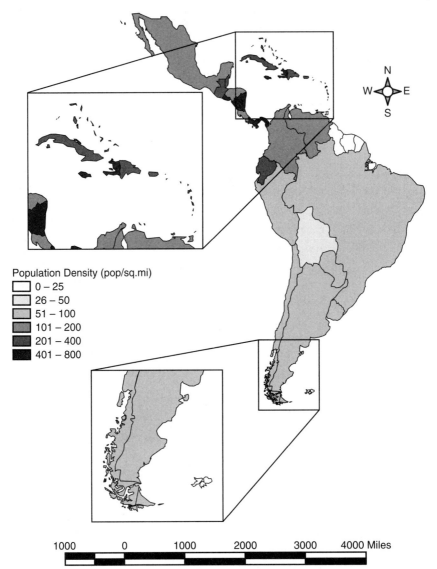

Making people modern has elevated some and failed many others. Population growth and demographic change make the struggle against grinding poverty a monumental one. In the twentieth century, the gap between the promises and the realities of modernization became the primary thrust of campaigns for social change, including such violent episodes as the Mexican revolution.

# 9

# Environments

The physical and natural setting for Latin America's history has undergone innumerable changes. Modifications, at times violent and at times nearly imperceptible, resulted both from natural causes and from the interaction between humans and the ecological surroundings and the ways in which Latin Americans have "viewed" or interpreted the landscape. In this chapter, we examine both kinds of modification, from earthquakes to socially determined descriptions of landscapes (for example, people have viewed the rain forest as their home, as an obstacle to progress, or as an economic opportunity). Over thousands of years—from the prehistoric to the pre-Columbian era, through three centuries of colonial elaboration and the two centuries after independence—humans have witnessed dynamic changes in the environments of Latin America. Understanding the physical character of the region—its geography and its ecology—requires us to remember that the environment has a dynamic constitution; even when apparently static, both nature and humans have initiated changes that have improved or degraded the Latin American environments. Works by foreign travelers reveal widely varying descriptions of the environment. Different views have also been depicted in paintings and photographs of Latin America. For this reason, this chapter stresses the changing forms of the physical and natural surroundings that we call the environment.

Geological and geographical factors helped in shaping the people and their empires, republics, and economies as well as in determining the extent and type of man-made changes imposed on the landscape. Thanks to the achievements of modern engineering and effortless passage across awesome barriers in the comfort of modern transportation, it is assumed that natural forces are under control. Nature frequently and violently challenges this technological arrogance.

Volcanic eruptions and earthquakes, among other natural disasters, shatter the complacent conviction that human beings control everything. Pacaya's lava and dust

Courtesy of the Latin America Library at Tulane University.

An earthquake can destroy centuries-old structures in seconds. A 1917 earthquake in Antigua, Guatemala, reduced this colonial church to rubble. Virtually all of Latin America must contend with frequent natural disasters and their negative economic consequences, dislocations, and loss of lives.

destroyed a number of Guatemalan villages in the 1960s. In the same decade, Costa Rica's Irazú, usually a placid tourist attraction, spewed debris, fumes, and dust across the central valley for years until it finally subsided. Nature's timing can be devastating. Cerro Negro, a 2,200-foot-high volcanic peak in Nicaragua, suddenly tossed ash some 1,000 yards into the air in November 1995. In nearby León, heavy layers of volcanic dust threatened to collapse roofs. The fine, powdery ash sifted into every conceivable crevice, disabling cars and machinery and contaminating water. Refugees, their heads covered with clothing, vainly sought to avoid inhaling the dust. Crops crumpled under the weight of ash while some 6,000 head of cattle verged on starvation. Cerro Negro's devastation spread across a 30-mile radius. Approximately 200,000 people suddenly had their lives altered, some permanently, by Cerro Negro's activity.

Earthquakes, in a similar fashion, regularly destroy cities and disrupt national regimes. Guatemala's capital moved three times because of such natural disasters. The present site endured a series of sharp, violent tremors in 1917–1918 that left few structures untouched.

Managua, the capital of Nicaragua, barely survived a 1931 earthquake. Incredible devastation struck again in 1972. The failure of the Anastasio Somoza regime to respond to the crisis, instead turning international relief efforts into governmental opportunities for graft and corruption, provided the final push for the Sandinista revolutionaries to launch their efforts on behalf of change—efforts that would quickly succeed. With volcanic eruptions, earthquakes, hurricanes, floods, and landslides it is difficult to name a settlement that has not experienced the harshness of nature at least several times over the past 100 years and untold times from the pre-Columbian era to the present. Despite such setbacks, human beings have worked both negatively and positively to alter the environment as far back as recorded history.

## ENVIRONMENTAL VISIONS AT INDEPENDENCE

After achieving independence, the leaders of the new nations developed different visions of the environment. The new national leaders during the nineteenth century focused on developing new commercial products based on their conceptions of their environments that included, of course, natural resources. They also formulated campaigns regarding human resources that resulted in the promotion of immigration and the abolition of slavery (in some cases pressured by Great Britain). The end of slavery (Brazil and Cuba were the last to do so), the promotion of immigration, and the rise of new commercial products, especially coffee, wheat, and beef, were all related and brought changes to both the urban and rural environments.

At least until the 1880s, the *criollo* (or Europeanized) view of the rural landscape saw "savage" wilderness in need of subjugation in the name of progress. Rural dwellers held a *mestizo* (hybrid) view of the environment that combined a religious feeling of interconnectedness with the idea that it was a place of liberty and a haven from oppressive outsiders. This view later broke down into many local appreciations of place, with ethnic interaction the key to the view of the ecosystem.

In formulating plans for the development of their peoples and their lands, Latin American elites appropriated European and U.S. views of nature and shaped them to their own uses. The sources for these foreign visual evaluations ranged from travelers (such as Fanny Calderón de la Barca), scientific expeditions (none more universally recognized than Alexander von Humboldt's), and historians (such as William Hickling Prescott, whose *History of the Conquest of Mexico* and *History of the Conquest of Peru* were internationally successful) to painters and other authors. The preeminent Latin American interpreter of the environment was Argentine Domingo Sarmiento.

Nature—as a landscape to be subdued through understanding and use—found its most persuasive and popular proponent in the German scientific traveler Alexander von Humboldt. He provided both a model to bring the environment under control by measuring, indexing, and locating it, and a method to "see" it through poetic description, landscape painting, and cultivation of exotic plants. Seeing the ecology of Latin America as Humboldt indicated permitted appreciation and control through the literary, visual, and practical arts.

By mid-century, Latin American ecology was widely known: Literary descriptions abounded while landscape painting astonished audiences across Europe and the United States. Governments (both national and municipal), universities, and private individuals established botanic gardens. Numerous painters went to Latin America in the first half century after independence (ca. 1820 to 1870). Among the artists and writers who contributed to the visual and written understanding of the region were Frederick Catherwood and John Lloyd Stephens in Central America and James Whistler and George Catlin in eastern South America. No single painting of Latin American nature had more impact in the United States than did *Heart of the Andes.* Frederic Edwin Church, inspired by the works of Humboldt, went to South America in 1853 and 1857. In 1859 he exhibited his large, 5-by-10-foot canvas in a one-painting show. *Heart of the Andes* stunned audiences first in New York, then across the United States, and finally in Europe. Church and other painters showed viewers untamed nature, unoccupied (or nearly so) space, and unlimited opportunities for those who would apply labor to profit from the environment.

The most significant explanation of the savagery, emptiness, and opportunities of the landscape outside of Latin America's few cities came from the Argentine Domingo Sarmiento. He wrote a melodrama about the confrontation between "civilization" and "barbarism." He and other civilizers taught Latin Americans how to see the criollo view of the landscape, with its need to subdue nature by understanding it, and to seize nature's opportunities through productive use of resources.

Those with a different visual understanding of the landscape—in Argentina, the nomadic gauchos and Indians—had no place in Sarmiento's urbanized worldview. Even Latin Americans who shared Sarmiento's view differed in their understanding of the environment and the regulation of nature depending on their particular region. Floods, storms, earthquakes, and especially volcanic eruptions challenged those who intended to dominate the environment. Clearly, the understanding of environment was a political, social, and cultural construct.

A dramatic example of an environmental construct occurred in 1877 when the Ecuadorian volcano Cotopaxi erupted, spewing ash to Quito and pouring lava into towns in its immediate vicinity. Elites deeply divided by religious and political views agreed that divine will had compelled the eruption. Church leaders and their political allies blamed the programs of their Liberal opponents, interpreting the reforms as an affront to God. Liberals, most of whom were practicing Catholics, saw the priests who had withheld the sacraments from the people as the cause for God's wrath. Later in the century, debates over divine will largely disappeared from public discussions of nature; but the explanations, the "views" of the environment, remained socially, politically, and culturally constructed.

A smattering of individuals saw the environment as something to be protected. In 1828, the newly independent Costa Rican government reserved a mile-wide strip of coast for fisheries and called on municipalities to provide for conservation of communal forests and lands. In 1833, the same government mandated green belts of permanent farmland, pastures, and woodlands around cities. These efforts were followed by laws in 1846 to set aside forested watersheds and in 1859 to prohibit the hunting of white-tailed deer. Then, in 1895, the Costa Rican government attempted to reserve all uncultivated lands in a 15-kilometer zone on both sides of the main rivers draining the central plateau of the nation.[1] These efforts ran counter to urbanization and development patterns in the region.

Beginning in the late 1880s, Latin Americans undertook major campaigns to attract foreign investors, industry, and immigrants with the goal of establishing productive control over nature. Leaders also sought recognition of national achievements that together represented "civilized" society. In nearly every case, these campaigns resulted from a particular view of the environment. Natural resources, raw materials, unoccupied fertile lands, acculturated indigenous peoples, and disciplined workers (often former slaves)—all became metaphors of progress, civilization, and a cultivated environment. World's fairs gave expression to these metaphors, beginning with the celebration of the centennial of the French Revolution, the Paris Universal Exposition. Latin American elites displayed their vision of the proper national ideology at the Paris Universal Exposition (1889), the American Historical Exposition (Madrid, 1892), and the Columbian Universal Exposition (Chicago, 1893).

The Ecuadorian exhibits created "a close relationship between technological progress, evolutionism, and scientific racism." Here "savages" or indigenous people were presented as part of "nature," "equal to animals," "without sensible speech," "stubborn," and "dirty." They were often graphically portrayed as fusing with nature, into the trees, often with a monkey-like appearance, and as such, to be conquered and civilized.[2] This attitude began to change at the end of the century, under the influence of *costumbrismo*. In Ecuador, a burst of naturalistic nationalism appeared that was especially prevalent in painting. It emphasized the details of the environment, including the Indians, and idealized the people and landscape, as part of a vanishing and romantic past.

Government planners adopted immigration programs because they wanted European migrants who could help change the relationship between individuals and the environment. The largest number of immigrants chose Argentina and Brazil because elites there shared the same attitudes toward the environment that Donald Worster has summarized as the "imperial ecology: to establish through the exercise of reason and by hard work, man's domination over nature."[3] These immigrants contributed to a general campaign to subdue nature in the name of progress. The result was that the world's fair exhibits of Brazil and Argentina featured agricultural production—beef, wheat, wool, coffee, and sugar—rather than raw materials, such as tropical woods and useful minerals.

Other Latin American countries based their claim to progress on their extractive industries, from minerals, timber, and bananas to, ironically, guano fertilizer. For centuries, mammoth flocks of seabirds along Peru's coast had deposited

---

[1]David Rains Wallace, *Quetzal and the Macaw: Costa Rica's National Parks* (San Francisco: The Sierra Club, 1996), p. 8.

[2]Blanca Muratorio, "Nationality and Ethnicity: Images of Ecuadorian Indians and the Image makers at the Turn of the Nineteenth Century," in Judith D. Toland, ed., *Ethnicity and the State* (New Brunswick: Transactions Publishers, 1993), pp. 21–54.

[3]Donald Worster, *Nature's Economy: The Roots of Ecology* (San Francisco: Sierra Club, 1977), p. 2.

guano until it reached the heights of hills. During the mid-nineteenth century, before the development of chemical fertilizer, guano became the leading additive to restore exhausted soils. By 1860, on the eve of the U.S. Civil War, Peruvian guano accounted for 43 percent of all the fertilizer used in the United States.

## NATURE AS RAW MATERIAL

Beginning in the 1880s, the symbols of national progress showed a landscape dominated by steam—portrayed as the smoke of locomotives or factories. These "productive" images ignored for the most part any negative or destructive aspects of the national projects or foreign enterprises that governmental leaders and national intellectuals viewed as progress.

The burst of mining enterprises in the last two decades of the nineteenth century in Mexico illustrates many of the environmental consequences of development projects assumed to bring modernization. In the far northwest state of Sonora, following the arrival of railroad connections to Arizona, a mining boom occurred. Local elites seized the opportunity to establish lucrative related enterprises. Besides commercial agriculture designed to supply the miners with provisions and to export to U.S. markets, entrepreneurs such as Feliciano Monteverde of Minas Prietas profited substantially from the sale of lumber to the mines for use as rail ties, shoring in mine shafts, and fuel for steam generators. The American consul estimated that the mines yearly consumed some "1,000,000 feet of lumber and over 200,000 cords of wood." Monteverde and others soon deforested their own lands and quickly began buying surrounding properties to continue their logging activities. As demand outstripped supply, they began importing lumber from the Pacific Northwest of the United States and coal from Gallup, New Mexico.

The main shaft in one of the La Colorada mines collapsed in 1909. Due to the depth of the shaft and the flooding that attended the landslide, the company made no attempt to rescue the workers. With the collapse of other tunnels, mining quickly declined in the area. Besides the damage caused by tunnel cave-ins, mining had severely changed and damaged the environment. The desolation starkly revealed the impact of deforestation. The region's lonesome beauty was marred by mountains of chemically leached tailings and pools of water polluted with potassium cyanide used to process gold, lime, cyanide, and zinc.

The disregard of environmental damage and threats to the local people resulted in a major dispute (1909) between El Rey del Oro Mining Company and the residents of Mulatos, Sonora. The miners dumped ore tailings and by-products next to the town, and the company released water containing potassium cyanide into the stream flowing by the town. The death of several cattle after drinking from the stream mobilized the residents of Mulatos, who had their mayor file a complaint with the company. When the company took no action, the town's authorities ordered it to construct a pipeline to discharge the chemicals away from the community or shut down. The company locked out employees and complained to the governor, hoping that unemployment and political clout would overturn the actions of a local town council. The governor intervened to order the mine reopened and the town's directive suspended. To embarrass the governor for his blatant capitulation to big, foreign-owned business, the council distributed his order throughout the community.[4] This pattern of environmental degradation became characteristic of Mexico's northern border states for the rest of the twentieth century. The government paid no attention at all to the issues involved.

Mexico's tropical forests, in contrast, received attention from the national government for the first time during the same period.[5] From the colonial years until the regime of Porfirio Díaz (1876–1911), the tropical lowlands, except for gulf ports such as Veracruz, had never been integrated into the politics or economics of Mexico City. This region, from the time Spaniards first arrived until late in the nineteenth century, had a reputation for disease (yellow fever and malaria) and danger (from pirates for a time and from discontented Mayas) that turned away would-be developers, except for those interested in exploiting tropical woods. This activity received its inspiration from British success, measured by the substantial profits generated in the Belize colony from both dyewood (*palo de campeche*) and cabinet woods (mahogany and cedar). Mexicans exploited tropical hardwoods in three stages: (1) logging along the shoreline, (2) harvesting along riverbanks, and (3) inland forest enterprises relying on railroad connections to either rivers or coastal ports. The coastal stage occurred in the seventeenth and eighteenth centuries as Mexican loggers searched out mahogany timberlands at the mouth of the Coatzacoalcos River and other gulf estuaries for wood for the shipyards of Havana. The chief concern of the colonial government was not to regulate these activities, but to defend against British or other foreign logging interests.

The demand for hardwoods after Mexican independence encouraged exploration of the rivers of southern Mexico, in particular the Usumacinta system that allowed riverbank exploitation of the Lacandon forest. The necessary workers arrived via the new road from Chiapas, built jointly by the federal and state governments. This enterprise resulted in the incorporation, for the first time into Mexican law (1861), federal regulations pertaining to reforestation, which required loggers to plant 10 mahogany or cedar seeds for every tree cut.

This reform law had much less impact than did the reform law of the Benito Juárez government, which allowed individuals access to vacant public and communally held lands (the 1856 Lerdo Law, written into the 1857 Constitution). An 1863 law specified that 2,500 hectares could be claimed through denunciation of

---

[4]Miguel Tinker-Salas, *In the Shadow of the Eagles: Sonora and the Transformation of the Border during the Porfiriato* (Berkeley: University of California Press, 1997), pp. 216–218, 232–233.

[5]This discussion of tropical forests and the demand for national regulations in Mexico is based on Herman W. Konrad, "Tropical Forest Policy and Practice during the Mexican Porfiriato, 1876–1910," in Harold K. Steen and Richard P. Tucker, eds., *Changing Tropical Forests: Historical Perspectives on Today's Challenges in Central and South America,* proceedings of a conference sponsored by the Forest History Society and IUFRO Forest History Group, 1992, pp. 123–143.

vacant public lands—the classification of virtually all forested tropical regions. Neither law had an immediate impact on the tropical forests, but they did set a precedent for national regulation of this resource and for establishing increased economic production as the purpose of national lands.

Subsequent planners alternated between alarm because of extensive deforestation in the effort to bring more land into the productive economy and impatience at the pace of development. Tropical forests were identified as either uninhabited or indigenous communal properties and therefore remained a great untapped resource. Concern for the forests resulted in an 1881 law that included the 1861 provision that 10 seeds must be planted for every tree cut in the national forests. The government also passed the Colonization Law of 1883, a provision that eliminated the 2,500-hectare limit on the size of individual denunciations. The law also encouraged surveys of national territory by offering one-third of the lands measured as payment to the surveying companies that did the work. Under these provisions, family firms in both Chiapas and Tabasco moved quickly to expand their claims deep into the forests.

Foreigners recognized the new opportunities provided by the Díaz government. In 1892, London capitalists formed the Mexican Exploration Company to obtain a concession in Quintana Roo. Businessmen in Mérida, Yucatán, using German capital, soon moved into the northern part of the same territory. French capital quickly found its way into the Lacandon region. Given the success of the programs to attract investment in undeveloped regions, the Díaz government undertook regulation of forest activities with the law of 1894 (see the Profile, "Law for the Exploitation of Forests and Vacant and National Lands, Mexico, 1894," page 215).

The Law for the Exploitation of Forests and Vacant and National Lands of 1894 served as the basis for all later forest legislation, including that of twentieth-century revolutionary governments. The law, providing for contracts of 2, 5, or 10 years with renewals, contained three other essential provisions: the government's right to regulate forest exploitation, the right to collect user fees, and the need for conservation to establish controlled exploitation and renewal of forests.

A national Society of Friends of the Trees, founded by Mexican intellectuals in the early 1890s, encouraged the planting of trees and the distribution of information on the negative affects of deforestation. Nevertheless, the group focused its concern on the highlands, rather than on the lowlands of the country. In the tropics, the goal was to increase, not limit, cutting programs.

Although Mexico's forest programs at the turn of the century focused on development, conservation could not be ignored. In 1909 Mexican, U.S., and Canadian representatives met in Washington, D.C., for the North American Conference on Conservation of Natural Resources. Again, the Mexican officials focused their attention almost exclusively on the temperate regions of the country, with only passing references to the tropical forests. The Porfirian program shaped governmental policy on tropical forests well into the twentieth century. The principal issues informing the policy were the potential for economic growth, the need for development, the presence of allegedly indolent, sometimes hostile indigenous peoples, and the problem of local disease.

---

**P R O F I L E**   Law for the Exploitation of Forests and Vacant
and National Lands, Mexico, 1894

---

1. Permits required, issued by the Land Agency of the Ministry of Development;

2. All concession or permit holders obligated to manage their operations in complete conformity with the state regulations of the 1894 laws of the ministry, so that: The destruction of national forests will be avoided, ensuring, to the contrary, their repopulation by conserving necessary trees with fertile seeds, in order that the existing species in the forests have their reproduction guaranteed;

3. Specific restrictions placed on size of trees that can be cut, amount of gum or resin that can be taken from designated areas, quotas that must be paid per tree trunk or unit of resin and gum extracted, areas within forests that can be converted to agriculture, and heads of livestock that can be pastured;

4. All trees cut for export must be clearly marked by forest inspector;

5. Federal employees have the right, at all times, to monitor all phases of forestry operations, including transport from forests and ports;

6. At their own expense, concession holders are obligated to mark boundaries and produce a map of their holdings, to be provided to federal agents within two years of being granted their concession;

7. No transfer to third parties of any exploitation rights is permitted without prior permission by federal authorities, and under no conditions are such rights to be transferred to a foreign state or government; nor may a foreign or state government be admitted as partner;

8. No use other than that stipulated in contract is permitted;

9. If valid claims against land are presented by private individuals, the concession holders are obligated to turn over such lands to the government within six months;

10. Within rented areas, and subject to previous notice to the Ministry of Development, residences for workers and other buildings to house sawmills, supplies, and equipment may be constructed;

11. Students of national forestry schools must be admitted to observe operations when accompanied by a professor;

12. A guarantee of 2,000 pesos must be deposited in the national bank, to be forfeited upon violation of conditions of the contract;

13. All disputes to be settled by federal courts, with no recourse to foreign rights;

14. All concession and/or contract holders will always be considered Mexicans, . . . and are subject to federal laws. . . .

15. All concessions or contracts will be null and void, when so declared by federal agents—after having heard defense of holders—in the event of:

    i.   violation of any regulation governing forests,

    ii.   failure to pay quotas and fees,

    iii.   six-month interruption of activities without due cause,

    iv.   failure to make and present map within stipulated period,

    v.   failure to build constructions for extraction activities,

    vi.   transfer of area or part thereof to third party without consent,

    vii.   transfer to, or partnership with, foreign government or state, or agent thereof.

The developmentalist position prevailed over concern for regulation; nevertheless, the Porfirian government created an administrative structure for oversight of forests and other natural resources. The Ministry of Development, Colonization, and Industry housed a Department of Forests, including a Central Forest Council with local councils in each state, and a National Forestry School in Coyoacán, Federal District, which trained forestry guards and inspectors. Although greatly underfunded, these agencies held promise for the future.

Typical of Porfirian developmental programs was the attitude toward temperate-climate forests that had potential as a source of wood pulp for manufacturing newsprint and paper. The small paper industry produced high-quality stock from linen and cotton until the last decade of the nineteenth century. In 1892, Mexicans brought together European papermaking technology and recently introduced electrical power to create the first factory in the nation, the San Rafael industrial plant, to produce newsprint from wood pulp. By 1911, the managers of the San Rafael factory were accused of degrading the environment and threatening the economic activities of other entrepreneurs.

With the Mexican Revolution of 1910, officials were receptive to complaints regarding issues involving the environment. The manager of the Santa Cruz hydroelectric plant charged that San Rafael officials diverted Tlalmanalco river water, causing problems for the electricity-generating plant and contaminating the water used by the villagers of Chalco and other pueblos in the Chalco valley. Nicolás de San Juan, in his complaint to the Minister of Development, pointed out that his plant used the water only as a motive force whereas the paper plant used it in newsprint production, thereby polluting the resource. In early 1912, the minister sent an inspector, Leopoldo Villarreal, to investigate the complaint. Villarreal reported that the water below the plant was unsafe for humans, plants, and animals downstream. The owners of the Miraflores textile plant filed another complaint against the paper mill, charging that the mill was making the plant's operations impossible because of water contamination. They contended that the foam fouled the textile machinery, discolored thread, and threatened the villagers downstream.

José de la Macorra, general manager of the San Rafael paper mill, conceded the damage his plant did to the water system and proposed a solution. Protection of the river water required construction of a system to drain underground water used in the manufacturing process away from the river. Construction of the underground system required the approval of the Tlalmanalco town council. Negotiations to secure permission had been disrupted by the revolution during 1910–1911. The governor of the state of Mexico joined debate on the issue, securing a revised agreement from the city council and sending it to the factory for approval. At this point the paper trail ends, but the issue demonstrates the early and growing concern with questions of environmental degradation.[6]

---

[6]Blanca E. Suárez Cortez, "Las fábricas de papel de San Rafael y anexas, s.a., y un viejo problema, la contaminación del Río Tlalmanalco," *Boletín del Archivo Histórico del Agua,* 2 (1996).

# DEVELOPMENT VERSUS ENVIRONMENTALISM

After World War II, Latin America entered a period of dramatic efforts, in agriculture and in industry, to develop national economies. Agricultural programs focused on improved production through what was widely heralded as the Green Revolution, and industrial expansion moved into the "takeoff" phase. The Green Revolution successfully raised agricultural production, but at a high cost. Increased production required dependence on the use of pesticides, which resulted in social dislocations, public health hazards, and ecological damage.[7] After World War II, with the emergence of the Cold War, the U.S. government saw improved agriculture with increased food production and better nutrition as sure defenses against the spread of Communism in the Western Hemisphere. According to this line of thinking, commercial agriculture would generate enough capital to drive nascent industries to the takeoff point. The Green Revolution, with the aid of the United States (not just in Latin America, but throughout the developing world), called for the introduction of high-yield crops, more effective irrigation systems, improved farm machinery, and the use of agricultural chemicals—both fertilizers and pesticides. The problems associated with the introduction of certain pesticides have been aggravated by the emphasis on commercial crops, especially cotton.

Export crops received the largest percentage of insecticide treatment. Coffee, corn, bananas, beans, cotton, and fresh-cut flowers were sprayed. In several Central and South American countries, bananas were coated with from 75 percent (Honduras) to 35 percent (Costa Rica) of all the pesticides in use. Cotton, more than any other crop, illustrates the problems associated with this practice. The wonder pesticide developed during World War II and released by the U.S. War Production Board in August 1945 was dichloro-diphenyl-trichloroethane, or DDT. The introduction of DDT was followed during the next decade by the development of an additional 25 new pesticidal compounds. The release of chemicals to control boll weevils and malaria-carrying mosquitoes followed. One result was a cotton boom on the Pacific coastal plain from Chiapas, Mexico, to Costa Rica. By 1978 the region had become the world's third leading producer of cotton behind the United States and Egypt.

Like cotton, the Colombian fresh-cut flower industry appeared to be yet another economic success story, aided by the availability of rapid air transport from producers to the United States, Canada, Europe, and Japan. During the 1990s, Colombia exported 3.5 billion cut flowers a year. Just over 50 percent of all cut roses and 95 percent of all single-stem carnations that entered the U.S. market were grown in Colombia. Just before Valentine's Day 1998, some 14 million roses were flown to the United States. Mother's Day and Easter were also peak periods. The industry directly employed more than 72,000 workers, mostly women, in

---

[7] On these issues, see N. Patrick Peritore and Ana Karina Galve-Peritore, eds., *Biotechnology in Latin America: Politics, Impacts, and Risks* (Wilmington, DE: SR Books, 1995); and Douglas L. Murray, *Cultivating Crisis: The Human Cost of Pesticides in Latin America* (Austin: University of Texas Press, 1994).

Colombia, and indirectly many more in several other countries. Reasonable prices and high quality (flowers with a single blossom, a bruise, or evidence of insects were rejected) assured continued demand. To keep prices low and quality high, low-paid labor applied large amounts of insecticides indiscriminately. Between 70 and 333.6 kilos of chemicals per hectare, including some banned chemicals, were used in the Colombian flower industry.

When the industry began in the western savanna region of Colombia in 1965, a handful of relatively small companies had a minimal impact on the environment. By the 1990s, more than 450 cut-flower enterprises operated in various regions of the country. The sheer size of the industry, coupled with the application of chemicals, resulted in widespread water contamination. Water used for irrigation soon became saturated with chemicals and polluted the groundwater. Moreover, the industry put great stress on the supply of available water. One flower grower consumed as much water as a rural community of 20,000 inhabitants. In some districts, the cut-flower industry consumed 75 percent of available water. Algae filled rivers and streams, and water tables dropped significantly. Water rationing and tank trucks became a regular way of life in the flower-growing regions. The Colombian government's failure to regulate chemical use and water consumption, as well as the worldwide demand for the perfect blossom at rock-bottom prices, has led to environmental degradation and a public health disaster. The long-range impact in Colombia has yet to be calculated.

Consequences of widespread pesticide use included environmental stresses—the rapid clearing of forests, soil degradation, and chemical contamination of soil and water—and widespread public health problems. Humans who experience repeated exposure to pesticides suffer damage to the central nervous system and may have impaired vision, muscle weakness, tremors, dizziness, paralysis, and cardiorespiratory failure. Neurological diseases, multiple sclerosis, Parkinson's disease, cancer, miscarriages, and premature births have also been linked to pesticide use.

The Green Revolution also increased human misery. Growing cotton and other nontraditional commercial crops—oriental vegetables from the Dominican Republic; fresh flowers from Costa Rica and Colombia; melons from Honduras, Guatemala, and Mexico—contributed to rising levels of landlessness and unemployment, food shortages, and poorer health among the general population of the region. Agricultural industry-sponsored seminars on the safe use of pesticides began in the 1970s with encouragement from various international agencies and Central American governments. Such programs created the illusion that the problem of pesticides could be solved simply by proper handling of the chemicals and thus served to promote pesticide-dependent development.

An effort began in the 1980s to encourage "integrated pest management" (IPM), an approach to pesticide control that combined biological, environmental, cultural, and legal methods into what Ray Smith of the University of California called "old traditional agriculture with a little bit of sophistication added in."[8] Nicaragua has been among the proponents of this system in Latin America, especially since 1981. Desperate for cotton for foreign exchange earnings to rebuild the country, the Sandinista government implemented a dynamic IPM

---

[8]Murray, *Cultivating Crisis,* p. 101.

program with financial and technical assistance from West Germany. By 1987, the success of the program had been largely undermined by the U.S. economic embargo and diplomatic efforts to restrict foreign assistance to Nicaragua.

In the years from 1950 to 1980, growth in Latin America was 5.5 percent, higher than the U.S. rate (4.8 percent) during its startup period (1870–1906). This economic growth coincided with a population explosion, chaotic city planning, political disorder, and further environmental degradation.[9] Neither government nor business leaders expressed much concern about the environmental consequences of economic growth and developmental programs. The few efforts at regulation were aimed chiefly at the activities of the poor and were scarcely enforced. In Mexico, for example, the government in 1941 ordered the introduction of oil stoves to replace wood-burning braziers. People were given one year to install the stoves. Nevertheless, charcoal-burning braziers, contributing to both air pollution and destruction of the forests, remain in evidence on city streets throughout Mexico today.

Besides law and business practices, other activities revealed new views of the environment. Portraits of domination of the Argentine environment appeared in the paintings of Cesáreo Bernaldo de Quirós. His depictions of gaucho scenes claimed to show earlier episodes of life on the pampas. Quirós painted scenes set in what were commonly believed to be natural surroundings. In reality, the earlier environment had been discarded, and the wilderness had come to be viewed not as a vast, untamed nature, as in Sarmiento's time, but as a constructed landscape dominated by cultural features.[10]

Along with the pressure for more material resources came new concerns, including soil conservation and rural development. A project funded by the World Bank, the Program for the Integrated Rural Development of the Humid Tropics (PRODERITH), was created to ease the negative impact of rapid urbanization. Although the program eventually had a global impact, it began with six test sites in southern and eastern Mexico. The Mexican government obtained technical assistance from the U.S. Soil Conservation Service. Established to increase agricultural production in the tropical zones, alleviate poverty, and expand the economic base of the region, PRODERITH soon included conservation goals, in particular programs to promote surface drainage, soil protection, pasture management, and training of conservation personnel. By 1985, Mexico's economic crisis required reorientation of the project. One change was to move toward the creation of a national conservation program. The administration of President Carlos Salinas de Gortari further altered the program by privatizing or localizing administration of the six sites. Emphasis during the Salinas administration went to developing irrigation programs and mechanisms to reclaim water from municipal and industrial treatment plants for use in agriculture. This integrated program has now lapsed as government attention has turned

---

[9]Sergio Zermeño, "Society and Politics in Contemporary Mexico: Modernization and Modernity in Global Societies," in Wil G. Pansters, ed., *Citizens of the Pyramid: Essays on Mexican Political Culture* (Amsterdam: Thesis Publishers, 1997), p. 158.

[10]Joe Foweraker, "Popular Movements and Political Culture in Contemporary Mexico," in Pansters, ed., *Citizens of the Pyramid,* pp. 179–181.

elsewhere. No Mexican government agency currently has the will, financing, or motivation to continue it.

Nicaragua, the country with the most extensive natural resources in Central America, had no environmental management policy until 1979. The new Sandinista regime nationalized natural resources previously conceded to domestic and foreign entrepreneurs. Forestry and mining concessions were reclaimed not just to halt the loss of valuable resources but also to prevent ecological damage. For example, the ecosystem was damaged as forests were destroyed for pasturelands and as gold extraction processes contaminated rivers with toxic wastes. To oversee its program, the government created the Nicaraguan Institute of Natural Resources and Environment (IRENA) to manage and protect natural resources. Unfortunately, the political commitment was not matched by effective implementation.

Protectionists soon clashed with developmentalist proponents eager to find profits for the state agencies of forestry, mining, and fishing. The conflict between protectionists and government developmental agency chiefs spread to other revolutionary programs. The agrarian reform program, for example, contained provisions requiring soil protection and erosion control. These requirements were never enforced, partly because officials lacked the necessary expertise to do so and partly because the officials ignored these concerns. Simply put, the importance of food production outweighed the need for erosion control. As one result, Nicaraguan crops received a massive dose of pesticides, which led to short-term increased harvests and long-term environmental costs.

Even more immediately detrimental to Nicaragua's natural resources was the war initiated by the *contras*, with backing from the U.S. government. Fighting destroyed forest areas and agricultural resources and required mobilization of all governmental agencies to support the defense effort, thus limiting their ability to carry out activities such as environmental impact studies of government-sponsored development programs. Specifically, the fighting partially destroyed rain forest preserves. In another crisis, 20,000 hectares of forest and coffee trees were destroyed to eliminate a coffee plague. The only positive effect of the war was the return of pioneer agrarians back to towns for safety. This allowed forests to regenerate.

The protectionist wing of the Sandinista regime undertook a new program of forestry management based on a Swedish model and with Swedish government financial support. Foreign assistance helped initiate new programs focused on rural development, alternative technologies, reforestation, and watershed protection. Most important, the revolutionary era spawned a generation of technicians trained in environmental sciences. The technocratic character of IRENA received additional encouragement from the successor to the Sandinista government, the regime of President Violeta Chamorro. The agency quickly formulated strategies—the Conservation Strategy for Sustainable Development, the Scheme of Environmental Territorial Planning, the Forestry Action Plan, and the Environmental Action Plan—to foster sustained environmental usage through land-use planning and utilization of biological diversity.

Internal government ambivalence about this vigorous environmental program appeared almost immediately in the economic initiatives from the Ministry of Economy and Development, which were designed to promote foreign investment in the nation's forest, energy, fish, and mineral resources. Support for this approach, including the plan to deregulate resources, came from the government's Neoliberal economic wing. By the end of 1995, the Chamorro government had privatized 17 percent of the national area and had an additional 24 percent in the process of privatization. Nevertheless, 13 percent of national territory remained protected as conservation areas. Three of the protected regions make up the largest and most important biological zones in Central America. The Indio Maíz and the Bosawás reserves contain the densest rain forest outside the Amazon in the Americas; and the Miskito Cays Biological Reserve, located on the Caribbean marine platform, includes the cays, coastal wetlands, and coral reefs and encompasses numerous marine ecosystems.

Nicaragua's environmental program received both encouragement and discouragement from the 1992 United Nations Conference on the Environment and Development (the Earth Summit), held in Rio de Janeiro, Brazil. Nicaraguan representatives presented the national program at the meeting and promoted Nicaragua as the environmental leader of Central America. The Chamorro government expected to receive financial assistance because of its leadership and because Nicaragua's rain forest is second largest in the Americas. The result was a presidential ecological summit in Managua in 1993, attended by world leaders including U.S. Vice President Al Gore. Despite the worldwide attention, financial assistance never materialized.

Nevertheless, environmentalist members of the Chamorro government pushed ahead with efforts to establish comprehensive environmental legislation, called the General Law on the Environment and Natural Resources. This package, which included specific legislation for each natural resource, died in debate in 1995. The inspiration for the central government's protectionist policies came from a Danish environmental model. The Danes, in turn, became the largest foreign donor to this program. Additional international support came from multilateral organizations, such as the World Bank. International funds currently support three programs: the cleanup and recovery of Lake Xolotán; the Protierra project to manage natural resources in the northwest; and the Socio-Environmental and Forestry Development Program in north-central Nicaragua. The diverse expressions of Nicaraguan civil society will have to share with the government the responsibility for the success or failure of national environmental programs to promote the sustainable use of natural resources. Success of the environmental program appears to lie in the hands of local governments and agencies that will have to insist on implementation of the environmental laws.[11]

Nicaragua's well-rounded program, even though it exists largely only in law, has no match elsewhere in the hemisphere. Other Latin American nations, when they have paid attention to the environment at all, have looked at single issues such as the rain forest. Typical of this focused approach is the forestry program in Paraguay. The Paraguayan government has attempted to enlist the support of the

---

[11]See Desirée Elizondo Cabrera, "The Environment," in Thomas W. Walker, ed., *Nicaragua without Illusions: Regime Transition and Structural Adjustment in the 1990s* (Wilmington, DE: SR Books, 1996), pp. 131–146.

pioneer agrarians for its forest conservation project. For much of the past 50 years, some 400 square miles of Paraguay's forest has been lost annually to loggers and to fire as farmers and cattle grazers burn trees to open space for their agricultural activities. In addition, the smoke from the fires impairs visibility and contributes a variety of air pollutants.

To halt the ecological destruction, two conservation groups purchased a 220-square-mile section now called the Mbaracayu Nature Reserve in eastern Paraguay. The region comprises subtropical hardwoods, grasslands, and wetlands and is home to thousands of species of plants and animals. The fauna includes jaguars, tapirs, peccaries, armadillos, bush dogs, king vultures, macaws, and bare-throated bellbirds. Ache Indians, hunters and gatherers, have used the park for their traditional hunting grounds for thousands of years. Officials plan to save the reserve by expanding its borders and by showing pioneer agrarians how to farm without cutting or burning the trees.

Inspiration for the park came from efforts to preserve the traditional hunting lands of the Ache, considered the most genetically pure and socially isolated Indians in South America. Moisés Bertoni, a Paraguayan environmentalist, secured the Aches' interest in the reserve by donating large amounts of money to enlarge their reservation. Nevertheless, it was only through a series of accidents that the Mbaracayu reserve was created. A logging company that owned the region defaulted on a World Bank loan in the 1970s. In following its policy to preserve wild lands, the World Bank sought an appropriate buyer to create a preserve. It took nearly a decade, but in 1991 Paraguayans formed the Moisés Bertoni Foundation to join with the Nature Conservancy from the United States to purchase the property for $2 million. Private contributions and the U.S. government aided in the purchase effort, with the understanding that the Bertoni Foundation would manage the reserve. The Paraguayan government, for the past 5 years a democracy after 35 years of dictatorship, had established a small national park system; but the nation has relied on private, nongovernmental agencies for its ecological conservation program.

The Aches have exclusive hunting rights in the reserve, but they are permitted to use only bows and arrows. The Indians also forage for wild honey, fruits, and insect larva. Settlers already in the reserve and others nearby have been encouraged to grow the *maté* herb, used to prepare the national tea, and to harvest palm hearts. Complaints have charged that the reserve was simply another plaything of well-fed, wealthy foreigners who could not comprehend poverty and despair. Poaching, illicit logging, and marijuana growing continued to threaten the reserve. Officials, trying to promote sustainable growth programs, also wanted to develop environmentally oriented tourism in the park.[12]

This perhaps overly simplistic division between ecologists and developmentalists, so apparent in discussions and planning about the use of natural resources, is abundantly evident in recent conflicts over the use of pesticides.

Production, disposal, and trade of hazardous wastes constitutes yet another issue on Latin America's environmental agenda. Traditionally, the disposal of

---

[12]Patrick Graham, "A Forest Fighting Back," *Fort Worth Star-Telegram*, November 24, 1995.

human and animal wastes from homes and businesses was a public health measure. The usual practice was to remove these wastes by dumping them in landfills or water. Disposal problems have multiplied with the increased exploitation of natural resources and growth in manufacturing in recent decades. In these cases, waste disposal often involved toxic and hazardous substances. At the same time, nations with more extensive manufacturing economies have been confronted by the difficult problem of finding a place to dump their dangerous waste materials—and increasingly they have turned to Latin America as a possible dumping ground. The U.S. Environmental Protection Agency (EPA) defined hazardous wastes as those that threaten health and environment from "toxicity, explosiveness, infectiousness, radioactivity, flammability, corrosiveness, irritation and sensitization potential, and genetic change potential," and identified the categories of waste producing these hazards as "asbestos, incinerator ash, rubber wastes, industrial chemical wastes, municipal wastes, slag, sewage, sludge, used paints and pharmaceutical manufacturing wastes." Toxic substances, such as heavy metals, dioxins, and furans, are part of most wastes or can be produced upon incineration. The EPA concluded that essentially any industry produces these types of toxics.

Toxic wastes enter the ecosystem through improper handling or disposal. The animal population is particularly at risk, because toxic compounds move through the upper levels of the food chain. Hazardous products can also affect plants as well as water, land, and air quality. Handling, especially transporting, these wastes carries with it the risk of spills. The most dramatic recent example of this danger was the explosion in April 1992 of Guadalajara's underground sewage pipes—caused by improper disposal of chemical waste—that killed some 1,500 persons. Increased awareness of the dangers of hazardous wastes has only slowly resulted in international negotiations. The first agreement dealing with these substances came on March 22, 1989, in the Basel Convention on the Control of Transboundary Movements of Hazardous Wastes and Their Disposal. This agreement, arranged with the support of the United Nations Environment Program, established global regulations for the international movement of hazardous wastes. The convention entered into force in 1992, with 52 signatories including the United States. Under the terms of the Basel Convention, exporters must notify recipient nations of shipments and must receive approval from them before proceeding. Developing nations advocated tighter restrictions, and other critics wanted all shipments banned.

The Lomé IV Convention of December 15, 1989, moved beyond the Basel agreement. This convention, agreed to by 12 European and 69 African, Caribbean, and Pacific countries, bans the transport of waste between these nations. The European Community agreed not to send wastes to the signatory nations, and the African, Caribbean, and Pacific signers pledged not to accept any waste shipments. (African nations went a step further in the 1991 Bamako Convention, banning all imports of hazardous and nuclear wastes into African nations.) The African campaign to prevent dumping of wastes raised the fear that Latin America would be targeted by the United States. Mexico, according to 1993 EPA estimates, was already receiving some 12 percent of the hazardous wastes exported from the United States.

The world's nations are concerned not only about the amount of hazardous wastes shipped to another country but also about that country's ability to properly dispose of them. In 1993, the United States sent 80 percent of its hazardous waste exports to Canada. Canadians, finding economic opportunity in this field, have modern waste treatment facilities not found elsewhere in the hemisphere. Most of Latin America lacks modern treatment equipment, and the region, located in the tropics, has a more fragile ecosystem than Canada does.

Latin America may become the world's dump for hazardous materials because of its proximity to the United States and the failure of Latin American nations to agree on a regional convention to regulate trade in these materials. As of 1992, 25 countries in Latin America and the Caribbean had established individual national bans. Mexico and the United States agreed in 1984 (with amendments in 1987) on the regulation of waste shipments to Mexico, requiring U.S. companies in Mexico to remove all their hazardous wastes. Consequently, Central America has become a major receiver of waste materials. Both Honduras and Nicaragua have acted to block these shipments. Free-trade agreements in the hemisphere have the potential to increase trade in hazardous wastes unless specific restrictions are included in any trade treaty.[13] These issues received significant discussion at the 1992 United Nations Earth Summit in Rio de Janeiro, where delegates proposed a number of international agreements—but none of them had materialized by the Earth Summit Plus Five in 1997.

The major issue at the Earth Summit was the preservation of Latin America's rain forests. Biological diversity of the Amazon basin—at least 60,000 species of higher plants, 2.5 million species of anthropoids, 2,000 species of fish, and 300 mammals—makes the region unique. For all its wonders, the basin's soils are generally poor and tend to become hardpan when cleared. Grasslands are interspersed throughout the Amazon region. In recent times, burning off the forest has expanded these grasslands.

Brazil has the largest rain forest reserves in Latin America. From Portuguese times to the present, the Amazon region has been regarded as an area of incredible wealth, if only the key to unlocking its riches could be found. Isolation and a difficult environment defeated most attempts at striking it rich. Collecting forest products, except for the brief rubber boom of 1880–1910, supported only a small population at a marginal level with minimal impact on the ecosystem. In the twentieth century, Brazilian government policies have focused on development of the entire nation. This approach led to programs designed to move people into peripheral areas such as the rain forest and to stimulate economic development.

Roads had the greatest initial impact. With the completion of the Brasília-Belém road in 1965 and the subsequent construction of the Trans-Amazonian Highway and its secondary arteries, thousands of immigrants took to the highway and arrived to establish settlements in the Amazon basin. By 1980, more than 3,000 kilometers of roads crossed the region, and work began on the 12,967-kilometer perimeter road circling Brazil's Amazonian frontier. Predictably, the world's largest rain forest

---

[13]"Trade and the Environment: The Legacy of Hazardous Wastes," *North-South Issues* 2, no. 5 (1993).

Public health, street sanitation, and the maintenance of an attractive city proved difficult as millions of rural inhabitants poured into cities of Latin America. Ernesto P. Uruchutu (governor-mayor of Mexico City, 1952–1966) attempted to meet the challenge with a fleet of modern garbage trucks, shown here in battle formation in Mexico City's zocalo, in about 1960. Today, many mega-cities have all but lost control over urbanization and can do little to meet the public health needs of their citizens.

experienced widespread degradation. Deforestation is becoming increasingly evident and has consequences for the hydrologic cycle, climate, and biological resources.

The highways cutting through the forest have exposed the remaining Indian groups to civilization, economic competition, and other disruptive influences. An estimated 90 percent of Indian groups have been directly affected. Migrants, often in poor health, introduce disease. One small group of 420 forest people was reduced to a population of 79 within two years. Indians who assimilate to the new reality are incorporated into the labor force at the lowest level. Increasingly, Indians demand legal rights and have learned to use the political process to reestablish their claims, but they have been unable to stop destructive development and the wasteful burning of the forest.

In Ecuador, rain forest development initially resulted from worldwide demand for tropical products. The country's coastal rain forest became the center of cacao production on large plantations, often of hundreds and even thousands of hectares. In the 1920s, plant disease ended the cacao boom, leading to the establishment of small-scale orange and coffee farms. Banana production, fueled by exploding demand, created a new boom and put further pressure on the coastal forest.

In Ecuador's Amazon region, rain forest destruction resulted from population pressure and the petroleum industry. As in the Brazilian Amazon, the process began in the 1960s. Until then the area had remained pristine, even missing out on the rubber boom because it had only a few stands of rubber trees. It missed out on the *chinchona* (herb used to produce quinine) collection boom for the same reason. Limited military efforts to establish settlements in the zone during Ecuador's war with Peru in 1941 had little success. Beginning in 1964, land reform measures led to classification of the Amazon region as unoccupied land, disregarding the existence of some 150,000 indigenous peoples.

Early planning efforts collapsed in the face of spontaneous migration, particularly with the oil boom of the 1970s. Significant petroleum reserves discovered by the Texaco-Gulf consortium in 1967 caused economic euphoria, and migration to the region soon began. The first barrel of commercial crude oil was carried through the streets of Quito as though it were the procession of one of the saints. Ecuadorians believed that petroleum would somehow make everyone rich, happy, and modern. People asserted that Amazonian crude oil had medicinal properties useful for the treatment of arthritis, balding, and other common maladies. They smeared their bodies with crude oil, lathered their thinning hair with it, covered their scalp with a plastic cap, and the next morning eagerly searched for results, after washing out the oil with diesel fuel. To Ecuadorians, petroleum promised national salvation—and little else, including the rain forest environment, mattered. Petroleum exports soon supplied 40 to 50 percent of export profits and underpinned the country's national budget.

Frantic road building opened promising locations. Texaco drilled 339 wells, of which a stunning 235 struck oil. Well-paying jobs for the few could be found in services, small-scale agriculture, and road building; these opportunities attracted desperate but hopeful migrants. Shanty settlements scarred the landscape and polluted the surrounding area. More serious than the negative impact of settlement was the casual disposal of industrial waste. The petroleum industry produced some 5 million gallons of toxic waste each day. Most of the toxic residue went into unlined pits or was discharged directly into rivers and streams. Road dust was controlled by coating the surface with industrial residues, resulting in further pollution.

Pipeline spills have poured some 16.8 million gallons of crude oil into the headwaters of the Amazon river system. Waters previously rich in fish supported little aquatic life, with serious consequences for food supplies at a time when more and more people were flooding into the rain forest. Migration into the region between 1960 and 1998 increased the population in the northeastern Ecuadorian Amazon from less than 25,000 to more than 200,000 people.

A class action lawsuit filed in 1993 accused the Texaco company of public and private nuisance and requested $1.5 billion in damages. Because of the negative international publicity, some companies have directed their Ecuadorian subsidiaries to observe better environmental practices, including the use of directional drilling, which allows up to 12 wells to be drilled and exploited from a single platform. Nevertheless, the government remained more interested in production than environmental protection. Minimal regulations in 1998 were not enforced, and remedial action often was left to the discretion and whims of on-site managers. "San Petróleo" in 1998 was no longer carried through the streets, but nevertheless continued to enthrall Ecuadorian government officials.

Some encouraging signs of a change in attitude became evident in 1990s. Quito's Municipal Training Institute (ICAM) created a program on environmental issues for municipal officials and law enforcement personnel in 1994. It also developed complementary programs to raise environmental awareness among schoolchildren and the general community. This educational effort provided a necessary, but long-range program. Rain forest restoration will be expensive and will require technology not yet available.

Migration of both people and industry to the Amazon basin results in general deforestation. Most Amazonian countries, except for Venezuela, began colonization projects in the 1940s. After 1960, accelerated migration began to have a noticeable impact on the rain forest. From 1975 to 1980, activity in the Brazilian Amazon resulted in the deforestation of 367,000 square kilometers and continues at an annual rate of some 2,800 square kilometers. In Colombia, satellite images indicate a cleared area of 2 million hectares with an equal expanse in the process of deforestation. In the entire basin, an estimated 800,000 square kilometers, over 50 percent in Brazilian territory, have been cleared. Burning these forest resources wastes the cellulose from the trees that have been cut, makes no use of exotic hardwoods, and destroys potentially valuable pharmacological resources.

Inappropriate use of land and resources characterizes the development process in all countries with Amazonian territory. Eager migrants overwhelm even the most well-conceived plans. Settlers dispose of garbage and sewage, and sawmills dump sawdust and scrap into streams and rivers. Unplanned deforestation in the Andean republics has created severe erosion; consequently, tons of sediment pour into the headwaters. An estimated 4.3 percent per hectare of soil washes out of cleared land, compared to an insignificant 0.3 percent per hectare for forested land. Deforestation of the land and contamination of the water reduces biodiversity, and in some areas native species have disappeared. Sedimentation has seriously damaged fisheries. Agricultural and livestock facilities established on cleared land tend to be extensive, and yields are generally low. Quickly exhausted land is abandoned, and more is cleared by burning. In the Brazilian Amazon alone, settlers have abandoned an estimated 5 million hectares of land, which is thought to be so eroded as to be unproductive.

Mining operations, many quite large, and a horde of small-scale miners are responsible for extensive chemical contamination. These miners use tons of toxic mercury to amalgamate gold and eventually dump it into rivers, where it is consumed by fish and enters the region's food chain. Some 6,000 to 7,000 dredges operate in the region of the Madeira River. Gold production requires removal of 1 cubic meter of sediment for each 2 grams of gold, resulting in the displacement of some 50 million cubic meters of soil annually. Mercury contamination, including the sediment that lines the area's heavily dredged riverbanks, poses a critical problem.

If a villain can be identified in the process of rain forest deforestation, it is government officials and their relentless desire to develop the Amazon (see the Profile "Chico Mendes, Green Warrior," page 229). They see land in the basin as a useful, almost inexhaustible social and political safety valve. Land reform—always difficult, often politically dangerous—can be avoided by directing the poor into frontier regions, including the rain forests. Government policy favors large-scale investors able to finance development and supply the tax revenues to build

## Major Vegetation Types

Grasslands

Desertic and semi-desertic

Mixed, semi-evergreen-deciduous
and coniferous forest

Open woodlands and savanna

Evergreen, semi-evergreen and
deciduous forest

Evergreen and semi-evergreen
forest

Mixed and broad leaved forest

1000        0        1000        2000        3000        4000 Miles

roads and encourage even more development. Wasteful government schemes have left derelict remains scattered throughout the forest. The Balbina dam project on the Uatumá River created a large lake in the heart of the Amazon. Decaying wood turned the water into a fetid, acidic stew low in oxygen. The ill-conceived project killed the river. The downstream population sank into absolute poverty, and many fled to overcrowded cities on the coast. Each megawatt hour costs $108 to produce—four times a rate considered competitive. The entire disaster cost an estimated $1 billion to construct and destroyed a formerly productive river and the habitat of thousands of plants and animals.

---

**PROFILE** Chico Mendes, Green Warrior

Brazilian government policy encouraged large-scale investments in the Amazonian rain forest. Large cattle, lumber, and industrial enterprises all accelerated deforestation. Talk of sustainable development did little to alter what appeared to be an unstoppable process of destruction. Those who lived in the forest and depended on it could not compete with the well-financed interests that profited from cleared land and uncontrolled development. Conflict between the new economy and the old found its expression in the life and death of Chico Mendes.

Mendes, a rubber-tree tapper, depended on the forest and its continued existence for his survival. As president of the Xapuri Rural Workers' Union, he became an adept ecological politician pressing for protection of what he characterized as Brazil's green inheritance. He called for small-scale enterprises that made adaptations to the rain forest to replace the large-scale operations that had received government encouragement. His active, public campaign to protect the rain forest as a complete ecosystem that included humans as well as many other life-forms soon attracted the attention of the international community. Both the World Bank and the Inter-American Development Bank consulted with Mendes on the suitability of development projects. The United Nations recognized his activism and awarded him its Global 500 prize. Other international honors followed from a host of environmental organizations. Mendes's international stature gave him influence in Brazil. Because of his activities, in October 1988 the government unveiled a new plan called *Nossa Natureza* (Our Nature) that in theory supported sustainable development and protection of the rain forest. Less than a month later, on December 22, 1988, the hired guns of an owner of huge tracts of the rain forest murdered Chico Mendes as he stood in the doorway of his home in Xapuri. Since his death, the forest is still being burned to clear it in the name of development.

---

Planned colonies seldom function as intended. Mass migration overwhelms even the best plan. For example, a projected large-scale rice plantation in a level area in the Mayo River Valley attracted so many squatters that three times the area planned for development was eventually and illegally cleared. The total or partial failure of colonies results in secondary waves of migration to fresh land. In the process, Amazonian towns have become slum cities. Manaus, made a free port in 1957 to jump-start development, succeeded all too well. Ten years later, it had a population of 245,000; in the 1990s, the population had reached an estimated 2 million. Manaus has become a giant rain forest *favela* without adequate public services, water, or reasonable garbage disposal. The surrounding forest has been seriously degraded. In the Peruvian Amazon, an estimated 268,316 people settled between 1976 and 1981 with similar results.

The highest deforestation rate in all of Latin America has occurred in Costa Rica, which lost almost half of its forest cover from 1950 to 1990. Much of this depletion came not through cutting for timber, but by the burning of forested land for pasturage to raise low-grade beef for export. Nevertheless, during the same period, millions of acres of forest lands survived because they were protected through Costa Rica's national park system. The park system's goal was "to perpetuate all of Costa Rica's biological resources—habitats and ecosystems as well as scenery and wildlife."[14] This goal went well beyond that of the traditional national park systems that tried to preserve remnants of wildlife and scenery for sentiment and recreation. The Costa Ricans have successfully placed 25 percent of their forests in these parks and another 25 percent in multiuse, sustainable growth reserves.

These national parks represent the culmination of programs that began during the 1930s. In 1939, legislation tried to establish a two-kilometer preserve around the Poás and Irazú volcanoes as well as along the summit of the mountain chain from Cerro Zurqui to Concordia. In 1945, another law created parklands along both sides of the newly built Pan American Highway where it crossed the mountains near San José. In 1940, Costa Rica signed the Western Hemisphere Convention on Natural Resources, although the legislature did not ratify it until 1966. But these early efforts failed because the government did not have, or did not allocate, the necessary monies to establish and maintain the parks.

Increasingly, transnational cooperation has resulted in preservation efforts. The System for the Vigilance of the Amazon, established in 1998, offers one example. This program involves the cooperation of the U.S. Export Import Bank, *AB Svensk Exportkredit* (the Swedish export bank), Raytheon Company, and the SIVAM Vendor Trust. The U.S. Export Import Bank is providing most of the financing, with loans totaling just over $1 billion. This project created an integrated information network that linked numerous sensors to regional and national coordination centers, supplying the Brazilian government with extensive data on the Amazon region. The potential use of these data extended beyond monitoring the rain forest; it assisted in air safety; weather forecasting; detection, prevention, and control of epidemics; managing land occupation and usage; and law enforcement.

The land and the environments increasingly have become a part of worldwide discussions about Latin America in recent years. Interest in the environment, new perceptions of the value of preservation, and new concerns for ecosystems have resulted in the growth of ecotourism in which visitors set out to see different environments and attempt to make their visit without affecting the ecosystem. This trend reverses the Sarmiento-developmentalist view of rural, unexploited regions. Rather than a savage landscape desperate for subjugation, these undeveloped areas, especially the tropical rain forests, express an ideal of wholesome nature, the organic whole of living things, and the repository of biodiversity, all of which must be cherished and respected. It remains to be seen whether ecotourism will help preserve the environment or become just another form of mass tourism.

## THE ENVIRONMENTAL IMPACT
## OF MASS TOURISM

Mass tourism came into being after World War II in the late 1940s and early 1950s. Now in the new millennium tourist traffic constitutes a more or less permanent demographic movement. At any given moment, it remains at a stable

---

[14]Wallace, *Quetzal*, p. xv.

level as individual tourists come and go to be replaced by others. This keeps their environmental impact constant. Ease of rapid travel makes it possible for people to enjoy several days or weeks in distant locations. In many small cities and towns, tourism results in a doubling of the population with a corresponding increase in demand on resources and services of all types.

The negative impact of mass tourism can be observed without difficulty. The evidence includes the erosion of beaches and the breakup of coral reefs and coastal and marine populations through usage, water sports, garbage disposal, and cutting of canals for cruise ships and pleasure boats. Coastal road building and drainage of swamps have an impact on fisheries. The greater the flow of tourists, the greater the negative impact when an area's carrying capacity has been exceeded. At that point, environmental degradation deters tourists who then find yet another holiday destination.

Tourism commercializes the environment, local culture, and anything else that might attract visitors. Indian rituals become entertainment, and their everyday activities become trivialized. Tourism sets up competing demands for land: golf courses versus farming or forests. It pushes up land prices and encourages expansion into fragile ecological areas. In short, mass tourism is a form of economic imperialism that displaces the native population and diverts its resources to meet the needs of outsiders. An alien invasion directed by travel agents rather than conquistadores overwhelms nature and determines the types of economic activities to be pursued. In certain regions, the industry functions as a form of monoculture (economic dependence on one activity or enterprise). When the carrying capacity is exceeded, little remains of the old life; the natives are left with a deteriorating tourist infrastructure, half utilized at cut-rate prices, with no way to go back or reverse the environmental damage.

Governments, anxious to generate revenues, collaborate in short-term, destructive projects for what is often portrayed as easy money. In many Latin American countries, tourism is a large part of export revenues. The Organization of American States estimated that from the late 1960s to the 1990s tourism brought $102 billion into Latin America. Mexico alone received $10 billion from tourism between 1988 and 1992. Guatemala reports an annual take of $207.5 million a year. The World Tourist Organization projects at least a 50 percent increase in the first decade of this century. Argentina, Uruguay, and Brazil already rely on tourism for 20 percent of export earnings. Tiny Belize receives some 76 percent of its foreign exchange from tourism. Such revenue figures do not take into account the costs, which are not always immediately evident. Nevertheless, the figures explain the reluctance of Latin American governments to regulate the environmental impact of the industry.

Efforts to preserve Latin American ecosystems require a realistic approach and discussion of the carefully calculated cost-benefit analysis as well as an understanding of the economies, politics, societies, and cultures of the region. These campaigns will also require careful thought about the nature of tourists and the environments.

# 10

# Latin America
# in the Global Context

Similar to a multidimensional chess game, Latin America's place in global politics and economics functions on several different levels. At any given moment, one piece may be the most active, but all will be in play. Economic, cultural, psychological, and geopolitical factors make the relationship a close one. For Latin Americans the inescapable and sometimes uncomfortable reality comes in their relationships, in both economic and political terms, with the United States. As a large, dynamic market the United States determines much of the profitability of the hemisphere's mines, fields, and factories; in turn, Latin America is an important, but not crucial, market for U.S. products. Latin America's dependency on the American market seems to be unavoidable and is therefore resented. Less obvious, but certainly more complex, is the cultural relationship between the two regions, which is characterized by strong attraction—at times infused with disdain and suspicion, admiration, and envy of the economic strength of the United States—along with astonishment at its seemingly endless creativity. To Latin Americans, North Americans often appear to be anti-intellectual, pragmatic to an amoral degree, crass, condescending, and superficially friendly. Compounding such cultural annoyances, Latin Americans experience the United States on a daily basis, whereas most Americans can scarcely name the major Latin American capitals or accurately locate Central or South American countries on a map. This unequal and casually disrespectful relationship at times results in hostile, sometimes rabid, often illogical anti-American outbursts that offend an uncomprehending United States.

Complicating matters, both sides experience periods of exaggerated infatuation with the other. In the United States all things Peruvian, Brazilian, Argentine, or Guatemalan suddenly become wonderful, exotic, and briefly admirable. New

## Latin America in the World

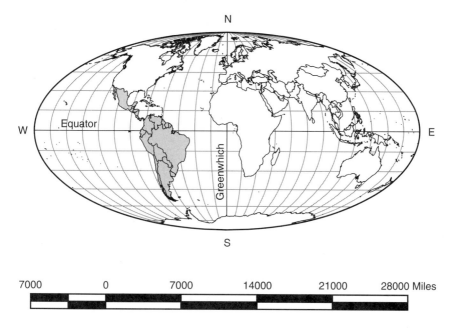

music or dance fads often precede the infatuation stage. Unfortunately, the roller-coaster ride from reality to euphoria and back often leaves Latin America with a burned-out sense of disappointment, which the United States does not appear to notice, care, or remember. Class, occupation, education, and mutual exposure all influence how each side sees the other; but in general, the points just noted are the important elements of a difficult relationship.

The individual Latin American nations have developed different and often enduring relationships with other nations of the world. Brazil and Argentina in the nineteenth century had extremely close economic and political ties with Great Britain. The French developed strong cultural influence throughout the region, but especially with the Chileans and Central America. In the twentieth century, at times the Japanese and the Germans have carried out extremely active diplomatic and economic campaigns in Latin America; and throughout the Cold War, the Soviet Union had important diplomatic, economic, and cultural missions in Latin America. Since his 1959 revolution, Fidel Castro has directed Cuban efforts to achieve global partnerships, especially in Africa, and national influence in international organizations, especially in the United Nations General Assembly and agencies such as the World Health Organization. The Cuban diplomatic corps today is one of the largest in the world. Although Cuba and the United States remain without formal diplomatic relations, the Cubans have strong representation throughout the rest of the Americas and the Southern Hemisphere. Nevertheless, for Latin America the United States remains the major international relationship.

## HISTORICAL ROOTS

The historical roots of the complex Latin American global relationships may be traced to the creation of new societies in the Western Hemisphere. From the moment Europeans arrived in the hemisphere they regarded it as exotic, different, and certainly not European. The eighteenth century added the intellectual under-pinnings of the already emotionally well-established idea of a different and unique New World. Many Europeans viewed the Western Hemisphere as a clean slate whereby human beings might reach a stage of natural perfection; others chose a negative but equally romantic approach that exaggerated America's vices. Nevertheless, both groups agreed that New World societies could not be fully Europeanized.

Europeans, as conquerors and reorganizers of an extensive pre-Columbian population, assumed the superiority of their own culture, including its religious foundations. Thus, Spaniards born in the New World (*criollos*) and mixed-ancestry *mestizos* went to great lengths to claim inclusion within European culture. Indians who accepted elements of the new language, religion, and other aspects of Spanish culture in a similar manner conceded the cultural reality. The Western Hemisphere developed a unique culture, but not to an exaggerated degree. Important elements of Europe, its languages, religious beliefs, and philosophical notions mingled with aboriginal and African cultures. A Spanish-American criollo might have a different accent or use certain Indian or African words in everyday speech that Spaniards found curious, but they understood each other with little difficulty. Moreover, the New World's political philosophy and structure reflected the model of the imperial mother country. Nevertheless, Spain as the imperial center exercised cultural superiority over its provincial, distant, and often rustic subjects in America. Inevitably, a sense of cultural inferiority infused the colonial elite as well as other social levels.

In English North America, various historical factors limited the extent of colonial inferiority. The religious dissenters who made up the first wave of settlers in effect rejected the mother country. Although well aware of their uncertain status, they were inclined to see cultural differences and isolation from the imperial center as desirable. The romantic glorification school of the eighteenth-century Enlightenment also tempered cultural anxieties in North America to a much greater degree than in Spanish America. Nevertheless, both groups retained lingering feelings of colonial inferiority, and they still do. The difference of degree may be explained by the century that separated the establishment of Spain's American empire and that of the English colonies and by the differing patterns of European-Indian relations. Spanish colonization tapped into the zeal and energy of the Counter-Reformation. The Protestant assault required a clear, even rigid, restatement of what it meant to be a Catholic and what Catholic culture stood for—in sharp contrast to the despised Lutheran heresy. Anything less than religious and cultural purity appeared dangerous. To those who believed themselves to be under cultural siege, religion constituted a barrier against the forces of disintegration. In contrast, 100 years later in English North America, religious dissenters could be tucked away in the forest, much to the monarchs' relief. Religio-cultural loyalty may not have been a major colonial concern for seventeenth-century England, but it was for sixteenth-century Spain.

In Spanish America establishment of a colonial empire involved the inclusion of a large, productive, and organized Indian population indoctrinated in the basic elements of Spanish culture. By contrast, in English North America the scattered and limited Indian population remained on the outer fringes of colonial society. The degree to which the Indians accepted or rejected English culture and religion concerned missionaries only. Nor did miscegenation occur to the same extent as in Spanish America; thus, a defined English–Native American mestizo culture never emerged. Moreover, the Scotch-Irish and lower-class English immigrants who arrived in the American colonies had few cultural pretensions. Although a sense of inferiority may be identified, its main component was class, not race or culture.

In various subtle ways, colonial powers defined the attitude toward themselves and their competition. Their American subjects generally lacked familiarity with the broader world and demonstrated limited tolerance of different cultures and religions, all of which made it relatively easy to enlist their support in the struggle for dominance in the New World. The average imperial subject imagined foreigners to be different to the point of peril.

Colonialism resulted in an exaggerated attachment to a cultural ideal, the focus of which lay in Europe. In Spanish, Portuguese, or English America, cultural uncertainties stemmed from the same causal root and shared a common Eurocentrism, but each group attached itself to distinct European cultures. In the nineteenth century the pan-Latinism of François Guizot, supported and popularized by Napoleon III, captured those already vast cultural differences, encapsulating them in the term *Latin Americans*. According to Guizot's notion, an Anglo-Saxon United States territorially and culturally threatened to destroy the hemisphere's "Latin" Americans. Pan-Latinism placed all Latin-derived language groups under the same cultural umbrella. Gratified, flattered, even relieved, Spanish Americans and Luso-Brazilians became Latin Americans—distinct, undoubtedly superior to, and unquestionably different from Anglo-Americans. In fact, such differences antedated Guizot by several centuries.

To the governing monarchies, the New World provided an arena for European conflicts and new imperial ambitions. Virtually all European pretenders secured territorial positions of widely varying size and importance, introducing competing cultures along with their flags. Spain and Portugal, the preliminary colonizers, would be joined by England and France as the major Western Hemisphere powers. By the second half of the eighteenth century France had abandoned Canada to the British. France then completed its withdrawal from North America in 1803, when Napoleon sold the Louisiana Territory to the United States. Thus Anglo-Saxon North America, Protestant with a few notable exceptions, countered a well-established Catholic culture stretching from New Spain (Mexico) to South America. Occasional alliances and increased contact in the eighteenth century acted to create a wary ambivalence between the North and the South—bridgeable on some levels, but not on others.

North American Puritans launched one of the first attempts to establish ties between the North and the South. At the close of the seventeenth century Cotton Mather, Samuel Sewall, and several other Boston Puritans targeted Spanish America, believing it ripe for conversion. Their grand plan envisioned a hemispheric cultural unity based on Protestant beliefs. The Boston Puritans began a process that continues today in the form of televangelists and Protestant missionaries. The zealous Cotton Mather learned Spanish—by his own account in a matter of weeks—and composed a tract titled *La religión pura,* published in Boston in 1699. Mather's work, the first Spanish-language book published in English North America, projected Puritan religious values rather than identifying common links. Samuel Sewall supported Mather's efforts in addition to developing his own project. Sewall, a well-to-do merchant and member of the Council of Massachusetts Bay Colony, envisioned a new Protestant Jerusalem in Mexico City. He believed that Puritan tenets had the revolutionary potential to separate the Spanish-American colonies from Spain. These early Puritan fantasies encompassed generous motives as well as religious rigidity. According to the Puritans, though Spanish America undoubtedly struggled with a benighted version of Christianity, it was worthy of redemption.

A more fruitful and secular approach sprang from one of the more admirable intellectual currents of the eighteenth-century Enlightenment, which sought universal truths and scientific unity within a "Republic of Letters." In British North America a nascent intellectual inter-Americanism may be noted in the growth of the book trade and foreign-language courses. In 1741, New York bookseller Garrat Noel, who served as the official Spanish translator of the Provincial Council of the Colony of New York, published a basic Spanish grammar text. His *A Short Introduction to the Spanish Language* sought to advance tolerant understanding as well as to impart the basics of Spanish grammar. In 1776 the College of Philadelphia offered the first advanced course in Spanish grammar and literature in English-speaking North America. Another Philadelphia institution, the American Philosophical Society, deliberately sought to develop contacts with the Spanish world. Mutual exchange of correspondence, proceedings, and honorary memberships created a worldwide intellectual network. The Count of Campomanes, one of Spain's most distinguished intellectuals, maintained a corresponding membership with the society (1784), as did other notable individuals. Thomas Jefferson sent Campomanes a personal copy of his own *Notes on Virginia.* Both Jefferson and Benjamin Franklin enjoyed widespread respect throughout the Spanish world for their well-publicized scientific studies. In 1801 the American Philosophical Society selected its first Spanish-American resident member. Alejando Ramírez, a botanist and member of the Spanish Academy of History, as well as a royal official, had served in several official posts in Guatemala and Cuba and as Intendant of Puerto Rico. The list of Spanish-American members of North American scientific societies, and vice versa, ballooned in the early nineteenth century, providing an intellectual bridge between the United States and the soon-to-be independent nations.

## DIVERGING INTERESTS

The relatively innocent phase based on respect for knowledge began to change as the Latin American republics and the United States each began consolidating independence within the first quarter of the nineteenth century and working out new economic and diplomatic relationships. With sovereignty came responsibilities and potentially conflicting objectives. Weak, insecure, fledgling republics sought to obtain a reasonable share of collapsing empires. The United States, because it achieved independence about four decades before most of Latin America did, went through the self-interested state first and indeed would be strong enough to play a minor provocative role in the subsequent Spanish-American process. Even as an enlightened Thomas Jefferson dreamed in 1801 of an intellectual unity binding all together, he also envisioned a time when Americans would spread across North America and perhaps even the southern continent creating a "people speaking the same language, governed in similar form and by similar laws."[1] Jefferson undoubtedly imagined a natural process rather than imperialist expansion. Nevertheless, he assumed that English would be the language, American democracy the form of government, and constitutionalism the basis of law. Jefferson's pleasant dreams provided the stuff of nightmares for others.

Both Great Britain and Spain conspired to cage the new republican United States between the Appalachian Mountains and the Atlantic seacoast. Spain moved to keep the United States as far away from the Mississippi River and the Gulf of Mexico as possible, while Britain viewed the Old Northwest (now the states of Ohio, Indiana, Michigan, Wisconsin, and Illinois) as a barrier to possible American expansion. Spain also contested the boundaries set between Britain and its breakaway colonies by claiming the Ohio River Valley and Lake Michigan. Moreover, the boundary between the United States and Spanish Florida remained vague and in dispute. Garrisons, military outposts, and alliances with Indian tribes discouraged American incursions. The French Revolution of 1789 and a series of European wars in its aftermath gave the United States some breathing room. President George Washington skillfully concluded a series of treaties that shored up the new republic's still shaky territorial integrity. A treaty with an increasingly desperate Spain allowed American merchants to use the Mississippi River system and even warehouse goods in New Orleans. Spain believed that such limited access would take some pressure off the boundary line, but the reverse occurred as Americans moved westward in ever-increasing numbers.

In Paris, Napoleon concluded that his plan to reestablish a French colonial empire in the New World was unrealistic, but perhaps the United States could be

---

[1] Quoted in Frederick Merk, *Manifest Destiny and Mission in American History* (Westport, CT: Greenwood Press, 1983), p. 9.

used to counter the British. Thus, Napoleon forced Spain to return the Louisiana Territory to France and then sold it (1803) to the United States, effectively encouraging the expansionist energy that Britain and Spain had worked so hard to block. Meanwhile, taking a lesson from its European protagonists, the United States jumped at the chance to weaken Spain and its then ally Britain, both confronting Napoleonic armies, to meddle in Latin American independence movements. Handled properly, the prize might well be Canada detached from Britain, Spanish Florida, and perhaps even Texas. Thus, the United States permitted Latin American agents to commission privateers to attack Spanish shipping. The city of Baltimore alone furnished 21 privateers that sailed under the rebel flag of Buenos Aires. At least a dozen more sailed from New Orleans, flying the flags of Mexico and Caracas. Only when the privateers began plundering non-Spanish vessels did the American authorities take action to stop the arrangement. Unfortunately for the United States, plans for a great "Empire of Liberty" literally went up in smoke as British troops seized Washington, D.C., and burned the capital during the War of 1812.

A chastened United States, still expansionist but now more circumspect, saw little future in direct confrontation with Europe. Prudent American leaders now advocated neutrality toward the rebelling Spanish colonies, but suggested to Spain that the United States might not recognize them officially if Spain conceded disputed territory. Faced with imperial collapse, Spain negotiated the Florida Treaty (1819), also known as the Transcontinental Treaty, which the American public greeted as a diplomatic triumph until learning that Spain had been prepared to throw in Texas. Nevertheless, significant territory in the west passed from Spanish to American hands. Spain paid dearly for little more than an implied promise by the United States not to be involved in the Latin American independence movement. Complementing the gains of the Transcontinental Treaty, an agreement with Britain over the Oregon Territory gave the United States a foothold on the Pacific coast. While the United States maneuvered to surround the core states of its fragile republic with territorial padding at the expense of the old colonial powers, a notion of a great and prosperous future inevitably developed and soon became the Doctrine of Manifest Destiny. Henry Clay, speaker of the House of Representatives, and others believed that a New World political system, under the guidance of the United States, would develop naturally as the various parts of the Spanish-American empire became independent.

The Monroe Doctrine (1823) merged two major strands of American foreign policy—isolationism and opposition to the European presence in the hemisphere. The Monroe Doctrine rejected any new transfer of territory from one colonial power to another—but not to an American state. Colombia, interested in protecting itself against a possible Spanish reinvasion backed by the Holy Alliance, first posed the question of how the United States intended to enforce the doctrine. In fact, as all realized, the Monroe Doctrine's success depended largely on the British navy. Nevertheless, the Monroe Doctrine became the central pillar of American foreign policy for the next 100 years and remains an important element into the twenty-first century.

While the United States took a unilateral approach, Spanish America, drawing on its sense of Hispanic cultural unity, attempted to devise a collective response to European meddling in the hemisphere. Simón Bolívar invited the various new nations to send delegates to a Panama congress to meet in 1826 with the idea of forming a league or confederation of American states. Bolívar, Juan Egaña of Chile, Ecuadorian Vicente Rocafuerte, and others understood that total fragmentation of the old empire was neither desirable nor necessary. Spanish Americanism never made the transition from an emotional reality to a formal structure. Rivalries between the new nations made unity impossible. Nevertheless, the shadowy aura of a departed empire persisted in the vague sense of Spanish Americanism shared by Latin American republics. Significantly, it excludes the other historical and cultural entities—Anglo-America, Anglo-French Canada, and Luso-Brazil. As an Argentine writer and academic bluntly noted in the 1920s, "the social community . . . of Spanish America does not extend to either Brazil or the United States."

## EXPANSION AND CONTRACTION

In the first half of the nineteenth century, the United States concentrated on transcontinental expansion. A sweep westward from the Gulf of Mexico and the Old Northwest became inevitable after the Louisiana Purchase, as Francisco Bouliney, the Spanish military commander in New Orleans at the time of the retrocession, so clearly and bitterly anticipated. The process entailed acquisition of territory held by Mexico as the successor state to Spain. The clash between Latin America's perception of what it meant to be a successor of a reasonably well-defined empire and the American strategy of breaking off bits and pieces of territory originally held by European colonial powers eventually led to war. It must be kept in mind that the Latin American republics were new politically, but not territorially or psychologically. They split into independent entities along jurisdictional boundaries, usually the internal divisions of kingdoms or *audiencias* (high-court jurisdictions) and major cities. Most parts of Spanish America had a sense of their own internal unity. In many cases the new capital was the old political center. Mexico City, Lima, Buenos Aires, Bogotá, Caracas, and Quito, among others, played essentially the same role after independence. When conflict between the new republics occurred, the disagreement was over actual physical boundary lines, often traversing unpopulated jungles, deserts, or barren areas. Most rejected the idea of using broad viceregal administrative boundaries but accepted secondary jurisdictional lines such as kingdoms and audiencias or, in certain areas, the authority of an urban center. Despite the assumption of sovereignty by various parts of the late empire, a sense of a broader unity based both on history and culture remained. Mexico thus entertained the notion that the Philippines and the Marianas, then still part of the Spanish empire, might join the Mexican Republic because they had been part of the old viceroyalty of New Spain and could furnish colonists to populate the empty spaces in northern Mexico, particularly California.

The inevitable clash of perceptions led to war between the United States and Mexico. Relations between the two rested upon opposing realities, one aggressively expansionist and the other defensively protectionist. One side stood to lose what the other sought to gain. The territory at stake, with a population of some 40,000—mainly Native Americans, acculturated as well as unassimilated—appeared to be a demographic vacuum. The "empty" space had drawn Spaniards and Mexicans from the south, Anglo-Americans from the east, and even Russians from the far north who advanced to within 100 miles of San Francisco.

Indeed, the confrontation over the Southwest from Texas to California represented the last act of a drama begun by colonial powers, with the existing native population cast as incidental to the process and prior European activity crucial. Mexico rested its claims upon sixteenth-century Spanish explorations and its role as a successor state. Meanwhile, the United States saw little reason to alter its successful strategy of pressure, diplomacy, and purchase. Mexican officials wanted to increase the number of settlers in the northern territories, particularly in Texas, in order to counter the silent invasion of Protestant Americans; but they believed they would prevail in any military confrontation with the Americans. Many European observers shared their confidence.

The revolt and independence of Texas appeared to offer the possibility of yet another American ploy. President Andrew Jackson urged the Texans to claim territory all the way to the Pacific coast, so that when annexation eventually occurred, the various U.S. interests would be united behind it. Easterners could not be convinced of the utility of annexing Texas, but they could be brought around if the territory in question included Pacific harbors. President John Tyler, just before leaving office, pushed through Congress a joint resolution supporting the annexation of Texas. The Lone Star Republic entered the American Union in December 1845 as the twenty-eighth state. President James K. Polk succeeded in making the annexation of Texas acceptable by linking it with the acquisition of Oregon (1846), following Jackson's general suggestion. Polk then proposed buying a new border from El Paso, due west, for $25 million. The outbreak of war changed the situation, but the United States returned to its old strategy when it purchased the Mesilla Valley (Gadsden Purchase) in 1853. The territorial concessions of the Treaty of Guadalupe Hidalgo (1848), along with the Gadsden Purchase, completed the process of continental expansion. Article 21 of that treaty provided for the resolution of future disputes in the spirit of peace and "good neighborship." Unfortunately, a bitter Mexico continues to brood over the "loss" of its "national" territory. Each side's differing historical perceptions constitute an apparently unbridgeable psychological gap between them.

## FANTASY AND NEGLECT

Following its acquisition of a Pacific coast, the United States showed little interest in Latin America. American commercial interests, thrilled at the prospect of expanding trade with Asia, designed railway schemes to link the nation's industrial

East as well as an ambitious South with Pacific ports. The United States directed its energy to the Far East rather than southward into Latin America, which except for Mexico appeared to be a British economic preserve. Mexico received attention from American investors due in part to the Asian fantasy of trade connections and in part to its proximity. American entrepreneur Albert Kimsey Owen dreamed of transforming Topolobampo, Sinaloa, into a transpacific port linked by rail to Norfolk, Virginia. His "express route to the Orient" ended in bankruptcy, but not before stretches of track were laid. Another exciting possibility involved building a railway across the Isthmus of Tehuantepec, only 810 miles from the port of New Orleans and the Mississippi River network, to dramatically reduce travel time and distance between American manufacturing centers and Asian markets. The scheme seemed plausible but ended (but perhaps not permanently) with the opening of the Panama Canal in 1914.

Meanwhile, the hemisphere measured its progress by a European yardstick. Within the hemisphere itself, nations strove to be more modern and progressive than their neighbors, beautification of cities being only one of many symbolic indicators of their standing in the race for modernization. In the process, Latin America became aware of the incredible pace of modernization in the United States. Thanks in large measure to European capital by the latter half of the nineteenth century, it seemed likely that the United States would overtake Europe. Initially, Latin Americans perceived northern progress as more of an embarrassment than a threat. Indeed, few Latin American countries dealt with the United States directly. Cuba, Mexico, and illegal filibustering activities in Central America were the exceptions. Latin America eventually realized, however, that the Anglo-Saxon North might emerge as the dominant force within the hemisphere, overwhelming them in unforeseen ways if they remained passive.

By the turn of the twentieth century many Latin American intellectuals publicly warned that U.S. economic strength verged on controlling the future of the entire Western Hemisphere. Worse yet, they cautioned that such control would extend beyond trade and commerce into social and cultural realms. Guizot's warning had been prophetic. Uruguayan José Enrique Rodó laid out what many Latin Americans believed to be at stake. His book *Ariel* (1900), still widely read and admired, sounded a stern warning. Rodó's work demonstrated his own intellectual refinement and wide reading in French, British, Spanish, and American literature and philosophy. He suggested that such exquisite learning would be in jeopardy if the United States and its crass materialism penetrated the region. Mediocrity and a lowering of culture to its lowest possible level appeared to him to be the fruits of America's materialistic democracy. Rodó urged Latin America to elaborate its own "rationally" conceived democracy, including an "indispensable element of aristocracy." Rodó could accept the elitism of Thomas Jefferson but hated what he perceived to be the common leveling of Andrew Jackson and the coarsening of culture.

*Ariel's* unabashedly aristocratic tone seems strangely archaic today. Carlos Maggi, lamenting Latin America's uneven progress, expressed frustration when he decried the tendency to nurture and keep under glass the enchanting but absolutely "worthless orchid" of elite culture and advised, "Close the tomb of *Ariel*

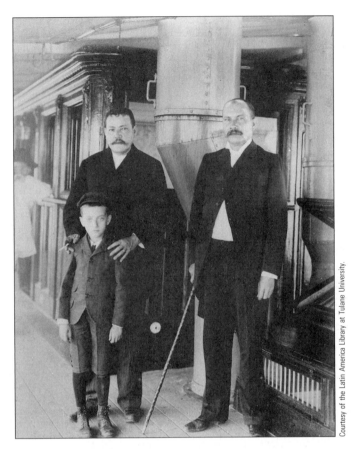

Courtesy of the Latin America Library at Tulane University.

The governor of Ceiba, Honduras, posed aboard ship with friends in the early decades of the twentieth century. Well-dressed in modern attire with a handsome cane, the governor could easily be mistaken for a merchant or a banker from New Orleans, the destination of many such ships. Maritime links and bananas pulled Honduras into the modern world commodity economy, providing plantation jobs for coastal inhabitants and money for the national treasury, and encouraging over-concentration on one product (monoculture), a problem unrecognized at the time in many parts of Latin America.

with seven padlocks and [move] forward." Maggi's reaction indicates that Rodó lost, perhaps as he feared and knew he would. Nevertheless, Rodó's strain of cultural elitism remains alive today, evoked to separate Latin America spiritually from the materialistic North and its presumptive crassness.

U.S. influence, economic as well as cultural, over Latin America expanded concentrically as the country developed. First Mexico, then Cuba and Central America, entered the orbit. The plan for a canal drew the United States southward to the very fringe of South America. An American diplomat wrote in 1909 that the

Orinoco River—which flows with its tributary, the Apuré, more or less horizontally across Venezuela—marked the natural maximum reach of American influence. Within that sphere the United States would act to reinforce its interests. President Theodore Roosevelt's brazen detachment of the Isthmus of Panama from Colombia, preparatory to taking over the canal project, made the point. As many observed, an American canal would transform the Caribbean from a "blind alley" into the high road to the Pacific. As for the other countries south of the Orinoco line, the diplomat suggested a disinterested friendliness aimed at cultivating trade.

A new version of Manifest Destiny revolved around the canal project. President Benjamin Harrison's (1889–1893) secretary of state, James G. Blaine, supplied much of the vision. Blaine's imperial imagination roamed the globe. He revived the notion of buying the Danish West Indies (today the American Virgin Islands) and projects for coaling stations throughout the Caribbean, and he pressed for naval bases in the Pacific and the occupation of Hawaii. He envisioned a broad arc of naval bases from Puget Sound to Pearl Harbor to Samoa to Chimbote, Peru, extending American power well into the Pacific with the then contemplated canal as the centerpiece. Blaine convened representatives from all the Latin American republics in Washington, D.C., in 1889 for the First International American Conference. He hoped to establish the notion that the United States served as a concerned but maternal big sister for the hemisphere. Although few of the more concrete projects suggested at the conference came to fruition, all participants understood that the United States saw its leadership role as a natural prerogative that came with its undeniable power.

Despite all the posturing and maneuvering, both the United States and Latin America remained tied to Europe culturally and economically. Each knew much more about events on the other side of the Atlantic than about what occurred in other parts of their own hemisphere. Often travelers to and from South America had to pass through Europe first and then backtrack by steamer to New York or a South American port. For the adventuresome, a trip from Rio de Janeiro to New York via Liverpool required at best a month. The absence of direct and regular steamship connections meant that even news passed through a European filter. Misunderstandings, cultural distortions, and deliberate falsifications also passed through transatlantic cables controlled by European companies. American and Latin American perceptions could be manipulated by a not necessarily trustworthy or sympathetic Europe. Indirect contact and transmission of information remained a reality until the 1920s, particularly in South America.

## THE MAKING OF THE AMERICAN MEDITERRANEAN

American expansion into the Caribbean initially centered on Cuba. Prior to the American Civil War, Cuba had been envisioned as a possible slave state to balance the free states in the U.S. North. By the end of the nineteenth century, however,

Cuba had become an important part of a larger geopolitical strategy. Planners pointed out that if Cuba and Puerto Rico could be brought under the control or sovereignty of the United States and if the Danish West Indies could be purchased, the U.S. Navy could control the northern passage through the Leeward Islands. A string of islands, a virtual barrier reef cutting across the principal sea approaches, would make it possible for the United States to deny military access to the Caribbean and the Gulf of Mexico. From an economic standpoint, the United States already dominated Cuba. Cuban sugar relied on the American market, and the island's prosperity rose and fell based on the ups and downs of the sugar tariff. It remained only for the United States to exert direct political control. The Cuban insurrection of 1895 provided the opportunity.

Cuba had been plagued by civil unrest for most of the nineteenth century, and the events of 1895 conformed to the pattern of violence. What made this situation different, however, was that for the first time, a Cuban insurrection caught the American public's attention as well as imagination. The yellow journalism of American newspapers is often blamed for fanning war fever, but in reality the country itself was psychologically ready to extend its reach into the Caribbean. Annexation, the obvious objective, lost its clarity of purpose due to a tremendous amount of posturing over the benefits of extending American-style liberties to the allegedly downtrodden remnants of Spain's American empire. In the end such talk served to save Cuba from outright annexation. Puerto Rico and the Philippines, also part of Spain's empire, enjoyed no such protection. If Cuba could not be absorbed outright, at least it could become a protectorate of the United States under the terms of the Platt Amendment. The peace treaty worked out when Spain transferred Puerto Rico and the Philippines to American sovereignty and provided for the nominal independence of Cuba. The United States was also granted a permanent naval base at Guantánamo Bay—although the entire Cuban "reef" had eluded the geopolitical planners, at least a portion fell into their hands. The rest of the pieces dropped into place with minimal difficulty.

The matter of acquiring a canal remained to be worked out in order to assure easy transit between the oceans. President Theodore Roosevelt contrived to achieve this goal in 1903 when he detached the Isthmus of Panama from Colombia. A canal treaty with the new Panamanian republic allotted the United States a 10-mile-wide canal zone from sea to sea, to be governed as if it were a sovereign part of the United States. The immorality of the blatantly self-serving actions of Teddy Roosevelt would be partly admitted when the United States made reparation to Colombia in 1921, but only after Roosevelt's death.

Geopolitically driven imperialism had not yet run its course. The United States continued to be concerned about the possible transfer of territory to a European power. Washington's concerns centered on the possibility that a Caribbean country would unwisely contract debt and then default, making itself vulnerable to territorial demands, including long-term leases or even the concessions of permanent coaling stations. Such footholds would give imperial competitors a threatening presence close to the United States. Initially, commercial relations between Latin America and Europe seemed harmless enough. Thus, in his message to Congress in 1901, President Theodore Roosevelt declared that the Monroe Doctrine did not shield

Courtesy of the Latin America Library at Tulane University.

Ill-trained and ill-equipped Colombian militiamen, photographed in about 1900, offered scant resistance to the contrived rebellion in Panama. The virtually instantaneous recognition of an independent Panamanian republic by Theodore Roosevelt shocked Latin Americans. The episode exemplified the arrogant self-interest often displayed by the United States in the Caribbean.

Latin America from punishment for commercial misdeeds, provided the settlement did not involve the transfer of territory. Such diplomatic naïveté ended as a result of European retaliation against Venezuela over a series of claims. Joint action by Britain and Germany off the coast of South America led to the sinking of Venezuelan ships and the naval bombardment of Puerto Cabello. Italy, with its own claims, joined in the blockade of Venezuela's coast. Hostile public reaction in Latin America surprised European bankers. Argentine statesman Luis María Drago formulated the Drago Doctrine (1902), which declared that public debt should not be collected by force or occupation. The United States realized the extreme danger of a miscalculation. Washington now viewed Latin American–European commercial relations as potentially dangerous. To make matters worse, a tribunal of international judges drawn from the Permanent Court of International Arbitration ruled that any state that incurred the expense of forcefully collecting debts had a preferred position in any subsequent debt settlement. Such a decision encouraged the use of force.

European creditors, well aware of the apprehension caused by the Venezuelan incident, sought a compromise solution. They made it known that they would not intervene to collect delinquent payments if the United States assumed that responsibility. In effect, Europe recognized American hegemony in the hemisphere conditioned upon Washington's acceptance of the role of fiscal policeman or, as an alternative, joint intervention with the United States. Reluctantly, the big sister accepted the sterner role of the schoolmarm. An exasperated Teddy Roosevelt is reputed to have complained, "These wretched republics cause me a great deal of trouble." The root of the problem, in the U.S. view, was a fatal political incapacity. Irresponsible governments could not be allowed to make themselves vulnerable and consequently endanger the security of the United States. The Roosevelt Corollary to the Monroe Doctrine (1904), unlike the 1823 doctrine itself, turned inward to threaten Latin America with American intervention unless those countries behaved themselves. Moreover, if Latin America insisted on financial dependency, American banks had to step forward. Acting on the new perceived responsibilities, Roosevelt, with the permission of Dominican authorities, appointed an American as receiver of the Dominican Republic's customs receipts. American officials then divided the proceeds, paying 55 percent to foreign creditors and setting aside the rest for the Dominican treasury. Money became the tool to teach political responsibility. Inevitably, other tools had to be added, leading eventually to armed occupation.

## ON THE BACK OF THE JAGUAR

President Woodrow Wilson's Latin American policy reflected personal ambivalence toward the hemisphere's republics. He had no knowledge of the nations involved, little interest in acquiring it, and scant respect for a region he deemed hopelessly backward. His worldview revolved around Europe. Ironically, Wilson shared the Eurocentric approach of Latin America's elites—a position that left both sides with a better understanding of France than of each other. Wilson's reaction to the confusing events of the Mexican Revolution, following the resignation of Porfirio Díaz in 1911, demonstrated the danger of well-intentioned ignorance.

Prior to World War I, most U.S. investments in Latin America went to Mexico and Cuba, with only insignificant amounts to other countries of the hemisphere. Thus, when revolutionary violence swept Mexico, approximately $1 billion worth of American property, railroads, mines, plantations, ranches, and businesses appeared to be in jeopardy, as well as the lives of some 40,000 American citizens living in the country. Several members of Wilson's cabinet had personal economic interests in Mexico, or connections with companies that did. Colonel Edward M. House, an influential advisor to the president as well as an honorary Texas colonel, owned shares in several Mexican silver mines. Wilson's close friend Cleveland Dodge worried over the impact of revolutionary violence on the copper industry. Key representatives in Mexico, John Lind and Duval West, had important ties with the Mexican Land Company. Wilson received plenty of advice about what to do in Mexico, all of it based on self-interest.

Wilson's immediate predecessor, President William Howard Taft, had been able to avoid intervention by temporarily placating various interests with such tactics as deploying U.S. troops along the border. Taft's Mexico policy became an issue in the 1912 elections. During the last few weeks of the outgoing Taft administration, Francisco Madero died violently as the regime of Victoriano Huerta consolidated its illegal seizure of power. An appalled Washington withheld formal recognition pending the receipt of more information. After Wilson's inauguration, he decided to drive Huerta from office. In 1913 President Wilson issued his *Declaration of Policy with Regard to Latin America,* in which he stated his opposition to any government established by force—Huerta would not be recognized. Wilson's hostility toward Huerta began a chain of events that ended with the U.S. Navy seizing the Mexican port of Veracruz (1914). The objective, to prevent a German vessel from delivering arms by seizing the docks, inevitably led to a battle for the entire city and resulted in many civilian casualties. Public reaction in Mexico shocked Wilson—after all, he hoped to oust a murderous, illegitimate military pretender. The Yankee invasion of Mexico's principal port set off a violent wave of anti-American nationalism. Fortunately, Wilson extricated himself from Veracruz under cover of a conference jointly sponsored with Argentina, Brazil, and Chile in Niagara Falls, Ontario. When the United States pulled out, it left arms and ammunition for Venustiano Carranza's forces, which Wilson deemed worthy of support. Carranza publicly denied any support from Washington, due to the level of public anger over the Veracruz incident. Wilson was not quite free of Mexico. Pancho Villa's raid on Columbus, New Mexico, in 1916 forced Wilson to deal with an aroused American public calling for military action. The punitive expedition into northern Mexico, led by General "Black Jack" Pershing, appeared to be yet another violation of Mexican sovereignty. The eventual withdrawal of the expedition, without a catastrophic incident and without capturing Villa, caused a heartfelt sigh of relief within the Wilson administration. Veracruz was another item on Mexico's list of historical grievances against the United States.

## HAITI, THE DOMINICAN REPUBLIC, AND NICARAGUA

The opening of the Panama Canal in 1914 transformed serious concerns over perceived instability into vital security considerations requiring immediate action. Haiti appeared to be the most dangerous problem. From 1908 on, one individual after another seized the presidency, sacked the treasury, and left violently. One erstwhile president died of poisoning; another was blown to bits; and just before the American intervention, one was yanked out from under a bed and hacked to pieces by an outraged mob that then paraded his body parts triumphantly through the streets. The collapse of order, worrisome in itself, became more critical when rumors circulated about Germany's interest in establishing a naval presence in Haiti. American banks and railroad investors pressed for action. In July 1915, U.S. Marines from the USS *Washington* seized control of the Haitian government, beginning a 19-year occupation. American officials replaced Haitians at all vital levels, installing a series of puppet presidents. The United States also introduced racial segregation, alienating virtually every Haitian in the process. The occupation resulted in few reforms and no lasting beneficial effects. As a result, by 1930 the United States began returning control to Haitians; in 1934 President Franklin D. Roosevelt withdrew the marines, leaving only an economic mission in place until 1941. Haitians viewed the end of the American occupation as a second emancipation.

American intervention on the other half of the island of Hispaniola, the Dominican Republic, occurred the year after the Haitian takeover. In the Dominican Republic, the United States dispensed with puppet presidents and governed directly under military law. The heavy-handed military government jailed its critics, including the poet Fabio Fiallo, causing widespread outrage throughout Latin America. As in Haiti, the marines trained a constabulary to maintain order, under the illusion that an American-trained force would be a strictly professional one and hence apolitical and willing to function within a democratic structure. The fact that no such structure existed did not seem to be a concern. Predictably, the constabulary became the most powerful and effective institution in the Dominican Republic. After the American withdrawal in 1924, the constabulary functioned as a personal instrument of its chief, Rafael Leonidas Trujillo Molina, who then seized the presidency in 1930. The barely nascent democracy collapsed in the face of a well-equipped, professional force that made possible Trujillo's 31-year rule.

Oddly, Woodrow Wilson never considered himself an interventionist, despite U.S. actions in Veracruz, Haiti, and the Dominican Republic. Undoubtedly, President Wilson preferred other methods of controlling the Caribbean, such as the purchase of the Danish West Indies in 1917 in the midst of World War I. Significantly, the transfer of sovereignty from Denmark to the United States took place on March 31, 1917, the fiftieth anniversary of the purchase of Alaska.

In Nicaragua, President William Howard Taft, Wilson's predecessor, appointed a collector of customs and encouraged American bankers to become involved in fiscal management of the country. Following a widespread revolt in 1912, Taft dispatched a contingent of marines. Sterner actions and even more marines were sent after the civil war in 1927. The United States decided that the army should be replaced by an American-trained constabulary, as in Haiti and the Dominican Republic. The new *Guardia Nacional* (National Guard) soon dominated the country. When the United States withdrew in 1933, it abandoned the country to a well-trained and well-equipped force with no other institutional counterbalance. Only General Augusto César Sandino, along with his ill-equipped and ragged guerrilla band, opposed the de facto marine protectorate. When he finally accepted reality in 1934, he was shot by the Guardia Nacional. Almost inevitably, the chief of the Guardia, General Anastasio Somoza, assumed the presidency in 1937, holding onto power until his death in 1956, to be followed in succession by his two sons.

To Latin Americans, dollar diplomacy and armed intervention demonstrated several unpleasant realities. First, American motivation seemed to be based on self-interest. The United States, excessively concerned with the security of the Panama Canal and overly suspicious of European intentions, all too readily took unilateral action no matter what the impact might be on Latin America. While Latin Americans worried about their survival as sovereign entities, the United States appeared single-mindedly focused on its own national security. Second, by assuming the role of hemispheric policeman, without consultation with or participation of the Latin American republics, the United States indicated an arrogant belief in its legitimate right to use power to gain compliance. Finally, Americans believed that their moral values and political principles had universal application across cultures and that anything short of full acceptance of such values and principles by Latin Americans indicated backwardness.

In a futile attempt to deny the United States an excuse to intervene in Latin America, Mexican Minister of Foreign Relations Gerardo Estrada formulated the Estrada Doctrine (1930), which asserted that diplomatic recognition should be accorded any government, whether it had taken power by force or elections. The minister sought to end the moral imperialism so exemplified by Woodrow Wilson. What Estrada and many others failed to grasp was that all American presidents, to varying degrees, reflected the public's view that the foreign policy of the United States should mirror its own moral values. As communications technology improved, and news and information traveled faster, politicians increasingly had to cater to public opinion. The American public saw little contradiction in forcing others to measure up to its moral standards. The events of the twentieth century intensified Latin America's suspicions of the United States and its motives. As the noted Peruvian legal historian Francisco García Calderón wrote early in the century, "To save themselves from Yankee imperialism, the Latin American democracies would almost accept a German alliance, or the aid of Japanese arms. Everywhere the Americans of the North are feared."

## GOOD NEIGHBORS?

Economic collapse in the wake of the stock market crash of 1929 forced the United States to look inward, first to stabilize the economy and then to begin the process of recovery. Shuttered factories, lines of the unemployed, and a sharp drop in consumer spending made recovery difficult even to imagine. Demand for Latin American raw materials dropped worldwide as the gray pall of depression spread to one industrial country after another. Even more unnerving, people now questioned the future of capitalism as an economic and social system. The rise of militant competing ideologies, fueled by desperation, acted to challenge the liberal democratic capitalism that had enjoyed a virtual monopoly from the period of the independence of Latin America in the early nineteenth century into the twentieth century, despite the best efforts of anarchists and socialists. In the 1930s the wave of the future seemed to be either fascist or communist, or at best a completely revamped capitalism. The Communist International, charged by the Soviet Union to support communism worldwide, established a presence in Uruguay in the 1920s, and a series of national Communist parties sprang up throughout Latin America. Of more immediate concern, German and Italian fascists assumed control over their respective nations, giving them immense status and influence in a Latin America accustomed to viewing Europe as its preferred model. The victory of General Francisco Franco in Spain's civil war, assisted by Germany and Italy, added another element of uncertainty. Many immigrant communities in Latin America supported fascism, advocating it as a suitable model that could guarantee order and establish a social balance. In Brazil, the paramilitary *Integralistas*—known as the Green Shirts—became a major political force. Fascist ideas filtered into major institutions including the Brazilian, Chilean, and Argentine armies. Mexico had its own paramilitary Gold Shirts. Managed trade and skillful propaganda projected a positive image of fascist economic recovery and a moral revitalization—a powerful, although profoundly deceptive, message.

Even before the crash of 1929 the United States understood that Latin America harbored a tremendous amount of ill will toward the colossus of the north. Thus Charles Evans Hughes, secretary of state under President Warren G. Harding, asserted time and again that the United States supported the unimpaired sovereignty of Latin American states. Herbert Hoover made a preinaugural trip around South America, promising to withdraw marines and making other appropriately soothing overtures. President Franklin D. Roosevelt stated in his inaugural address in 1933 that the United States intended to be a "respectful good neighbor." Roosevelt, who admitted the policy required self-restraint, initially had some difficulty adjusting to the new role. When Dr. Ramón Grau San Martín assumed the presidency of Cuba (1933–1934), the United States refused to recognize his government and dispatched warships to patrol Cuban waters. Later, in 1944, when Grau San Martín, again the Cuban president, visited Washington, President Roosevelt received him warmly and commented, "And to think that I did not recognize you eleven years ago." With the exception of Cuba, Roosevelt made good on his promise to be a good neighbor and abide by the "doctrine of good manners," in the words of a Peruvian politician. Secretary of State Cordell Hull committed the United States to a convention on the Rights and Duties of States, which forbade interference in the internal affairs of other states. In 1934 Washington ended the Platt Amendment and two years later removed the clause in the original Panama Canal treaty that gave the United States the right to intervene in Panama. Few in Latin America were convinced the United States would be able to resist the temptation to interfere, no matter what agreements and conventions Washington signed. But to everyone's surprise, when Mexico expropriated foreign-owned oil companies in 1938, Roosevelt resisted pressure for intervention. Unfortunately, the timing of the Good Neighbor policy robbed it of much of its moral impact. Many interpreted the policy as the ploy of a temporarily economically crippled giant making a good thing out of necessity. Brazilians, always inclined to paranoia about others coveting their immense territory, saw the Good Neighbor policy as an attempt to establish an American economic sphere along the lines of Japan's coprosperity sphere, then unfolding at China's expense. Skepticism that a new era had indeed arrived may have been warranted, but what Latin Americans failed to grasp was that Roosevelt and his advisors had lost confidence in their neighbors' ability to accept reasonable reforms as well as in U.S. power to impose the preferred model on the hemisphere. The liquidation of dollar diplomacy reflected that negative assessment. By the mid-1930s, the United States had reached the point where it would settle for order, provided that those who imposed it did so in a manner that did not excessively embarrass Washington. The reality of a string of dictators—Trujillo, Somoza, Papa Doc, and Batista, all in the American Mediterranean—became tolerable if not pleasant. Roosevelt privately observed that Anastasio Somoza of Nicaragua might well be a "son of a bitch," but at least he was our "son of a bitch." One can imagine Roosevelt had equally pungent assessments of other Latin American dictators.

## WORLD WAR II AND THE POSTWAR PERIOD

Shortly after the German invasion of Poland in 1939, the American republics met in Panama and announced that the entire hemisphere constituted a neutral zone. At the same time, the Inter-American Economic Committee studied the potential impact of a European war. Nazi advances in Western Europe resulted in subsequent conferences in Havana about what to do if Dutch and French possessions in the hemisphere were threatened with German occupation. The United States proposed a joint inter-American occupation. Argentina, sympathetic to Germany, opposed the idea, claiming that the United States could use the threat to create new colonies for itself. Following the Japanese attack on Pearl Harbor on December 7, 1941, most Latin American republics severed relations with the Empire of Japan, Germany, and Italy and eventually declared war. The Central American countries, including Panama as well as Cuba, Haiti, and the Dominican Republic, declared war on the Axis powers almost immediately. Bolivia and Colombia did so in 1943. Chile, Ecuador, Paraguay, Peru, and Venezuela delayed until early 1945. Argentina gave in to economic and political pressure to join the rest of the hemisphere in declaring war but did not do so until March 27, 1945.

The United States viewed hemispheric security as a matter of absolute necessity. Latin America's harbors and coastline had to be denied to enemy shipping and submarines and secured against possible invasion, and its raw materials had to be made available to the Allies. Although Latin Americans understood the reasoning behind such measures, many worried that they would be forced into an American-dominated economic bloc. The United States had little patience with such concerns. In particular, Brazilian ambivalence about the impending war was worrisome. President Getûlio Vargas, only three days after the fall of France, delivered an address aboard the warship *Minas Gerais* in which he noted, "We march toward a diverse future . . . the age of liberalism has passed." Just what Vargas meant remains unclear, but an apprehensive United States interpreted the statement as a troubling sign. In reality, Vargas's attitude stemmed from his belief that Brazil's long-range interests and freedom from economic dependency lay with a broad and mixed economic and cultural network. As a member of the Brazilian elite, Vargas preferred European culture to that of a crass United States. Thus he reluctantly contemplated the demands of Washington. Any alliance with the United States, in his view, endangered Brazilian culture and opened the gates to Americanization. In the end, Vargas had little choice. The sinking by German U-boats of several Brazilian ships in 1942 forced his hand. Meanwhile, the United States pulled out all the stops. Besides offering to fund a modern steel complex at Volta Redondo, the United States sent a contingent of seasoned diplomats to pressure the Brazilian government to cooperate. A newly established Office of Inter-American Affairs (OIAA), headed by Nelson A. Rockefeller, worked to bring Latin America into a firm alliance with the United States. The OIAA engaged in low-level espionage and organized cultural activities designed to tie the alliance together psychologically. Lectures sponsored by the OIAA or the State Department and given by writers, academics, artists, and filmmakers appeared to be effective, particularly those of actor Errol Flynn and filmmakers Walt Disney, John Ford, and Orson Welles. Welles, who became somewhat of a trophy foreigner for members of the elite who liked to show him off, developed close ties with Brazilian officials. When Brazil finally declared war on Germany, he attended the ceremony. News photographs, with Welles seated next to Foreign Minister Oswaldo Aranha, circulated throughout Latin America. Vargas and the Brazilian elite tolerated the cultural campaign but viewed such efforts as crude and overbearing. The influence of American cultural propaganda on the middle and lower classes, not immediately evident at the time, became obvious in the postwar years, much to the distaste of cultural nationalists.

Most Latin Americans understood that a fine line existed between angling for advantage at a moment of great peril for the United States and being obstinate. Mexico officially aligned itself with the United States when German submarines torpedoed Mexican oil tankers. Mexico quickly moved beyond a declaration of hostilities (1942) to accept responsibility for coastal defense, and the nation soon accepted military aid from the United States. On a more active level the Mexican government allowed the U.S. Army to open recruiting offices in Mexico City and sent an air squadron to engage the Japanese in the Philippines and in Formosa. It is important to remember that aircraft and fighter pilots represented some of the most sophisticated military technology and personnel then available; thus the participation of Latin America at this level symbolized a new sense of military ability and competence. Brazil, well aware of its bargaining position, insisted on a major role in the ground war. The Brazilian army envisioned a force of 50,000 but in the end settled for a 25,000-member expeditionary force. The U.S. Army, reluctant to accept Latin American armed participation due to the potential problems of language and logistics, saw little advantage in including Latin Americans in the active war effort. The Brazilians, however, made it clear that while they would supply raw materials and permit the establishment of American air bases in northeastern Brazil, they must also have a direct military role. Indeed, in Brazil World War II is referred to as the *a guerra atual* (the actual war). In the end, the United States accepted Brazilian combat troops. To the surprise and relief of the U.S. Eighth Army, these troops acquitted themselves with distinction in several hard-fought campaigns.

After the war, the hemisphere's republics had no intention of returning to the old prewar relationship of being either ignored or patronized by the United States. The old Pan American Union had long been a major irritant. The United States had used the Pan American Union as its own instrument, reserving the right to appoint several of its directors and in effect establishing the organization's agenda. Cynical Latin American diplomats referred to it as the American Ministry of Colonies. In 1948, the Ninth Conference of American States staged a gentle revolt, insisting upon a democratic restructuring of the organization with a governing board representative of the various member states, supported by a multinational staff. Moreover, full-time representatives to the organization would be accorded the rank of ambassador. Even the name changed, becoming the Organization of American States (OAS). Nevertheless, the headquarters remained in Washington. While unquestionably the OAS enjoys more prestige than the Pan American Union did, suspicion lingers that the organization remains an extension of the U.S. State Department.

More significant for relations between the United States and Latin America, the war's aftermath forced a heavy concentration on European affairs and required both U.S. aid and diplomacy. The rapid spread of communism in the wake of the ruin and despair caused by World War II alarmed the United States to the point that all else was pushed off the agenda. The Good Neighbor policy ended abruptly as security concerns came to dominate foreign relations world-wide. Little energy, time, or money remained for Latin American concerns, a state of affairs greatly resented throughout the hemisphere. Latin Americans viewed such neglect as a betrayal of regionalism in favor of globalization and an ideological struggle that did not involve them. Eventually, Washington's concern for hemispheric security against communism came to be seen as some sort of inexplicable paranoia that required humoring perhaps, but could not be taken seriously.

Secretary of State John Foster Dulles stretched Latin America's willingness to humor the United States to the limit. He insisted on bringing concerns over communist influence in Guatemala to the Tenth Inter-American Conference in Caracas (March 1954). Only six republics, all dictatorships, supported Dulles until threats of economic and political measures brought a favorable vote on the issue of the dangers of international communism. The United States crafted the Declaration of Caracas, with Mexico and Argentina abstaining. Eventually the Eisenhower administration organized a counterforce (1954) in Guatemala under Colonel Carlos Castillo Armas and succeeded in driving out Colonel Jacobo Arbenz's regime. Castillo Armas then acted to restore the traditional social order in Guatemala. The Good Neighbor policy died at that moment.

President Eisenhower's unilateral action in Guatemala ignored the inter-American system. The decision indicated a complete lack of respect for the opinion of the Latin American republics and appeared to be a blatant exercise of power. The most troubling aspect of the action—the willingness of the United States to use force, albeit indirectly, to forestall reform—appeared to support an unworkable status quo. Fear that a reform movement might be hijacked by radicals or communists could not justify quashing the attempt. Many now feared that Latin America would be forced into a rigid mold, politically and socially, by Washington's need for control over "its home hemisphere" as it faced worldwide and hostile competition from the Soviet Union.

The extent of Latin America's apprehension could not be grasped easily by those who saw themselves as involved in the defense of the West. In the United States, disagreements were viewed as economic, as they still are. Trade, tariffs, and finances could be understood and seemed basic, while everything else fell into the nonproductive emotional category. Nevertheless, to placate the Latin American nations, Vice President Richard M. Nixon was dispatched to Argentina in 1958 to attend the inauguration of the country's first elected president following years of imposed leadership. The trip to Buenos Aires included a goodwill tour of seven South American countries. All went reasonably well until Nixon arrived in Peru. There he encountered a student mob in Lima, but he acquitted himself with dignity and in the end received the grudging respect of his opponents. The confrontation in Lima did not, however, prepare him for the defining moment of his trip—the violent hostility in Caracas. Even before the American vice president left the airport, he passed through a jeering, spitting crowd. On the road into the city a mob stopped his car, broke windows, and stoned the party, including the car of Mrs. Nixon. It became obvious that the Venezuelan government had done little, if anything, to ensure the visitors' safety. In retrospect, Nixon was lucky to have escaped alive. A panicked Washington ordered a small contingent of marines to stand by in case the vice president had to be rescued. Fortunately, Venezuelan army troops moved into Caracas and restored order.

The complexity of anti-Americanism during this period offered a wide panorama of possibilities eagerly pursued by many groups on the Left and the Right. Left-wing intellectuals framed their hostility in the broad global terms of American imperialism. Communists pushed for a political realignment beneficial to the Soviet Union, while cultural nationalists sought to roll back American influence and refocus on traditional Eurocentric values. The possibility of political legitimacy based on radical anti-Americanism alarmed Latin American conservatives. While they shared elements of anti-American feelings, they feared that radical anti-Americanism could now be used to upset order and open the floodgates of radical political and social reform. Traditional politicians responded in nimble, if opportunistic, fashion. They viewed Washington's bewildered hand-wringing as an opportunity to press the United States to pour development money into the region—in effect finally getting their own Marshall Plan. These Latin American political figures sensed that the United States would be grateful for a simple economic explanation for Latin American hostility, as well as an easily understood solution. Thus Brazil's president, Juscelino Kubitschek, counseled

Eisenhower to establish a joint development program, Operation Pan American, to address the region's problems. Although Eisenhower decided against the proposal, he did withdraw opposition to the formation of an Inter-American Development Bank, capitalized at a billion dollars with 45 percent contributed by the United States. Subsequently, the U.S. Congress appropriated $500 million to create a social development fund to be administered by the new bank.

The Cuban Revolution of 1959 convinced many in Washington that social reforms not only could not be ignored, but that in fact change needed to occur in advance of a crisis. The abrupt shift of Cuba into the socialist camp came as a shock, with implications throughout the hemisphere. To Latin Americans it appeared that Cuba, the central core of the American Mediterranean and just 90 miles from Florida, had managed to accomplish the impossible. Overnight it had slipped out from the orbit of the United States, apparently establishing complete independence. At the time few people realized that Cuba had simply abandoned its dependency on one great power—to become dependent on another. As a result, Fidel Castro, the charismatic Cuban leader, outfitted in military fatigues and carrying a large cigar, became a Latin American folk hero—the David who had out-maneuvered the American Goliath. Fidel would soon make much of his underdog status.

The best way to handle the Cuban situation seemed clear to the United States. In its case before the OAS, at a meeting in San José, Costa Rica, the United States charged that Castro had encouraged extra-hemispheric intervention—a policy that historically both the United States, with its Monroe Doctrine, and Latin America had rejected. In the end, the OAS condemned all intervention, not just Soviet action in the hemisphere, but ruled out a combined OAS military action against Cuba. The perceived failure of Latin Americans to understand the gravity of the Cuban situation led Eisenhower to approve a plan to use Cuban exiles to over-throw the Castro regime—somewhat along the lines of the Guatemalan episode. When President John F. Kennedy took office in 1961 he approved the invasion plan, but he made modifications that had negative military consequences. The subsequent debacle of the Bay of Pigs invasion proved a sobering experience to the new president.

The mismanaged invasion led the United States to reassess Latin American vulnerability. Poverty, the slow pace of development, and a host of needed but long-delayed reforms had allowed pressure to build to the point of possible widespread revolutionary violence. Cuba provided a smoldering fuse, which might set off a wave of violence elsewhere in the hemisphere that communist opportunists could seize upon. Latin America had long complained that the United States ignored stalled development south of the border while it poured money into European assistance programs. Thus the Alliance for Progress, an-nounced by President Kennedy in broad detail in 1961, seemed to be the ideal instrument to stimulate economic development, encourage reforms, and mitigate poverty in Latin America. The alliance would also serve to forge a solid anti-communist Latin American bloc linked with the United States. This ideological objective conflicted in part with the developmental thrust of the program. The United States had to work with existing governments that did not necessarily share the desire for reform, democracy, or social change. To have attempted to circumvent such governments would have caused an outcry and charges of American intervention in internal affairs. Washington hoped that eventually, developmental prosperity would force reforms; meanwhile, at least something would trickle down to the bottom. The Alliance for Progress succeeded from an inter-American political standpoint more than in social and economic terms. Nevertheless, John F. Kennedy became, and remains, one of the most popular American presidents in Latin America with innumerable schools, some in the most improbable places, named in his honor.

In 1962, Cuba precipitated yet another crisis. The Soviet Union constructed missile sites in Cuba and stationed aircraft there capable of delivering nuclear bombs to virtually the entire United States. A dismayed United States placed an arms embargo around the island and demanded a Soviet retreat. The OAS moved to support Washington, and a number of Latin American republics contributed naval forces to take part in the arms blockade, mobilized troops, and offered other forms of assistance. Coordinated Latin American actions in support of the United States during the Cuban Missile Crisis indicated that Latin American nations understood the danger and responded accordingly. The compromise agreement with the Soviet Union called for removal of the offensive threat in exchange for an American promise not to invade the island. Gradually, neighboring nations realized that a neutralized Cuba could still be used for other purposes, including an attempt to export revolution. Castro's involvement in Venezuela and elsewhere alienated many Latin American governments, and by 1964 all of Latin America except Mexico had suspended diplomatic relations with Cuba. These nations also saw the utility of accepting American counterinsurgency training. Nevertheless, Latin America only reluctantly accepted the economic embargo imposed on Cuba by the United States, believing it to be a violation of the principle of nonintervention.

For most of the 1960s and 1970s Moscow did its best to capitalize on the wave of Latin American nationalism that followed the Cuban Revolution. President Lyndon B. Johnson provided more fuel for hostile propaganda by dispatching 23,000 troops to the Dominican Republic in 1965 to prevent the return to power of Juan Bosch. Johnson insisted that communism was the issue—but few in Latin America believed him. By 1975 the Soviet Union had signed trade agreements and established diplomatic relations with most Latin American countries. Socialist experimentation in Cuba, its economic diversification and focus on industrialization, coupled with social reforms and the extension of benefits such as education and public health to the lower classes, was glorified. Cuban propaganda claimed that socialism had broken the historical pattern that had kept Latin America subordinated to American capitalism.

Fully aware of the importance of culture in Latin America in 1960, the Cuban regime founded the *Casa de las Américas* to promote the work of Latin American novelists, poets, and playwrights. The Casa's program emphasized Cuba's allegiance to Hispanic culture as it struggled to free itself from American influence. In the propaganda war, Cuba easily outplayed the United States.

In the 1960s dependency theory swept the hemisphere. The works of André Gunder Frank became immensely popular in Latin America and indeed throughout the Third World. Frank described economic relations between the developed world (the center) and the periphery as parasitic and imperialistic and declared that revolutionary action was required. Frank's extremism would be modified by others, who nevertheless agreed with the general notion. Fernando Henrique Cardoso may have been the most influential Latin American proponent of dependency theory. Cardoso avoided extremism, but did not see the situation in quite the bleak fashion of many others. The many varieties of dependency theory all fell into the aptly titled "global accusation" mode. Dependency theorists attacked national elites who had failed to fend off external forces as well as the developed economies of the north. The theory was based on Marxism, although most who embraced it did not consider themselves Marxists and certainly not communists. To Washington, dependency theory appeared to be an attempt to saddle the United States with guilt for Latin America's failure to develop, and it helped to create an overall climate of hostility toward capitalism and its representatives. It set up a north–south division that briefly threatened to solidify into opposing blocs along the lines of the Third World model. Dependency theory and the apparent success of socialist Cuba combined to put the United States on the psychological defensive.

The election of Marxist Salvador Allende Gossens to the Chilean presidency (1970) surprised both Washington and Moscow. When it became evident that a Marxist might assume the presidency in Santiago, Washington, fearing another Cuba, authorized covert action; but it proved to be too late. Nevertheless, from the very beginning the United States adopted an openly hostile attitude toward Chilean socialism and spent vast amounts of time and money on efforts to destabilize the regime. In retrospect, covert intervention by the United States may have been unnecessary. It is clear that divisions within the Left and economic mismanagement combined to guarantee the inevitable failure of the Allende presidency. The military coup of 1983 and the death of President Allende in the national palace constituted yet another episode in the long saga of political leaders allegedly crushed by the United States. Washington lost the propaganda war, but the end of Allende's regime was gratefully received by the U.S. State Department. Negative association of the United States with the often brutal dictatorship of General Augusto Pinochet that succeeded the Allende regime and evidence of the role of the U.S. Central Intelligence Agency in Allende's overthrow embarrassed the United States into the 1990s.

The assumption of power by the *Frente Sandinista de Liberación Nacional* (FSLN) in Nicaragua posed yet another unwelcome challenge to the United States during the 1980s. The fact that the FSLN, or *Sandinistas,* had toppled the Somoza dictatorship, essentially created and supported by the United States over many decades, added to the difficulty, although the United States had withdrawn its support of Somoza some time before the collapse. The administration of President Jimmy Carter, unfortunately seen as weak, uncertain, and naïve, wanted to avoid the use of force. Moreover, President Carter's willingness to relinquish control over the Panama Canal implied to many observers a withdrawal from involvement in Latin America. The facts that the canal had become somewhat obsolete and that the American withdrawal was stretched out over time seemed immaterial. Both the Sandinistas and Moscow misjudged the situation.

When Ronald Reagan assumed the American presidency (1980), the United States moved to confront the FSLN as well as strengthen the Salvadoran regime in San Salvador, then under extreme pressure from guerrillas supplied by Nicaragua and Cuba. American policy, highly unpopular in Latin America as well as among powerful elements in the U.S. Congress, nevertheless succeeded in keeping the FSLN off balance and signaled to the Soviet Union that easy gains could not be expected. Washington's willingness to ignore Latin American opinion when it believed the U.S. national interest was involved may have seemed more blatant than in the past because of President Reagan's political style; consequently, few American presidents were the target of more bitter personal attacks in the Latin American press. In the early 1980s, the tiny Caribbean island of Grenada was ruled by a vicious group apparently aligned with Cuba. Evidence suggested that the Cubans were building an air base on the island, within striking distance of the Venezuelan coast. Reagan's decision to invade Grenada (1983) illustrated U.S. willingness to use force in the early stages of a crisis. Although Latin Americans objected mildly, they resigned themselves to the reality that the United States was unable to deal with Latin America and the Caribbean outside the context of the Cold War.

Hemispheric solidarity came under unexpected strain when the Argentine military challenged British sovereignty over the long-disputed Falkland (Malvinas) Islands and seized the islands in 1982. The United States had long favored negotiations over control of the islands, located some 300 miles off the Argentine coast. Nevertheless, the United States supported the British in the ensuing war. Britain soundly defeated Argentina and resumed control of the islands. Ironically, the discredited military regime then in control of Argentina had to permit the return of democratic civilian rule. Argentina's use of force limited the extent of Latin American support as well as the degree of anger over American support for Britain.

By the end of Reagan's second term, the Soviet Union had slid toward eco-nomic collapse and political disintegration, making it difficult for the Soviets to challenge U.S. policy. As a result, in early 1989 President George W. Bush pressed the Soviets to support free elections in Nicaragua; by May, the FSLN gave in and agreed to hold elections in February 1990 under the watchful eyes of the OAS and the United Nations. In El Salvador the flow of weapons from Cuba through the Nicaraguan pipeline continued. The crash of a plane carrying surface-to-air missiles brought a stern protest by the United States—and by 1989, the end of Soviet involvement in Central America. The Soviet Union also began to reduce its economic and military assistance to Cuba. Imperial overreach became evident as the Soviet economy imploded at an alarming rate. U.S. dominance in the hemisphere had been briefly contested by its Cold War adversary, but the United States soon resumed its traditional role. When the United States invaded Panama and arrested General Manuel Noriega in 1989, to end Noriega's alleged support for drug cartels, Moscow and the Latin American republics said little. Two years earlier the Soviets and the Latin Americans had defended Noriega vigorously on the basis of the quasi-sacred principle of nonintervention, thereby forcing the

United States to weigh its actions carefully and to delay removing the Panamanian strongman from power. Latin America and the United States had moved into the post–Cold War era.

## ECONOMICS OVER POLITICS: THE ENTERPRISE FOR THE AMERICAN INITIATIVE

The Bush administration unveiled a plan (1990) that called for bilateral free trade negotiations and the creation of a free trade zone in the Americas. Earlier Mexico had proposed a free trade agreement with the United States. The United States envisioned a Mexican agreement as the first step to be followed by trade arrangements with other countries. The United States, no longer obsessed by the Cold War, and Latin America, just beginning to pull out of the debt crisis of the 1980s, both appeared ready for a new relationship. Few recognized that while Latin America responded to the economic reality that impelled the region to move beyond vertical import substitution into the larger global market, the United States had arrived at a political, not economic, watershed with the end of superpower competition. Latin America, driven by economic imperatives, made the mistake of assuming that Washington fully shared its motivation. American ambivalence toward hemispheric free trade, temporarily obscured by the campaign for the North American Free Trade Agreement (NAFTA) energetically pursued by Mexican president Carlos Salinas de Gortari, reasserted itself almost at the moment NAFTA went into effect (1994). The North American Free Trade Agreement reflected American political concerns, including worries about labor conditions and environmental protection. A preliminary agreement to establish a U.S.–Mexico Integrated Border Plan (1992) dealt with noneconomic quality-of-life issues that required major political concessions. Side agreements appeared more important to the United States than the core economic terms of the agreement. The permanence of the arrangement cannot be assumed. Escape clauses and protectionist safeguards to protect domestic industries, along with the right of each party to withdraw from NAFTA, reflected Washington's conditional acceptance of the entire agreement. In the end, the United States preferred bilateral agreements that did not impose hemisphere-wide economic responsibilities.

President Bill Clinton moved the process along in a rhetorical sense when he convened the Summit of the Americas in Miami (1995). Called for the purpose of creating a whole new architecture in which "words are turned into deeds," the meeting produced a consensus that a free trade hemisphere should be established by 2005. Meanwhile, Brazil, the driving force behind a tariff union (MERCOSUR) made up of Argentina, Brazil, Paraguay, and Uruguay, created its own trading bloc. The success of MERCOSUR promised to revitalize other trade groups. Instead of one Americas-wide organization, there may eventually be several groups. The United States retreated from the grand scheme of creating a hemisphere-wide trade zone in favor of a modest bilateral approach. A Chilean-U.S. agreement set a pattern. Passage of a free trade area in Central America and the Dominican Republic in 2005 added minor trading partners. Meanwhile, Brazil resisted pressure to support an

Americas-wide free trade zone out of concern that it would lead to American domination both politically and economically.

## THE INTER-AMERICAN DRUG WAR

The U.S. "War on Drugs" has created new anxieties and a new arena for dispute in recent years. What began as a squabble over whether consumer demand for drugs in the United States encouraged Latin American production, or vice versa, has become an issue of mutual concern—that illegal production and use of drugs will corrupt and destroy the state, shred the social fabric throughout the hemisphere, and leave the Latin American economy in ruins. Challenges posed by the illegal drug industry—crime, corruption, economic, and financial distortions—have forced all sides to acknowledge common dangers as well as shared vulnerability. It is a mistake to view the War on Drugs as solely an American public relations invention. The core explanation for a high level of inter-American cooperation is the issue of state survival. Why states allowed the situation to get to such a dangerous point is a legitimate question. The difficulty of dealing with the problem appears to be traceable to the elaboration of a culture of vice control. Regulation and suppression of deviant social behavior, at one time left to moral codes, has slowly shifted to the state.

Conflict over use of narcotics may be traced to the nineteenth-century opium trade. Opium trading, a legal industry for the British, generated handsome profits that moved into the banking and economic systems, as would the rewards of any other acceptable commerce and industry. The Chinese, who had to deal with the human costs, failed to force an end to the opium trade. Subsequently, the development of manufactured substances—morphine, cocaine, and heroin—broadened the drug trade, particularly in Asia. Chinese laborers brought an acceptance of drug use with them when they arrived in the hemisphere. The United States, after acquiring the Philippine Islands as a result of the Spanish American War, became concerned over the extent of opium consumption at its Asian outpost. A conference called in Shanghai in 1909 brought together 13 nations to consider the issue. Little came out of the conference besides the identification of the problem and an impulse to control it.

In Latin America traditional use of various narcotics antedated European arrival in the Western Hemisphere. Use of coca leaves in Peru, Bolivia, and Ecuador and tobacco, peyote, and marijuana in Mesoamerica evolved to meet environmental, political, religio-cultural, and economic needs. Drug use became embedded in custom and tradition.

In the early colonial period, demographic decline temporarily decreased demand. Spanish mining activity and population recovery slowly increased demand and expansion of the coca-growing industry. Spanish colonial authorities viewed coca use with some ambivalence. Although fully aware of its usefulness, especially at high altitudes and in the mines, administrators noted that it appeared to be an indirect challenge to Spanish cultural hegemony. Opposition to consumption and production of coca reached a high point with the Second Council of Lima (1567–1568), where many clerics advocated its suppression on the grounds that it played a central role in Indian religious rites and that its hunger-curbing properties substituted for adequate food intake with disastrous consequences. In the latter part of the eighteenth century, the leading coca planter, don Tadeo Díez de Medina, marketed coca in what is now Bolivia through his merchant operations in La Paz. By 1780 he employed a large number of workers on several pieces of property. Coca planters formed an organization with legal status in 1830. Although production involved non-Indians as well as Indians, it nevertheless met a demand rather than actively seeking or creating new markets. In the nineteenth century coca seemed exotic, interesting, and useful. In his essay "The Turning Point in My Life," Mark Twain noted that but for lack of transportation, he would have gratified his "longing to ascend the Amazon [and] open up a trade in coca with all the world." The Coca-Cola Company of Atlanta, Georgia, incorporated the leaf into its secret beverage formula. The company still imports coca leaves legally for flavoring.

The nature of narcotics use on a global level changed with the British opium trade, which stimulated what today is referred to as casual or recreational drug use. Escapism, self-indulgence, new addicts, and market expansion became important to opium traders. The development of chemically altered drugs in the late nineteenth century created new products—more refined, concentrated, and easier to transport and market. Chemical drugs also increased demand for the vegetable product, the raw material required for the initial production process. Manufacturing drugs also added value far beyond that of raw coca leaves or opium. Thus, by the beginning of the twentieth century, the stage had been set for social, political, and economic conflict.

Changing attitudes and differing cultural perceptions became evident when the United States pressed Latin America to ratify the 1912 Hague Opium Convention. The response, cool and unconcerned, indicated no sense of urgency. In 1914 the United States passed the first federal antidrug legislation—the Harrison Narcotic Act. The legislation stimulated calls to control the emerging problem by cutting off the source of supply and thereby eliminating drug use. In the 1930s Mexico, the Caribbean, and Central America, particularly Honduras, appeared to be the source of drugs. The Federal Bureau of Narcotics (FBN), established in 1930, proved largely ineffectual. Nevertheless, the issue became a matter of bureaucratic and diplomatic concern. Putting pressure on foreign governments and implying corrupt complicity at the highest levels ignored the ability of Honduras or Mexico to suppress production. They did not have the financial resources to attempt even minimal efforts. Denunciation of Latin American drug policies before the Opium Advisory Committee in Geneva merely ruffled feathers. Andean coca growers did their best to rally political and public support. In Peru, the National Institute of Andean Biology attempted to dispel criticism of coca use.

The scope of the issue widened in 1937 when the United States passed the first federal antimarijuana law. By the end of the 1930s, with all the prohibitions in place, the extent of the task facing state authority had yet to be fully understood. Sporadic efforts to develop cooperative drug control had limited results. But while enforcement efforts seemed difficult to get off the ground, negative social perception about drug use promised some hope. Mexican officials associated marijuana with criminals, and in the Andean coca areas governments noted

Chewing coca leaves to control fatigue and altitude sickness is an ancient custom in the Andean region. A La Paz, Bolivia, market vendor, photographed in about 1952, has no shortage of customers. The processing of coca leaves into the much more potent cocaine in the 1980s and 1990s has led to demands by the United States and other countries plagued by the drug trafficking for control of the growing of coca.

the increase of cocaine consumption among the urban populations—in a departure from the traditional pattern of chewing the coca leaves. Nevertheless, resistance to international controls that might infringe on traditional use remained strong.

The failure of state policy to control drug use and production inevitably led to an escalation of use and eventually to the War on Drugs. In the United States, the alarming increase in drug use among all social and economic classes threatened moral and civic society. The approximately 250,000 addicts in 1900 had swelled into the millions by the 1990s. Crime and urban degradation appeared linked with drug use. General Paul C. Gorman, then head of the U.S. Southern Command in Panama, testified before a congressional committee in 1988 that drug cartels were dramatically more successful at subversion than our Cold War adversary. Allied with terrorists and revolutionaries, able to corrupt military and civilian institutions and high officials, the drug cartels jeopardized American foreign policy objectives throughout Latin America. The Omnibus Drug Act and the Defense Authorization Bill of 1988 provided for a limited militarization of the Drug War. Operation Blast Furnace in 1986 and Operation Snowcap the following year influenced the decision to escalate counter-narcotics efforts. Blast Furnace, an armed assault on cocaine laboratories in Bolivia supported by the American military, led to a significant drop in the price of coca leaves.

The possibility of at least a semipermanent disruption of the production chain led to Snowcap, in which Drug Enforcement Agency (DEA) agents trained in military tactics, along with a small group of army special forces, established forward bases in Peru and Bolivia. In Santa Lucía in the heart of Peru's coca region, the United States constructed a fortified base complete with helicopters. The objectives, fairly modest despite the high drama of military assaults, included disruption of the trade as well as efforts to diminish the usefulness of the producer-terrorist connection—essentially a protective alliance. Low-intensity warfare, with limited involvement of American troops, aimed at containment rather than suppression.

Along with direct enforcement activity, the United States offered counter-narcotic equipment, helicopters, trucks, weapons, and training for the national military, the police, and special antidrug units. Government officials, always sensitive to charges that they are compromising national sovereignty, nevertheless have had little choice but to accede to the presence of foreign enforcement personnel, whom officials generally referred to as advisors. Efforts to secure reluctant participation in the War on Drugs centered on the "decertification" process—a public pronouncement by Washington that a particular country has not done enough to control drug production. Decertification results in cessation of certain types of U.S. assistance and obligates the American government to vote against loans to decertified nations by various multinational banks. The process also allows the American government to suspend decertification in the national interest—in effect holding the sword just above some alleged offending country's economic head. Colombia, often threatened, was decertified in early 1996. The extradition of known drug kingpins became a sensitive issue. Over the years Colombia has at times dispatched its nationals to the United States for trial and sometimes not, depending on the politics of the moment.

The War on Drugs is characterized by public posturing, endless eradication campaigns, and innumerable international conferences, with little accomplished. The 1990 Drug Summit held in Cartagena, Colombia, provided political theater but little substance. Most of the world wondered whether President George Bush, the star attendee, could be adequately protected. Few expected new initiatives or a solution. Crop substitution programs to encourage farmers to switch to legal crops, in theory a good idea, have proved in reality to be yet another example of mutual posturing by both Latin American countries and the United States. Coca can grow in any tropical region, but much of the land now used for its cultivation is unsuitable for marketable agricultural crops. Moreover, lack of roads, bridges, and distribution systems makes it virtually impossible to market lower-value crops. In Peru's Upper Huallaga Valley, crop substitution projects, along with an American-supported eradication effort, eliminated some 18,000 hectares of coca. Coca cultivation actually increased from 30,000 to 42,000 hectares in the early 1980s. The figure had doubled by the 1990s—two to three hectares were planted for each one eradicated. The farmers planted additional coca as insurance against destruction and at the same time anticipated higher prices because of the eradication program. Law enforcement activities appear to be an unintended price support system. Counter-narcotic obstacles add value, as does the processing. According to the Peruvian National Anti-Drug Directorate (1996), a kilo of opium—a relatively new drug crop in the region—worth $1,500 in Peru jumps to $3,000 at the Colombian border, and once converted into heroin, jumps to $15,000 at the U.S. border. A similar value-added scale could be constructed for coca. A market functions along standard economic lines, whether legal or illegal.

The impact of the War on Drugs on inter-American relations is conditioned by the basic concern that all states and societies are vulnerable. State survival in Latin America is the issue. Thus old sensitivities are ignored, albeit reluctantly, by Latin American governments. Officials, from the top down, are painfully aware that the War on Drugs led by the United States has resulted in a loss of sovereign control. Moreover, physical protection of both foreign and national personnel involved in counter-narcotic programs gives the appearance of an occupation force operating in hostile territory. As Peruvian President Alberto Fujimori lamented (1992), "No government may fight against [its] entire population." Pro-coca elements in Bolivia are quick to point out violations of sovereignty. The visit of General Lawson Magruder, Commander of the U.S. Army's Southern Command (August 1996), prompted Evo Morales, president of the Coordinating Board of Tropical Region Coca Growers, a legal body, to claim that the visit represented a violation of Bolivian "dignity and sovereignty." He made his charges on La Paz radio and speculated that the United States wanted to establish a military base in central Bolivia to facilitate control of antidrug operations in all the Southern Cone countries. A resigned attitude precluded any anti-American demonstration or action. In Colombia (September 1996), the finance minister requested authorization to sell war bonds to provide the armed forces with new weapons and equipment. The Revolutionary Armed Forces of Colombia (FARC), which originated as a pro-Soviet Marxist group in 1964, has become rich because of its involvement in the drug industry and threatens to control the country.

By the 1990s many believed that Colombia and Mexico had become narco-democracies and that other Latin American countries, including Brazil, had been infiltrated by drug interests. Colombian President Ernesto Samper's 1994 campaign for the presidency received contributions from drug traffickers, and it would be naïve to believe that drug money had not made its way into other campaigns elsewhere in the hemisphere. The transnational scourge of the trade is beyond denial by any hemispheric nation. Mexico has emerged in the 1990s–2000s as the main conduit into the largest drug market, the United States. An estimated 92 percent of cocaine entering the United States passed through Mexico in 2005. Mexican drug gangs control 11 of the 13 largest drug markets in the United States, dealing in cocaine, heroin, methamphetamine, and marijuana. The Sinaloa cartel, also referred to as the "Federation," emerged as the dominant force in 2005. Unless social attitudes change in the United States—the largest market for illegal substances—or the War on Drugs succeeds, current concerns driving cooperation in the War on Drugs may well become major divisive issues as desperate governments legalize the drug trade.

---

**P R O F I L E** The Big Sting—Operation Casablanca

The War on Drugs declared by the United States has never been popular in Latin America. Who is to blame for the drug problem, the drug producers, or the consumers who create the demand? This question identifies a central and divisive issue. All agree that the vast amount of illegal money flowing from the drug business has corrupted officials, the police, and in some cases, the army. In the United States many officials believe that Mexico, Colombia, perhaps Paraguay, and even Brazil are influenced by narco-money. The possibility that Mexico and Colombia are narco-democracies already concerns American officials. Operation Casablanca demonstrated the depth of mistrust between the U.S. and Latin American governments as well as the potential for serious intra-hemispheric tensions resulting from the War on Drugs.

Casablanca's almost three-year sting operation involved setting up the Emerald Empire Corporation to provide money-laundering services to illegal drug distributors. The operation quickly made contact with the Juárez, Mexico, mob, which works with the group in Cali, Colombia. Over a period of time, American agents uncovered extensive drug contacts in Mexican financial circles. Finally, Emerald Empire Corporation invited several suspects to an all-expenses-paid meeting in Las Vegas, Nevada, and arrested them on American territory. Three major Mexican banks were implicated. Bankers, in exchange for channeling money into the legal financial system, received 2–3 percent. Several Venezuelan bankers also fell into the trap. In all, some 112 individuals appeared to be involved.

Both the banks and the Mexican government protested the sting. The banks noted that they have a large number of employees, and a few bad apples should not be allowed to discredit the entire staff. The Mexican government protested that the investigation had been conducted without its knowledge and, moreover, involved extensive undercover activities by American agents on Mexican soil without permission, in clear violation of Mexican law and political sovereignty. Operation Casablanca, although a successful counter-narcotic scheme, resulted in damaged relations between the United States and Mexican officials with possibly negative impact on future antidrug cooperation in the War on Drugs.

---

# THE INTER-AMERICANIZATION
# OF THE UNITED STATES

In the last half of the twentieth century, the influx of Latin American immigrants into the United States created a critical mass. Clearly, a demographic shift took place that was at least equivalent to the wave of European immigration in the first quarter of the same century. By 1999 some 30 million Latin Americans lived in the United States, and the figure is projected to reach 40 million by 2010. The growth of the Latin American population did not happen overnight, nor is it solely an immigrant community. Generation after generation were born in the United States; they claim roots as deep as, and in certain regions deeper than, those of the descendants of various European immigrant waves. Nevertheless, the twentieth-century wave of Latin American immigration created a new dynamic, reflected in relations between Latin America and the United States.

Sizable ethnic groups have always played a role in formulating American foreign policy toward their putative original land. In the case of Latin Americans, they have had a more direct and functional impact, made possible by what anthropologist Roger Rouse has characterized as the social space of post-modernism. In effect, the doleful old departing lament captured in popular song, "Soon you'll be sailing far across the sea," has been replaced by the offhand, "I'll call you in the evening." Transportation and communications technology have made it possible for new immigrants to stay in close, constant touch with their native countries. The latest events in Argentina, for example, are reported and discussed in the United States within hours. Spanish-language television, talk shows, and newspapers rapidly inform the audience at virtually the same moment the U.S. Department of State is grappling with the implications of a particular event. The physical and psychological distance between Buenos Aires, Miami, or New York City is no greater than that separating the "Big Apple" from Los Angeles or Honolulu. Low-cost air travel makes it possible to return "home" frequently. Even working-class and relatively poor individuals can maintain close contact with at least two different worlds.

Immigrant circuits, often involving minimum-wage jobs or undocumented workers, are common. The towns of Aguililla, Michoacán, and Redwood City, California, are tied together in such a fashion. San Pedro in the western highlands of Guatemala and Houston, Texas, are in effect dual homes of Mayan villagers. The residents go back and forth, send their children to school in San Pedro, or spend vacations with relatives; and in postmodern fashion, many of these individuals see nothing strange about it. Alausi, Ecuador, a declining rail center, developed a similar association with Newark, New Jersey. Patterson, New Jersey, has a huge Peruvian population able to fill direct flights from Newark to Lima. Los Angeles, the second-largest "Mexican" city after the Mexican capital itself, is the American terminus of innumerable immigrant circuits, as are Chicago, Illinois, Waterloo, Iowa, and other cities and towns throughout the United States. Owing to recent changes in Mexican law, Mexicans abroad may now vote in national elections. It will soon be routine for Mexican politicians, presidential candidates, and others to campaign throughout the United States. The Mexican vote in Los Angeles, Phoenix, or Chicago could become the swing vote in a Mexican election. Brazilians have established a significant presence throughout the United States. There is scarcely an American city without obvious signs of Latin American cultural influence, or a municipal library without an extensive Spanish- and Portuguese-language section.

The extent of the inter-American book trade would shock José Enrique Rodó, as would the fact that the United States is the fifth largest Spanish-language book market in the world after Spain, Mexico, Argentina, and Colombia. Mexico relies on the United States for much of its imported printed material, and the American market is the best one for Mexican books. Most major Latin American publishing houses think in terms of a unified Spanish-language market that includes the United States. *Reader's Digest* and Walt Disney children's books in Spanish and Portuguese have influenced readers throughout the Americas for decades. Benjamín Fernández, a Mexican publisher, has distributed Disney material for over 40 years and claims that children read Disney books more than anything else except schoolbooks. Disney's Latin American branch, headquartered in Miami, coordinates activities in Argentina,

Brazil, Colombia, Mexico, and elsewhere in Latin America. Unlikely transcultural best sellers in Latin America include *Chicken Soup for the Soul* and *The 7 Habits of Highly Effective People,* both translated into standard Spanish and devoid of local slang or peculiar usage so that they can be promoted in all Spanish-language markets. On the other side of the market, English translation of Latin American authors has broadened beyond the literary stars; although the market is still modest, it is clearly growing. The Spanish-language television network, Univision, moving to tap the huge Latin American consumer market in the United States, announced in 1999 that it would run programs with English subtitles. Bilingual television mirrors the emerging cultural reality.

Of all the groups involved in the inter-Americanization process, Cubans play a unique role. The circumstances of Cuban immigration after 1959 created a population with distinct characteristics. Before the revolution, Cuban immigration to the United States had been constant but relatively modest, drawing upon the lower middle classes on down. More-favored individuals visited, perhaps purchased property, but did not contemplate permanent residence. In the nineteenth century, New York City, Key West, New Orleans, and *Ybor City* (Tampa) already had Cuban communities. New York remained the destination of choice for Cubans until 1959. Rail and the road to Key West, with ferry service to Havana, loosely tied Florida with the island. Airline service between Miami, Key West, and Havana began in the 1920s. By 1948 Cuba led all countries in the number of airline passengers entering the United States. The ebb and flow of people traveling in both directions—constant, natural, and unremarkable—changed abruptly in 1959.

The initial disruptions and uncertainty of life under the new Castro regime set in motion an outward trickle that soon turned into a flood as people began to understand the implications of Cuban socialism and its impact on their own lives and those of their families. The United States extended refugee status to these people, provided resettlement money, and offered other benefits. Washington believed that Cuban refugees, voting with their feet, illustrated in a graphic way the evils of communism—a lesson that the rest of the world, including Latin America, could not ignore. All Cuban refugees, whether they remained in Miami or moved on to other destinations, had to be registered at Freedom House in Miami. Post-1959 Cuban immigration clearly had a political component. The refugees and the American government shared a similar worldview, dominated by hostility toward the Castro regime and the ardent desire to see it replaced by a democratic government duly elected in open and free elections. All assumed that Castro would lose any such election.

The Cuban refugees differed from previous exile groups, which customarily had hoped to stage a return to power from a safe haven, in that they formed an anticommunist alliance with the host government. Moreover, the Cuban community in Miami constituted a complex immigrant enclave made up of all classes, complete with a professional class, artisans, workers, and entrepreneurs. In this environment the residents received from other compatriots all necessary daily services, as well as an amazing array of specialized ones such as plastic surgery and other medical specialties. Graduates of the University of Havana, from engineers to humanists, settled in the enclave or moved to a smaller one in New Jersey.

Rarely in U.S. history has such a complex and complete immigrant community developed so rapidly—with the possible exception of the Eastern European Jewish community in lower Manhattan in the early 1920s.

The Cuban influx must be viewed as a demographic movement rather than a simple assembly of refugees. The Cuban community immediately plunged into foreign affairs and domestic policies, pressuring Washington to adopt a stern and uncompromising approach to the Castro regime. They became the group to consult before taking any action that might affect the Caribbean. The Cuban American National Foundation, well financed and politically connected, acted as a foreign policy think tank, providing the material for lobbyists and others to pressure elected officials. President Ronald Reagan, addressing a Cuban American National Foundation Independence Day gathering in the Dade County auditorium (1983), related a string of Cuban American success stories including those of Cubans in his own administration. He concluded by charging the audience to help him explain the Central American situation to their fellow citizens. The Cuban community contributed both a perspective on Latin American affairs and an impressive array of individuals who bridged cultures, mingling with non-Cuban elements at all levels. President Clinton's brother-in-law, Hugh Rodham, married Mariá Victoria Arias, a politically active Cuban American lawyer. She became part of a small group that hammered out foreign policy issues over dinner at the Colonnade Hotel in Coral Gables or at "Little Havana's" Versailles restaurant. Wealthy businessman Paul Cejas, an occasional overnight guest in the White House, and others, including Arias, constituted an influential informal advisory body directly linked to the top of the political structure by political contributions, friendship, and family ties. Political involvement among Cuban Americans is broader and more issue-focused than that of any other Latin American group. Cubans in Dade County, Florida, have income levels considerably above those of other Latin Americans and high levels of educational achievement. Because of their legal status, they have become citizens and participate actively in politics. Their special relationship with Washington encouraged them to engage in political life at the local, state, and national levels. As a result, Cuban Americans hold high national and municipal office. The first super-mayor of Dade County—Alex Penelas, the son of Cuban exiles—swept into office (1996) largely because Latinos made up 40 percent of the electorate. Miami's importance to the American economy translated into political influence. Cuban American economic activity, reinforced by that of other Latin American immigrants, made South Florida an economic center linking the United States with Latin America and the Caribbean. Significantly, as well as symbolically, the U.S. Army Southern Command (Southcom), previously headquartered in the Panama Canal Zone, relocated to Miami in 1997.

To what extent inter-Americanization will change the relationship between the United States and Latin America in the future remains to be seen; that it will seems obvious. The Americanization of culture, which Latin Americans have long complained about, has its counterpart in the Latin Americanization of the United States. The inevitable compromises and accommodations between these two cultural realities may soon merge the parts together in the hemisphere in a manner few can envision today. Moreover, the Latin American nations, especially Mexico and Brazil, seem poised to play greater roles in international organizations such as the United Nations.

# A Selected English Language Bibliography

We have selected works which in their totality provide a vast fund of general knowledge about Latin America. While all of these studies have been drawn upon to construct our work, we have excluded many other scholarly books in English which may be too specialized as well as valuable contributions in Spanish, Portuguese, and French which we also relied upon in our own study. Readers and researchers will find that the works we list here contain useful, more topic-oriented, bibliographies to facilitate an in-depth view of a particular subject.

Two sources that offer concise information as well as short essays on major historical periods, movements, people, and events are The Encyclopedia of Latin American History and Culture, edited by Barbara A. Tenenbaum, (New York: Simon and Schuster MacMillian, 1995) and the Cambridge Encyclopedia of Latin America, 2d ed. (Cambridge: Cambridge University Press, 1992). For a guide to the current literature, see The Handbook of Latin American Studies edited by the staff of the Hispanic Division of the Library of Congress.

Andrews, George Reid. *Blacks and Whites in São Paulo, Brazil, 1888–1988*. Madison: University of Wisconsin, 1991.

Arrom, Silvia Marina. *The Women of Mexico City, 1790–1857*. Stanford: Stanford University Press, 1985.

Atkins, G. Pope. *Latin America in the International Political System*. 3d ed., Boulder: Westview Press, 1995.

Bagley, Bruce M. and William O. Walker, III, eds. *Drug Trafficking in the Americas*. New Brunswick, Transaction Publishers, 1994.

Bakewell, Peter. *Silver and Entrepreneurship in Seventeenth-Century Potosí: The Life and Times of Antonio López de Quiroga*. Albuquerque: University of New Mexico Press, 1988.

Barman, Roderick J. *Brazil: The Forging of a Nation, 1798–1852.* Stanford: Stanford University Press, 1988.

Beezley, William H. *Judas at the Jockey Club and Other Episodes of Porfirian Mexico.* Lincoln: University of Nebraska Press, 1987.

Brandenburg, Frank. *The Development of Latin American Private Enterprise.* Washington, D.C.: National Planning Association, 1994.

Britton, John A., ed. *Molding the Hearts and Minds: Education, Communications and Social Change in Latin America.* Wilmington: SR Books, 1994.

Bulmer-Thomas, Victor. *Economic History of Latin America Since Independence.* Cambridge: Cambridge University Press, 1994.

Burns, E. Bradford. *The Poverty of Progress: Latin America in the Nineteenth Century.* Berkeley: University of California Press, 1980.

Bushnell, David. *The Making of Modern Colombia: A Nation Inspite of Itself.* Berkeley: University of California Press, 1993.

Bushnell, David, and Neil Macaulay. *The Emergence of Latin America in the Nineteenth Century.* 2d ed. New York: Oxford University Press, 1994.

Camp, Roderic Ai, ed. *Democracy in Latin America: Patterns and Cycles.* Wilmington: SR Books, 1996.

Carlson, Marifran. *Feminismo: The Women's Movement in Argentina From Its Beginnings to Eva Perón.* Chicago: Academy Chicago Publishers, 1988.

Cole, Richard R., ed. *Communication in Latin America: Journalism, Mass Media and Society.* Wilmington: SR Books, 1996.

Collinson, Helen, ed. *Green Guerrillas: Environmental Conflict and Initiatives in Latin America and the Caribbean.* London: The Latin America Bureau, 1996.

Collier, Simon and William F. Sater. *A History of Chile, 1808–1994.* Cambridge: Cambridge University Press, 1996.

Crowley, Frances Geyer. *Domingo Faustino Sarmiento.* New York: Twaynes Publishers, 1972.

Davis, Darién J., ed. *Slavery and Beyond: The African Impact in Latin America and the Caribbean.* Wilmington: SR Books, 1995.

Dietz, James L., ed. *Latin America's Economic Development: Confronting Crisis.* 2d ed., Boulder: Lynne Rienner Publishers, 1995.

Drake, Paul W., ed. *Money Doctors, Foreign Debts and Economic Reforms in Latin America from the 1890s to the Present.* Wilmington: SR Books, 1994.

Foweraker, Joe and Ann L. Craig, eds., *Popular Movements and Political Change in Mexico.* Boulder: Lynne Rienner Publishers, 1990.

Gay, Robert. *Popular Organization and Democracy in Rio de Janeiro: A Tale of Two Favelas.* Philadelphia: Temple University Press, 1994.

Gilbert, Alan. *The Latin American City.* London: Latin American Bureau, 1994.

Gootenberg, Paul. *Between Silver and Guano: Commercial Policy and the State in Post Independence Peru.* Princeton: Princeton University Press, 1989.

Greenfield, Gerald M. *Latin American Urbanization: Historical Profiles of Major Cities.* Westport: Greenwood Press, 1994.

Guillermoprieto, Alma. *The Heart that Bleeds: Latin America Now.* New York: Alfredo A. Knopf, 1994.

Hahner, June E. *Emancipating the Female Sex: The Struggle for Women's Rights in Brazil, 1850–1940.* Durham: Duke University Press, 1990.

Hamill, Hugh M. ed. *Caudillos: Dictators in Spanish America.* Norman: University of Oklahoma Press, 1992.

Harrison, Lawrence E. *Underdevelopment is a State of Mind: The Latin American Case.* Lanham: University Press of America, 1985.

Johnson, John J. *Political Change in Latin America: The Emergence of the Middle Sectors.* Stanford: Stanford University Press, 1958.

Joseph, Gilbert M. And Mark D. Szuchman, eds. *I Saw a City Invincible: Urban Portraits of Latin America.* Wilmington: SR Books, 1996.

Karasch, Mary C. *Slave Life in Rio de Janiero, 1808–1850.* Princeton: Princeton University Press, 1987.

Kizca, John E., ed. *The Indian in Latin American History: Resistance, Resilience and Acculturation.* Wilmington: SR Books, 1998.

Klein, Herbert S. *Bolivia: The Evolution of a Multi-Ethnic Society.* 2d ed. New York: Oxford University Press, 1992.

———. *Haciendas and Ayllus: Rural Society in the Bolivian Andes in the Eighteenth and Nineteenth Centuries.* Stanford: Stanford University Press, 1993.

Kleymeyer, Charles David, ed. *Cultural Expression and Grass Roots Development: Cases from Latin America and the Caribbean.* Boulder: Lynne Rienner Publishers, 1994.

Lewis, Paul H. *The Crisis of Argentina Capitalism.* Chapel Hill: University of North Carolina Press, 1992.

Lomnitz, Larissa Adler, and Marisol Perez-Lizaur. *A Mexican Elite Family, 1820–1980.* Princeton: Princeton University Press, 1987.

Loveman, Brian and Thomas M. Davies, Jr. *The Politics of Antipolitics: The Military in Latin America.* Wilmington: SR Books, 1997.

MacLachlan, Colin M. And William H. Beezley, *El Gran Pueblo: A History of Greater Mexico.* 2d ed. Englewood Cliffs: Prentice Hall, 1998.

Marichal, Carlos. *A Century of Debt Crises in Latin America: From Independence to the Great Depression, 1820–1930.* Princeton: Princeton University Press, 1989.

Mariz, Cecilia Loreto. *Coping with Poverty: Pentecostals and Christian Base Communities in Brazil.* Philadelphia: Temple University Press, 1994.

Martínez, Oscar J., ed. *U.S.-Mexico Borderlands: Historical and Contemporary Perspectives.* Wilmington: SR Books, 1996.

McClintock, Cynthia. *Peasant Cooperatives and Political Change in Peru.* Princeton: Princeton University Press, 1981.

Menchú, Rigoberta. *I, Rigoberta Menchú: An Indian Woman in Guatemala.* London: Verso, 1984.

Munro, Dana G. *Intervention and Dollar Diplomacy in the Caribbean, 1900–1921.* Princeton: Princeton University Press, 1964.

Murphy, Arthur D. and Alex Stepick. *Social Inequality in Oaxaca: A History of Resistance and Change.* Philadelphia: Temple University Press, 1991.

Nickson, R. Andrew. *Local Government in Latin America.* Boulder: Lynne Rienner Publishers, 1995.

Nunn, Frederick. *The Time of Generals: Latin American Professional Militarism in World Perspective.* Lincoln: University of Nebraska Press, 1992.

Penglase, Ben. *Final Justice: Police and Death Squads Homicides of Adolescents in Brazil.* New York: Human Rights Watch, 1994.

Pérez, Louis A. *Cuba and the United States: Ties of Singular Intimacy.* 2d ed. Athens: University of Georgia Press, 1997.

Phillips, Lynne, ed. *The Third Wave of Modernization in Latin America: Cultural Perspectives on Neoliberalism.* Wilmington: SR Books, 1998.

Pike, Frederick B. *Spanish-America, 1900–1970: Tradition and Social Innovation*. New York: W.W. Norton, 1973.

——. *The United States and Latin America: Myths and Stereotypes of Civilization and Nature*. Austin: University of Texas Press, 1992.

Place, Susan E., ed. *Tropical Rainforests: Latin American Nature and Society in Transition*. Wilmington: SR Books 1993.

Portes, Alejandro and John Walton. *Urban Latin America: The Political Condition from Above and Below*. Austin: University of Texas Press, 1976.

Rock, David. *Argentina, 1516–1982: From Spanish Colonization to the Falkland's War*. Berkeley: University of California Press, 1985.

Rodó, José Enrique. *Ariel* with a Foreword by James W. Symington and a Prologue by Carlos Fuentes. Austin: University of Texas Press, 1988.

Rodríguez, O., Jaime. *The Independence of Spanish-America*. Cambridge: University of Cambridge Press, 1998.

Rodríguez, Linda Alexander, ed. *Rank and Privilege: The Military and Society in Latin America*. Wilmington: SR Books, 1994.

Rodríguez, Linda Alexander. *The Search for Public Policy: Regional Politics and Government Finances in Ecuador, 1830–1940*. Berkeley: University of California Press, 1985.

Russell-Wood, A. J. R. *Fidalgos and Philanthropists: The Santa Casa de Misericórdia of Bahia, 1550–1755*. Berkeley: University of California Press, 1968.

Salvucci, Richard J., ed. *Latin America and the World Economy: Dependency and Beyond*. Lexington: D.C. Health and Company, 1996.

Sater, William F. *Chile and the United States: Empires in Conflict*. Athens: University of Georgia Press, 1990.

Schoonover, Thomas D. *The United States in Central America, 1860–1911: Episodes of Social Imperialism and Imperial Rivalry in the World System*. Durham: Duke University Press, 1991.

Scobie, James R. *Buenos Aires: From Plaza to Suburb, 1870–1910*. New York: Oxford University Press, 1971.

Simonian, Lane. *Defining the Land of the Jaguar: A History of Conservation in Mexico*. Austin: University of Texas Press, 1995.

Stein, Steve. *Populism in Peru: The Emergence of the Masses and the Politics of Social Control*. Madison: University of Wisconsin Press, 1980.

Suchlicki, Jaime. *Cuba: From Columbus to Castro*. New York: Charles Scribner's Sons, 1974.

Topik, Steven. *The Political Economy of the Brazilian State, 1889–1930*. Austin: University of Texas Press, 1987.

Tussie, Diana. *The Inter-American Development Bank*. Boulder: Lynne Rienner Publishers, 1995.

Vélez-Ibañez, Carlos C. *Rituals of Marginality: Politics, Process and Culture Change in Central Urban Mexico, 1969–1974*. Berkeley: University of California Press, 1983.

Walker, William O., ed. *Drugs in the Western Hemisphere: An Odyssey of Cultures in Conflict*. Wilmington: SR Books, 1996.

Weber, David J. *The Spanish Frontier in North America*. New Haven: Yale University Press, 1992.

Weber, David J. and Jane M. Rausch, eds. *Where Cultures Meet: Frontiers in Latin American History*. Wilmington: SR Books, 1994.

Wood, Bryce. *The Dismantling of the Good Neighbor Policy*. Austin: University of Texas Press, 1985.

Yeager, Gertrude M. ed. *Confronting Change, Challenging Tradition: Women in Latin American History*. Wilmington: SR Books, 1994.

# Photo Credits

This page constitutes an extension of the copyright page. We have made every effort to trace the ownership of all copyrighted material and to secure permission from copyright holders. In the event of any question arising as to the use of any material, we will be pleased to make the necessary corrections in future printings. Thanks are due to the following authors, publishers, and agents for permission to use the material indicated.

**Chapter 1.** p. 37, Courtesy of Champion Latin American Collection, Tucson, Arizona.

**Chapter 2.** p. 52, Courtesy of the Latin America Library at Tulane University.

p. 67, Courtesy of the Latin America Library at Tulane University.

**Chapter 3.** p. 69, Courtesy of the Latin America Library at Tulane University.

p. 74, Courtesy of the Latin America Library at Tulane University.

p. 79, Courtesy of the Latin America Library at Tulane University.

**Chapter 4.** p. 86, Courtesy of the Latin America Library at Tulane University.

p. 103, Courtesy of Eladio Ortiz, *El Financiero International Edition,* March 23–29, 1998, p. 13.

**Chapter 5.** p. 114, Courtesy of the Latin America Library at Tulane University.

p. 115, Courtesy of the Latin America Library at Tulane University.

p. 121, Courtesy of Champion Latin American Collection, Tucson, Arizona.

p. 127, Courtesy of the Latin America Library at Tulane University.

p. 129, Courtesy of the Latin America Library at Tulane University.

p. 132, Courtesy of the Latin America Library at Tulane University.

**Chapter 6.** p. 139, Courtesy of the Latin America Library at Tulane University.

p. 145, Courtesy of Champion Latin American Collection, Tucson, Arizona.

p. 150, Courtesy of the Latin America Library at Tulane University.

**Chapter 7.** p. 158, Courtesy of the Latin America Library at Tulane University.

p. 162, Courtesy of Museo del Banco Central de Reserva de Perú.

p. 175, Courtesy of the Latin America Library at Tulane University.

**Chapter 8.** p. 189, Courtesy of the Latin America Library at Tulane University.

p. 194, Courtesy of the Latin America Library at Tulane University.

p. 196, Courtesy of the Latin America Library at Tulane University.

**Chapter 9.** p. 208, Courtesy of the Latin America Library at Tulane University.

p. 225, Courtesy of the Latin America Library at Tulane University.

**Chapter 10.** p. 242, Courtesy of the Latin America Library at Tulane University.

p. 245, Courtesy of the Latin America Library at Tulane University.

p. 262, Courtesy of the Latin America Library at Tulane University.

# Index